MATHEMATICAL APPROACHES TO POLITICS

Edited by

HAYWARD R. ALKER JR.
KARL W. DEUTSCH
ANTOINE H. STOETZEL

Elsevier Scientific Publishing Company
Amsterdam · London · New York 1973

For the U.S.A. and Canada:
JOSSEY-BASS INC. PUBLISHERS
615 MONTGOMERY STREET
SAN FRANCISCO, CALIF. 94111 U.S.A.

For all other areas:
ELSEVIER SCIENTIFIC PUBLISHING COMPANY
335 JAN VAN GALENSTRAAT
P.O. BOX 1270, AMSTERDAM, THE NETHERLANDS

Library of Congress Card Number: 71-190676

ISBN 0-444-41050-3

Printed in The Netherlands

MATHEMATICAL APPROACHES TO POLITICS

Preface

The science of politics is the oldest of the social sciences but still perhaps the most dependent: it derives much of its methodology from statistics (the science of the state turned into the science of numerical data), from economics and from sociology and it steals much of its substance from anthropology, from history and from law. Yet there is little doubt about the core of the subject: it focuses on the ways in which decisions are taken by men acting within territorially or functionally defined networks and constellations of organizations. And the hallmark of the discipline is *systematic analysis*, whether couched in verbal and literary terms or in the formalized language of statistics or of mathematical logic.

The International Political Science Association has throughout its existence endeavoured to encourage a variety of styles of systematization: it has been a pluralist organization open to all promising innovations, all efforts to develop new insights and new lines of explanation.

Karl Deutsch has throughout his career been one of the great innovators of the discipline. He was the first to see the potentialities of the communication models developed by the cyberneticists and he was one of the first to build up large-scale data banks for computer analyses of information on political systems and their interactions. The International Political Science Association was quick to recognize the world-wide importance of his initiatives and encouraged him to set up an extensive network of contacts across all continents. He organized a brilliant series of sessions at our World Congress in Munich and has since organized a Research Committee under the Association to serve as a forum for exchanges of ideas and experiences in the use of mathematical techniques in the analysis of political processes and structures.

This volume is a tribute to Karl Deutsch's great achievements. It is edited in cooperation with two of his brilliant disciples, Hayward Alker and Antoine Stoetzel, but it is first of all a monument to the great mind of Karl Deutsch. The International Association is proud to sponsor this publication by one of its leading scholars.

Stein Rokkan
President,
International Political
Science Association

Contributors

HAYWARD R. ALKER *Massachusetts Institute of Technology*
PETER H. ARANSON *University of Minnesota*
RICHARD W. CHADWICK *University of Hawaii and Harvard University*
FRANTIŠEK CHARVÁT *Czechoslovak Academy of Sciences*
KARL W. DEUTSCH *Harvard University*
DAVID G. GORDON *University of Michigan*
MELVIN J. GUYER *University of Michigan*
MELVIN J. HINICH *Carnegie-Mellon University*
RAYMOND F. HOPKINS *Swarthmore College*
JAROSLAV KUČERA *Czechoslovak Academy of Sciences*
JEFFREY S. MILSTEIN *Department of State, Washington, D.C.*
PETER C. ORDESHOOK *Carnegie-Mellon University*
ANATOL RAPOPORT *University of Toronto*
SIMON SCHWARTZMAN *Escola Brasileira de Administracao Publica*
PAUL SMOKER *University of British Columbia*
MIROSLAV SOUKUP *Czechoslovak Academy of Sciences*
ANTOINE STOETZEL *University of Paris, Sorbonne*
MICHAEL TAYLOR *University of Essex*
HARRISON C. WHITE *Harvard University*

Contents

Quantitative Approaches to Political Analysis: Some Past Trends and Future Prospects

*KARL W. DEUTSCH**

Since 1950, political science has begun to undergo a transformation similar to that which occurred in economics after 1930. At that earlier time, economics was transformed by the data of national income accounting, the methods of econometrics, and the advances in theory by J.M. Keynes and others. Political science experienced only in the 1950s and 1960s the cumulative impact of large amounts of quantitative data and data collections, including both survey research and aggregative data. Methods of statistical analysis, mathematical modelling and the use of computers entered political science on a relatively large scale only in the 1960s, with varying results. Theoretical work in political science in regard to conflict models, the theory of games and coalitions, systems analysis and systems theory, communication and control theory began to accelerate in the 1950s but made a larger impact only in the decade that followed.

So far, however, we have had no recent contribution in political

*An early version of this essay was given as the Rapporteur General's report at the Plenary Session on Quantitative and Mathematical Approaches to Political Science at the VIII World Congress of Political Science at Munich, September 1–5, 1970. In rewriting it for the present volume I have benefitted greatly from the criticisms and suggestions of Professor Hayward R. Alker, Jr., but the responsibility for the judgments in the present text remains entirely mine.

theory that would be comparable to the combined breadth, specificity, elegance and usefulness of work of J.M. Keynes and his successors. In the search for such a theory of politics centers now a major task for political science in the 1970s and 1980s.

Earlier Advances in Quantitative Political Thought

The Stage of Broad Theories, 1890–1940

Quantitative and mathematical elements in political thought are as old as systematic political theory itself. The Pythagorean thinkers stressed the need for proportion and harmony in all matters, including government. Plato wanted no one ignorant of geometry to enter his Academy. Aristotle defined the largest desirable size of a city-state by the same principle as the largest desirable size of a ship: not larger than could be controlled by the rudder. Similarly, Aristotle delimited the largest desirable size of a city–state's terrritory – not larger than could be surveyed from a single vantage point – and of its population: not larger than to permit its assembled citizens to listen to a single speaker who did not have the voice of Stentor, an unusually loudvoiced Homeric hero. These questions are quantitative; they seek answers in terms of quantitative limits.[1]

It was not until the half-century between 1890 and 1940, however, that the quantitative elements in political and social theory increased to a remarkable degree. Many thinkers about society and politics developed theories with major quantitative implications. Vilfredo Pareto's concept of the circulation of elites involved inescapably some notion of measurable rates and proportions; later, in 1936 and 1950, Harold Lasswell, first alone and later jointly with Abraham Kaplan, developed further the quantitative aspects of the elite concept, and of the agglutination of values as a measure of the general, rather than the specialized, character of a particular elite.[2]

[1] Aristotle, *Politics* [Ernest Barker translation] (New York: Oxford University Press, 1962); Werner Jaeger, *Aristotle* (Oxford: Clarendon Press, 1962) 2nd ed.; Bertrand Russell, *History of Western Philosophy* (New York: Simon and Schuster, 1945).

[2] Vilfredo Pareto, *The Mind and Society* (New York: Dover Publications, 1935, 1963) 4 vols. in 2; Harold D. Lasswell, *Politics: Who Gets What, When, How* (Cleveland: The World Publishing Co., 1958); H.D. Lasswell and Abraham Kaplan, *Power and Society* (New Haven: Yale University Press, 1950).

Max Weber defined key concepts of his theories in terms of probability, such as "domination" as "the chance to be obeyed;" this implicit mathematics of Max Weber still remains to be made explicit through the systematic measurement of compliance rates.[3] Werner Sombart formulated his prediction of the declining relative importance of foreign trade as a proportion of national income – a prediction which in the main was not confirmed between 1890 and 1914 but which turned out to contain a great deal of truth in the half-century that followed.[4] Roberto Michels' proposition of the "iron law of oligarchy" in the leadership and organization of political parties; Rudolf Hilferding's and V. I. Lenin's theories of the increasing concentration of private business enterprises and the increasing importance of monopolies; Lenin's theory of the unevenness of economic and political development; Thorstein Veblen's prediction of both rising prices and increasing numbers of competitors in the course of monopolistic competition (and hence a persistence and possible growth of a middle class of self-employed small businessmen); Karl Mannheim's "principle of fundamental democratization" in society and politics through a general increase in social and political mobilization and participation – all these theories included major quantitative propositions, capable of being tested and measured, and offering from a measurement of their rates of change some possible bases for further theoretical inferences and predictions.[5]

[3] Max Weber, *The Protestant Ethic and the Spirit of Capitalism*, translated by Talcott Parsons (London: Allen and Unwin, 1930 and New York: Scribners, 1930); K.W. Deutsch, *Max Weber und die Soziologie heute: Verhandlungen des fünfzehnten deutschen Soziologentages* (Tübingen: J.C.B. Mohr (Paul Sieback) 1965), pp. 139–145; and on compliance rates, *Politics and Government: How People Decide Their Fate* (Boston: Houghton Mifflin Co., 1970), pp. 15–16.

[4] Werner Sombart, *Der moderne Kapitalismus* (München: Duncker and Humblot, 1928) 3 vols.; Andreas Predöhl, *Aussenwirtschaft: Weltwirtschaft, Handelspolitik, und Währungspolitik* (Göttingen: Vanderhoeck & Ruprecht, 1949); for data, see K.W. Deutsch and Alexander Eckstein, "National Industrialization and the Declining Share of the Economic Sector, 1890–1959" in *World Politics*, 13:2 (Jan. 1961), pp. 267–299.

[5] Roberto Michels, *Political Parties* (Glencoe, Ill.: Free Press, 1958); Rudolf Hilferding, *Das Finanzkapital* (Frankfurt: Europäische Verlaganstalt, 1968); V.I. Lenin, *Imperialism, The Highest Stage of Capitalism* (New York: International Publishers, 1939); Thorstein Veblen, *The Theory of Business Enterprise* (New York: Charles Scribner's Sons, 1904); Karl Mannheim, *Man and Society in an Age of Reconstruction: Studies in Modern Social Structure*, revised ed. (New York: Harcourt, Brace and World, 1940), pp. 44–49. See also H. Stuart Hughes, *Consciousness and Society: The Reorientation of European Social Thought, 1890–1930* (New York: Knopf, 1958).

All such broad theories implied a thrust toward the questions "How much? How soon? How fast? How far?" and they implied further questions: "How new? How different? With what new side effects?" In this manner, these broad theories of the half-century before 1940 raised the interlinked questions of both quantity and quality in political and social change.[6]

A Wave of Empirical Descriptions, 1920–1960

The broad theories, of which the foregoing examples have been given, were scientific in intent, and partly in performance. To a significant extent, each could be corroborated or disconfirmed by reproducible and often quantitative evidence. Overlapping with this period was the work of several outstanding historians with a scientific and partly quantitative orientation. These men were motivated by the ancient desire *rerum cognoscere causas* – to know the causes of things – but they made critical use of both broad social and political theories and of specific historical and in part quantitative data in order to account for the origins and outcomes of major historical processes and events.

Sidney B. Fay's work on the origins of the First World War, Crane Brinton's work on the French Revolution and his study of the Jacobins, William L. Langer's work on the diplomacy of the classic imperialist age, and somewhat later David Potter's and C. Vann Woodward's work on the North–South conflict and on race relations in American history; all these were informed by a broader and more differentiated understanding of social and political theories than had been the writings of most of their predecessors.[7] These historians went beyond the stress on the economic factor in history, which in

[6] Daniel Lerner, ed., *Quantity and Quality* (New York: Free Press of Glencoe, 1961).

[7] Sidney B. Fay, *Origins of the World War*, 2 vols. (New York: Macmillan, 1934); Crane Brinton, *A Decade of Revolution, 1789–1799* (New York: Harper, 1934); C. Brinton, *The Jacobins* (New York: Macmillan, 1930); William L. Langer, *European Alliances and Alignments*, 1871–1890 (New York: Knopf, 1950); *The Diplomacy of Imperialism*, 2 vols., (New York: Knopf, 1951); David M. Potter, *People of Plenty: Economic Abundance and the American Character* (Chicago: University of Chicago Press, 1954); C. Vann Woodward, *Origins of the New South* (Baton Rouge: University of Louisiana Press, 1951), *Reunion and Reaction* (Boston: Little, 1951). *The Strange Career of Jim Crow* (New York: Oxford University Press, 1957).

the United States Charles A. Beard had pioneered.[8] They sought to elucidate the interplay of political, economic, social, cultural, and psychological processes and conditions, searching for verifiable data and consistent theories in regard to all of them.

Another stream of empirical and descriptive contributions came from the fields of anthropology and psychology. Inspired in part by the primarily qualitative ideas of Sigmund Freud, Oswald Spengler and others, these contributions stressed configurations of culture. The work of such scholars as Alfred Kroeber, Ruth Benedict, Margaret Mead, Henry A. Murray, Erik H. Erikson, and Charles W. Morris contained few, if any, explicit quantitative data, but it offered potential new patterns of recognition.[9] Eventually this body of ideas would contribute, directly or indirectly, to the development of both qualitative and quantitative content analysis, computer simulation of affective cognition, and quantitative cross-cultural studies.[10]

From the 1930s through the 1950s, empirical description of political attitudes and behavior was given new scope and powers through the reception of sampling theory and practice, together with improvements in the technique of interviews. Suitably chosen samples

---

[8] Charles A. Beard, *The Idea of National Interest: An Analytical Study of American Foreign Policy* (New York: Macmillan, 1934), *An Economic Interpretation of the Constitution* (New York: Macmillan, 1913).

[9] Sigmund Freud, *Group Psychology and the Analysis of the Ego* (James Stachey translation) (New York: Liveright Publishing Corporation, 1951); Oswald Spengler, *The Decline of the West* (New York: Alfred A. Knopf, 1926–28), 2 vols.; Alfred L. Kroeber, *Configurations of Culture Growth* (Berkeley: University of California Press, 1944), *Style and Civilizations* (Ithaca, New York: Cornell University Press, 1957); Ruth Benedict, *Patterns of Culture* (New York: Pelican-Mentor 1947); Margaret Mead, "The Study of National Character," in D. Lerner and H.D. Lasswell, eds., *The Policy Sciences* (Stanford: Stanford University Press 1951), pp. 70–86, and "National Character," in A.L. Kroeber, ed., *Anthropology Today: An Encyclopedic Inventory* (Chicago: University of Chicago Press, 1953), pp. 642–647; Erik H. Erikson, *Childhood and Society* (New York: Norton, 1950) and Charles W. Morris, *Varieties of Human Value* (Chicago: University of Chicago Press, 1956).

[10] Bernard Berelson, *Content Analysis in Communications Research* (Glencoe, Ill.: Free Press, 1952); Harold D. Lasswell and Nathan Leites, *The Language of Politics* (Cambridge: M.I.T. Press, 1965); Harold D. Lasswell, Daniel Lerner and Ithiel de Sola Pool, *The Comparative Study of Symbols* (Stanford: Stanford University Press, 1952); Ithiel de Sola Pool, ed., *Trends in Content Analysis* (Urbana, Ill.: University of Illinois Press, 1959); Philip J. Stone, Dexter C. Dunphy, Marshall S. Smith and Daniel M. Ogilvie, *The General Inquirer: A Computer Approach to Content Analysis* (Cambridge: M.I.T. Press, 1966), and Charles E. Osgood, George J. Suci and Percy H. Tannenbaum, *The Measurement of Meaning* (Urbana, Ill.: University of Illinois Press, 1957).

permitted the reduction of large universes of possible observation to manageably small numbers of cases which were still representative. Survey research now became possible, and it soon was applied to the study of voting behavior, political attitudes, audience reactions and the effect of mass media by Harold Gosnell, George Gallup, Elmo Roper, Hadley F. Cantril, Paul F. Lazarsfeld, and many others.[11]

Large-scale empirical descriptions and comparisons were also attempted in political science, even though at first often without much use of the new quantitative tools and methods. Only a few examples can be given here. Charles E. Merriam directed in the 1920s a ten-volume comparative study of civic education in various Western countries. Quincy Wright directed and wrote a monumental study of war. In Britain, W.A. Robson carried out studies of municipal and metropolitan government. In France, going beyond the older French traditions of electoral geography and quantitative history, Raymond Aron applied his approach of historical sociology to the analysis of war and peace, and Maurice Duverger undertook a widely noted comparative analysis of political parties.[12]

---

[11] Harold F. Gosnell, *Non-voting* (Chicago: University of Chicago Press, 1924), *Getting out the Vote* (Chicago: University of Chicago Press, 1927), *Grass Roots Politics* (New York: Russell & Russell, 1942, 1970). Herbert Hyman, *Political Socialization: A Study in the Psychology of Political Behavior* (Glencoe, Ill.: The Free Press, 1959); George Gallup, *The Pulse of Democracy* (New York: Simon and Schuster, 1940), *A Guide to Public Opinion Polls* (Princeton: Princeton University Press, 1944); Elmo Roper, "Where Stands Freedom? " (New York: *Time*, 1948), *You and Your Leaders* (New York: Morrow, 1957); Hadley Cantril, ed., *Public Opinion 1935–1946* (Princeton: Princeton University Press, 1951), and Hadley Cantril, *The Politics of Despair* (New York: Basic Books, 1958), *The Pattern of Human Concerns* (New Brunswick, N.J.: Rutgers University Press, 1965), *The Political Beliefs of Americans: A Study of Public Opinion* (New Brunswick, N.J.: Rutgers University Press, 1967); William B. Buchanan and Hadley Cantril, *How Nations See Each Other* (Urbâna, Ill.: University of Illinois Press, 1953); Paul F. Lazarsfeld *et al.*, *The People's Choice* (New York: Columbia University Press, 1948); Bernard Berelson, Paul F. Lazarsfeld and William N. McPhee, *Voting* (Chicago: University of Chicago Press, 1954); Angus Campbell, Philip E. Converse, Warren E. Miller and Donald E. Stokes, *The American Voter* (New York: Wiley, 1960).

[12] Charles Edward Merriam, *The Making of Citizens; a Comparative Study of Methods of Civic Training* (Chicago, Ill.: The University of Chicago Press, 1931); Raymond Aron, *Peace and War: a Theory of International Relations* (Garden City N.Y.: Doubleday, 1966); Maurice Duverger, *Political Parties: Their Organization and Activity in the Modern State*, 2nd English Ed., rev., translated by Barbara and Robert North (New York: Wiley, 1963); William Alexander Robson, *Great Cities of the World: Their Government, Politics and Planning*, 2nd ed., (New York: Macmillan, 1957); William A. Robson and D.E. Regan, eds., *Great Cities of the World*, 2 vols., (Beverley Hills, Calif.: Sage, 1972); François Goguel-

Combined Empirical and Theoretical Approaches after 1950

In the 1950s, and particularly in the 1960s, there followed more broadly-based efforts at empirical and theoretical synthesis in political studies, now including a greater and more rigorous use of quantitative data. Harold Lasswell, Daniel Lerner, Ithiel Pool and their associates combined elite studies and content analysis in the worldwide political changes and revolutionary trends. Gabriel Almond and Sidney Verba combined political analysis and survey research for the comparative study of the "civic culture" in five countries. Clyde Kluckhohn, Raymond Bauer and Alex Inkeles applied anthropological, psychological and sociological analysis, together with extensive interviews among defectors from the Soviet Union, in an attempt to elucidate the working of the Soviet political and social system in the Stalin era. Pool, Bauer and Lewis Dexter applied a variety of quantitative and qualitative research methods to a study of the attitudes of American businessmen to issues of United States policy in regard to foreign trade. C. Wright Mills, Floyd Hunter, Robert A. Dahl, Nelson W. Polsby, and Raymond Wolfinger made increasing use of quantitative methods in the study of elite composition and influence in the politics of the American cities. Jean Stoetzel used psychological analysis and opinion research data for a study of the changing attitudes of Japanese youth after World War II; the problem of attitude change among all age groups in Japan was later investigated in a major series of surveys and studies by C. Hayashi and other scholars in Japan; and a large-scale survey of the semantic differentials of over 600 concepts, many of them political, in 23 countries and language areas, was carried out by Charles Osgood and his associates putting "the measurement of meaning" on a new broad and quantitative basis.[13]

Nyegaard, *Géographie des Elections Français Sous la Troisième et la Quatrième République* (Paris: Colin, 1970): Fernand Braudel, ed., *Histoire Economique et Sociale de la France* (Paris: Presses Universitaires de France, 1970); Oszkar Jászi, *The Dissolution of the Habsburg Monarchy* (Chicago, Ill.: University of Chicago Press, 1929); Stuart A. Rice, *Quantitative Methods in Politics* (New York: Alfred Knopf, 1928).

[13] Harold D. Lasswell and Daniel Lerner, eds., *World Revolutionary Elites* (Cambridge: M.I.T. Press, 1965); Ithiel de Sola Pool, Harold D. Lasswell and Daniel Lerner, *The Prestige Press* (Cambridge: M.I.T. Press, 1970); Gabriel Almond and Sidney Verba, *The Civic Culture* (Princeton: Princeton University Press, 1963); Alex Inkeles and Raymond A. Bauer, *The Soviet Citizen* (Cambridge: Harvard University Press, 1959); Raymond A. Bauer, Ithiel de

Another large-scale attempt at synthesis was undertaken by Gabriel Almond and his associates in regard to political modernization and development, in a multi-volume series which combined functional and quantitative analysis with some quantitative reasoning and use of data.[14] A similar combination had been used earlier to good effect by Daniel Lerner in his well-known study, *The Passing of Traditional Society*. By the end of the 1960s, an analysis of a number of political development concepts and models, which Latin American political scientists had worked out, revealed a strong element of implicit feedback concepts and quantitative reasoning in their essays, and an important volume on mathematical models had been edited by Oscar Varsavsky and Alfredo Calcagno.[15]

Sola Pool and Lewis A. Dexter, *American Business and Public Policy* (New York: Atherton Press, 1963); C. Wright Mills, *The Power Elite* (New York: Oxford University Press, 1956); Floyd Hunter, *Top Leadership, U.S.A.* (Chapel Hill: University of North Carolina Press, 1959); Robert Dahl, *Who Governs: Democracy and Power in an American City* (New Haven: Yale University Press, 1961); Nelson Polsby, *Community Power and Political Theory* (New Haven: Yale University Press, 1963); Jean Stoetzel, *Without the Chrysanthemum and the Sword: A Study of the Attitudes of Youth in Post-War Japan* (New York: Columbia University Press, 1955); Chikio Hayashi, *et al.*, (Research Committee of Japanese National Character, The Institute of Statistical Mathematics), *A Study of Japanese National Character* (Tokyo: Shiseido Publishing Company, 1961) (in Japanese with English summaries). For Charles Osgood, see note 10.

[14] Gabriel A. Almond and James S. Coleman, *The Politics of Developing Areas* (Princeton: Princeton University Press, 1960); Gabriel A. Almond and G. Bingham Powell, Jr., *Comparative Politics: A Developmental Approach* (Boston: Little, Brown, 1966); Lucian W. Pye, ed. *Communications and Political Development* (1963), Joseph LaPalombara ed., *Bureaucracy and Political Development* (1963), Robert E. Ward and Dankwart A. Rustow, eds., *Political Modernization in Japan and Turkey* (1964), James S. Coleman, ed., *Education and Political Development* (1965), Lucian W. Pye and Sidney Verba, eds., *Political Culture and Political Development* (1965), Joseph LaPalombara and Myron Weiner, eds., *Political Parties and Political Development* (Princeton: Princeton University Press, 1966).

[15] Daniel Lerner, *The Passing of Traditional Society: Modernizing the Middle East* (Glencoe, Ill.: The Free Press, 1958); Karl W. Deutsch and Jorge Dominguez, "Political Development toward National Self Determination: Some Recent Concepts and Models," *Comparative Political Studies*, January 1972, pp. 461–475; and in more detail, "Politische Entwicklung zur Nationalen Selbstbestimmung. Einige Neuere Begriffe und Modelle," in Klaus von Beyme, ed., *Theory and Politics – Theorie und Politik: Festschrift zum 70. Geburtstag für Carl Joachim Friedrich* (The Hague: Martinus Nijhoff, 1971), pp. 417–455; Oscar Varsavsky and Alfredo Calcagno, eds. *America Latina; Modelos Matemáticos* (Santiago de Chile: Editorial Universitaria, 1971); José A. Silva Michelena, *The Illusion of Democracy in Dependent Nations* (Cambridge, Mass.: M.I.T. Press, 1971); see also Frank Bonilla and José A. Silva Michelena, eds., *A Strategy for Research on Social Policy* (Cambridge, Mass.: M.I.T. Press, 1967), and Frank Bonilla, *The Failure of Elites* (Cambridge, Mass.: M.I.T. Press, 1970). The last-named three books constitute volumes 1, 2 and 3 respectively of a larger study, *The Politics of Change in Venezuela.*

Quantitative Data Collections and Broad Inventories of Behavioral Research Results

Efforts in the large-scale use of quantitative data had been made by Pitirim A. Sorokin, but the more systematic collection of quantitative data on a comparative and worldwide basis had been pioneered as a modern practice by W.S. Woytinski, first in a five-volume work published in Germany in 1927, and then in two large volumes in English, published in 1953 and 1955 in the United States. The other volumes of data and projections focussed on needs and resources, first of the United States, and later of the world, were published by J. Frederic Dewhurst and his associates. During the 1930s, the development of national income accounting by Simon Kuznets, Colin Clark and others led to the collection and eventual publication of a great volume of national and cross-national economics data which were of direct relevance to political analysis.[16]

Other combined attacks, including the use of quantitative data, on major problems of political behavior were carried out by Seymour Martin Lipset, Stein Rokkan and Mattei Dogan in the United States, Norway and France, and by Pavel Machonin and his associates in Czechoslovakia.[17] Finally, combined research approaches were used

---

[16] In the most extensive work by Pitirim Sorokin, quantitative data often were selected on a more subjective basis and cannot be readily retraced to their sources. Cf. Pitirim A. Sorokin, *Social and Cultural Dynamics* (New York: American Book Company, 1937–41). More limited and verifiable data are given in P.A. Sorokin, *Social Mobility* (New York: Harper, 1927); W.S. Woytinsky, *Die Welt in Zahlen*, 5 vols., (Berlin: Mosse Verlag, 1927); W.S. Woytinsky and E.S. Woytinsky, *World Population and Production: Trends and Outlook* (New York: Twentieth Century Fund, 1953), and *World Commerce and Governments: Trends and Outlook* (New York: Twentieth Century Fund, 1955); J. Frederic Dewhurst and associates, *America's Needs and Resources* (New York: Twentieth Century Fund, 1947), and *Europe's Needs and Resources* (New York, Twentieth Century Fund, 1961): Simon Kuznets, *National Income and its Composition, 1919–1938* (New York: National Bureau of Economic Research, 1941), *Modern Economic Growth* (New Haven: Yale University Press, 1961); Colin Clark, *The Conditions of Economic Progress* (London: Macmillan, 1st ed. 1940, rev. eds. 1951 and 1957). For examples of the use of quantitative data in political analysis, see Karl W. Deutsch, *Nationalism and Social Communication* (Cambridge, Mass.: MIT Press, 1953, rev. ed. 1966).

[17] Seymour Martin Lipset, *Political Man* (Garden City, N.Y.: Doubleday, 1960); Mattei Dogan and Stein Rokkan, eds., *Quantitative Ecological Analysis in the Social Sciences* (Cambridge, Mass.: MIT Press, 1969); Pavel Machonin, ed. *Sociálni Struktura Socialistické Společnosti; Sociologické Problémy Soudobé Československé Společnosti.* (Prague: Svoboda, 1966).

not only on problems of the past and present but also for projections of the future. The work of Daniel Bell, Bertrand de Jouvenel, R. Delapalme, Radovan Richta, Fritz Baade, Robert Jungk, Herman Kahn, Anthony Wiener and many others has made the projecting of future trends and possibilities, and the suggestion of suitable provisions to meet various contingencies projected as possible or even probable (though *not* predicted as certain) a significant field of political and social science.[18]

The Development of New Mathematical Models and Methods of Analysis

During the same decades since World War II, a wide range of mathematical approaches to political analysis were developed, or else carried forward to broad application. The most far-reaching of these developments was the shift from the search for single causes of political outcomes or events to multivariate analysis. This type of analysis sought for a plurality of independent variables, or antecedent conditions in the past, each of which would contribute both singly and in interaction with other conditions, to the likelihood of some later political outcome; and it sought not for a single outcome of any such combination of conditions but rather for a distribution of several more or less probable subsequent outcomes. Particular applications of this method might be controversial, since they depended on the realistic identification of all major relevant antecedent variables and of all important subsequent outcomes, but the breadth, power and flexibility of the method made it in most cases superior to the single-cause method and its search for just one "master link" that all too often remained vague, poetic or rhetorical.

One result of this work was an accumulation of what J. David Singer has called the "correlational knowledge" of which variables appeared correlated how strongly and how significantly with what

[18] Daniel Bell, *The End of Ideology* (rev. ed. New York: The Free Press, 1966); Bertrand de Jouvenel, ed, *Futuribles: Studies in Conjecture* (Geneva: Droz, 1963); Radovan Richta, *Civilization at the Crossroads: Social and Human Implications of the Scientific and Technical Revolution.* Translated by Marian Šlingová. 3rd ed. (White Plains, N.Y.: International Arts and Sciences Press, 1969); Fritz Baade, *Der Wettlauf zum Jahre 2000. Unsere Zukunft: Ein Paradies oder Selbstvernichtung der Menschheit* (Oldenburg: Stalling, 1960); Robert Jungk and Johan Galtung, 1st International Future Research Conference, Oslo, 1967. *Mankind 2000* (Oslo: Universitetsforlaget; London: Allen & Unwin, 1969).

types of outcomes, and under what conditions. Controlling for additional conditions often meant unmasking spurious correlations due to some additional variable which had been previously unidentified or neglected; in other cases it meant the discovery of some discriminating variable which would sort out a previously weak correlation among two variables, in a large but heterogeneous universe of cases, into two different but more clear-cut correlations in two different subsets of cases. Thus Bruce Russett found only a weak correlation between the inequality of land holdings and political unrest in a large number of countries, but when he separated the countries into those where agriculture accounted for a large portion of the gross domestic product and the labor force employed, and those where the share of agriculture in these terms was small, he found a strong connection between agrarian inequality and political unrest – and particularly violence – in the first group of countries but not in the second.[19]

Eventually, analyses of this kind – as exemplified by the work of Lazarsfeld, Russett, Singer and Rudolph J. Rummel – lead to the use of methods of multiple regression and covariance analysis, designed to show how much any one of several variables contributes, positively or negatively, to the probability of a particular outcome, both directly by itself and indirectly through the efforts of an interaction with other variables. Further developments of this approach lead to Simon–Blalock causal modeling and the rediscovery of biometric path analysis, which aims at identifying the main paths from causes to effects in a system with pluralities of input and outcome variables.[20] (It should be noted that these early approaches and models

[19] Bruce Russett, Hayward R. Alker, Jr., Karl W. Deutsch and Harold D. Lasswell, *World Handbook of Political and Social Indicators* (New Haven: Yale University Press, 1964) (henceforth cited as *World Handbook I*), pp. 237–242.

[20] Paul F. Lazarsfeld and M. Rosenberg, eds. *The Language of Social Research: A Reader on the Methodology of Social Research* (Glencoe, Ill.: Free Press, 1955); Paul F. Lazarsfeld, ed. *Mathematical Thinking in the Social Sciences* (Glencoe, Ill.: Free Press, 1954); J. David Singer (ed.) *Quantitative International Politics* (New York: Free Press, 1968). For a discussion, see Hayward R. Alker, Jr. *Mathematics and Politics* (New York: Macmillan, 1965), Chs. 5 and 6, pp. 89–129. For examples of important recent work, see J. David Singer and Melvin Small, *The Wages of War, 1816–1965* (New York: Wiley, 1972); Bruce M. Russett, ed., *Peace, War and Numbers* (Beverley Hills, Calif., and London: Sage Publications, 1972); Rudolph J. Rummel, *Dimensions of Nations* (Beverley Hills, Calif.: Sage, 1972); and John V. Gillespie and Betty A. Nesvold, eds., *Macro-Quantitative Analysis: Conflict, Development and Democratization* (Beverly Hills, Calif.: Sage, 1971).

were unidirectional, more or less explicitly suggesting a one-way flow from causes to effects. To deal with cases of circular causation, feedback loops and interdependent processes, other methods had to be devised, which will be discussed below.)

Differential Equations for Action–Reaction Processes

Another important approach to cases of mutual interaction between two processes or actors was based on pairs of differential equations, representing the mutual actions and reactions, friendly or hostile, of the participants. This method was developed by Lewis F. Richardson and applied by him to arms races between the great powers. The Soviet biologist G.F. Gause applied differential equations to calculating the chances for survival of each of two competing species of beetles in a bag of flour, as well as the conditions and chances for their peaceful coexistence. Later, Anatol Rapoport and Kenneth E. Boulding deepened this method of analysis and applied it to a wider range of problems of political and military conflict and defense.[21] Most recently, Urs Lutterbacher and Paul Smoker, among others, have attempted to develop this type of conflict and arms race model with some further refinements.[22]

The Theory of Games, Coalitions and Decisions

Another major mathematical approach to the study of conflicts, coalitions and decisions in politics – as well as in other fields – has been through game theory. The classic work by John Von Neumann and Oskar Morgenstern was published in 1944, following upon an earlier paper by Von Neumann in 1928. A major summary text by Robert Duncan Luce and Howard Raiffa followed in 1957, and the works of Thomas C. Schelling and Anatol Rapoport initiated a great

---

[21] Lewis F. Richardson, *Arms and Insecurity* (Chicago: Quadrangle Books, 1960); G.F. Gause, *The Struggle for Existence* (Baltimore: The William and Wilkens Co., 1934); Anatol Rapoport, *Fights, Games and Debates* (Ann Arbor: The University of Michigan Press, 1960); Kenneth Boulding, *Conflict and Defense* (New York: Harper, 1962).

[22] Urs Lutterbacher, *Dimensions historiques de modèles dynamiques des conflicts: Application au processes de course aux armaments, 1900–1965*. PhD thesis, (University of Geneva, Switzerland, 1972); Paul Smoker, "International Relations Simulations: A Summary", this volume.

and often productive discussion of the possibilities and limits of the applicability of game theory to political analysis, and to the tempting but dangerous notions of threats, deterrence, pre-commitment, and conflict escalation and deescalation among nation states, and particularly among nuclear powers.[23] In the course of this discussion, and out of the extensive empirical research carried out by Rapoport and his associates, important contributions emerged on the "prisoners dilemma" games, and on problems of communication and rationality in situations of mixed motive confrontation where elements of both cooperative and adversary interests are intermingled.[24]

A particularly important innovation seems to me Rapoport's combination of mathematical analysis of various types of games and conflict situations with large-scale experimentation on the actual behavior of men and women in making decisions about their strategy in such situations during long runs of repeated plays of each particular game. This highly effective combination of mathematical analysis and behavioral research has shown that in normal prisoners' dilemma games the saintly tactic of always giving in to the adversary tends to bring out the worst in the latter, turning most people into ruthless exploiters of the concessions so gratuitously offered to them. But the experiments also show the futility of the "hard-boiled" tactic of refusing all cooperation and always attempting to exploit one's adversary or partner; this type of behavior merely tends to elicit retaliations, and as both players persist in distrusting and penalizing each other, they both continue to lose. The best tactic, Rapoport's subjects found, consists in initiating cooperation, persisting in it so long as it is reciprocated, retaliating on a "tit-for-tat" basis for acts of betrayal and hostility but then always initiate new acts of cooperation and maintain cooperative behavior so long as the

[23] John Von Neumann and Oskar Morgenstern, *Theory of Games and Economic Behavior* (Princeton: Princeton University Press) 1947; Robert Duncan Luce and Howard Raiffa, *Games and Decisions* (New York: John Wiley & Sons) 1957; Thomas C. Schelling, *The Strategy of Conflict* (Cambridge, Mass.: Harvard University Press) 1960, *Arms and Influence* (New Haven: Yale University Press) 1966; Anatol Rapopc ., *Fights, Games and Debates* (Ann Arbor: University of Michigan Press) 1960, *Strategy and Conscience* (New York: Harper & Row) 1964.

[24] Anatol Rapoport, *Two-Person Game Theory: The Essential Ideas* (Ann Arbor: University of Michigan Press, 1966); Anatol Rapoport and Albert M. Chammah, *Prisoner's Dilemma* (Ann Arbor: University of Michigan Press, 1965).

other side will match it. A high degree of awareness of the pay-off matrix of the prisoners' dilemma game under way, with its rewards for mutual cooperation and penalties for mutual hostility, turned out to increase the likelihood of cooperation among the players; when this matrix was kept on prominent display in front of them, their frequency of cooperation doubled. It would be interesting to test what happens if this matrix were displayed to only one player and not to his adversary; would the more ignorant player gain a marginal advantage from tending to try more often to exploit his adversary, in accordance with George Orwell's satirical formulation "Ignorance is Strength," or would he, too, lose as a result of his ignorant behavior?

The more recent work of Rapoport and his collaborators opens up a new area of substance. In the "threat games" discussed in their paper in the present volume, one player is clearly in the situation of the "underdog" while his adversary is in a favored or "top dog" position. If each player follows his own dominant rational strategy, then the underdog remains permanently disadvantaged, receiving little or nothing in the way of a pay-off while his top dog adversary keeps getting most or all of the reward. In such an asymmetrical situation, Rapoport's mathematical analysis shows it will pay the underdog to act in a seemingly irrational way to his own short-run detriment. By accepting an immediate loss to himself, the underdog can also inflict a significant loss on his adversary, so as to make it now rational for the latter to change his earlier tactics and to concede in the end to the underdog a more equitable division of rewards. The applicability of this reasoning to strikes in industry, student unrest in universities, protest of women, and generally to the strategy of many disadvantaged groups deserves careful and thorough exploration.[25]

Here again, Rapoport and his collaborators have combined mathematical analysis with behavioral experimentation. They made their subjects exchange roles, so that each was playing half of the time in the privileged and half of the time in the underprivileged position. Their choices of strategy in these two situations then created four distinct types of behavior, suggesting possible corresponding styles of political culture or types of personality. There is

[25] Anatol Rapoport, *et al.*, "Threat Games: A Comparison of Performance of Danish and American Students in a 'Threat Game'", this volume.

the conformist – what Rapoport calls the SS-type of personality, selfish when in power but submissive or slavish when weak. There is its rare opposite, the good Christian, generous or meek or submissive both when weak and when in power. There is the power-oriented type, pushing his advantage to the utmost when in a powerful position but refusing to accept subordination and resisting and rebelling against it even at a high cost of sacrifice. And finally there are the generous rebels, who resist and revolt when oppressed or disadvantaged but who, when in power, are generous and cooperative toward their weaker partners. The relative proportions of these four types of behavior among American and Danish students, playing identical games with identical pay-off matrices, makes fascinating reading in the essay in the present volume. It demonstrates an important step toward turning the study of national character, as well as of its possible change, at long last into an experimental science. (To pursue this line of exploration, however, it will be necessary to control as far as possible all relevant parameters of the experiment; Rapoport's Danish subjects were students of engineering, while his Americans were graduate students of the social sciences – this occupational difference may have contributed to the very high frequency of conformist and situation-accepting SS-type behavior among the Danes but it suggests no obvious explanation for the relatively high frequency of power-oriented behavior among the American subjects which rather seems to tally with other data about American culture.)[26]

Other important work on games and coalitions has been done by William Riker and his associates, and by Duncan Black, Robin Farquhar and Robert Axelrod.[27]

Econometric Models and Approaches

Another significant line of contributions to the application of mathematical and quantitative reasoning to politics has come from a

[26] *Ibid.*

[27] William H. Riker, *The Theory of Political Coalitions* (New Haven: Yale University Press) 1962; Duncan Black, *The Theory of Committees and Elections* (Cambridge, England: Cambridge University Press, 1958); Robin Farquhar, *Theory of Voting* (New Haven: Yale University Press, 1969) Robert Axelrod, *Conflict of Interest: A Theory of Divergent Goals with Applications to Politics* (Chicago: Markham Publishing Co.) 1970.

development or transfer of econometric models and methods to this field. Outstanding here have been the contributions of Herbert Simon and Kenneth J. Arrow, and the work of Anthony Downs and Mancur Olson. The authors included in the survey by William C. Mitchell and the book of readings edited by Bruce M. Russett have attracted wide attention; and a new journal, *Public Choice*, is to deal with problems of this kind.[28]

Econometric models and approaches to political problems such as electoral competition have been praised for their simplicity and elegance; they have permitted a wider application of cost-benefit analysis; and they have had the advantage of the availability of a large stock of existing models, methods and calculating techniques from the field of economics proper. At the same time, they have been criticized for their limited and partial nature. Much of the political context, of the multiplicity of relevant values, of the sociological, psychological, historical and cultural aspects, of the decisions of individuals and of the effects of the larger social and political environment – all these, it has been pointed out, tend to be excluded or tacitly assumed as constant in most econometric approaches to political analyses. Despite the partial convergence of econometrics, sociometrics and psychometric approaches to one-way and even two-way causal analysis, it appears that such methods at their present level of development can be used effectively on parts of a problem but rarely on the whole. They tend to be good servants but bad masters in political analysis. If a wider range of relevant conditions are to be considered, a broader analytic framework is needed, and the proponents of general systems theory have attempted to fill this need.

---

[28] Herbert A. Simon, *Models of Man: Social and Rational: Mathematical Essays on Rational Human Behavior in a Social Setting* (New York and London: John Wiley & Sons) 1957; Kenneth J. Arrow, *Social Choice and Individual Values* (New York: John Wiley & Sons) 1963 2nd ed.; Mancur Olson, Jr., *The Logic of Collective Action* (Cambridge, Mass.: Harvard University Press) 1965; William C. Mitchell, "The Shape of Political Theory to Come: From Political Sociology to Political Economy" and Mancur Olson, Jr. "The Relationship between Economics and the Other Social Sciences: The Province of a 'Social Report'", both in Seymour Martin Lipset, ed., *Politics and the Social Sciences* (New York: Oxford University Press, 1969), pp. 112–143 and 144–169, respectively; Anthony Downs, *An Economic Theory of Democracy* (New York: Harper and Row, 1957); Bruce M. Russett, ed., *Economic Theories of International Politics* (Chicago: Markham Publishing Company, 1968).

General Systems Theory

The term "general systems theory" was first made popular by a biologist, Ludwig von Bertalanffy, and it has been popularised in the biomedical and social sciences by James Grier Miller, utilizing more specialized work by Nicholas Rashevsky, Ralph Gerard, Anatol Rapoport and John R. Platt.[29]

During the 1950s and 1960s, general systems theory has merged with the theory of information, communication and control, or cybernetics, as developed by Claude E. Shannon, Norbert Wiener, Warren McCulloch, W. Ross Ashby, Gray Walter, Colin Cherry, George A. Miller and Georg Klaus.[30] By now these communication

[29] Ludwig von Bertalanffy, "General Systems Theory" in *General Systems: Yearbook of the Society for the Advancement of General Systems Theory*, 2 (1956); James G. Miller, "Living Systems: Basic Concepts" in *Behavioral Science* 10 (July 1965) pp. 193–237, "Living Systems: Structure and Process" in *Behavioral Science* 10 (October 1965) pp. 337–379, "Living Systems: Cross-Level Hypotheses" in *Behavioral Science* 10 (October 1965) pp. 380–411; Nicholas Rashevsky, *Mathematical Theory of Human Relations: An Approach to a Mathematical Biology of Social Phenomena* (Bloomington, Ind.: Principia Press) 1947, *Mathematical Biology of Social Behavior* (Chicago: University of Chicago Press) 1951; Ralph W. Gerard, "A Biologist's View of Society" *Common Cause*, 3 (1950), p. 360, reprinted in *General Systems*, I (1956), pp. 55–62, "Higher Levels of Integration", *Science*, 95 (1942), pp. 309–313, R.W. Gerard, C. Kluckhohn, and A. Rapoport, "Biological and Cultural Evolution", *Behavioral Science*, I (1956), pp. 6–14. Anatol Rapoport, "Some System Approaches to Political Theory" in David Easton, ed. *Varieties of Political Theory* (Englewood Cliffs, N.J.: Prentice-Hall, 1966), pp. 129–141; John R. Platt, "Hierarchical Restructuring" in *Bulletin of the Atomic Scientists*, Nov. 1970, pp. 2–4, 46–48, also in *General Systems*, Vol. 5 (1970), pp. 49–54. Cf. also Roy F. Grinker, ed., *Towards a Unified Theory of Human Behavior* (New York: Basic Books, 1954, 2nd ed.) esp. the chapters by Talcott Parsons, Anatol Rapoport, K.W. Deutsch and John P. Spiegel.

[30] Claude E. Shannon and Warren Weaver, *The Mathematical Theory of Communication* (Urbana, Ill.: University of Illinois Press, 1949); N. Wiener, *Cybernetics*, 2nd ed. (Cambridge, Mass.: M.I.T. Press, 1961), and *The Human Use of Human Beings* (Boston: Houghton Mifflin, 1950, and New York: Avon Books, 1967); Warren S. McCulloch, *Embodiments of Mind* (Cambridge, Mass.: M.I.T. Press, 1965); A. Ross Ashby, *An Introduction to Cybernetics* (New York: Wiley, 1956), and *Design for a Brain*, 2nd ed. (New York: Wiley, 1960); W. Grey Walten, *The Living Brain* (New York: Norton, 1953); Colin Cherry, *On Human Communication* (New York: Wiley, 1957); George A. Miller, "The Magical Number Seven, Plus or Minus Two: Some Limits on Our Capacity to Process Information," *Psychological Review* 63 (March 1956), pp. 81–82; J.R. Pierce, *Symbols, Signals and Noise* (New York: Harper & Row, 1965); Georg Klaus, *Kybernetik und Gesellschaft* (Berlin (East): VEB Deutscher Verlag der Wissenschaften, 1965). On automata theory and artificial intelligence, see the articles by George A. Miller and N. Chomsky in D. Luce, ed., *Handbook of Mathematical Psychology* (New York: Wiley, 1963–65) 3 vols.; Herbert Simon, *The Sciences of the Artificial* (Cambridge, Mass.: MIT Press, 1969); Allen Newell and Herbert Simon, *Human Problem Solving* (Englewood Cliffs, N.J.: Prentice-Hall, 1972).

and control oriented approaches, often referred to by Norbert Wiener's term *cybernetics* – a term earlier proposed by Ampère – may be considered a part of general systems theory. More specific work on automata theory and artificial intelligence has informed computer science, mathematical linguistics and the various other social sciences. Certainly, no general systems model nowadays could be considered well developed if it ignored the cybernetic aspects – the communication channels, information flow, storage and recall feedback processes, perception and recognition, information screens or filters, and the like – of the government or political system which it purported to resemble. The models of political systems, and generally of complex organizations, proposed by such writers as David Easton and Amitai Etzioni, show significant advances in just this direction.[31]

The approaches and models of general systems theory have led to significant insights and hypotheses for further testing. James G. Miller has proposed 168 cross-level hypotheses, that is, hypotheses applicable to more than one system level; and John R. Platt in his essay on hierarchical restructuring has stressed the crucial role of the interplay of processes of change on at least three system levels – not only the system level on which the main phenomenon studied actually occurs but also at least the levels immediately below (the subsystems) and above (the suprasystem).[32] But in these and most other cases, the connection between relatively more complex systems models and actual data has not yet been established. To produce just such a connection between complex systems models and specific data is one of the main tasks of the growing amount of work on computer simulation.

---

[31] David Easton, *The Political System* (New York: Knopf, 1953), *A Framework for Political Analysis* (Englewood Cliffs, N.J.: Prentice-Hall, 1965), and *A Systems Analysis of Political Life* (New York: Wiley, 1965); Charles A. McClelland, "Applications of General Systems Theory in International Relations," *Main Currents in Modern Thought*, 12 (November 1955), pp. 27–34; Amitai Etzioni, *The Active Society* (New York: Free Press, 1968); Herbert A. Simon, *The Sciences of the Artificial* (Cambridge: MIT Press, 1969); Herbert Simon and Allen Newell "Information Processing in Computer and Man," *American Scientist* (Sept. 1964), pp. 281–300; Hayward Alker, Le comportement directeur, *Revue Française de Sociologie*, Supplement 1972.

[32] James G. Miller, "Living Systems: Cross-Level Hypotheses" in *Behavioral Science* 10 (October 1965), pp. 337–411; and John Platt, "Hierarchical Growth" in *Bulletin of the Atomic Scientists*, November 1970, pp. 2–4, 46–48.

Simulation of Political Systems, Processes and Structures

Already in the early 1950s, teams of mathematicians, scientists and engineers had succeeded in simulating on the computers of the time the behavior of river systems, including the effects of changing frequency and amount of rainfall, freezing or melting of ice and snow, the operation of dams and locks, and the probable extent, times and areas of flooding. Similarly, they had succeeded in simulating the behavior of electric power systems, including the network of thermal and water power stations, transmission lines and transformer facilities, the distribution and timing of anticipated demands for power, the effects of changing water levels in the reservoirs serving hydro-electric power plants, and the effects of temporary damage or other sudden or "transient" changes in any part of the system.

Since the late 1940s, economists such as Lawrence Klein, J. Orcutt and later D. Suits had simulated the operation of the economy of the United States, and similar simulations were developed for the British economy and for the economy of Venezuela.[33]

In the field of political science, simulation developed later. The first approaches depended almost always on role-playing, with human actors taking the role of various governments, individual statesmen, or of particular bureaucratic agencies, non-governmental organizations, interest groups, or parties. Such role-playing simulation experiments were reported on early by Lincoln Bloomfield and Hans Speier, and later developed particularly by Harold Guetzkow and his collaborators.[34] Eventually they were relatively widely

[33] Irma Adelman, "Simulation: Economic processes," *International Encyclopedia of the Social Sciences*, (New York: Collier-Macmillan, 1968), vol. 14, pp. 268–274, with references; Cf. also Charles F. Hermann, "Simulation: Political Processes, *Ibid.*, pp. 274–281, with references; Martin Shubik, "Bibliography on Simulation, Gaming, Artificial Intelligence and Allied Topics," *Journal of the American Statistical Association* (1960), 55: 736–751, and *Simulation of Socio-Economic Systems. Part 2: An Aggregative Socio-Economic Simulation of a Latin American Country.* Cowles Foundation for Research in Economic Discussion Paper No. 203, (New Haven: Cowles Foundation, 1966); Edward P. Holland and Robert W. Gillespie, *Experiments on a Simulated Underdeveloped Economy: Development Plans and Balance-of-Payment Policies* (Cambridge, Mass.: MIT Press, 1963).

[34] Lincoln Bloomfield, "Three Experiments in Political Gaming" *American Political Science Review* 53, (December 1959) pp. 1105–15; Harold Guetzkow, *et al.*, *Simulation in International Relations: Developments for Research and Teaching* (Englewood Cliffs, N.J.: Prentice–Hall, 1963), and Harold Guetzkow, ed., *Simulation in Social Science: Readings* (Englewood Cliffs, N.J.: Prentice-Hall, Inc., 1962); "Some Correspondences between Simu-

accepted in schools, universities, and parts of the armed services and their intellectual ancillary institutions as tools for education, personnel training and, less frequently, problem exploration.

Already in the purely role-playing games, objective reality was represented to some extent by the different resources and strategic options placed at the disposal of each player, and often by the decisions of one or several umpires who decided whether some particular move or outcome was permissible within the framework of the game. Eventually, as more data became available and their relevance was more widely recognized, such data were stored in a computer, together with some simple programs representing the most obviously anticipated countermoves of other players and the outcome of the interplay of this entire round of moves and countermoves on the situation of the game and of each player. In Oliver Benson's "diplomatic game," each player, representing a country with a configuration of economic, military and diplomatic resources, based on the recent actual statistics for that country, has a choice of several moves. He can make or dissolve an alliance with another country, he can attack another country or desist from an attack already underway, or he can choose to do nothing. Whatever "move" he makes is reported to a computer which quickly informs him and all other players about the outcome of this move. Players thus receive constant feedback information about the consequences of their actions. The simulation exercise develops in this manner from a purely human role playing game to a mixed man–machine simulation in which the computer represents the large social, economic and political facts, structures and forces which are specific to a particular time, place and situation, and which cannot be simply overridden by the mere decision of an individual.[35]

---

lations and 'Realities' in International Relations," in Morton A. Kaplan, ed., *New Approaches to International Relations* (New York: St. Martin's Press, 1968), pp. 202–269. For an important critical summary of comparisons of simulation results with real world events, see Harold Guetzkow. In a tabulation of the results of 55 comparisons drawn from 24 studies, Guetzkow found that "almost two-thirds of the entries consist of assessments in which the findings from the simulations correspond with "Some" or "Much" similarity to the findings in the reference materials," *Ibid.*, p. 252.

[35] Oliver Benson, "The Use of Mathematics in the Study of Political Science" in *Mathematics and the Social Sciences*, ed. James C. Charlesworth (Philadelphia: The American Academy of Political and Social Science) Monograph No. 2, June 1963, pp. 30–57; and "A Simple Diplomatic Game" in James N. Rosenau, ed., *International Politics and Foreign Policy: A Reader in Research and Theory*, 1st ed. (New York: Free Press, 1961), pp. 504–511.

As this approach was carried further, particularly in the field of international politics by Harold Guetzkow, Paul Smoker and Hayward Alker, the computer-operated share of the simulation was increased until all-computer simulations were developed. It then became possible to compare for one and the same situation or problem simulated the outcomes of several "all-human" role-playing simulations (differing for example in the skill and expertise of personnel, such as high school students, or non-commissioned officers, in contrast to experienced diplomats, high-ranking officers, or business executives) with the results of mixed man–machine simulations and with those of several "all-computer" simulations incorporating somewhat different data sets and operating rules; and all these different simulations could then be compared with the actual outcomes of one or several comparable real-world cases. So far, these new opportunities for systematic comparisons across different system levels have not been followed up in depth, and such systematic empirical and critical comparisons remain yet for the most part to be carried out.

Thus far, the most important work toward a world-wide model of the international system of trade, with clear political implications, has been developed by a Swiss economist, Bruno Fritsch, and his collaborators. The ecological world model developed by J.W. Forrester, D. Meadows and their associates, represents an impressive demonstration of the technical potentialities of computer modelling but omits all political data and, indeed, most data about economic and social learning behavior, and it employs no systematic empirical validating procedures.[36]

Somewhat better progress has been made with simulations at the level of the national political system. Here models were developed that no longer depended on role-playing but rather used explicit quantitative data and relationships suitable for computer processing. A massive use of public data from a longer period permitted Ithiel Pool, Robert Abelson and Samuel Popkin to construct a process model of the American electorate that could be operated so as to derive single case implications; it was used successfully in 1960 to

[36] René Codoni, Bruno Fritsch, *et al.*, *World Trade Flows: Integrational Structure and Conditional Forecasts* 2 vols., (Zurich: Schulthess Verlag, 1971), J.W. Forrester, *World Dynamics* (Cambridge, Mass.: Wright Allen Press, 1971); Donella H. Meadows *et al., The Limits to Growth* (New York: Universe Books, 1972).

predict probable voter responses to various political issues and contingencies. To predict the issues which would in fact become salient in any particular campaign, however, had to be left to the subjective judgement of the investigators! A few years later, Gerald Kramer developed an econometric probabilistic model of the general tendency of American voters to respond to the rise or fall of economic prosperity and the tenure of office by one or the other of the two major parties. This model differed in kind from the Abelson-Pool-Popkin one. It did not predict well all single-case results but it accounted successfully for nearly two-thirds of the variance of the percentage share of the Republican Party in the major party votes cast in Presidential elections in the United States from 1924 to 1964; and it permitted an estimation of the extent to which particular candidates had done better (such as President Eisenhower in 1956) or worse (such as Senator Barry Goldwater in 1964) than the anticipated vote for their party, as predicted by Kramer's general model. More limited computer simulation research was carried out in the German Federal Republic by Werner Kaltefleiter who tested the expectable effects of various proposed changes in the West German electoral laws by applying them to the actual votes cast at earlier national elections.[37]

More elaborate all-computer models of the political systems of developing countries have been worked out by José A. Silva Michelena and Frank Bonilla for Venezuela, and by Ronald Brunner and Gary Brewer with the aim of applicability to a wider range of developing countries.[38]

At the present stage, most of the all-computer simulations are not broadly enough based on data about all of even the most relevant aspects of the political system to permit any broader modeling of expectable political responses to a wider range of problems or contingencies, and over a more extended period of time. With the partial exception of the studies in the Varsavsky-Calcagno and Bonilla-Silva Michelena volumes, almost all existing political computer models

---

[37] Werner Kaltefleiter, oral communication, Harvard University, Cambridge, Mass., 1970.

[38] José A. Silva Michelena and Frank Bonilla, eds., *Strategies for Research on Social Policy*, Vol. 1, *The Politics of Change in Venezuela* (Cambridge, Mass.: M.I.T. Press, 1967); José A. Silva Michelena, *The Illusion of Democracy in Dependent Nations* (Cambridge, Mass.: M.I.T. Press, 1971); Frank Bonilla, *The Failure of Elites* (Cambridge, Mass.: M.I.T. Press, 1970). For a discussion of Brunner's thesis, see the chapter by Hayward Alker in this volume. On the important work by O. Varsavsky, see ref. 15, above.

contain no quantitative data or estimates about *inequalities* of income, prestige, political representation, propensity to organize and similar matters of obvious political significance. Most models also make no use of data about the differences in attitudes, behavior and resources among different *age groups* and *age cohorts.* (The latter are persons born in about the same period, and thus likely to have experienced the same highly salient political or social event at about the same impressionable or "formative" age in their lives.)

Nor do present all-computer models make any explicit assumptions about the *frequency and magnitude of errors* of perception or judgment, or failures of communication or execution, and the like, except insofar as models of "satisficing" behavior, or else the use of Monte Carlo Methods, imply some allowances for errors on the part of the actors. Such models, however, are not widely used in political science. Rather, many studies treat more naively a policy decision as equivalent to its execution, and errors in perception or action as non-existent or insignificant. No engineer would dare build an elaborate machine without some estimate of the frequency of errors by its operators and of failure of some of its components. Most of our all-computer models of political systems have not yet reached this level of sophistication. They do not use numbers to take into account the expectable frequency and size of errors, and hence their probable effects. Only some studies of crisis decision-making form here a laudable exception. Generally, however, we are only beginning to collect empirical data on such error or failure frequencies. Armies have long collected data on the frequency of desertions by soldiers but they do not appear to have done so for the frequency of major errors by generals, governments or heads of state. Among civilian scholars, J. David Singer has been the first, so far as I know, to have systematically collected data about all wars within political systems from 1816 through 1965, making it possible to compute the frequency with which wars were initiated by governments who subsequently lost them. If we define "losing" a war one has started as "failing to win the major stated objective for which the military initiative was undertaken," – or else the major "real" objective as identified by historians and analysts of policy – then the decision to initiate a war (that is large-scale organized hostilities across an international boundary or line of demarcation) turned out to be erroneous for the initiating government in one-third of all cases. This average error rate 1816–1965 conceals a historic change. From 1816 through 1910, starting a war ended in failure for the initiator in only about one-fifth of the cases; but from 1911 through 1965, this error rate was as high as three-fifths of all cases. (The Vietnam war, which was deliberately escalated by the United States under President Lyndon Johnson in 1965 but had no definite outcome in that year, is not included in this tabulation.)[39]

It is here, in supplying data, or at least evidence for estimates, of human behavior in situations which are crucial but hard to observe, that "manned" or role-playing types of simulation, pure or in combination with the use of computer data and responses, can make a continuing and important contribution. How often do players in games, simulating some international situation or conflict, grossly misperceive the intentions or even actions of their adversaries, or their current allies? What are their likely reactions to future surprises? By how much or how little are these error frequencies reduced by the educational level, specific expertise, general executive experience, age, rank, sex or other characteristics of the personnel playing the decision-making roles? Harold Guetzkow and Charles Herman have reported that in identical world politics games, played once by Navy petty officers, and once by senior officers, diplomats, or business executives, the players with the simpler cognitive structure were more likely to choose policies of force and to make decisions leading to war than were their more sophisticated counterparts.[40] It would be important to establish the amount as well as the

[39] On "satisficing" behavior, see Herbert Simon, in Paul F.Lazarsfeld, ed., *Mathematical Thinking in the Social Sciences* (New York: Russell and Russell, 1969), pp. 388–415. On crisis decision-making, see Ithiel de Sola Pool and Allan Kessler, "The Kaiser, the Tsar and the Computers: Information Processing in a Crisis," *American Behavioral Scientist*, 8 (May 1965), pp. 31–38; Charles F. Hermann, ed., *International Crises: Insights from Behavioral Research* (New York: Free Press, 1972). For the frequency of errors in initiating wars, see K.W. Deutsch and Dieter Senghaas, "Die brüchige Vernunft von Staaten" in D. Senghaas, ed., *Kritische Friedensforschung* (Frankfurt: Suhrkamp, 1971), pp. 105–163, esp. 106, 146, 156; J. David Singer, *The Wages of War* (New York: Wiley, 1972); and J. David Singer, S. Bramer and J. Stuckey "Capability Distribution, Uncertainty, and Major Power War, 1820–1965" in *Peace, War and Numbers*, ed. Bruce Russett (Beverly Hills, Calif.: Sage Publications, 1972).

[40] Harold Guetzkow, ed. *Simulation in Social Science: Readings* (Englewood Cliffs, N.J.: Prentice-Hall, 1962), and H. Guetzkow, Charles Hermann, *et al. Simulation in International Relations* Englewood Cliffs, N.J.: Prentice-Hall, 1963); H.R. Alker, Jr. and Ronald Brunner, "Simulating International Conflict: A Comparison of Three Approaches," *International Studies Quarterly*, 13, 1 (March 1969); William Coplin, ed., *Simulation in the Study of Politics* (Chicago: Markham Publishing Company, 1968).

direction of this difference, and generally to use role-playing simulations to gain quantitative behavioral data of this kind, such as the effects of time pressure, fatigue, fear and threats on the greater or lesser rationality or propensity to decisions for policies of violence on the part of decision-makers in crises and deterrence situations.[41] These data, or estimates compatible with them, could then be put into the appropriate terms of a new generation of improved all-computer models; and this dialog between wholly or partly human-operated role-playing simulations and fully automated all-computer versions could then continue for the mutual development of both.

As regards simulations on the level of the national political system, we need a continuing dialog between the present highly abstract, or else sectorally limited computer models and much richer information available from aggregate data, survey research, from political analysis, and from historic, descriptive and institutional studies. Too often in the past, simulation methods in economics as well as politics have omitted the health, culture, habits, motivations, skills and values of the population, the work force or the electorate, as well as of management and of important sectors of consumers. Gunnar Myrdal has forcefully criticized these persistent sins of omission in most of the currently conventional Western theories of economic development, but with minor modifications his criticisms might apply to much current theorizing about political development as well. Abstract models in theory and computer simulation can help to free mere historic knowledge and area expertise from their usual incapacity to produce testable extrapolations, projections and predictions, but without the richness and depth of many kinds of knowledge, abstract models and theories may well remain arid and their predictions and policy advice misleading.[42]

If this reasoning were accepted, it would follow that we should

---

[41] Cf. the earlier work reported in Roy W. Grinker and John P. Spiegel, *Men under Stress* (San Francisco, Calif.: University of California Printing Department, 1964); Herbert Kelman, ed., *International Behavior: A Social-Psychological Analysis* (New York: Holt, 1965).

[42] Cf. Gunnar Myrdal, *The Challenge of World Poverty* (Harmondsworth, Middlesex: Penguin Books, 1971), pp. 22–59, *Value in Social Theory: A Selection of Essays on Methodology* (New York: Harper, 1958; London: Routledge, 1958), and *Objectivity in Social Research* (New York: Pantheon Books, 1969); Stanley Hoffmann, ed., *Contemporary Theory in International Relations* (Englewood Cliffs, N.J.: Prentice-Hall, 1961).

give priority of attention during the next few years to simulations of the national political systems of highly developed countries, such as the United States, France, West Germany, Britain, Norway, and the Netherlands. For all of these there are available rich statistical and survey data, analytic and descriptive political studies, and historical, economic, sociological and literary information; and we should not try to go directly to attempt simulating the political system of some less developed country about which much less is known in most or all of these respects. There are many competent scholars in each of these highly developed countries, as well as in the United States, who would be able and willing to cooperate in such attempts at turning political theory to some extent into an experimental science and making simulation work in regard to countries about which we know enough to make speedy and multiple testing of the models possible. To the extent that sub-national or supra-national political systems or actors should prove to be more important in their influence on political outcomes, the simulation of such systems might also deserve priority attention, if at least a minimum of requisite data should be obtainable. On the same grounds of relevance to world politics, simulation models of the Soviet Union, Japan, China, and India should be attempted as soon as practicable – perhaps within the next 5 or 10 years.

Until now, at least in the United States, public and private funding agencies have in effect refused to permit such a development. They have had little interest in supporting a better understanding of the politics of a country which the United States cannot manipulate as a junior ally under hegemony, and need not fear as an enemy. Moreover, most executives imagine that the politics of highly developed countries are already adequately understood, or else that they are unintelligible except in terms of personalities. These imaginings are false. Mutual understanding of one another's political system and processes is far from adequate among highly developed countries, but it can be improved most easily and thoroughly among countries of this type. Less developed countries may seem to offer more opportunities – and temptations – for the exercise of power to the policy-makers of the United States and some other highly developed countries. With luck, these policy-makers may at least know that they need more and better knowledge of the peoples and political systems of the countries that may look like more "power vacuums" and "dominoes" to those who view them from a great geographic and intellectual distance. Consequently, some of the more thoughtful decision-makers and other elite members have tended to encourage political research on these countries, although often within narrow pre-conceived frames. But such research, if its results are not to be misleading, requires the application of better and more deeply understood political theories, and methods of research and simulation, which do not as yet exist. The creation of this knowledge may well be in part a roundabout process, and it may have to start to a larger extent through the simulation of the political systems of highly developed countries – or else be delayed for a good many years.

In the meantime, of course, efforts at modeling the political systems of various developing countries will continue, albeit with less than adequate cognitive and financial resources, and subject to the risk of manipulative pressures or misuse from outside. Even so, this work, too, will be worth supporting. Particularly when scholars from the less developed country or region itself carry on this work it may yield valuable insights, and it may help to develop the intellectual capabilities and personnel of the developing country toward earlier and more far-reaching self-determination.

While the material support for large-scale simulations of national and international political systems is thus still lagging, the intellectual resources for carrying this work forward have increased substantially. Even partial simulations of particular institutions, functional areas, and the like may be carried on now, so as to prepare the ground for their later integration into more comprehensive models of a larger and more relevant system. Some of the past developments in this direction have been sketched in the preceding pages. Perhaps even more important contributions are now being developed, or appear within reach. The rest of this introductory essay will be devoted to these new departures and to what seem to be some of the most promising directions for further work.

Some Promising Developments

From One-Way Causation to Feedback Process Models

Perhaps the most important major development would be the

transition from one-way causal thinking and causal modeling to genuine cybernetic models, embodying causal loops and circuits of feedback processes, as well as their results in the direction of homeostasis, goal-seeking, or cumulative change and eventual systems transformation. Mathematical methods and models from which performance characteristics and changing output variables can be computed have long been in existence in the field of control engineering. Many actual control systems are in operation in many countries ranging from thermostats in buildings and laboratories, to automatic pilots in aircraft and to entire automatic factories in modern industry. Yet many of the mathematical and designing skills involved in these practices have been transferred so far only very incompletely to the modeling of economic systems, and to an even lesser degree to the modeling of political systems and processes.

Many negative feedback controls are so organized that they tend to bring the system into a goal state or target state in relation to the outside world, and then to keep it in that state. Some subsystem may control the setting of this goal or target value toward which the system then will tend. In most man-made machinery of this kind, such as in the familiar thermostat, this goal value is set from the outside by a human operator, for we want our machines to pursue our goals and not their own. Several writers have concentrated their attention on this process of setting the target values for the goal-seeking system. Who sets the target values, they have argued, and who controls the target-setting subsystem, (such as the appropriate pointer or dial on the thermostat), controls the entire system.[43]

There is some truth in this observation and some merit in the preoccupation with following up its implications for research and analysis. But as we have noted, these externally manipulable target-setting subsystems are characteristic of man-made machinery deliberately designed to be subservient to us; they are absent in this form in most of the cybernetic systems which we find in nature or in human society. The large feedback system of meteorology and ecology, the social, cultural, political or economic feedback systems of human society, and the physiological and neurological feedback systems of living organisms do not have any such convenient knobs, dials or

[43] Cf. Georg Klaus, *Kybernetik und Gesellschaft* (Berlin (East): VEB Deutscher Verlag der Wissenschaften, 1965, 2nd ed.); Helmar Frank, *Kybernetische Maschinen* (Frankfurt am Main: S. Fischer Verlag, 1964).

buttons attached to them through which their behavior can be conveniently manipulated from outside. On the contrary, most of these naturally or historically developed systems are to some degree autonomous and tend to make outside manipulation quite difficult or even impractical. They may possess, however, some internal feedback processes by which their goals or target values may be changed and the performance of their goal-setting subsystems modified. They are thus often capable of goal-changing feedback or even of far-reaching self-transformation. Natural autonomous systems with these characteristics are capable of goal change, and of mutation and evolution; and these are indeed found throughout the world of organisms, and to a lesser degree, even in many non-living systems, from molecules to planets, stars and galaxies.

In societies and political systems, too, the autonomous processes of goal change and evolution are found, and the rise of new forms of organization, of writing, record-keeping and communication, and of historical, social and political awareness are observable. Conscious efforts to influence the fate of societies, states, and of all mankind may then also be seen as a new set of goal-changing and perhaps even structure-transforming feedback processes, arising autonomously within a society or being brought to it from the outside and thus eliciting more or less autonomous responses. It is these at least partly autonomous goal-changing and structure-transforming processes for which we most urgently need mathematical models of the feedback type, perhaps using the technique of multiple equations, and freeing ourselves from the narrower framework of one-way causal thinking.[44]

The Data Revolution and Its Implications

The development of new models implies the need also for new

---

[44] See the draft paper by Hayward R. Alker, Jr., presented at the VIIIth World Congress of Political Science, Munich 1970, "Multivariate Methods in Political Science: A Review, Critique and Some Further Suggestions" (Brussels: International Political Science Association, multigraphed); Hayward R. Alker, Jr. and William Greenberg, "The United Nations Charter: Alternate Pasts and Alternate Futures," in *The United Nations: Problems and Prospects*, E.H. Fedder, ed., (St. Louis: Center for International Studies, University of Missouri, 1971); Ronald D. Brunner, "Processes in Political Development: Simulating Theories of Political Systems," (PhD Thesis, Yale University, 1971); and the comments on this last-named work in Alker's chapter in this volume.

data, in larger amounts, in longer time series, and often of new kinds, serving as indicators of processes not previously highlighted in analysis.[45] In addition, there is much more need for *derived data*, developed from the raw data directly available from various sources. We need ratios, rates of change, statistical distributions; indices of inequality, and sometimes the rates of change in these; breakdowns by sub-populations and sub-periods; percentage shares; coefficients of correlation and determination, and often again their rates of change. Many of these derived data have been generated but they need to be kept available for quick preliminary comparisons and testing, and for new secondary analyses in the light of new theories and questions.

How can these new amounts and kinds of data be obtained? And once obtained, how can they be maintained and kept available? In all these respects, the 1960s have seen substantial progress. International organizations, particularly the United Nations and its affiliated economic and social agencies, have greatly increased the quantity and quality of published economic and social data which are highly relevant for political analysis. The United Nations *Survey of the World Social Situation*, the United Nations *Statistical Yearbook*, the *Annual Reports* of the United Nations Economic Commissions for Europe (ECE), Latin America (ECLA), Africa and Asia and the Far East (ECAFE), the statistical publications of the United Nations Education, Scientific and Cultural Organization (UNESCO), the International Labour Organization (ILO), the World Health Organization (WHO), the United Nations Food and Agricultural Organization (FAO), the International Monetary Fund (IMF) and the International Bank for Reconstruction and Development (IBRD), the Organization for Economic Cooperation and Development (OECD) – all these are examples of the large new data sources that have become available during the last quarter century, and that in the 1970s, together with their predecessor organizations, now offer information with a time depth of two or more decades.

In addition, the statistical data available from national govern-

[45] For some of the difficulties of operationalizing some of the new theories and models, and their key variables, see the thoughtful criticisms of Wolf-Dieter Narr, *Theoriebegriffe und Systemtheorie* (Stuttgart: Kohlhammer Verlag, 1969), pp. 108–110, 178–182; Frieder Naschold, *Systemsteuerung* (Stuttgart: Kohlhammer Verlag, 1969), pp. 122–127, 135–136, 144–145, 158, 161–166; and W.D. Narr and F. Naschold, *Theorie der Demokratie* (Stuttgart: Kohlhammer Verlag, 1971), pp. 240–252.

ments have increased greatly in the 1950s and 1960s. In many of the less developed countries, statistical services have been organized and personnel trained with United Nations assistance, with significant gains in the scope, uniformity, comparability and quality of data.

During the same decade of the 1960s, the availability of survey data has increased greatly, and data archives and data centers have developed in the United States and in Western Europe, with significant beginnings in Latin America, Japan, India, and to some extent in Subsaharan Africa. The Inter-University Consortium for Political Research at the University of Michigan at Ann Arbor, Michigan, the Roper Center for Public Opinion Research at Williamstown, Massachusetts, the public opinion and survey research activities at Columbia University, at the University of California at Berkeley and at Los Angeles, and at the University of North Carolina in the United States, the European Zentralarchiv für Empirische Sozialforschung at the University of Cologne, the Institut Français d'Opinion Publique (IFOP) at Paris, the INFAS/DATUM Institute at Bonn-Godesberg and the Institut für Demoskopie at Allensbach in Germany, and to some extent the Institute of Behavioral Sciences at Tokyo, Instituto Torcuato Di Tella at Buenos Aires, the Behavioral Sciences Centre at New Delhi, and Rajni Kothari's Center for the Study of Developing Societies – all these are outstanding examples of the wealth of survey data and institutions that have carried on work during this period.

In response to these new opportunities, as well as to the need of theorists for more ample and more appropriate data to test their theories, several university data centers or programs have developed. Major examples are the Yale World Data Program, founded originally by H.D. Lasswell and K.W. Deutsch, and long led by Bruce M. Russett, with major support at various times by Hayward R. Alker, Jr. and Richard L. Merritt, and more recently continued by Michael Hudson and Charles L. Taylor;[46] the *Cross-Polity Survey* by Arthur

[46] Bruce M. Russett, Hayward Alker, Karl Deutsch, Harold Lasswell, *World Handbook of Political and Social Indicators*, 1st ed. 1964; Michael Hudson and Charles L. Taylor, *World Handbook of Political and Social Indicators*, 2nd ed., 1972 (New Haven: Yale University Press); Richard L. Merritt and Stein Rokkan, eds., *Comparing Nations: The Use of Quantitative Data in Cross-National Research* (New Haven: Yale University Press, 1966); Charles L. Taylor, ed., *Aggregate Data Analysis* (Paris–The Hague: Mouton, 1968); Ellen Mickiewicz, ed., *Handbook of Soviet Social Science Data* (New York: The Free Press, 1973). See also Bruce Russett, *International Regions and the International System* (Chicago: Rand McNally, 1967), and *Trends in World Politics* (New York: Macmillan, 1965).

Banks and Robert Textor published by M.I.T. and the statistical series published by Arthur Banks at the State University of New York at Binghamton, N.Y.,[47] the work by Robert Holt, John Turner, William Flanigan and Edward Fogleman at the University of Minnesota; and the promising work undertaken by Raymond Bauer, Bertram Gross and others, mostly at Washington, D.C., in the search for a system of social indicators as an aid in the evaluation of the social state of the nation and of the results of particular governmental policies and programs.[48] Examples in Europe are the work of Wolfgang Zapf on long-term data series at the University of Frankfurt; in Hungary, the volume of data edited by Alexander Rado; and in Czechoslavakia the somewhat uneven two volumes of data compiled by a team of scholars.[49]

Toward a Second Data Revolution?

Many of the readily available data about the performance of governments and of national political and economic systems have been oriented toward various forms of economic output, – such as the production of steel or electric energy, or such aggregate indices as the gross national product (G.N.P.), the gross domestic product (G.D.P.), the net national product (N.N.P.), or national income, and the like – and to the amount and productivity of work performed. Data of this kind have been criticized on the grounds that they do

---

[47] Arthur S. Banks and Robert R. Textor, *A Cross Polity Survey* (Cambridge, Mass.: M.I.T. Press, 1963); A. Banks, *Cross–Polity Time Series Data* (Cambridge, Mass.: M.I.T. Press, 1971).

[48] Robert Holt and John Turner, *The Political Basis of Economic Development* (Princeton: Van Nostrand, 1966); William Flanigan and Edward Fogleman, *The Minnesota Political Data Archive* (Minneapolis; University of Minnesota) and (eds.) *The Methodology of Comparative Research* (New York: Free Press, 1970); Raymond Bauer, ed., *Social Indicators* (Cambridge, Mass.: M.I.T. Press, 1966); Bertram M. Gross, ed., *Social Goals and Indicators for American Society* (Philadelphia: *The Annals,* Vol. 371, May 1967).

[49] Wolfgang Zapf, manuscript data, Harvard University, 1968, unpublished; W. Zapf and Peter Flora, "Some Problems of Time Series Analysis in Research on Modernization," *Social Science Information*, 10 (1971), pp. 53–102; William Flanigan and Edwin Fogleman, "Patterns of Political Violence in Comparative Historical Perspective," *Comparative Politics,* 1, (Oct. 1970) pp. 1–20; "Patterns of Political Development and Democratization: An Historical Comparative Analysis," both in John Gillespie and Betty Nesvold, eds., *Macro-Quantitative Analysis* (Beverly Hills, Calif.: Sage, 1971).

not measure adequately the well-being of the population and what is called the "quality of life." (By which is often meant the degree of satisfaction or dissatisfaction which they feel themselves, or else which they ought to feel, according to some critical observer.)

A new detergent, it is pointed out, is counted as an addition to the gross national product, but any river pollution or other environmental damage caused by it is not deducted, and if expensive devices are built to undo or reduce this damage, these are counted as further additions to the G.N.P., although they merely might have restored the river to its earlier state.

It is useful to remember, therefore, that the G.N.P. and similar production data do not measure well-being, welfare, subjective satisfaction, or the agreement with particular philosophic or esthetic standards. They merely measure economic resources which are more or less available for recommitment by political or social decisions, either in an emergency or in the course of cultural, political or social change. They indicate resources for possible uses, old or new, good or bad, rather than any particular type of use or achievement. But as such indicators of social resources and potentialities, this kind of data remains indispensable for political analysis.

In response to the genuine merits of the new criticism, however, new kinds of data will have to be added to our equipment. These data must be oriented toward a plurality of values, such as those suggested by Harold Lasswell and Abraham Kaplan.[50] They must notably include data on life expectancy and physical and mental health; disposable income and economic security for individuals and families; social and human ties, answering to needs for affiliation and affection; resources for individual's experiences of rectitude, respect and self-respect, and for every person's experiences of some control over the circumstances of his own life, and of some participation in the decisions affecting it.

This approach will require data about uneven *distributions* of the relevant values, resources and opportunities – about their variance over social strata, age groups, the sexes, regional, ethnic or cultural communities, and about the changes or fluctuation of all such distributions over time.

---

[50] Harold Lasswell and Abraham Kaplan, *Power and Society: A Framework for Political Inquiry* (New Haven: Yale University Press, 1950); K.W. Deutsch, "Some Quantitative Constraints on Value Allocation in Society and Politics," *Behavioral Science*, 11:4, July 1966, pp. 245–252.

Similarly, we shall need data about the distribution of indicators of failure in such matters, again differentiated by social classes and strata, and by regional, ethnic, or social groups and categories, in regard to, for example, mortality and morbidity; suicide, murder and other crimes; numbers of persons in prisons or prison camps; numbers of reported cases of desertion, divorce, abandonment or ill-treatment of children; failures of motivation for work or study; drug abuse, and many more.

Moreover, we shall need data about the correlations and feedback effects among many of these data, such as between inequality of wages and incomes, on the one hand, and labor productivity, capital formation, economic growth, and motivation for sustained work or study, on the other. Similarly we need to know more about the effects of censorship and other restrictions on the freedom of inquiry, criticism and expression on the rates of discovery and innovation in science, technology and economic life. We need to know whether such effects are negligible or significant, and in the latter case, whether they are positive or negative, and whether they are relatively large or small in comparison to the effects of other conditions or contingencies on the same kind of outcomes.

A beginning has been made in many of these questions through the study of medical and social statistics, the study of time budgets by Alexander Szalai and others, supported by UNESCO;[51] the work on experimental data, recently surveyed by Jean Laponce; the work on quasi-experimental data by Donald T. Campbell; and indirectly through the work of Charles E. Osgood and his associates on a cross-national atlas of semantic meanings; [52] but most of this work is still

---

[51] Alexander Szalai, *The Use of Time* (Paris–The Hague: Mouton 1972), "Differential Evaluation of Time Budgets for Comparative Purposes" in R.L. Merritt and Stein Rokkan, eds., *Comparing Nations* (New Haven: Yale University Press, 1966), pp. 239–258. Cf. Harrison White, "Uses of Mathematics in Sociology" in *Mathematics and the Social Sciences*, ed. James C. Charlesworth, pp. 77, 87 (1963).

[52] Donald T. Campbell, "Reforms as Experiments," *The American Psychologist* Vol. 24, No. 4 (April 1969) pp. 409–429; Donald T. Campbell and Julian C. Stanley, *Experimental and Quasi-Experimental Designs for Research* (Chicago: Rand McNally 1969, 1963); J.A.Laponce and Paul Smoker, eds., *Experimentation and Simulation in Political Science* (Toronto: University of Toronto Press, 1972); Charles E. Osgood, "Exploration in Semantic Space: A Personal Diary," *The Psychologists* (ed. T.S. Krawiec), (New York: Oxford University Press, 1972); Charles E. Osgood, William H. May and Murray Miron, *Cross-Cultural Universals of Affective Meaning* (Urbana: University of Illinois Press, 1973).

to be done. If and when much of it will be done, its impact on political and social science may well amount to that of a second data revolution.

Waiting Line Theory: A New Tool for Political Analysis

"The German fate," wrote the satirist Kurt Tucholsky many years ago, "is to wait in front of an office window; the German dream is to sit behind one." In many countries, waiting lines have long been a symbol of government, of bureaucracy, and of the unresponsiveness of large organizations, both public and private, to the needs of individuals. Only in recent years, however, have the growth and decline of waiting lines become susceptible to mathematical analysis, and has waiting line theory become an established field of study. As Harrison White's paper in the present volume illustrates, political scientists and students of public administration stand to gain much from the reception of waiting line theory into their own fields, not only for its application to specific technical problems but also as a more general point of view.[53]

In essence, waiting lines arise in the course of attempts to match the time of a client who needs some service with the time of some server who has the capacity to supply it. The client may need a government permit, or a postage stamp, or a seat on a bus or airplane, or a drink of water. The server may be some person, organization or inanimate device, such as a government official, a ticket salesman, a government agency or committee, a bus, a vending machine, or a drinking fountain. The clients arrive at the service point at some average rate, per unit of time, trying to obtain the service; this is called their rate of arrival. Usually their actual rate over shorter time periods varies around this average, ranging from slack times to peak loads, or even varying randomly, and the actual distribution of their arrivals over time has a large influence on the outcome. Servers have a capacity to service on the average, so many clients per unit of time; this is their *potential rate of service.* If the servers are absent for some time, or if the service equipment is sometimes out of order, the *actual rate of service* will be lower than the potential one.

[53] For a general introduction to waiting line theory, see J. Riordan, *Stochastic Service Systems* (New York: Wiley, 1962); D.R. Cox and W.L. Smith, *Queues* (London: Methuen, 1961). See also Harrison White, "Everyday Life in Stochastic Networks," this volume.

The relationship between these two actual rates – the actual rate of arrival (or demand) and the actual rate of service (or accommodation) – is critical for the outcome. If the rate of service exceeds the rate of arrival by a safe margin, no waiting lines will form; or if a temporary fluctuation in either rate would lead to the formation of a waiting line, it would sooner or later be absorbed again. If the rate of service should be less than the rate of arrival, however, waiting lines will form and grow, towards infinity if the process should continue long enough.

What happens if arrival rate and service rate are equal? In that case, the amount and kind of their fluctuations will be decisive. If the arrival rate should vary *randomly*, so that (by the definition of randomness) no variations in the service rate are likely to match it, then waiting lines will grow here, too, and tend to grow toward infinity, as this situation continues. This is because whenever the current arrival rate falls below the rate of service and there is no waiting line, the unused excess service capacity is permanently lost, and when later the arrival rate exceeds the service rate – as it must, if the long-term average of the two rates is to be equal – this excess must produce a waiting line. As the arrival rate continues to fluctuate randomly, the amounts of wasted service capacity will accumulate, but so will the later periods when the arrival rate exceeds the service rate, and the length of the waiting line corresponding to this excess. Given such random fluctuation around an equal *average* rate of actual arrivals and potential service capabilities, waiting line theorists assure us, such waiting lines will slowly tend towards infinity.[54]

It follows that for each average (but fluctuating) arrival rate the average service capacity must be larger, if growing waiting lines and congestion are to be avoided. But how much larger? Just what is the size of the critical margin of excess service capacity which will reduce to a tolerable level the expectable amounts and fluctuations of waiting lines and congestion within the system? And what are the most important conditions – such as perhaps the range and distribu-

[54] Robert Dorfman, oral communication, Harvard University, 1970. See also Harrison White, "Uses of Mathematics in Sociology," in J.C. Charlesworth, ed., *Mathematics and the Social Sciences*, (ref. 35 above), pp. 77–94, esp. pp. 87–89; Philip M. Morse, *Queues, Inventories and Maintenance: The Analysis of Operational Systems with Variable Demand and Supply* (New York: Wiley, 1958); Harrison C. White, *Chains of Opportunity: System Models of Mobility in Organizations* (Cambridge, Mass.: Harvard University Press, 1970).

tion of the variations in the arrival rate – which influence the size of this necessary margin of excess (or reserve) capacity?

Answers to these questions could have far-reaching implications for many problems in politics and economics. If the required margin of excess service capacity should only amount to two or three percent, the problem of providing and maintaining such a margin is likely to be often trivial. But if this needed margin should be between five and fifteen percent, the problem often would be less easy, and if this margin should be between twenty and thirty percent, or even higher, the situation must be serious indeed. At present, we do not know at all well in many cases even the order of magnitude of the required margins of excess capacity to protect the system from frustratingly long waiting lines and waiting periods. Without any realistic order-of-magnitude notion of this kind, however, we may not be able to think effectively about the problem; and as yet we are usually even farther away from the detailed calculations; taking account of the complex interplay of many specific factors and conditions, from which we might discover the actual margin of excess capacity needed in a concrete case.

Possible Implications for Unemployment and Customs Unions

Many examples of such waiting line problems from the fields of government, public and private bureaucracies, production scheduling, traffic and transportation planning, telecommunications and the service industries should be obvious. But even the general problem of unemployment might have a waiting line component that goes well beyond what used to be called "friction" in the traditional economics textbooks. If a certain number of jobs opens up each year through the death, retirement or migration of their present incumbents, these openings occur at least in part in random fashion; and many jobseekers – with the important exception of relatively inexperienced high school and college graduates – also enter the labor market at more or less random times. If we think of each jobseeker as a request for placement in a job acceptable to him, and each hiring of a new employee as a service satisfying such a request, then we can see that waiting lines are likely to arise and grow, unless the number of acceptable job openings remains in excess of job requests by some critical margin. Full employment, and tolerably brief periods of job search for persons seeking to be placed, will thus require a margin of economic growth and of expanding employment opportunities. If this critical margin should be larger – as it well may be – than what the automatic processes of the market under the classic equilibrium models are likely to provide, political interventions in the economic process may be necessary.

A similar line of reasoning calling for more research, may well apply to *customs unions* and to the general problem of *economic integration* among hitherto separate markets or sovereign states.

According to classical economic theory, an effective customs union between two previously separated countries would merge their economies into a single market within which competition would have free play. In such a situation, the classic theory predicts, the less efficient industries in each country (less efficient in the sense of producing less output sold per unit of employed capital, land and labor) would be forced to shrink. In particular, capital would soon be diverted away from them and rechanneled into more efficient industries, yielding higher profits to capital in the new customs union. The shrinking industries then would have to discharge labor into market, while the expanding industries would increase their number of jobs and employees. Classical theory often seems to suggest that the number of new jobs created in expanding industries in each country of the customs union would eventually balance the number of jobs in the shrinking industries there, and that after some adjustment period, total employent would be just as high as if the two countries or markets had remained separated from each other.[55]

All these arguments, however, still ignore the waiting line effects. The less efficient industries will not all close on one day in response to their loss of tariff protection, nor will the more efficient industries expand their job offerings on the same day in response to their enhanced sales opportunities in the larger common market. Rather, workers discharged by the shrinking industries are likely to appear in

[55] Actual classical forecasts are more complex. If the efficient expanding industries should use more modern labor-saving machinery, and hence relatively more capital and less labor, and if the less efficient shrinking industries on the average should be more labor-intensive, then even by classic economic reasoning a customs union might wipe out more old jobs than it would create new ones. Conversely, if a customs union should increase the average profits of capital, as it might under some conditions, then it could stimulate additional domestic savings and investments or attract additional investments from abroad, so that the total volume of employment in the customs union area might increase.

the market gradually and more or less at random times, looking for new jobs, and the new job offerings from the expanding industries will also appear in the market only gradually and more or less at random.

If the number of new jobs created by the custom union should be less than, or even equal to, the number of new jobs created, then waiting line theory under these circumstances would predict that the waiting lines of unemployment in the labor market would tend to keep growing throughout the period of industrial adjustment. A balance of jobs lost and jobs gained, in short, would not be good enough. Only an expansion of the economy and its job structure, keeping the new jobs created ahead by a critical margin of the old jobs lost, could prevent the long-term unemployment in such a customs union.

A first rough implication of this reasoning is that customs unions ought to be attempted only in the early stages of periods of economic expansion, if avoiding protracted additional unemployment is a goal of policy.

A second implication is that the size of the required margin of additional employment opportunities, above and beyond those merely offsetting the jobs lost, may well be critical for the unemployment levels and perhaps for the political stability of the new customs union. Research on appropriate waiting line models and margins of necessary additional employment opportunities might thus throw significant new light on the problems of customs unions, economic integration, and their expectable levels of political opposition or support.

The Politics and Economics of Spontaneity

Once we embark on this line of reasoning, it will take us further. It can suggest to us a quantitative approach to a core problem of political theory, the problem of freedom. In particular, it suggests a possible mathematics of spontaneity, and thus a perspective on a major aspect of freedom. If freedom can be defined from one operational viewpoint as a range of choices, spontaneity can be defined as the opportunity to act out one's impulses, and thus to act in consonance with one's own psychic structure, character, and inner processes.

To be able to act or behave spontaneously implies further not only the capacity or probability to initiate an action in this manner but also a significant probability to complete successfully the spontaneous action thus initiated. What appears as such a probability of success from the viewpoint of the acting individual or group, appears from another viewpoint as the responsiveness of his environment, that is, of the larger system within which his action must be completed.

This responsiveness can be defined as the probability that an attempted action will be completed successfully within the system (or that an acceptable system response will be forthcoming) within tolerable limits of error and delay. Thus the responsiveness of a telephone system could be measured by the probability that an attempted call to a local telephone number will reach the desired station within one minute. The responsiveness of an automobile to the steering efforts of its driver can be measured by the probability that the car will change its course to an acceptable extent within half a second of the driver's moving the steering wheel, and so on.[56]

From the viewpoint of most individuals, of course, spontaneous behavior and the responsiveness of their social environment refers most often to their efforts to deal with their own lives rather than to any efforts to control or change society at large. If I want on a Saturday morning in late May, to go spontaneously with my wife for a weekend to the White Mountains, how likely am I at this late point in time still to get acceptable hotel accommodations in that popular resort area in response to my telephone call?

The answer is likely to depend on the vacancy rate, and hence on the current excess capacity, of hotel rooms in the area. If the vacancy rate is high, spur-of-the moment trips to these mountains will be practicable, if it is lower, I may have to spend an hour of my Saturday morning on the telephone in search of last-minute accommodations, and if the vacancy rate is very low or zero, then I may have to give up my spontaneous project. Indeed, if the vacancy rate of such hotel rooms were always very low, people might have to book their reservations in advance by several months, or even a year, so that

[56] For a discussion of the concept of responsiveness in an international context, see Dean G. Pruitt, "Definition of the Situation as a Determinant of International Action," in Herbert C. Kelman, ed., *International Behavior* (New York: Holt, Rinehart and Winston, 1965), pp. 393–432.

they would have to decide in November to go on a "spontaneous" week-end next May.

The chances for successful spontaneous behavior thus depend upon the margin of excess capacity of the requisite facilities over the rate of arrivals, or requests for service or accommodation, during the relevant time period. Here, too, a service rate that is merely equal to the rate of arrivals or requests will not be enough. A margin of excess capacity will be needed to avoid congestion and the stifling growth of waiting lines. If this needed margin turns out to be small, spontaneity in behavior will be more easily attainable, but if the requisite margin should be substantive, successful spontaneous behavior may become difficult or unattainable.

If society generates a large volume of requests for some service or opportunity, and if it tries to give each request an equal chance to succeed while lacking a service capacity exceeding the volume of requests by an adequate margin, then the outcome may well be not simply gratitude for their efforts but a growing amount of waiting, lines, delays, frustrations and complaints.

So long as such waiting line problems remain severe, they may contain a built-in incentive to the preservation, or even the new creation, of a *class system.* It is well known that any overloaded service system implies some temptation to the imposition of priorities, that is, privileges in allocating scarce opportunities or services. Such privileges may go with money, as in markets; or with rank, as in armies; or with ascribed nobility or virtue, as did the medieval prerogatives of noblemen and clerics; or with membership in a presumably more revolutionary class, as in the case of factory workers at some times and places in Communist countries; or with achieved performance of some socially rewarded function, as in the treatment of heroes, meritorious government or party functionaries, or outstanding producers or artistic, scientific or economic contributors in many countries.

A system of such priorities is not yet a class system. It becomes a class system, however, when it becomes linked to the family system prevalent in the society so that its privileges are transmitted across generations by heredity, regardless of personal achievement.

It has long been known that such tendencies are inherent in most situations of growing demand and continuing scarcity, where services and opportunities persist in falling short of social and political demands. Waiting line theory now suggests that these problems of general frustration and special privilege will persist even if such shortfalls were reduced to zero; that nothing but an adequate margin of excess service capacity and facilities is likely to cure them; and that the order of magnitude of this margin, as well as the main conditions affecting it, are yet to be discovered, together with their implications for our political ideas.

Another line of reasoning leads from the analysis of waiting lines to the study of *power*. In many situations, those who keep others waiting in line are relatively powerful, and those kept waiting are relatively powerless. Individually, customers making small purchases may be less valuable to the management of a department store, supermarket or quick-lunch counter than the cost of an additional service point with one employee to staff it, so as to make the client's waiting lines shorten or obviate the need for them. Hence, when the usual waiting lines shorten, sales clerks may be withdrawn from some department store counters, some check-out counters at the supermarket may be closed, and so may be whole sections of lunch counters or restaurants while customers at other sections wait in line. In stores where the customers are more affluent, and likely to make larger purchases, more sales clerks are provided, even though they may not all be busy every moment. Here we find the equivalent of an invisible waiting line of unused service points and partly idle service personnel, waiting in line for requests for their services.

In business relations, who waits in line for whom is usually decided by economic costs and gains. In the case of hospital ambulances and fire departments, where facilities are kept waiting on standby for urgent calls, it is largely the social consensus on the relative urgency of the service that determines how much is to be spent in order to ensure the appropriate expectable speed of response. Here, political power may be significant if poorer or less influential groups or neighborhoods may have to wait longer, on the average, for emergency service.

In government services, finally, this element of power may be still more prominent. The political culture of a country or a city may determine how much in resources and personnel is to be spent on quick and responsive service to anyone, how much on service to favored groups or classes, and how large a cost in the form of delays and waiting is left to be borne by the clients, without appearing in the books of the agency that is so tardily serving them.

A client-centered service system, of course, would have to take the clients' waiting costs into account, just as it would have to include the cost of partly redundant service facilities and personnel in the total cost of the system.[57] How these costs of waiting lines, on the one hand, and of additional service facilities and personnel, such as government officials, on the other, will be balanced against each other – and how these balances may change – should tell us much about the power relations within the government and the community it rules or serves.

Most present-day public service systems, of course, are not client-centered in design and operation. Rather, as Adam Yarmolinski once put it, most agencies and their personnel tend to arrange their service so as to suit their own convenience and not that of the public they are supposed to serve. Waiting lines then may well help to perpetuate this situation. For a waiting line is an engine to undermine the solidarity of its victims. Each of them wants to get served and leave the line as soon as possible, and each competes with his neighbors for earlier service. Few clients, if any, are likely to stay for sustained efforts to improve the service or to modify the system.

Almost inevitably, waiting lines contribute to each individual's experiences of frustration, dependence, and of being dominated by the official or agency for whose service one is waiting, or by some impersonal system that sends one from waiting line to waiting line. A major problem of affirmative political theory – the design of a freer and more responsive society with a minimum of inequality and domination – is thus related to a better understanding of the theory of waiting lines.

Some New Perspectives in Game Theory

Recent developments in game theory are leading toward new departures in several directions, all relevant for political analysis. The article by Anatol Rapoport and his associates in the present volume

---

[57] Cf. Manfred Kochen and K.W. Deutsch, "Toward a Rational Theory of Decentralization: Some Implications of a Mathematical Approach," *American Political Science Review*, Vol. 63, No. 3, (September 1969), "Decentralization and Uneven Service loads," *Journal of Regional Science*, Vol. 10, No. 2, (1970), "Pluralization: A Mathematical Model," *Operations Research*, Vol. 20, No. 2 (March–April 1972), "Decentralization by Function and Location," *Management Science Application* (forthcoming).

is a good example. It continues Rapoport's earlier work of combining the mathematical analysis of games with relatively large-scale experimentation with the actual behavior of players in the face of various pay-off matrices and other contingencies, and with the statistical analysis of the results.[58] What is new in regard to method is that this paper deals with an *asymmetrical* pay-off matrix which presents one of the two players with a very different situation from that faced by the other. The entire field of asymmetric games has thus far been explored very little; but if games are to be viewed as possible models of conflict situations in real life, then it is worth noting that in real conflicts the situation of the parties is rarely identical with only the positive and negative pay-off signs reversed, as is the case in so many of the more popular game models. A more thorough exploration of many asymmetrical games thus would make the use of game models in conflict models more realistic.

The article by Rapoport *et al* also makes an important contribution in regard to substance. It shows how under certain conditions it may be rational for the weaker party – disfavored by the pay-off matrix and seemingly relegated to a permanent "underdog" position – to disregared its short-run interest, accept a temporary loss, and by forcing its favored "top dog" adversary to change his behavior and to consent to a less unequal division of the pay-offs between the two players. Rapoport's "threat game" model demonstrates that the most rational and hence dominant solution for a single play of the game may be different from the solution for a sequence of plays, and that a tactic of threat, sacrifice and eventual compromise may be the most rational for the "underdog" player to follow. The applicability, in principle, of this general model to many situations of strikes in labor relations, student unrest in universities, and riots in rural or urban poverty areas is evident, and it deserves wider and more detailed exploration.

Here again, Rapoport and his collaborators have joined actual experimentation and observation of behavior with their theoretical analysis. This time, their experimentation has been cross-national, comparing American and Danish students in both the "top dog" and "underdog" roles. The actual findings reported in the paper may

[58] Anatol Rapoport, Melvin Guyer, David Gordon, "A Comparison of Performance of Danish and American Students in a 'Threat Game' ", this volume. See also references in note 24, above.

reflect, however, also the influence of another variable, thus far uncontrolled: the Danish subjects, it appears, were engineering students while the Americans were graduate students of the social sciences. Future replays of this game, one may hope, will succeed in separating the effects of occupation from those of national character or culture.

Already, it seems clear that we are here at the start of the development of an array of experiments in game-playing behavior that could give us new reproducible distribution of conflict behavior among the members of different groups and subcultures, distinguished by nation, race or ethnicity, class, education, occupation, age, sex, professed ideology, or even by medical or psychiatric history or background. In a still broader framework, Rapoport's approach, if carried further, should permit us to explore, and perhaps eventually to map, the interplay of the effects of a conflict situation – as symbolized by a game matrix – with the effects of the behavioral propensities of the particular players of the game or parties to the conflict. Carrying this work still further, perhaps into the richer context of the Guetzkow or Smoker environments, could then yield still further fruitful insights and data.

A supplement to these combinations of mathematical game analysis and human experiments consists in replacing the human players on both sides by computer programs which simulate various patterns of reinforcement learning. The use of such learning programs in an all-computer simulation of a game could throw additional light on critical parameters and threshold values, either in the pay-off matrices or in the results of the early stages of each run of plays, with possibly critical lock-in effects on the course of the rest of each run. In addition, comparisons of the results of various learning programs, each modeling some kind of "rational" learning behavior, could teach us more about the nature of rationality in conflict situations; and a comparison of the behavior of such computer learning programs with the behavior of human players could tell us to some extent whether – and if so, how – human behavior in conflict situations, even under relatively placid labor conditions, deviates from the types of rationality that we have mathematically modeled. If sucessful, such all-computer experiments may develop beyond mere supplements to human game playing into a major line of investigation on their own, possibly leading to new analytic solutions, new questions, and perhaps new theorems.

Another promising line of development for game theory are game models of conflict behavior which take account of the limited resources of the players, including their limited capacity to think and to compute within the time period within which each has to chose his move, and hence his strategy (which is the sequence of his moves). Classic game theory, as developed by John von Neumann and Oskar Morgenstern, avoided this problem by simply assuming that each player had the capacity to survey instantaneously and exhaustively all alternative moves and strategies with all their consequences, at no cost to himself. This assumption was convenient at that early stage in the development of game theory but it has always been patently unrealistic. Thinking and computing always have had costs in time and resources. Many games, such as chess, derive much of their interest precisely from the task of each player to choose his move within a time that does not suffice to survey exhaustively all possible moves with all their combinations and consequences. Rather, he must choose his seemingly most promising tentative strategy, while being caught between a complex situation and an adversary confronting him, and the clock ticking at his back. Such situations of time pressure and large decision loads pressing down upon limited decision resources are more similar to conflict situations in real life; and there it is often not the best move or strategy that is chosen by an actor but rather one which he finds cheapest to compute.

Another hitherto neglected dimension of game models and conflict analysis are the resources of the players which permit them to stay in the game for an extended number of plays. If one takes the existence of such limited resources into account, many additional considerations become relevant, such as whether a particular strategy seems likely to conserve resources or to squander them; which strategy seems most likely to reduce the threat of gambler's ruin; how large a part of one's total resources is to be staked upon a single play or move; and many more.

Here again considerations of possible asymmetry ought to be introduced. How much of an advantage in terms of a larger supply of chips, money or other resources will make a critical difference to the outcome of a protracted game, such as a game of many plays? More precisely, how much of a change in the resource advantage of one player over his adversary makes how much of a difference to his chances to win the game, or to win by eliminating his opponent?

Rapoport's threat games, referred to above, might be fairly sensitive to asymmetry between the players in regard to resources and reserves.

If such questions can be asked about a rich player, in terms of resources, when confronting a poor one, they could be similarly asked about a "smart" player, in terms of his computing and decision-making equipment and its capacity and speed, against an opponent who is slower or otherwise limited in these qualities.

Finally, the combination and probable trade-offs between these different types of capabilities could be explored. What are the chances of a resource-poor but smart player to prevail against a rich but slow one? How much superiority in thinking and computing scope or speed would just suffice to offset how much of a margin of advantage in resources? What other conditions and contingencies – such as the number of possible plays, the amount of the stakes in each, and hence the expectable length of the game – would have a major effect on the expectable outcome – such as win, lose, or draw?

Many of these questions can be approached through further developments in game theory. Many of them, however, can also be attacked through the development of random walk models of conflict, which are part of a wider class of stochastic process models applicable to political analysis.

Random Walks and Other Stochastic Process Models

Stochastic process models of confict situations were developed in the 1940s and early 1950s by Paul F. Lazarsfeld and T.W. Anderson, and independently by the physicist Max Born.[59] Essentially, these models assumed two opposite and incompatible states, such as voting preference for one of two rival political parties in the Lazarsfeld and Anderson study, and one or more intermediate states, such as being undecided, or not intending to vote at all. Each of these possible

[59] T.W. Anderson, "Probability Models for Analyzing Time Changes in Attitudes" in *Mathematical Thinking in the Social Sciences* ed. Paul F. Lazarsfeld. (New York: Russell & Russell, 1969), pp. 17–66; Max Born, letter to Carl Lienau, February 7, 1961, unpublished, summarized in Karl W. Deutsch, "Social Conditions and Political Behavior: the Need for an International Data Program", paper delivered at the Vth World Congress, International Political Science Association, Paris, 1961. These results also seem consistent with the implications of the mathematical model reported in note 60 below.

states would then appear as the rows and columns of a matrix of transition probabilities, with the rows representing an earlier point in time and the columns a later one. Each cell entry then would represent the transition probability of a voter from an earlier state into a later one, such as the likelihood that a former Democratic sympathizer would become undecided, or that a former Republican supporter would shift his preference to the Democrats. The entries along the main diagonal of such a matrix would then describe the probabilities that the initial members of each group (or persons who were earlier in each state) would still be there at the end of the cycle or period modeled. If the transition probabilities should remain unchanged, it then would be easy to repeat the calculation for any number of cycles and to project the respective expectable future numbers of Democratic and Republican voters, as well as of the undecided, and of the non-voters, into the future. Even if some or all of the transition probabilities should change over time, such calculations could be made, so long as these changes were known or could be estimated with some confidence. Work of this type is not new in some other fields but its application to political science still needs much development. In time, of course, these relatively simple Markovian models are likely to be replaced by more complex models of a different kind, based on systems and processes under investigation.

Models of Recruitment and Attrition Rates

In the work of Max Born and his associates at the time of the Battle of Britain in 1940, the row and column entries consisted of airplanes and/or pilots flying for Britain; airplanes and/or pilots flying for Germany; airplanes being repaired or pilots being rehabilitated for return to duty; airplanes and/or pilots permanently lost to duty for their side by destruction, death, or enemy capture; and new airplanes in production and new pilots in training. (There was no significant probability of pilots or airplanes changing sides). As may be recalled, that battle lasted several months, and owing to the substantial initial quantitative superiority of the German *Luftwaffe*, it was mainly fought in the skies over southwest England. From a study of early data and a projection of the transition probabilities derived from them, however, Born and his associates found that British pilots, if forced to parachute out of their damaged planes, were much more likely to return to combat duty than were the German ones, who in the same situation, were likely to parachute into captivity. Together with the larger figures for aircraft production and pilot training, these conditions could be expected to reduce gradually the margin of German superiority, then produce a period of temporary equality of the two airforces, and end up with substantial Allied superiority and the collapse of the German attack. Born's predictions appear to have been borne out by events, and to have paralleled similar, but secret, calculations made by the British Air Ministry at the time.

A similar quantitative reasoning seems to be implied in Mao Tse-Tung's verbal theory of guerilla war. Here again, the relevant variables are the respective initial strengths of the government forces and the guerillas; the recruitment and attrition rates of each side; the size, distribution and probable outcome of engagements and the expectable length of the conflict, as determined by the interplay of all these conditions. The side with the greater initial strength but the less favorable recruitment–attrition balance would stand to gain from large engagements and a short campaign while the initially weaker side, if its recruitment–attrition ratio should be more favorable, would benefit from Fabian tactics, keeping the engagements small and the conflict protracted.[60]

In principle, this approach can be generalized into a mathematical model of any conflict between two sides or opposite states of affairs – let us call them A and B – within a system composed of countable actors or resources. Such a system then can be represented by a matrix of transitional probabilities, with the rows representing an earlier stage in time and the columns a later one. The rows might then represent shares at time 1 in the populations of voters, or of persons of military age, representing respectively, new entrants, active voters (or fighters) for A, passive sympathizers for A, neutrals or uncommitted, passive sympathizers for B, active voters (or fighters) for B, persons leaving the system through death, emigration, or captivity. If the columns of this matrix then show the same categories at time 2, and each cell entry shows the transition probability of individuals for staying in the same category, or for moving into another category between time 1 and time 2, the state of the system after one or

[60] See Mao Tse-Tung, *On Guerrilla Warfare*, 1936. (Translated) (New York: Praeger, 1963).

several such cycles up to time n can be computed. Where the critical units are not persons but pieces of equipment, such as airplanes, tanks, ships or nuclear warheads, similar computations can be made. In this general manner, the expectable outcome of electoral campaigns, wars, civil wars, or guerilla campaigns (with or without outside intervention) can be estimated, provided that the initial levels of strength and all the transition probabilities are known, and that the latter remain constant, or that their rates of change are known. The validity of such projections will depend, of course, on the realism of the key assumptions – such as constant transition probabilities – and on the reliability and accuracy of the data or estimates on which they are based, but they will at least help to extract more information from such data than could otherwise be done.

Matrix Models of International War and Peace

Another application of such transition matrices can be made to the state of affairs in the international system. The units here in a simple 5 x 5 matrix would be nation states; the rows representing the situations at time 1 could show new states entering the system through secession from old states, or mergers among them; states at war; states at high levels of defense preparedness (defined as spending more than one percent of their GNP on defense); states at low levels of preparedness, or relative peace (i.e. spending only one percent of GNP or less on defense); and states leaving the system by being absorbed into other states by conquest, partition, or federation or other forms of voluntary union. By using columns to represent the state of the system at time 2, and noting the transition probabilities, it is once again possible to project the development of the system over several time periods into the future. A transition matrix of this kind, based on approximate data for 1959 and 1961, has been recently published.[61]

Projections of this kind can show toward what expectable state of affairs the international system is moving, if past transition prob-

---

[61] K.W. Deutsch and Dieter Senghaas, "A Framework for a Theory of War and Peace," in Albert Lepawsky, E.H. Buehrig and H.D. Lasswell, eds., *The Search for World Order: Studies by Students and Colleagues of Quincy Wright* (New York: Appleton-Century-Crofts, 1971), pp. 23–46.

abilities should persist: whether most or all states eventually would become engulfed in war; or whether on the contrary, war should tend to die out in the system; or whether most states should tend to swing back and forth indefinitely among the states of war, high war preparedness, or low preparedness and relative peace in international relations.

A somewhat more complex model could then use a 7 x 7 matrix, distinguishing limited conventional war from all-out war with nuclear weapons or equivalent means of mass destruction. Another increase in the complexity of the model would consist in making the outcome for each state at time 2 depend not only on the state of affairs at time 1 but also at one, two or several earlier time periods, such as time 0, time −1, time −2, and so forth. Whether such additional complexities are worth introducing into the model, and if so, to what extent, is not only a question of available computing capacities but mainly of our knowledge of the real-world process or situation to be modelled.

An interesting problem in any case will be to discover and map the border conditions between classes of expectable outcomes of such transition matrices. What are the configurations of conditions beyond which the world is likely to drift eventually into general war? What are configurations of such conditions and transition probabilities within which war could be expected to die out? What are the transition probabilities and boundary conditions of the international system within which not only war but even high levels of armaments could be expected to disappear, so that low levels of defense spending and relative international peace would become general? And how could any or all of the relevant parameters and probabilities be changed, so as to make the transition to a peaceful world more probable? Answers to all these questions are yet to be found, but methods for seeking them are now available to investigators, promising significant progress within the next few years.

A Random Walk Model of Survival in Unequal Conflicts

In an otherwise trivial adventure novel, the hero is made to gamble at roulette against the villain in such a manner that whenever the villain bets on black, the hero bets on red, and vice versa. If black and red come up in random sequence, the theorem of "gambler's ruin" predicts that the player with more chips may be expected to win the contest, since his wealth will permit him to survive an adverse run of luck which would ruin his opponent. This, as I recall, is what duly happens in the novel; the hero wins, backed by large funds from the British government, and his less well supported adversary is temporarily frustrated.

This trivial story suggests some serious questions. How much of a margin of superiority in resources is likely to have how much of an effect on the expectable outcome of a contest of this kind? And supposing that someone wished to load or bias the roulette wheel in favor of the more indigent player, just how much of a bias in the wheel – or correspondingly in dice or coins – would be needed in order just to compensate the inequality in gambling chips or similar resources of the two players?

These questions can be answered with the aid of a mathematical model of a random walk between barriers. Let us imagine a person drunk enough to make his next step random but sober enough to remain upright and walking. His path will then be the result of the interplay of a random process (his step) with a deterministic one, since he must take that step each time from where he is at that moment. If we now assume that our random walker is blundering down a corridor one side of which is wet with paint while the other side has a comfortable upholstered couch along its entire length we may bet on whether he will end up first by touching the wet paint – our equivalent for his being ruined – or by finding a safe rest on the couch – our equivalent for victory. Starting our random walker nearer to one wall then would make more probable the outcome which that wall represents; it would correspond to giving one of two opposing gamblers a bigger pile of chips. Biasing somewhat in the opposite direction each step taken (perhaps by inclining somewhat the floor of the corridor, so that the steps are no longer wholly random) would have the opposite effect.

What then are the trade-off terms between more initial gambling chips (or soldiers, or favorably disposed voters) and a slightly higher probability of prevailing at each single step or encounter (such as each military skirmish, or each incident or time period of an electoral campaign)? Calculations using such a model have been made and will be published. Some of their results are by no means trivial. Thus if we set the sum of the total chips or similar resources possessed by both players as equal to 100, and note how equally or unequally it is divided between at the outset, it turns out that for moderate levels of resource superiority – approximately between 4:1 and 1:4 – an advantage of one percent in the likelihood to win a single encounter will balance as much as a 7.5 percent advantage in resources. For intermediate ranges of resource superiority, however, – between 4:1 and 9:1 – one percent of higher probability to win any single encounter will only offset about one additional percent of resource superiority; and if this resource superiority should be higher than 9:1, every additional one percent added to it will balance the effects of an additional two percent, approximately, of single encounter winning probability on the opposing side. King Frederick II of Prussia's cynical assertion that God tended to side with the stronger battalions thus seems somewhat dubious at superiority levels below 4:1, if simple-encounter winning probabilities tend in the opposite direction.[62]

Here again, the average proportion of total resources that is at stake in each encounter has a major influence upon the outcome. The larger that relative stake, the fewer encounters or plays will suffice to decide the game by ruining one of the players, and the greater the effect of any superiority in resources; the smaller each such stake, the longer the game will take until producing a decision, and the greater will be the effect of any advantage in the likelihood to win each single encounter.[63] The implications for the advantages or disadvantages of escalation (i.e. increasing the stakes of each encounter) or of Fabian tactics (i.e. limiting these stakes and protracting the conflict) for each side in any unequal contest of this kind should merit further explanation.

Modeling Processes of Drift and Processes of Control

Many of the models discussed so far are well suited to represent processes of drift which unroll automatically in producing a distribution of possible outcomes. Something similar holds true of some

[62] For details, see K.W. Deutsch and Victor Marma, "Survival in Unfair Conflicts," in *General Systems Yearbook*, vol. 18, 1973 (in press).

[63] *Ibid.*

other models used in political analysis and published elsewhere, such as the matrix analysis of transaction flows and the computation of indices of relative acceptance, which are also treated in Richard W. Chadwick's paper in the present volume,[64] and the modeling of processes of social mobilization, linguistic or ethnic assimilation, and changes in the political and social predominance of ethnic groups as treated also in Raymond F. Hopkins' chapter in the present book.[65] All these models focus on the outcome of more or less automatic processes of social, political and economic drift, with little, if any, explicit provision of deliberate human goal choice and goal-pursuing intervention.

Models of drift process usually involve relatively large-scale automatic processes represented by differential equations or by simple programs of reinforcement learning. Models of steering processes, by contrast, would involve far richer and more complex learning programs, often operating on a smaller scale, with significant capabilities for feedback, self-corrections, memory, goal-setting and goal change, partial self-monitoring or consciousness, and partial self-closure or self-filtering or will – in short, the basic process of an autonomous steering and self-steering system. [66] Some aspects of the problem of modeling such a system have been discussed above.

What interests us here is how drift processes and steering processes are related to each other in real life, and how their models could be related to each other in our analyses.

Only some of the most general questions can be indicated here. What are the most likely shares of drift processes and steering proces-

---

[64] See Richard W. Chadwick's paper in this volume; and R.W. Chadwick and K.W. Deutsch, "International and Economic Integration: Further Theoretical and Applied Developments in the Effects of Background Conditions vs. Political Controls" in *Comparative Political Studies*, April 1973 (in press).

[65] See Raymond Hopkins' paper in this volume; and K.W. Deutsch, with the aid of Robert M. Solow, "A Crude Mathematical Model of Assimilation and Mobilization Processes," Appendix V in K.W. Deutsch, *Nationalism and Social Communication*, 2nd ed. (Cambridge, Mass.: M.I.T. Press, 1966), pp. 235–239; Paul Werbos and K.W. Deutsch, "Succesful Prediction of Assimilation and Mobilization: a Case Study of Practical Methodology in Political Science", Harvard University, 1971, unpublished.

[66] Cf. Richard W. Chadwick, "Power, Control, Social Entropy and the Concept of Causation in Social Science," (paper delivered at the Albany Symposium on Social Power, 1971, at the State University of New York at Albany).

ses that could account for the observed distribution of political and social outcomes in some class of real life cases? What are necessary ratios between the size of a drift process and the size of direct effector resources of a steering system in order to modify or control the former to some critical degree of effectiveness, under various contingencies? What capacities, resources, response speeds, and other performance characteristics would a steering system need in order to control or modify a given drift process, so as to exceed a given level of outcome specifications or steering effectiveness? If a single condition or characteristic should prove crucial, what would be its critical threshold? If several conditions should be about equally important, what would be their critical configurations?

Combined drift-steering-feedback models could begin to answer such questions, and some work on such models has been started by Richard W. Chadwick and others.[67] Most of the work in this direction, however, remains as yet to be done.

Putting Models Together: Toward a World Model of Political and Social Change

Most quantitative models available today are severely limited in their *scope*, (the aspects of human behavior with which they deal), or in their *domain* (the set of persons and/or territories to which they refer), or in the *systems level* to which they are to be applied.[68] The richer the spectrum of human needs and activities dealt with in a model, or even in a simple description study, the lower is usually the level of the political system to which it applies. (For example only to individuals, small groups, or at most small villages or small towns) and the more restricted is the domain of populations or countries to which even these low-level models are intended to apply, such as a Mexican Indian village, a small town in the Mid-west region of the

[67] *Ibid.*

[68] For a discussion of the concepts of scope, domain, and systems level, see Harold D. Laswell and Abraham Kaplan, *Power and Society: A Framework for Political Inquiry* (New Haven: Yale University Press) 1963; K.W. Deutsch, *The Analysis of International Relations* (Englewood Cliffs, N.J.: Prentice-Hall, Inc., 1968); and J. David Singer, "The Level-of-Analysis Problem in International Relations" in *World Politics* 14 (October 1961), pp. 77–92.

United States. Conversely, the higher the system level and the wider the domain of the model or study, the poorer and more restricted its scope is apt to be, so as to limit it to one or a very few functions only, such as world trade, or world finance, world agriculture, world industry, world population, world raw materials, world migration, world labor relations, world science, world politics, world armaments, or even the world distribution of nuclear weapons.

These limitations originally were required by the limited capacities of the investigators, as well as of the models and of the facilities for computing, data storage and recall. These limitations were real, and for a long time compelling, but they always were external to the substance of the political and social processes to be studied. Politics and real life are rarely, if ever, split up along the lines of special disciplines or functions. Food, resources, population, industry, economic prosperity or poverty, social communication, political stability or discontent, immobilism or reform, war or peace, all interact with one other, and none of them can be projected or predicted to an acceptable approximation of the future without taking account of the rest.

To accomplish this task, three acts of synthesis must be performed. First of all, we need to combine several functionally specialized models into one more general multi-functional one; and this will need to be done separately at different system levels. On the level of world system, existing functionally specialized models must be brought together and their expectable interactions traced, so as to permit us to estimate their probable joint results. Similar syntheses of specialized functional models may have to be attempted at the levels of world regions, such as Western Europe or Latin America; at the level of nation states, such as the United States, other relatively much-studied countries such as Britain, France, the German Federal Republic, and perhaps eventually Japan, India, the Soviet Union, and China; at the level of provinces, states or other intra-national regions, such as Quebec, the United States South, or northern Ireland; at the level of large cities or metropolitan regions; and down to the level of community studies of some small towns and villages. Each of these units, at its own level, is to some extent a multi-purpose political and social system, and can be analyzed and, in principle, eventually simulated as such. Some work along these lines at each system level is likely to be done within the next five or ten years, but much of it may well occupy political scientists during several of the coming decades.

In the second place, models may have to be developed for large organizations, such as political parties, government agencies, social classes, interest groups, and private business corporations, which usually serve a smaller range of functions than do the territorial political systems, and which are likely to cut across several system levels, from the local to the national or international one.

In the third place, models of multipurpose political subsystems, such as of cities, districts, and cross-level multifunctional organizations may have to be assembled into models of national political systems; and models of nation-states and other international actors (such as supra-national or international organizations, and multinational political parties, churches, and business corporations) may have to be assembled into a world model, representing at least the most important – or at first, the most easily traceable – of their interactions.

World models of political and social change thus can be developed in three ways, singly or in combination: through the integration of models of more or less world-wide functional subsystems; or the combination of models of more limited organizations and agencies, usually pursuing more than one goal and serving more than one function; or through the joining together of models of multipurpose territorial political subsystems, such as nation-states or some of their major intra-national components.

Let there be no illusions. The task of modeling even the main political, economic and social trends of the world system is likely to prove enormously complex. There will be failures along the way, and even some intellectual disasters. But it would be still worse not to try; for we are likely to need for our survival every bit of true information as to where the world is going. Certainly, attempts at building up a useable world model will have to be made not once but many times. The poorer the component models are in their range and detail, the poorer and less complete and accurate the early world models will be. But even at this primitive stage, our early world models can suggest in what direction some of our component models need to be developed, and at the world level they soon will be likely to give us information about connections and processes which no single component model – nor any collection of disconnected component models – could reveal. The journey to a good world model will be long indeed, but it should be worth starting now.

Major elements for the beginning of such an enterprise are now at hand. A dynamic model of world population, basic tangible resources for production, and possible levels of environmental pollution and exhaustion has been developed by J.W. Forrester, D. Meadows and their associates under the sponsorship of the Club of Rome, and has been widely publicized.[69] This model represents a genuine step forward in its use of multiple interdependent feedback loops and in its effort to take account of material balances of demographic and industrial needs, against the supply of land, water and basic raw materials, as well as against possible levels of environmental deterioration as a by-product of haphazard economic growth.

Despite these virtues, the model and the projections and publicity derived from it are dubious in the extreme; and they seem likely to prove a caricature of world realities. Its outcomes depend critically upon the *elasticities* of the relationship between variables, that is, upon the ratios between changes in one variable and consequent or concomitant changes in others. Moreover, the effects of these elasticities may cumulate in the operation of the model. The elasticities assumed in the Club of Rome model are simply assumed, not derived from empirical research. Thus it is assumed that the ratio of increases in industrial production to increases in pollution are 1 to 1, so that doubling production will automatically double the amount of pollution of the environment. If this ratio should in fact be 10:1, or 1:10, the resulting projections would be very different; and the Club of Rome model does not even pretend to tell us what the real ratios are.

At the same time, the Club of Rome model pays little attention to technological change and its effects in changing and possibly reducing the amounts of resources – as well as of pollution – per unit of output. In a still more fundamental omission, it hardly concerns itself with the rates of change in human habits and institutions, and it ignores almost all of politics, economics, and the other social and behavioral sciences. As a result, not only the validity of some variables but the entire structure of the model remains problematic.

---

[69] See J.W. Forrester, *World Dynamics* (Cambridge, Mass.: Wright Allen Press, 1971); Donella H. Meadows, *et al., The Limits to Growth* (New York: Universe Books, 1972).

As it stands, therefore, the Club of Rome model appears less than a realistic image of the world's future and more like an elaborate alarm signal or publicity device.

It should be possible, however, to do more thoroughly what thus far has only been done in such small part. There are matrices of world trade flows at Harvard University, the Swiss Federal Institute of Technology (E.T.H.) at Zurich, and the University of Geneva; and there is a world model of national export-and-import projections (and their discrepancies), as developed by Professor Bruno Fritsch and his associates at E.T.H. Work on the world social system is being undertaken at the University of Zurich by Professor Peter Heintz, at Oslo by Johan Galtung, and at Stanford by Professor Alex Inkeles. Event data on violence and political instability have been collected and analyzed, together with a large number of dimensions of nation-states, by Rudolph Rummel at the University of Hawaii, by I. Feierabend at San Diego State College; data on world regions have been analyzed by Bruce M. Russett at Yale and Joseph Nye at Harvard; voting data in the United Nations General Assembly have been collected and studied by Thomas Hovet, and by Hayward Alker, Jr. and Bruce Russett; and the work of Alker, Christensen and Greenberg on the United Nations collective security system is relevant to the discussion of a world model with system-changing feedback processes.[70] At the same time, data and partial models of social

---

[70] For the work at Harvard, see note 62 above; for Zurich, Peter Heintz, ed., *A Macrosociological Theory of Societal Subsystems, I: With Special Reference to the International System* (Bern: Hans Huber, 1972), and the work by R. Codoni and B. Fritsch (note 36, above); for Geneva, Dusan Sidjanski, ed., *Méthodes Quantitatives et Intégration Européenne* (Geneva: Institut Universitaire d'Etudes Européennes, 1970); for Oslo, Johan Galtung, "A Structural Theory of Imperialism," *Journal of Peace Research*, (1971) pp. 81–117; Professor Inkeles' work at Stanford University is still in progress. For event data and national attributes, see Taylor and Hudson, *World Handbook II* (note 46 above); Rudolph J. Rummel, "Dimensions of Conflict Behavior Within and Between Nations," *General Systems Yearbook*, 8 (1963), pp. 1–50; Raymond Tanter, "Dimensions of Conflict Behavior Within and Between Nations, 1958–1960," *Journal of Conflict Resolution*, 10 (1966) pp. 41–64, and "Dimensions of Conflict Behavior Within Nations, 1955–1960: Turmoil and Internal War," Peace Research Society, *Papers* 3 (1965); Ivo K. Feierabend and Rosalind L. Feierabend, "Aggressive Behaviors Within Politics, 1948–1962: A Cross-National Study," *Journal of Conflict Resolution*, (Sept. 1966), pp. 249–71; Jack Sawyer, "Dimension of Nations: Size, Wealth and Politics," *American Journal of Sociology*, 73 (1967), pp. 145–72; Steven J. Brams, "The Structure of Influence Relationships in the International System," and Charles A. McClelland and Gary D. Hoggard, "Conflict Patterns in the Interactions among Nations," both in James N. Rosenau, ed., *International Politics*

mobilization, on national integration and secession, and more generally of political development, have become available for many countries.[71] By putting these various data and partial models together with the demographic, environmental, and material resources data organized in the Club of Rome model, it should be even now possible to start toward the construction of a political, social and economic model of world development.

Let us remind ourselves once more that these first world models will be primitive and that the way to better models will be long. Nonetheless it is necessary to take it, sooner or later. For it represents our best hope to answer on a world scale an ancient and most basic question: how men and women have made their own history in the past, and how they can do so again.

---

and Foreign Policy, rev. ed. (New York: Free Press, 1969), pp. 583–599 and 711–724, respectively. For national characteristics, compare also Irma Adelman and Cynthia Taft Morris, *Society, Politics and Economic Development: A Quantitative Approach* (Baltimore: Johns Hopkins Press, 1967); Simon Kuznets, *Modern Economic Growth: Rate, Structure and Spread* (New Haven: Yale University Press 1966). For studies of United Nations voting, see Thomas Hovet, Jr., *Bloc Politics in the United Nations* (Cambridge, Mass.: Harvard University Press, 1960); Hayward R. Alker, Jr. and Bruce M. Russett, *World Politics in the General Assembly* (New Haven: Yale University Press, 1965). See also Arend Lijphart, "The Analysis of Bloc Voting in the General Assembly," *American Political Science Review*, 58 (December 1963), pp. 402–417. For studies of regionalism, see Bruce M. Russett, *International Regions* (note 46, above); R.W. Chadwick and K.W. Deutsch, "International and Economic Integration" (note 64, above); Joseph S. Nye, Jr. *Peace in Parts: Integration and Conflict in Regional Integration* (Boston: Little, Brown and Company, 1971), and (ed.), *International Regionalism* (Boston: Little, Brown and Company, 1968).

[71] See sources cited in notes 46–49 and 63, above.

Part One:

Statistical Models and Data Analysis

Introduction

The papers in this volume are organized into four sections. In part, this division is one of convenience, reflecting their dominant forms of mathematical reasoning (including statistics). Thus each of the papers of the present section at some point uses conventional descriptive or inferential statistics; each of the papers in the next section focuses on issues in the development of rational models of political choice; the subsequent two papers are distinctive in their emphasis on network and communication structures; and all the papers of the last section suggest or discuss simulation models. But, as the reader will discover, statistical procedures are used or suggested in many different parts of this book; a concern with purposive, rational, or "irrationally rational" political behavior is certainly not limited to the authors of the second section. And concern with the tensions of political modernization and systems transformation informs every part of the book.

Therefore a deeper justification may be sought for the present organization. A clearly inadequate alternative would have been an exclusive structuring in terms of analytic purpose, although such a possibility might on other occasions be useful. Thus none of the papers is merely a descriptive measurement exercise, although each of the historically oriented papers by Milstein and Schwartzman in the present section, the analysis of "Threat Games" below, and Hopkins' study of mobilization/assimilation processes provide many interesting measurements. Nor do all the papers merely claim to be exercises in the development of explanatory empirical theory. Each author has normative concerns motivating his work and is, in one way or another, an advocate of his empirical interpretation or his theoretical and methodological approach. Although in the tradition of international political science, no paper advocates explicit policy positions, relevant methodological suggestions, including the interesting discussion of forecasting problems by Milstein and Hopkins, will be discovered at a number of points by the attentive reader.

Perhaps a deeper organizing principle is one in terms of mathematical approaches to political analysis. As imperfectly reflected in section titles, a number of orientations to mathematical applications exist in political science, sometimes simultaneously in the work of a single scholar. Partly they are a reflection of intellectual disposition, partly methodological training and research experience, partly of different theoretical schools of analysis. A more rigorous treatment of a similar distinction has been developed by Thomas Kuhn for the natural sciences in his *The Structure of Scientific Revolutions.* Although we do not subscribe to all his arguments about the paradigmatic character of normal, mature science, clearly his analysis of certain periods of scientific development in terms of competing paradigms (or preparadigms) has influenced us here. Moreover, since he emphasizes the important role of key mathematical formulas and methodological training via exemplary solutions of classical dilemmas or puzzles, it seems useful to present a combination of reviews, extensions, and applications of various mathematical approaches in this way. Given the controversial nature of such an argument in the history and sociology of the social sciences, we have, however, structured and labeled our section titles more loosely.

Chadwick's "Steps toward a Probabilistic Systems Theory of Political Behavior, with Special Reference to Integration Theory" is clearly an appropriate one to begin the volume. It is eclectic and programmatic, with provocative criticisms of earlier statistical practices in measuring power and integration. The explicitly systematic cybernetic orientation blends well with the information-theoretic treatment of power and dependence in section 3. And its discussion of decision-making processes compliments and contrasts nicely with the decision-making models presented and reviewed in sections 2 and 4. The notion of politics as "collective learning processes which manipulate goals and actual conditions either against or through socio-ecological conditions and drift processes" is provocatively elaborated – especially in the integration context. It should continue to stimulate those with a cybernetic, statistical orientation, and might also serve as challenge to other less dynamic or systematic approaches.

If anything, Milstein's paper is likely to be more controversial: not so much because of the statistical treatment, which is a sophisticated, pre-causal use of simultaneous regression systems, but, happily, because of its substantive content. Using official United States sources, plus an ingenious blend of American public opinion data and black market piastre rates, he provides an empirically based assessment of the choices facing United States policy-makers. Given that public data sources omit substantively important information on allocative decisions, Viet Cong and North Vietnamese opinion, and Allied terroristic activities, such a perspective is perhaps the most appropriate one for interpreting his findings. His analysis rings true in terms of Allied decisional dilemmas and perceptions, without affirming the political choices that were made.

The paper by Schwartzman represents an impressive achievement. It uses a Parsonian pre-theoretical orientation to structure a number of insights into twenty years of representative democracy in Brazil, 1945–64. A suggestive differentiation of co-optation and mobilization orientations helps inform us as to the bases underlying subsequent regime changes. His is a careful use of selected regional and national aggregate census and voting statistics. Without the benefit of recently developed ecological inference or multivariate analysis procedures, however, some of his theses will require further disaggregated analysis, when and if such becomes possible. One is struck, for example, with how Schwartzman's arguments might benefit from a richer formal analysis along lines suggested by the authors in the final section.

Steps Toward a Probabilistic Systems Theory of Political Behavior, with Special Reference to Integration Theory

*RICHARD W. CHADWICK**

Introduction

Speaking of man as a *political* animal is to say *social* man is organized with sufficient cybernetic capability to purposefully manipulate social and ecological environments, that goals exist to which this capability is applied, and that such goals are subject to cybernetic

---

*University of Hawaii and Harvard University. The first part is a substantial revision of this paper, since it was first presented at the IPSA Congress in Munich, 1970, while the second part is practically unaltered. I wish to thank Drs. Lawrence Alschuler and Joseph Firestone for their aid in making this revision. In the early stages of my thinking, Prof. Dieter Senghaas sharpened my thoughts with numerous incisive questions and criticisms. Among those who read earlier drafts, Hayward Alker, George Kent, and I. Richard Savage contributed usefully to the final form. The substantive stimulus for the theoretical framework and applications presented here came from Karl W. Deutsch, who has more than any other man guided my thinking since 1966. Support for the development of this paper, and some empirical applications to be reported elsewhere, has come from a variety of sources: The Dimensionality of Nations Project under Rudolph J. Rummel; the Center for International Affairs, Harvard University, sponsored my work through the support of the Cambridge Project, with Karl W. Deutsch, for the computer programming I undertook, and later collaborated in with Carey A. Mann. To these projects, and to Rummel's and Deutsch's personal encouragement over many years, I am deeply indebted. Needless to say, I alone am responsible for the errors of commission and omission in this paper, portions of which will appear in Chadwick, Deutsch, and Savage, *Regionalism, Trade, and International Community.*

controls. Political behavior, in this sense, is cybernetic, or goal-directed, activity; it is *adjusted* in response to evaluations with reference to its relative success in attaining some goal. The purpose of this paper is to contribute to a probabilistic *systems* theory of political activity, that is, to a theory about the effects of coordinated goal-directed activity on large scale systems, such as nation-states or metropolitan areas. Moreover, this formulation was made with a view toward further development and application within the context of system simulations, referent system (real world) data analyses, and policy generation.

Associated with the concept of *politics, power* has long referred to both the capabilities and successes of individuals, groups, and large political systems in their pursuit of common or interrelated goals within some relevant socio-ecological environment. Robert A. Dahl (1951) once characterized power as a *change in the probability of an action* , y, performed by a social actor, B, in consequence of another act, x, performed by another actor, A; thus:

$$\text{Power}(Ax \text{ over } By) = P(By|Ax) - P(By|\overline{Ax});$$

and was modified by Harsanyi (1962) to include the cost-effectiveness of change. It is evident, however, that Dahl's notion of power (and Harsanyi's modification) are not, in general, empirically tractable concepts; for the measurement of a *change* in the probability of the act, y, requires that we have for comparison a large number of putatively identical conditions under which the act, x, is performed only sometimes. In general this is possible only under controlled experimental conditions. Moreover, we need to determine whether the act, x, was performed in order to achieve a goal, that is, whether it was part of the output of a cybernetic system, subsystem, or actor. But this requirement leads us to a more profound consideration, namely, whether one can adequately define the boundary of political phenomena, that is, where political behavior ends and something else begins or vice versa.

While not pretending to be able to distinguish at the level of discreet actions those which are predominately caused by goal-directed processes and those caused by something else, we nevertheless may hope to distinguish analytically at higher levels of aggregation the overall strength of cybernetic processes over others. In order to accomplish such a task in present-day research environments, however, it is not enough merely to record actions performed by a number of social actors (such as political parties, pressure groups, community organizations, nation-states, international corporations and organizations, etc.) and classify them by content; for acts that "look like" they were goal directed according to content may not have been at all, and vice versa. Much of international relations interaction, for example, is putatively goal directed (threats, wars, trade); yet actual levels of interaction and changes in these levels are often explained not by rational or calculative processes with reference to attaining some goal, but rather by aggregative national attributes (such as population size, gross national product), dyadic attributes (distance, levels of hostility or integration), or "blind" processes such as Richardson processes. Moreover, even when actions might safely be assumed to be the product of goal-directed processes, precise (or even crude) measurement of the goal-states toward which such action is directed is not functionally possible for the researcher. If, then, we are to use the traditional concepts of *politics* and *power* in a behavioral science research context, we need a new approach to their measurement and modeling. Part One of this paper is devoted to first steps toward developing such a new approach; Part Two applies them to integration theory in the context of international relations.

A Probabilistic Systems Theory of Social Change through Political Power

The model in this section consists of seven basic concepts which are graphically integrated in Figures 1, 2, and 3. The first three are system *states*: goal, actual condition, and socio-ecological expectation; the last four are *processes*: drift, steering, feedback, and learning. The concept of *politics*, as previously described, is developed in terms of collective learning processes which manipulate goals and actual conditions either against or through socio-ecological conditions and drift processes. *Power* is seen as the ability to attain goal-states against socio-ecological expectations and drift processes. As such, power phenomena at the level of collective action are inherently part of political behavior, but political behavior includes in addition collective learning processes which intelligently direct the use of power potential.

Goals, Actual Conditions, and Socio-Ecological Expectations

Two types of actual conditions, denoted by a_{ik} and a_{ijk}, are distinguished here: a_{ik} refers to some *ith* actor's attribute, *k*, such as *i*'s population size, level of development, and so on; a_{ijk} refers to some frequency of action, type *k*, of *i* toward another actor, *j*, such as threats or trade sent from *i* to *j*.

These attributes or actions may differ from those desired by the actors themselves. When we presume that the concept of a collective goal is applicable (to be discussed below), we will denote it by g_{ik} when it refers to attribute *k* of *i*'s, g_{ijk} when it refers to some (quantity of) action from *i* to *j* of type *k*, and allow for *i*'s goals for *j* by denoting them as ${}_ig_{jk}$ and ${}_ig_{jik}$ (*i*'s goal: for *j* to perform acts of type *k* toward *i*). More indirect goals could be postulated, but are not considered below. Transposed notation will be used for actor *j* (that is, g_{jk}, g_{jik}, ${}_jg_{ik}$, ${}_jg_{ijk}$, respectively) to refer to *j*'s goals.

The notion of a socio-ecological expectation is theoretically related to the notion of a *social habit*, as aggregated by such organizing concepts as social institutions, social structure, role-behavior, and ecology in the bio-physical sense. Empirically, it is related to standard regression methods in social science, when some actor attributes and/or behavior are used to "explain" (account for variance in) attributes and/or actions in other actors. For example, trade between nations is often explained in terms of relative levels of gross national product, population sizes, and distance between two nations. The notion of a collective goal does not enter into such an "explanation", though a theory of the aggregate effects of un-coordinated individual or subsystem actor goals might, such as the goal of maximizing profit in classic economic theory. Such connections between aggregate studies and background theories are normally very loose, the latter usually being the "inspiration" for the former, without any rigorous attention being paid to the precise theory-model-method interrelationships. The key concept here, however, is that socio-ecological models do not postulate, model, and make empirical inferences about the effects of collective goals and collectively co-ordinated goal-directed actions. They aggregate individual or subsystem attributes and actions, and use process models that are at least consistent with the inference that the system as a whole "drifts" (see following section for further elaboration). In this sense, while the "profit motive" may be postulated at the individual actor (corporation) level, collective consequences of this process are merely the aggregative effect of many individuals independently acting to "maximize" their individual gains, *not* co-ordinating their activities to "maximize" collective gain.

Gaps between the goal-state, actual state, and socio-ecological expectation each have special meaning. If we consider the difference between the goal state g_{ijk} and the actual state a_{ijk} of i's actions of type k toward j, it is evident that we have a measurement related to the psychological sense of *frustation*, i.e., between what i would like to do and what i actually does. Because *frustration* in this sense does not refer to an emotional or drive state, but rather to a behavioral and empirical condition of a group or organization or social system, we can not impute to it a priori a motivational basis for collective action which would aim at reducing the gap. Whether such a social mechanism exists is an empirical question which may be answered differently depending upon the particular system we study. With this caveat clearly in mind, the notion of collective or system-level frustration is defined as

$$\begin{aligned} f_{ik} &= g_{ik} - a_{ik}, \text{ for } i\text{'s attribute } k, \\ f_{ijk} &= g_{ijk} - a_{ijk}, \text{ for } i\text{'s act, type } k, \end{aligned} \tag{1}$$

with similar definitions for ${}_i f_{jk}$ and ${}_i f_{jik}$ corresponding to ${}_i g_{jk}$ and ${}_i g_{jik}$ previously defined.

The problem of aggregating frustration across a variety of attribute and behavioral conditions is left unresolved here. Figure 1, below, indicates one possibly fruitful line of investigation. Two types of behavior are distinguished: conflict and co-operation, and a combined goal state, g_{ij}, and combined actual behavior, a_{ij}, are plotted. The distance F_{ij} is an interactive function, $F_{ij} = \sqrt{} \, (f_{ijx}^2 - f_{ijy}^2)$, representing the smallest Euclidean distance (a straight line) between the points g_{ij} and a_{ij}.

The gap between a goal condition or interaction and a socio-ecologically expected condition or interaction (denoted in Figure 1 by b_{ij}) is similarly relatable to a traditional psychological concept: alienation, a difference between how i desires to behave toward j, in this case, and how, in the sense of a statistical norm, he is expected to behave. Here, however, there is a departure from the usual notion

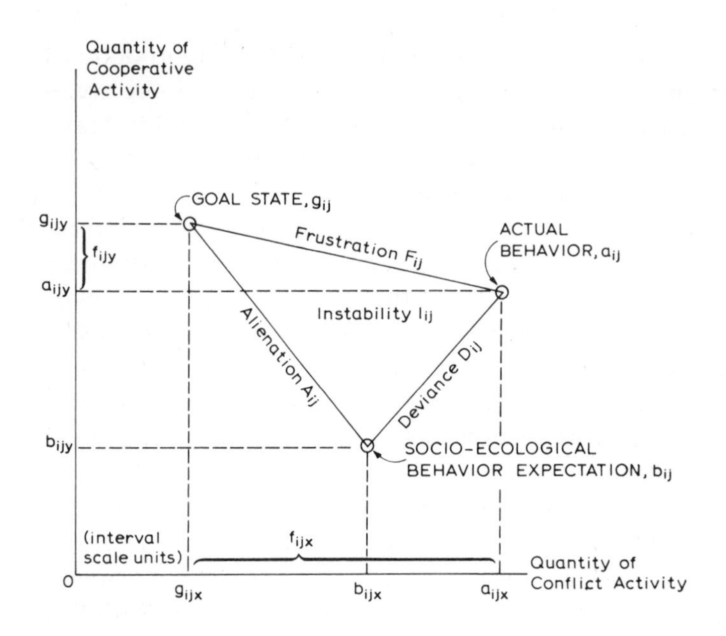

Fig. 1. – Alienation, Frustration, Deviance, and System Instability: A simple conceptual framework

of alienation in two ways: (1) we are identifying a group or organizational level characteristic, not an individual's emotional state; (2) we are employing a statistical norm, not a psychological norm or a sociological norm in the sense of a normative belief. There is good reason for making the latter departure, which is not meant to preclude, but rather to extend, normal usage. The notion of a departure from a statistical expectation or from a behavioral probability is valuable because of the cybernetic or political system context within which it can be interpreted. Alienation of a collectivity (group, organization), in this sense, means the degree to which its goal-state deviates from a behavioral social habit, i.e., from a socio-ecological expectation. As such, it implies two things: (1) the collectivity is dissatisfied with its "normal" attribute and/or interaction location in society; (2) it is aiming to do something about changing its "normal" location. Presuming that such a "normal" location – the socio-ecological expectation – is a "location of least resistance", so to speak, to move actual behavior into line with the goal-state, away from the expectation, requires social co-ordination of effort in non-habitual patterns; it requires overcoming a degree of social resistance.

This leads us to a third gap which is related to the traditional concept of social *deviance*, the gap between the socio-ecological expectation, b_{ij}, and actual behavior, a_{ij}, depicted in Figure 1. Again, the departure from tradition here is much like that with "alienation". We do not attribute to the gap a necessary relationship to normative deviance in the sense either of a social norm or a psychological expectation. It has its use in describing the degree to which a collectivity deviates from a statistical expectation. In the cybernetic context, it may partially index the degree to which a group has been successful or unsuccessful in moving toward its goal-state.

A derivative measure of these gaps between actual, expected, and goal-states of a system, is related to the traditional concept of instability, denoted by I_{ij} in Figure 1. Instability, which might be made operational in terms of the area formed by the triangle (g_{ij}, a_{ij}, b_{ij}), in this sense implies that the gaps themselves are highly likely to change significantly over short periods of time. How the gaps might change, under what conditions, and in what manner (direction), are questions which require answers in terms of dynamic processes.

Drift, Steering, Feedback, and Learning Processes

Figure 2 illustrates a simple analytic model of a total system con-

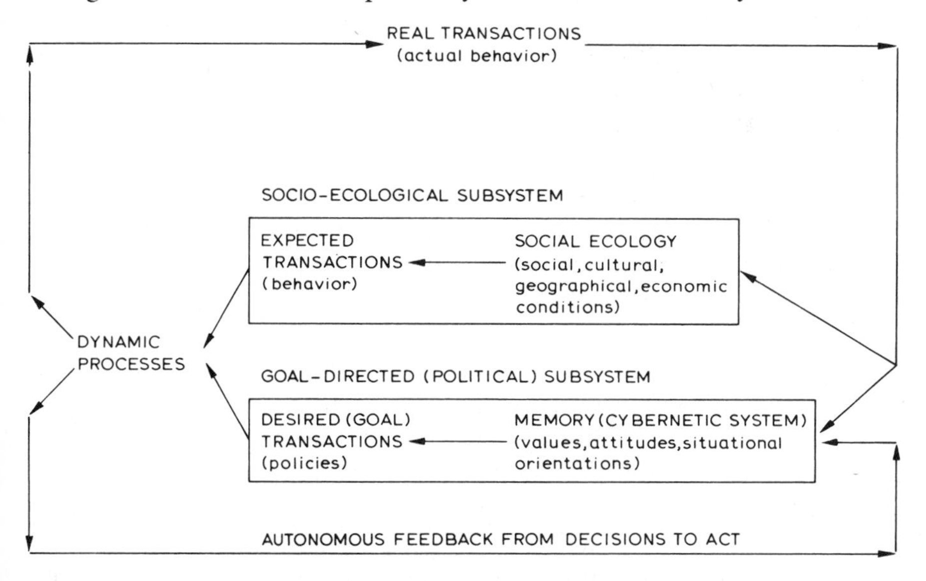

Fig. 2. – A simple sketch of a general global socio-political system

taining all the processes described herein. A "drift" process is depicted as a causal chain of events which excludes the "goal-directed subsystem" and "autonomous feedback loop". A "drift" explanation of, say, a pure conflict system, would assume that the socio-ecological system contained no coherent collective goals (such as specific "national interests") and/or no ability to translate these goals into co-ordinated activity which would evaluate relations between past actions and present conditions and modify future behavior. Other factors, such as population change, size, levels of development, and cultural differences, would act in a random fashion to allow nations to "drift" into war, other less hostile conflict processes, or peace (absence of war).

The use of such "drift" process explanations may lead to an overlay of "steering" process explanations. In such cases, the use of a socio-ecological expectation is to provide a floating zero-point against which to measure deviations in behavior; such deviations would then represent efforts to steer a system toward some other behavior pattern or new condition. As regards international trade flows, for example, the estimation of non-political, hypothetical probabilities of transactions began with the preliminary analysis of global systems by I. Richard Savage and Karl W. Deutsch (1960). By assuming that the only systemic factor influencing such flows was the relative size of each nation's share of the world export-import market, they created socio-ecologically expected values for trade between each pair of nations, proportional deviations from which permitted, they felt,

> tentative inferences about the distribution of preferences among pairs of larger groups of actors; about degrees of clustering or integration among actors; and about changes over time, if several matrices are used.[1]

Presumably, nations are steered toward more or less trade than probabilistically expected by the efforts of statesmen to make and enforce policies in accord with a set of operational goals, and the result is the pattern of exhibited preferences. This form of explana-

---

[1] Savage (1960, p.551). The inferences referred to are obtained through the "*RA*" index, which is defined on pp. 556, 569. In the present notation, this is $RA_{ij}=(t_{ij} - \hat{t}_{ij})/\hat{t}_{ij}$, where i and j are nations, t_{ij} is the actual frequency of transactions of some type per unit time, and $\hat{t}_{ij}$ is the estimated frequency of transactions from i to j over that same period of time.

tion would involve modeling a "goal-directed" system as indicated in Figure 2, but without the "autonomous feedback" linkage, for the notion of "steering" does not necessarily imply feedback altering the steering system or the goal itself.

It has been said that those who forget the past are condemned to repeat it. If a government or other social cybernetic mechanism is not equipped, through its recruitment, training, and administrative systems, to change its behavior in accord with feedback from the environment, interaction is likely to exhibit such over-time patterns as runaway growth (or decline), perhaps sigmoid curves as activity depletes resources, and other regular patterns based upon the assumption that no feedback process, or goal-directed collective behavioral modification, exists. Learning is a feedback process, but of a very special kind. A simple reinforcement learning process is described in Figure 3, which is a representation of a model used by Day and Tinney (1968) which they used to describe the decision processes of economic organizations. Adapting their reinforcement learning model to the concepts of Figures 1 and 2 above, the following interpretation is made:

1) "u" or the utility of an actor, i, is inverse to the gap F_{ij};
2) "a" is the set of actions, a_{ijy} and a_{ijx};
3) the constants, "k^+" and "k^-", so long as they are held constant over time, represent the "reinforcement" aspect of the feedback loop, but not the learning aspect;
4) the constant, "c" in the last two equations of Figure 3 represents a simple type of learning process, in that it involves a change not in behavior but in the criterion for how much behavioral change will take place.

More sophisticated forms of learning might be postulated, for example:

(1) change in the goal state, g_{ij}, upon repeated frustration;
(2) more generally, expansion of the number of time-points or decision-nodes (t, $t+1$, $t+2, \ldots, t+n$) with more complex functions describing alternative strategies, selected contingently upon over-time behavior of other actors influencing attainment of the goal states previously described (g_{ik}, g_{ijk}, ${}_ig_{jk}$, ${}_ig_{jik}$).

Conditions[b]	I	II	III	IV	V	VI	VII
				Strategies			
$u_t > u_{t-1}$	X	X				X	
$u_t < u_{t-1}$			X	X			X
$a_t > a_{t-1}$	X		X				
$a_t < a_{t-1}$		X		X			
$a_t = a_{t-1}$						X	X
$r_t < e$					X		
Actions[c]							
$a_{t+1} = (1+k_t^+)a_t$	X			X		X	X
$a_{t+1} = (1-k_t^-)a_t$		X	X				
$a_{t+1} = a_t$					X		
$k_{t+1}^+ = k_t^+$	X	X		X	X		
$k_{t+1}^- = k_t^-$	X	X	X		X		
$k_t^+ = k_o^+$						X	X
$k_t^- = k_o^-$						X	X
$k_{t+1}^+ = ck_t^+$			X				
$k_{t+1}^- = ck_t^-$				X			

Fig. 3. A decision table with learning (feedback) criteria[a]

[a] This table is an adaptation of Day and Tinney (1968, pp. 586–87).

[b] The symbols denoting various conditions are defined as follows:

- *u*: a utility of some type, such as profit,
- *t*: a time period during which a decision is to be made,
- *a*: an action quantity, such as production of a product,
- *r*: marginal utility, defined as $(u_t - u_{t-1})/(a_t - a_{t-1})$
- *e*: a satisficing criterion, below which marginal utility changes are treated as irrelevant.

[c] The symbols denoting various action strategies are defined as follows:

- *a*: an action, as before, measured in some quantity, $a \geqslant 0$,
- k^+: a parameter indicating how much more action (*a*) will be taken, $1 \geqslant k^+ \geqslant 0$,
- k^- : a parameter indicating how much less action (*a*) will be taken, $1 \geqslant k^- \geqslant 0$,
- *t,o*: time (*t*) incremented and decremented $(t+1, t-1)$ from decision to decision; "*o*" indicates some arbitrary initial condition, e.g., k_o^+ or k_o^-,
- *c*: a conservatism factor altering the willingness (k^+, k^-) of an actor to make as strong changes in his actions (*a*) as he heretofore had $(1 \geqslant c \geqslant 0)$.

Whether any such forms of learning are behavioral properties of large scale systems such as the governments of metropolitan areas or some nation-states, remains an open question, and one likely to be answered only through the use of simulation techniques.

The general model developed above will be applied to the problem of understanding the phenomenon of international integration, below, but any form of organized social behavior should be amenable to the type of analysis suggested here. Despite an extensive literature on the subject, incredibly little of a mathematical/empirical nature has been undertaken to date.[2] In fact, with the exception of the field theory developed by Rummel (1965, 1969), and the extensions and applications of the Savage-Deutsch model[3], only the field of arms races has been continuously exposed to theoretical and empirical mathematical modelling efforts, that is, in the general area of international relations.

The Phenomenon of International Integration[4]

Any useful theory of integration must include both a basic con-

---

[2] Deutsch and Savage had completed in 1960 the development of indices of integration and Deutsch briefly reported some of the results as applied to world trade flows in Deutsch (1960) (esp. pp. 46–48). Steven Brams, though not directly relating his work to the development of integration theory, took a significant next step by using the *RA* index (see footnote 1 above) as one of two "null"-model related criteria for constructing a derived matrix of linkages, which then would be used to *determine* (by definition) "most tightly-linked clusters" (Brams, 1966a). In another work, Brams further extended the use of the *RA* to a brief study of *system transformation*, in particular by examining the shifting membership of West Germany in various clusters of western European countries through several time periods (1954, 1958, 1962): Brams (1966b). Work similar to Brams, but with different emphases, has been done by Bruce M. Russett, who cites Brams' work (1967); and in J. David Singer (1968), an article by Russett entitled "Delineating International Regions." Application of the Savage-Deutsch method to later periods of data on the North Atlantic Area was extended by Hayward R. Alker, Jr. and Donald J. Puchala, "Trends in Economic Partnership: The North Atlantic Area, 1928, 1963", in Singer (1968). Also to be noted is Karl W. Deutsch (1966a); the transaction flow model utilized there, however – as with the model applied by Alker and Puchala (cited above) – is due to be made obsolete by Chadwick, Deutsch and Savage, *Regionalism, Trade, and International Community*, forthcoming.

[3] The works cited by Deutsch, Brams, and Alker and Puchala were previously cited in footnote 2 above. The others are as follows: Hayward R. Alker, Jr., Leo A. Goodman (1963) (1964), Harrison White (1963).

[4] The general definitions of *integration, amalgamation*, and *community* discussed in the three paragraphs immediately below are Karl W. Deutsch's, paraphrased from taped conversations with him.

cept of and operational tests for measuring integration. Commonsensically, to be integrated means to have a high probability of behaving as a unit, as a single whole. This implies both structural correspondence of subunits in a static sense and operational interdependence in a dynamic sense. Like the right lock for a key, an integrated economic system, for example, implies observable complementarities in commodity production among producing units. Operational interdependence implies not merely the existence of trade, or even large amounts of trade, between units within the system, but of amounts of trade *in excess of what might be expected by chance*, that is, above and beyond what might be expected given gross attributes (e.g., population size, gross national product, total value of exports and imports, geographic distance, etc.) of the interacting units.

Depending upon the degree of integration in the sense described above, we might also expect other behavioral properties. Internally destructive behavior, such as the preparation for and actual involvement in open hostilities or war, should be below a socio-ecologically expected volume. In this sense, a *security system* combines both high operational interdependence and relatively low levels of conflict-related behavior.

Beyond these minimal properties of an integrated system, higher levels of integration may be identified by an increasing capacity of the system to pursue collective goals or undertakings of a kind and on a scale beyond the reach of any of the subsystems separately. For example, this is a characteristic of most nation-states, which can pursue many different goals common to their component smaller groups and political units, but not attainable by them in isolation. If integration is thus thought of as a gradient, a matter of more or less, with certain thresholds demarcating levels of development, this capacity to pursue many common positive goals may be used to demarcate the point at which the system has become a general purpose *community*. The institutionalization of such a collective goal-directed decision-making system through the formation of political organizations marks a threshold of political *amalgamation*.

Within the abstract framework developed in the previous section, the measurement of integration in a social system requires that we (1) devise a model of the socio-ecological structure of the system and of its probable behavior patterns, under the assumption that no integrative subsystem exists; (2) make empirical measurements on behavior patterns to assess the explanatory power of such a model, and assess thereby the degree of non-predictability of its behavior, its non-randomness; (3) devise a model of the goal-directed (political) subsystem or decision-making system if the behavior is sufficiently unpredictable to so warrant; (4) test the explanatory power of the political subsystem model. It is an empirical question as to the type of feedback process and level of development which might exist.

We do not know enough about the dynamics of *development* of integrative processes to argue convincingly in favor of a given sequence of thresholds as most probable. For example, it may be that *amalgamation* at the political institutional level might be followed by increasing acceptance and use by politically relevant strata, thus *leading* to integration as previously discussed. Conversely, limited integration for special purposes, if producing positive, rewarding feedback, may later lead to more general amalgamation of institutions. The general discussion of the literature below will be used as a vehicle for further substantive development of the above theoretical framework, and will lay primary emphasis upon learning processes at the system level as the mechanism through which integrated systems evolve and devolve.

Concepts and Operationalizations of Integration in the Literature: A Partial Review and Critique

Current in our literature are a wide variety of concepts of integration. Some are deceptively simple, such as Amatai Etzioni's: "The ability of a unit or system to maintain itself in the face of internal and external challenges", while earlier he had remarked:

> Statements about the level of integration of a particular international system are in effect a composite score of the three dimensions of integration: monopolization of force, allocation of resources, and dominant identification (Etzioni, 1965, pp. 330, 10).

For a performance criterion – the ability to face challenges – to be made operational, a set of standardized "challenges" would have to be "administered" or observed through a content analysis schema in a manner controlling for situational (socio-ecological system) contexts. But aside from this near impossibility, Etzioni's earlier remarks suggest a hypothesis, rather than a definition, of integration, namely that *the ability to withstand challenges is a monotonic function of the degree of force monopolization, (system) resource allocation, and (system) dominant identification.* Is an integrated system one in which this hypothesis is true? One that has the three "independent" variable characteristics to a great degree? Or one that effectively faces challenges?

We do not raise these questions lightly; nor is the problem inherent in the above conceptualization unique to Etzioni's remarkable work. Consider one of the earlier, and still widely quoted, definitions of integration:

> . . .the attainment, within a territory, of a "sense of community" and of institutions and practices strong enough and widespread enough to assure, for a "long" time, dependable expectation of "peaceful change" among its population (Deutsch *et al.*, 1957).

If the institutions and practices referred to *are not the causal agents* in the generation of the dependable expectations of peaceful change, shall we say the system is *not* integrated? An alternative formulation presented by Deutsch (1966b), analogous to the composite score concept of Etzioni, begins with the definition of covariance between two systems:

> . . . I would define interdependence between two systems as covariance and a high flow of mutual transactions.
>
> We infer interdependence between two systems – let us call them i and j – when we observe that when something changes in System i, something varies in close correlation with it in System j.

Then Deutsch asserts:

> If covariance is positive, that is, in line with what each of the two acting systems – or self-steering – treats as a reward (or positive reinforcement, in behavioral terms) we speak of a condition of integration.

If the concept of *power* (as developed in the introduction) is added to this definition, so that the interdependencies generated through transactions are not only rewarding but *planned* (or more weakly, regulated), it is suggested that Deutsch's conceptualization of integration as *a condition of transaction flows over time* is sufficient for many purposes. But in conjunction with the previous definition of integration, it might be presumed from the general theory of reinforcement learning that the joint occurrence of significant interactions and rewarding effects together produce increasingly dependable expectations of peaceful change. It might also be presumed that these associated transactions and rewards themselves define, in their patterns over time, the institutions and practices also mentioned. Such presumptions, however, should be given the status of hypotheses, not definitions, if they are to be exposed to empirical tests of their utility.

More difficulties are uncovered when one moves from the structural form of these definitions of integration to their substance. At the core of many concepts of integration is the presumption that integrated systems have populations that are characterized by psychological identification with their systems, that is, possess a sense of *community*. One might wonder, therefore, whether integration and community are separable concepts. Donald J. Puchala's treatment of psychological identification would seem to suggest such a separation. He states that: "Integration refers to the merger of peoples into a transnational society and polity (and a transnational economy also. . .)." He then goes on to describe the "structural, political, and societal" characteristics of "*contemporary* regional integration," (my italics) which can be paraphrased as: (1) central governmental *institutions* affecting the allocation of resources and rewards (a cybernetic function in my terminology); (2) the development of a supra-national *political process* (cybernetic process) with transnational political actors competing without recourse to violence; and (3) the development of a transnational *community or society* with a *high probability of interaction* across national boundaries and a popular *emotional or identitive affinity* with the institutions through which these interactions take place (Puchala, 1968). The question of whether identification should constitute a component of a *universal* definition of integration (as opposed to a "contemporary" definition not including all cases from the past) is left open.

David W. Minar and Scott Greer, working in the context of concept formation as regards *community* in general, went one step further than Puchala by suggesting a causal relation between *political* activity and *integration*, and between integration and developing a sense of community. First they identify the identitive affinity which individuals share in a community, and relate it to nationalism (and we may note the similarity between their conception and Puchala's as regards contemporary regional integration):

> Among the elements of nationhood is a sense of community (or something very much like it): a feeling of identity, shared fate, common loyalty. The modern notions of nationalism and patriotism have much in common with the concept of community as it is projected on the nation-state scale (Minar *et al.* 1969, p. 121).

They then present a more generalized and specific conception of community:

> We have used the term community to refer to a group, united in space, function, or other interest, and sharing perspectives that bind them together for some degree of common action (p. 187).

Given the context, it would seem that "perspectives" here can refer to community *perceptions* as well as to value rankings or priorities among goals and actions. They then present the rough hypothesis that political activity

> . . . is often integrative in intent, consequences, or both. . . . In other words, as government goes about doing what it does, it may generate feelings of satisfaction, dependency, and loyalty among those it serves. These feelings in turn bind that population together[5].

---

[5] To be sure, governments also may deliberately aim at keeping certain groups separate as in the classic imperial policies of divide and rule; or they may produce disintegrative effects by their actions without intending to do so, such as by failures of coordination or responsiveness, or by inflicting severe deprivations on one of several groups, as happened in the secession of Ireland.

The implicit hypothesis here that "feelings" bind people together is somewhat at odds with the notion of "united in space, function, or other interest." The latter is fundamentally a *cybernetic* concept; from this perspective, *it is function that binds*, and the dividend of satisfaction may serve to *limit efforts to change the functional structure of the system*, or ultimately to destroy it. By contrast, the concept of "feelings" binding is a *franchise* concept, much more related to simple notions of exclusion and inclusion. *Patriotism* excludes people from abroad; *nationalism* excludes people not of your own nation; both in effect give a government a *franchise*, that is, *a chance to function* without significant outside competition. It is *probable* that, over a long period of time, a government that remains structurally stable will have achieved (or maintained) a *sense* of community in the population over which it exercises a franchise. But simply being a member of a nation-state, with all that this implies about cultural affinities and relatively good communications, does *not* imply *functional unity* (i.e., operational interdependence). Moreover, to the extent that stable functional unity is maintained over time *solely* by such franchise concepts as patriotism and nationalism, the system is increasingly likely over time to become less stable and ultimately disintegrate. For this implies that the relative degrees of satisfaction and dissatisfaction with the operational properties of the system (income growth and distribution, etc.) are not relevant for the government in making its decisions; eventually such governments must lose their credibility and rely upon the unity of the military and the threat of force, neither of which have been traditionally reliable sources of power.

If the two elements of functional performance and satisfaction are linked together, as Minar and Greer have done, it would seem to be a sound hypothesis that *identification* with the system by the population follows. This perspective on identification would seem to comport well with Henry Teune's conception of identification (in Jacob and Toscano, 1964, pp. 247-82):

> "Identification" may be defined as a *learned* pattern to respond to one set of stimuli as the most relevant for a given range of activities and to ignore significant competing stimuli for that range of activities. . . . If a substantial portion of the population living within a political boundary has *learned* that political identification

is rewarding or has a learned pattern to be politically *identified* with a specific set of political stimuli, then this collectivity of people could be called a political community. (Italics mine)

Here, through processes of reinforcement learning, satisfaction with functional performances produces the response set which Teune is willing to refer to as "identification".

From the Recognition of Integration to the Development of Integration: Input Conditions Favoring Integration

In discussing the properties by which integration can be recognized, we have already begun to indicate some of the conditions by which integration is produced, created, or increased. These conditions can be thought of as independent variables or *inputs* into integrative processes. The recognizable operating characteristics of integrated systems in general and communities in particular may then be viewed as the dependent variables or *outputs* of integrative processes.

For the purpose of developing this input–output model, let us now briefly summarize the concepts introduced so far, and their (apparently accepted) interrelations. Following Deutsch, *integration* as a *condition* (a state of affairs) refers to *aggregate properties of transactions* within and between systems. Being integrated represents one end of a continuum, defined by combinations of (1) relatively *high volumes* of transactions, (2) relatively greater interrelatedness or *covariance*, and (3) relatively high *reward* or positive affect stemming from those transactions[6]. To this definition is added (from Puchala, Minar and Greer, Teune, and the work of the Princeton group[7]) the

---

[6] It is to be noted that these conditions "define" integration only in a probabilistic sense. No theory of the dynamics of integrative processes per se is put forth here; consequently we are putting forth an empirical proposition here about the properties of the transaction, covariance, and reward structures we *expect* these systems to possess, in *consequence* of the build-up of effective integrative processes, *and* as *input conditions* leading to further development of integrative processes. Note that since we are dealing with a feedback system (see Figure 2), these conditions are both dependent and independent, the directions of cause and effect being separable only through over-time analyses of the processes themselves.

[7] The "Princeton" group referred to is the group who wrote the text cited as Deutsch *et al.* (1957).

political organization of these transactions, i.e., their *coordination around goals that apply to total systems. Community* is then conceived of as *an integrated system with which its members identify*. Depending upon the scope and intensity of coordination of transactions, we would expect greater and greater probabilities of expectations of peaceful change, and greater capability of pursuing joint goals not possible for any given system participating in the network of integration or community. In short, the higher the level of integration, the more probable it is that *a cybernetic system or supersystem is developing*. Thus *integration* and *political development*, seen as increasing the *power* (per the conceptualization in the introduction) of a system over a given social and ecological domain, are equivalent concepts.

Within the above analytic framework, we may postulate a simple four-stage growth process which we might consider a "most probable" *voluntary* incremental development of an integrated system and community: (1) the emergence of (*a*) relatively large volumes of transactions, and (*b*) covariance among these transactions, creating a condition of interdependence; (2) the development of positive affect (reward) in consequence of these transactions as greater control (political) capability develops in regulating these transactions; (3) the emergence of coordinative social mechanisms which we may refer to as regional organizations or governments, as the case may be, in consequence of the intensified political control of transactions; (4) the emergence of identitive affiliation or community as the relevant populations become accustomed to the organizational structure and its apparently rewarding effects. It is clear from historical precedents that these "stages" need not be attained in the sequence shown here. Nevertheless, departures from this sequence may be presumed to induce relatively severe strains on the process, which should be manifested with relatively high volumes of *conflict* and/or reliance on the threat or use of force. The presence of an external threat, for example, may prematurely induce formal organization and political controls, as in the early history of the United States and the Soviet Union, resulting in a period of doubt and inefficiency, not to mention serious conflict.

If we consider the possibility of *community preceding integration* (integration is but *one* of several possible sources of identitive affiliation, e.g., racial or ethnic identifications), it might be more useful to conceive of community from a perceptual perspective, to wit: a community is an identitive system, the members of which *tend to believe* that they share a common concept of what the system should be, will become, or is, and which they try, through their transactions, to bring into being. Then, the more widespread is this belief, the more it characterizes the *actual belief structure*, and the more *actual behavior* is *coordinated* around the maintenance and/or realization of this *goal image* (the greater the *integration* in the sense previously described), the higher is the level of *community*. In this sense, the United States *began* as an organization against external threat, established the basis for community in the sense of *franchise* (*belief* in sharing a common concept of growth and development *excluding* others, i.e., patriotism and nationalism), and slowly *integrated*.

In making the above distinctions, we have in mind several utilities, not the least of which, as Nye has suggested, is that they permit the relationship between behavioral interdependence and integration with identitive affiliation to become an empirical question[8]. Another utility is that they permit the relationships between goals, ideals (goals with which we identify), and realities to become amenable to empirical investigation. In this connection, we have in mind a distinction between the ideal and the real that has been well expressed by Minar and Greer (1969, p. 187):

> The importance of the concept of community lies in its very ambiguity. Like the concept of the human, it embodies both the descriptive and the ideal; it recalls to us our power to make as well as to accept, to act as well as to behave. Community refers to whatever groups exist; it also refers to our aspirations for the groups. Social science began with the efforts of the Greeks to make what existed into something nearer to their hearts' desires. Since no effort succeeds perfectly, since all achievement entails unanticipated side effects, since we must pay for any achievement by yielding alternative opportunities, it is probably best to think

[8] For a good review of integration concepts, see Joseph S. Nye (1968). While we do not wish to limit the usage of the term *integration* to our own, we agree with Nye that one must pick one's definition and make it operational if one wishes to test hypotheses about integrative phenomena. This section does not contain a comprehensive treatment of others' concepts of or related to integration, but rather only those we see as directly relevant to our work.

> of community as a variable, existing to some degree in many collectivities, to an extreme degree in a few.

This notion of the ideal is hardly new, either in recorded history or in contemporary integration theory. But it is often submerged in the more general concept of a goal or an end, and in the concept of goal-oriented behavior. Such behavior may exist without the goal or end being an *ideal*, that is, in behavioral terms, without having an identitive psychological status. Thus an ideal is a *type* of end or goal. We will, accordingly, use the term *socially coordinated behavior* to refer to interaction (transactions) *consciously* designed to achieve goals or ends. If such behavior is linked to the attainment or maintenance of a social system as a goal, and if such a system is *idealized* (identified with), then we will speak of *community-building or maintaining behavior*. This latter form of behavior was, in all likelihood, referred to by Ernst Haas (1964, p. 29) when he remarked:

> We must avoid reification of an analytical system. Hence I conceive of integration as referring exclusively to a process that links a given concrete international system with a dimly discernible future concrete system.

And we may contrast this usage with the more inclusive conceptualization put forth by Levi (1965), who conceived of "integrated behavior as end-oriented behavior," which "end determines the nature, kind, and importance of the integrative factors"; while the terminology is nearly identical, integration in his context seems to refer to a community-building process. Finally, at least two writers, Philip E. Jacob and Henry Teune, seem to be willing to refer to *politically* integrated behavior in the same manner we do:

> Political integration, defined roughly as a state of mind or disposition to be cohesive, to act together, to be committed to mutual programs, refers to more than one aspect or dimension of behavior. . . . More rigorous research on political integration should sharpen the definition of what is being analyzed[9].

[9] Jacob (1964, pp. 10–11). For a Parsonian approach to the concept of integration in this sense, see Karl W. Deutsch, "Integration and the Social System: Implications of Functional Analysis," in the same volume; for his discussion of goal relationships in particular, see pp. 182–3; and for his discussion of building large-scale communities, see pp. 206–8.

Presumably, their notion of a disposition to be cohesive implies behavioral interdependence which has become organized, that is, *socially* integrated behavior.

Having laid out our basic concepts of community and integration, we can now relate to many of the other conditions and processes mentioned earlier. Etzioni's reference to the ability of a system to maintain itself under challenge becomes a *probable* behavioral property of a system with a high degree of community – not an identity by definition. And it may be, as he seemed to suggest, that the presence of a nation-state organization within the system, one that monopolizes force, allocates social "resources", and tends to be the dominant focus of identification, would tend to increase the *probability* of succesfully resisting challenge. But whether this is so, and to what degree the nation-state is an asset *or liability*, become empirical questions quite independent of the basic concepts of, or operational tests for, integration and community[10]. The importance of this point may be illustrated by current efforts at economic integration and the emergence of the international corporation. From the point of view of these systems, "political" organizations such as political parties and nation-states are of mixed value, often hampering or negating further integration or the development of communities along lines of economic function. Similarly, referring to Deutsch (1957), whether the institutions and practices discussed

---

[10] Deutsch (1966b) has an interesting set of speculations regarding the efficacy of relatively "powerful" nation-states, insofar as the government apparatus is concerned. Countering Etzioni's suggestion about the function of the state per se, Deutsch speculates as follows:

> Will is to a considerable degree the ability *not* to learn, and power is the ability not to have to learn. Thus the exercise of power tends to degrade and reduce the learning capacity and the information-processing capacity of the power wielding organization.
> We have already seen, however, that the ability to communicate, to steer oneself, and to learn and respond is of major positive importance for integration. It therefore turns out that the relationship between power and integration is not simple or straightforward but highly ambiguous. (from p. 312).

This argument followed an earlier speculation relating integration to cybernetic capabilities of systems involved in transactions:

> . . . if two systems are strongly coupled with each other and at the same time their steering capabilities are such that they find it difficult or impossible to coordinate their behavior (i.e., are interdependent through some common ecosocial system not under their control), a good deal of mutual frustration and negative covariance (unrewarding or punishing relationships) will result. In particular, the coupling of two systems tightly together, if each steers its behavior at random and if both these systems are of about the same order of magnitude, is likely to produce considerable mutual frustration (p. 303).

(such as amalgamated and pluralistic systems) contribute to the *probability* of expectations of peaceful change, or to some other relationships, becomes an empirical question. One of the results of this Princeton study was that coordination need not be manifested by a centralized, amalgamated system (Deutsch *et al.*, 1957). And as regards Deutsch's (1966) mutual relevance and (positive) covariance variables, it should be noted that the confluence of high mutual relevance (many transactions) and positive covariance (rewarding interdependence) are, in theory, only *highly probable*, not necessary or sufficient conditions for community; in and of themselves, they simply define socially integrated behavior. Whether they are, in a causal sense, sufficient for transforming an organized transaction network into a community over time is, again, an empirical question.

In terms of simple input-output analysis, the above relations may be sketched as follows in Figure 4.

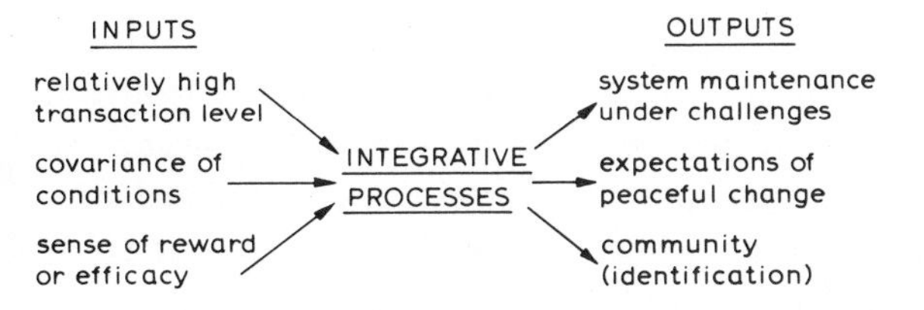

Fig. 4. – A simple input–output analysis of integration (see text p. 00)

Here, "integrative processes" belong to the "cybernetic processes" diagramed in Figure 2; the three "input" conditions represent the "transactions" and "attributes" portion of Figure 2; and the "outputs" represent *over time cumulated effects or stable conditions* characterizing the transactional and attribute matrices used to represent the global system. In terms of such matrices, the notion of "relatively" high transactions, covariance of conditions, and so on, would be exhibited operationally by *high densities*, or large numbers, *in the cells depicting the internal and external transactions and attributes of an integrated system, after the effects of ecosocial processes have been eliminated.* It must be noted carefully, however, that we assume that the above relations are *probable*, not *necessary* in all cases which we might observe. We do *not* have a theory or theoretical framework of integrative *processes* as such; hence we can not assert that all integrated networks will exhibit the relations shown in Figure 4. For example, some integrated networks might not consist of high volumes of transactions but of *critically significant* ones such as secret alliances, understandings, the exchange of classified information and strategic materials, and so on. Such a network would be characterized by at most two of the three input conditions shown, and perhaps not even that if sufficiently high volumes are not present to run ordinary probability tests to get a quantitative measure of the "non-randomness" (to be discussed in the next section) of the transactions. We do believe, however, that as a general rule such processes are not likely to be independent of the input characteristics shown; for the very fact that they *are critical* implies a larger political process which may exhibit itself in other ways.

A Partial Model for the Control of Socio-Ecological Effects in the Measurement of the Effects of Power and Integration

Integrative behavior is a subset of power behavior, or political (cybernetic) control activity. But not all influence is power; the political acts of statesmen, corporation directorates, and governmental agencies must be distinguished from the *effects on action* of the ecosocial (ecological and cultural) systems within which they are embedded. The notions of *relative* volumes of transactions, *relative* covariance of conditions, and *relative* reward levels refer to *departures from the ecosocially probable*. The task of this section is to suggest a number of models which may be used to measure the *net* effect of ecosocial variables on a given domain of transactions. Applications of such models will have utility to the extent that the models accurately represent such effects, and to the extent that measurements have been made on the relevant ecosocial variables and have been used in a given analysis.

Approaches to Measuring Ecosocial Probabilities

Another way of phrasing the notion of *departure from the ecosocially probable* is to refer to *political coordination. Coordination* may be somewhat more appropriate a term to use than *power*; while both refer to the *effects* of control activity, the habit of referring to the effects of power as constituting *success*, in contrast to Dahl's conception of power, may lead to some confusion in the following discussion. On the other hand, it must be noted that political coordination represents not only the short-term stimulus-response effect produced by an individual statesman's single act and immediate response, but to the long-term and more complicated effects *which they bring into existence*, such as derivative governmental agencies, planning boards, and so on. Political coordination, therefore, implies the measurement of the effects of large-scale organization on transaction flows of many different types, *sometimes only marginally related to statesmen's daily lives*, and not necessarily of a type which they would see as subjectively relating to their "power". Another term that has been suggested for this effect is political *organization*; but this implies the existence of *formal structure* to a transaction network, and we do not wish to limit ourselves to such systems. *Political coordination* is thus seen as encompassing what is traditionally referred to as *power*, as *political development*, and as *social control*, in that all of these imply cybernetic activity.

The fundamental concern in this section is with the analysis of *transaction matrices* (see Figure 2). These matrices – whether they be international trade, threats, or military action – contain *information* about the *effects* of political coordination. Our approach to detecting the effects of coordination on these matrices is to answer the question: what would they have looked like if coordination had not been present? If commerce and conflict would occur *anyway*, for example, how would it look *if the net effects of all efforts at coordination were zero*? We assume that political efforts at coordination are always present; to say that a *system* is coordinated, however, is to say that some stable communications network has been established among some set of individuals, with a stable value structure, decision-making procedure, and so on. To the extent such *systems* exist, departures from the ecosocially probable should occur. Measurement of these departures and various statistics derived from such measurements would tell us something about the strength, size, membership, perhaps internal organization of such systems of coordination. In conjunction with knowledge about the substance of the transactions forming the matrix, much more can be obtained.

The fundamental property of ecosocial probabilities which we assume here is that the elements of an ecosocial system *without* significant coordination behave in the aggregate as if they were *statistically independent*. This implies that knowledge of the *charac-*

teristics of the elements (individuals, groups) can be used to probabilistically estimate aggregate frequencies of their interaction. Obversely, this implies that *no knowledge of their communications network is necessary*. A simple analogy may be made here to the interaction of molecules of water. The interaction of one molecule with another requires knowledge of the individual characteristics of the molecules (location, momentum, direction). If we introduce a *piping system* with pressure valves, etc., we have introduced a simple *communications network* which must be taken into account if we are to adequately map the probabilities of interaction. Such "social piping" is in part what we refer to as coordination, but much more complex, as it goes about regulating the interaction of many individuals on a day-to-day basis.

There are essentially three approaches to designing a model which assumes a lack of political coordination in a transaction system. First, one may assume that all the information necessary to the analysis is contained in the transaction matrix itself. Second, one may assume that a simple probability model straightforwardly based upon the concept of independent events can be employed using *aggregate properties* (socio-ecological attributes in Figure 2) of the transaction system to estimate the independent probabilities of sending and receiving transactions. Third, it can be assumed that the transaction system has certain functional properties generating probabilities of interactions according to some composite effect not adequately represented by simply converting the measurement units on attributes into probabilities. These three possibilities will now be briefly developed.

Internal Analysis of Transaction Matrices: the Savage-Deutsch and Derived Methods. Consider the following transaction matrix of hypothetical trade between nations, *A, B, C,* and *D*. The probability of *A*

exports	A	B	C	D	
A	x	5	0	2	7
B	7	x	9	5	21
C	1	9	x	3	13
D	3	7	8	x	18
	11	21	17	10	59

$$\hat{T}(A \longrightarrow B) \doteq \frac{7 \cdot 21}{59} = \frac{147}{59} \doteq 2.5$$

$$RA(A \longrightarrow B) \doteq (5. - 2.5)/2.5 = 2.0$$

$$\Sigma \hat{T}_A \doteq 7(21+17+10)/59 \doteq 5.7$$

Fig. 5. – A simple probability calculation, showing error

sending in general is 7/59, that is, his proportion of total trade in the system; similarly the probability of B receiving in general is 21/59, B's proportion of total imports. Assuming that only these probabilities of sending and receiving are systemic predictors of the gross flow of trade from A to B, the expected value of trade from A to B is about 2.5, as shown (the probability is $7/59 \cdot 21/59$, but this has to be multiplied by total trade, 59, to obtain the expected value $\hat{T}$ shown in Figure 5; hence the formula).

Note that if this procedure were applied to all cells of the hypothetical trade matrix, a value $A \rightarrow A$ would also be possible to calculate. As we are not considering *internal* trade here, that calculation is ruled out, resulting in the total of all expected values of trade for A (A's expected total exports) to equal about 5.7 as shown in Figure 5. Thus a contradiction has arisen in the calculations; for by taking 7/59 as A's probability of exporting, we tacitly assumed that 7 equalled the *expected* value of A's total exports, but instead we obtained 5.7.

I. Richard Savage and Karl W. Deutsch (1960) invented a method to get around this contradiction, the mathematics of which need not be presented here. It is sufficient here to note that this method was invented so as to control for one ecosocial variable, relative size of market, so as to obtain the effects of other variables on transaction flows, in particular preference patterns for trade. Such a preference structure may be correctly labeled a cybernetic or truly political effect *only if the effects of other systemic (ecosocial) factors cancel each other out*. While this technique is useful, as they say, for the *preliminary* analysis of transaction flows – in particular trade flows – other methods employing their orientation but not the specific algorithms, may be tried with additional payoffs.

	A	B	C	D	s_1	y_1
A	3	5	0	2	10	7
B	7	4	9	5	25	15
C	1	9	7	3	20	20
D	3	7	8	12	30	40
s_2	14	25	24	22	85	
y_2	7	15	20	40		82

$$\hat{T}(A \rightarrow B) \doteq \frac{10 \cdot 25}{85} = \frac{250}{85} \doteq 3.0$$

with $RA = 0.67$

$$\hat{T}_y(A \rightarrow B) \doteq \frac{7 \cdot 15}{82^2} \cdot 85 \doteq 1.3$$

with $RA_y \doteq 2.9$ and $RA_{Ay} \doteq \frac{10}{7} - 1 \doteq 1.4$

Fig. 6. – A more complex probability calculation

Consider the following method, as illustrated in Figure 6. To relate the method to that shown above, a new $\hat{T}$ is calculated (3.0) and RA (0.67), this time based upon a matrix including diagonal (self-interaction) elements. Here we have used all cells because we wish to consider the probabilities of "self-trade", not in the sense of importing one's own exports, but in the sense of purely internal transactions. In this latter sense, we are considering both the probability of generating transactions as such, *and the probability of their diffusion to other systems*. Next, we introduce in y_1 and y_2 the concept of expected total probabilities of transactions. Suppose that system A for some substantive reason was expected to produce 7, not 10 transactions, B, 15 instead of 25, and so on. Under this assumption, $\hat{T}_y \doteq 1.3$, $RA_y \doteq 2.9$, and the total RA for A, $RA_{A\,y\,1} \doteq 1.4$. For simplicity, the proportion of transactions sent was made to equal the proportion received ($y_1 = y_2$). Such substantive expectations for total trade, or total transactions in general, can be generated in a variety of ways, which will be discussed in the next paragraph. It is important to note, however, that the simple extension of a transaction matrix to include a definition of internal transactions should not be quickly dismissed. As has been noted earlier, trade, population, and conflict behavior are all amenable to this sort of analysis. Analyses intercorrelating the patterns of deviation as determined by this method might show some useful results that would otherwise be missed[11].

Empirical (Inductive) Probabilistic Transaction Models. Notice that the Savage-Deutsch equation for predicting expected values of the total trade between each pair of nations may be written as

$$\hat{t}_{ij} = 0.0 + TU_iV_j, \tag{2}$$

where $\hat{t}_{ij}$ is the expected value of transactions, t, from nation i to nation j, T is the total number of actual transactions in a transaction matrix, U_i is the probability of i sending transactions in general, and V_j is the probability of j receiving transactions in general. Suppose U_i and V_j are variables other than the actual proportions of trans-

[11] Such work is currently in progress in my work with Deutsch, and separately on the analysis of international conflict data collected under Dimensionality of Nations Project auspices.

actions, that is, of the type shown by y_1 and y_2 in Figure 6 in contrast to the sums s_1 and s_2. Suppose further that the additive (0.0) and multiplicative (T) constants in Equation (2) are permitted to vary. We then have

$$\hat{t}_{ij} = a + bU_iV_j, \tag{3}$$

where a and b must be empirically determined. Moreover, we may extend this model by presuming that the bU_iV_j's are really the sums of many *mutually exclusive* factors *independently* contributing to the probability of a transaction between i and j. Such an extension would then take the following form:

$$\hat{t}_{ij} = a + b_1 x_{i1} x_{j1} + b_2 x_{i2} x_{j2} + \ldots + b_m x_{im} x_{jm}, \tag{4}$$

where x_{im} and x_{jm} are i and j's interaction probabilities associated with variable x_m, the mth variable beginning with x_1. Another type of extension of the model is to consider the prediction not of the individual ij interactions, but only the marginal sums $t_{i\cdot}$ and $t_{\cdot j}$ (i's total sent and j's total received, including the "self" transactions). Such marginal sums' expectations, $\hat{t}_{i\cdot}$ and $\hat{t}_{\cdot j}$, could then be used to calculate expected values after the manner shown in Figure 6. In terms of Equation (4), such a revision would become

$$\begin{aligned} \hat{t}_{i\cdot} &= a + b_1 x_{i1} + b_2 x_{i2} + \ldots + b_m x_{im} \\ \hat{t}_{\cdot j} &= a' + b'_1 x_{jm} + b'_2 x_{jm} + \ldots + b'_m x_{jm}. \end{aligned} \tag{5}$$

The equations for $t_{i\cdot}$ and $t_{\cdot j}$ would not necessarily be the same or even similar (identical up to a linear transformation); for the $t_{i\cdot}$'s and $t_{\cdot j}$'s are not necessarily equal or perfectly correlated. For example, nations do not necessarily send and receive similar numbers of total external and internal threats. It will be noted that equations (2), (3), (4), (5) are all linear in form, and (3), (4), (5) are amenable to the usual forms of multiple regression. What is extremely unusual about their use is that *the goodness of the model is not dependent upon the degree of correlation as such, but upon the value of the clustering patterns exhibited in the residuals*. For in all cases, the expected values are but the first step in detecting the effects of political controls on transaction flows.

There are several important implications of the above models. Behavioral scientists focusing upon international politics as a set of dependent variables have generated many analyses in which regression models of the above type have been employed. It is quite common these days to see such variables as gross national product (national income), population size, and other economic and demographic (or in general, ecosocial) variables used to predict conflict, trade, and so on, *basically under the assumption that the "error" term can be explained in terms of other similar variables*. Furthermore, the residuals are rarely if ever analyzed for patterning in their deviations. We suggest, on the other hand, that the most interesting part of much such research has hardly begun. We assume that much of the error term may not be explained by ecosocial variables, and that the strength and patterning of the residuals is of central, not peripheral, importance for *political* analysis. In fact, it is not too extreme to say that those who wish to assume that by carrying out such regression they are analyzing political behavior, are doing exactly the opposite. They are, from this perspective, analyzing the *ecosocial* effects on transactions, *not* the political (cybernetic) effects at all. This argument may be considered further in the light of empirical models below.

*Empirical, Inductive Transaction Models.*The models discussed so far are but simple extensions of the basic Savage-Deutsch Equation (2), and are generally consonant with the notion that transaction probabilities are a probabilistic function of mutually exclusive substantive ecosocial conditions such as population distributions, resource distributions, etc. However, transaction systems may have certain functional properties of their own which, while still amenable to the probability interpretation, are not representable by simple probability mathematics. For example, the probability of high levels of production may tend to increase with the square root of the population or some other exponential function. Communications capabilities may probabilistically decline with the square of the distance between point of origin and area of destination. Peculiar ecological circumstances may tend probabilistically to make one system more efficient than another. Furthermore, assuming a cybernetic (political) system with a "franchise" (as discussed previously above) over a given territory, such probabilistic effects may contribute to altering the probabilities of certain types or directions of political development.

Two types of empirical research may be used to exemplify the inductive research of the type described here. Hans Linnemann's work on international trade flows was based upon a multiplicative model with an unknown multiplier and exponents, as shown in Equation (6) below (Linnemann, 1966). Another type of model, more general in scope, is Rudolph J. Rummel's which assumes that interaction is a function of differences in attributes, as shown in (7) below (Rummel, 1965, 1969). Linnemann's model is somewhat

$$\hat{t}_{ij} = a\mathrm{GNP}_i^{b_1}\,\mathrm{GNP}_j^{b_2}\,\mathrm{POP}_i^{b_3}\,\mathrm{POP}_j^{b_4}\,\mathrm{DIST}_{ij}^{b_5}\ \ldots, \tag{6}$$

where GNP is gross national product,
POP is population,
DIST is a function of port-to-port distance,
t_{ij} is trade from i to j $(i \neq j)$,
and $a, b_1, b_2, b_3, \ldots,$ are empirical coefficients to be determined by regression.

$$\hat{t}_{ij} = a + b_1(x_{i1} - x_{j1}) + \ldots + b_m(x_{im} - x_{jm}), \tag{7}$$

where t_{ij} is some *dimension* of transactions,
x_{im} and x_{jm} are i and j's scores on some attribute dimension orthogonal to all other attribute dimensions $(m = 1, 2, \ldots)$.

clearer in interpretation because he does distinguish between ecosocial factors (GNP, POP, DIST) and others such as colonial ties or former colonial relationships which represent a cybernetic effect or past (residue) effect. However, neither his nor Rummel's model (an earlier version of which is shown by Equation (7)) can be given a simple ecosocial interpretation. In Linnemann's case, the multiplicative model is difficult to interpret probabilistically. In Rummel's case, since the *dimensions* are composite scores of all variables in an analysis, and since those variables are *both* ecosocial and cybernetic (such as type of political system), it is difficult to separate out the effects of each type of systemic variable. Nevertheless, the results of their work in practice suggest further development with the goal of clarifying their interpretation within the present analytic framework.

That such reinterpretation is possible seems indicated by the fact that they both use the *directed dyad* (i to j and j to i being considered separate units of analysis) in their work. By implication, each dyad is considered as an *independent* bit of information; knowing the values associated with i to j presumably tells us nothing about j to i, or about any other dyad. This implication is the functional equivalent of Savage and Deutsch's assumption of origin-destination independence.

Further Development of the Ecosocial Input–Output Model

Of the four probabilistic models previously mentioned, the model represented by Equation (4) is selected for further development here. It is more general than Equations (2) or (3) and is, therefore, more valuable as will become apparent in the development below. In contrast to (5) which assumes that each nation (or other system under analysis) has an ecosocial input–output function, (4) assumes that *dyadic opportunities for transaction* are the determining factors of the probabilities of interaction. And in contrast to the original Savage-Deutsch model, it permits the treatment of internal transactions on the same basis as external transactions. However, the only reason for preferring (4) to such empirical equations as (6) and (7) is that the first has a straightforward theoretical basis in the mathematics of probability. The latter two have their origin in theoretical frameworks that are only marginally related to the present work; and require far more substantive development before they can be used in the present context. (That they or other such models might in time prove superior to the simple model based directly upon probability mathematics is a real possibility). So that we can bring to bear the analytic developments in sections on integration, let us approach Equation (4) developmentally, starting from basic assumptions.

We have accepted a conception of integration as a variable or gradient. It is a condition brought about by *political coordination* of transactions, that is, the conscious efforts of statesmen and the organizations they create to achieve goals. The decision-making structure and the values embedded within it, of any system, represent *integrative processes* (see Figure 4) or *cybernetic processes* (see Figure 2) in a broader sense (some cybernetic processes may be *dis*integrative within a system). The *effect of*, and – through feedback effects shown in Figure 2 – *input to* such processes is a transaction pattern characterized by (*a*) relatively high volumes of transactions, (*b*) covariance of conditions, and (*c*) a derived sense of reward or positive affect within the systems integrated by *politics*.

Political coordination may be used and/or result in *community* (mass identification with the system); but it may also be used to generate *antisystems* and *conflict systems*, which may be characterized by relatively low volumes of transactions and negative affect, and by relatively high volumes of transactions with negative affect, respectively. We shall briefly discuss such combinations at the end of this section; they are important to point out here so that it becomes clear that *political coordination* and *integrative processes* are distinguishable concepts, in an operational sense. Let us now develop models which can be made operational for each of the three properties of integrated systems mentioned in the previous paragraph.

Relative Volumes of Transactions. To speak of political coordination (or *power*) in operational terms is to speak of *patterns of deviations* from the expected frequencies of transactions, where the expectations are derived from a probability model. In the case of coordination of transactions within and among regions or countries, such a probability model should be based solely upon aggregate properties of the geographic areas used to define the boundaries of a priori systems. If the coordination is integrative, by definition it is expected to become manifested by large *positive* deviations in transaction volumes which are *rewarding* for the system(s) with these positive deviations. In this section, we will develop the notion of *positive deviation patterns*; in the following section, we will develop the notion of *reward*.

At the atomic level (looking at a single region or nation's total internal transaction of some particular type, or at a particular pair of regions or nations' directed transactions), *coordination* refers to the *magnitude* of the difference between actual and expected transactions. We may represent this mathematically as follows:

$$D_{ij} = t_{ij} - \hat{t}_{ij}, \qquad (8)$$

where D_{ij} equals the difference between the actual volume (t_{ij}) of transactions (say trade, for example) from *i* to *j* (nations *i* and *j*, for example) and the expected volume of transactions ($\hat{t}_{ij}$).

When t_{ij} is greater than t_{ij}, D_{ij} is positive – one of the characteristics of integration if the transactions themselves are rewarding. If i equals j ($i = j$), then we are speaking of internal volumes (here, of internal trade, perhaps as indexed by gross domestic product), and such a condition would represent one aspect of *political development*.

One way of approaching the problem of predicting "random" transaction levels, that is, those that represent the "pure" effects of ecosocial conditions or attributes, is to consider the probabilities of i sending, $P(S_i)$, and j receiving, $P(R_j)$. Assuming these two probabilities to be *independent*, the probability of i sending to j with respect to some type of transaction is then $P(S_i) \cdot P(R_j)$, that is, i's probability of sending times j's probability of receiving. If we further *assume* that the *total volume* of all transactions between and within all i's (j's), as well as the totals sent (S_i) and received (R_j) are produced only by such random factors, then we may generate both the $P(S_i)$'s and $P(R_j)$'s from any observed, actual transaction matrix. If we let T equal the total volume of all transactions in such a real matrix, then the expected volume of transactions from any i to j, $\hat{t}_{ij}$, is given by the following equation (cf. Eq. (2); U_i is equivalent to $P(S_i)$ and V_j is equivalent to $P(R_j)$):

$$\hat{t}_{ij} = TP(S_i)P(R_j). \tag{9}$$

The expected values generated by (9) may then be used in (8) to generate the D_{ij}'s. For example, if the matrix shown in Figure 6 were a trade matrix between countries A, B, C, and D, and the diagonal cells were GDP (gross domestic product), we would be calculating $\hat{T}(A \rightarrow B)$ by (9) above (see Figure 6).

The basic trouble with this method is that the D_{ij}'s so calculated contain the implicit assumption that *coordination only redirects transactions dyadically* (pairwise with respect to all combinations of nations, including self-transactions). In this sense, *nations* are "preordained" to send and receive certain volumes of various types of transactions ($P(S_i)$ and $P(R_j)$ are fixed, as is total trade, T). Political coordination is limited in its effect to simply redirecting transactions, that is, altering the relative proportions any i sends to any j and any j sends to any i. For example, the United States can place an embargo on Cuban sugar, but this will not alter either the United

States' total import of sugar or Cuba's total export of sugar, assuming we are looking at the total number of all transactions involving sugar. We do not wish to limit the D_{ij}'s in this sense. Rather, we wish a model that permits both the total transactions to vary and the relative sending and receiving probabilities to vary. More substantively, we wish to assess the *effects* of political coordination upon both the *distributions* of *transactions* and the *total volumes of transactions sent and received* by each system (nation) within a total transaction network.

Starting from (9), we can develop in the direction of either (4) or (5) *under the assumption that the additive coefficient always equals zero* (a = 0.0); that is, that *the total of all expected values* ($\sum_{k=1}^{n} \sum_{g=1}^{n} \hat{t}_{kg}$) *equal the total of all observed transactions* (equal to the same summation but now over the t_{kg}'s). Substantively, such an assumption implies that while the $P(S_i)$ and $P(R_j)$ probabilities may vary, showing a possible impact of political coordination upon each nation's total input and output (and internal transactions) of some type, *the average total number of transactions within the global network can not vary*. Put another way, we would be assuming that the *world* was "preordained" to generate a certain number of transactions; and political coordination only affects the proportion produced by each nation, the proportion sent by each nation, and the direction in which these transactions are sent and received.

We wish to permit the total volume of transactions predicted to be variable. Thus, if more transactions are sent in total, T, than expected, $\hat{T}$, for example, we would interpret the *times as favoring cooperation* (coordination around positive or mutually rewarding goals); if *more* trade is predicted than observed, we would interpret the times as being unfavorable to this form of cooperation in general. Periods of expansion and depression would then be measurable quantitatively. In this sense, the notion of the *Zeitgeist* or "spirit of the times" or "mood" becomes an empirical concept, one that is amenable to being made operational. Thus the additive (a) coefficient in (4) or (5) should be empirically estimated.

As mentioned before, Equation (4) assumes that dyadic opportunities for transactions are more relevant determinants of interaction than the aggregate properties of each of the systems as a whole. For this reason (this assumption), we choose to further develop (4).

The a and b_m ($b_1, b_2, \ldots, b_m$) coefficients can be derived in such a way as to yield a simple probability interpretation. Consider that all transactions (such as trade, monetary transfers, mail flows; and in the communications sense of transactions: threats, accusations, military agreements such as alliances, secret treaties, etc.) involve communication and transportation capabilities for transacting, as well as the wherewithal to perform the transactions (natural resources, strategic locations, etc.): in short, they require ecosocial capabilities. Let us assume that there are M such inherent capabilities of nations, only m of which are measured (such as population, GNP, etc.), and let these be referred to as $x_{i1}, x_{i2}, \ldots, x_{im}$, for any nation i. Let the sum of any k^{th} such capability (k=1,2,. . . , m) equal s_k ($s_k = \sum_{g=1}^{n} x_{gk}$) such as world population, GNP, etc. Now, since a probability variable is, by definition, a real-valued function defined over a sample space, with a range $0 \leqslant p_{ik} \leqslant 1$, and a sum $\sum_{g=1}^{n} p_{gk} = 1$, all we need to do to transform each x_k into a probability variable p_k is to divide each datum x_{ik} by the appropriate sum s_k; thus we have

$$p_{ik} = x_{ik}/s_k, \tag{10}$$

where p_{ik} is nation i's proportion of the total s_k of the kth ecosocial variable, such as the United States proportion of world steel production.

At this point we will make a simplifying assumption, namely, that each p_k probability variable is symmetrically related to both the probability of sending and the probability of receiving; thus with respect to any pair of actors i and j, we have as the probability of i sending p_{ik} and j receiving p_{jk} and the probability of i sending to j as $p_{ik}p_{jk}$ (being multiplied together); and symmetrically, p_{jk} is j's probability of sending, p_{ik} *is* i's probability of receiving, and $p_{jk}p_{ik}$ is the probability of j sending to i. It is recognized that this is *only* a simplifying assumption for initial empirical investigations. It is easily conceivable that some probability variables may only be related to the probability of sending, while others may be related only to the probability of receiving. It is also conceivable that a non-distributive logic might be more appropriate, following the pioneering work of

Satosi Watanabe.[12] Only detailed substantive research into these possibilities will be able to determine which ecosocial variables play what kinds of roles during which periods of time.

The question now arises: how do we cumulate the m-number of ecosocial probability variables' impact on some particular type of transaction? The critical concept here is that we must weight each of the m $p_{ik}p_{jk}$ (hereafter referred to simply as p_{ijk}) probabilities such that their sum is unity, that is, that

$$\sum_{g=1}^{n} \sum_{f=1}^{n} \sum_{k=1}^{m} p_{gfk} = 1.$$

Since the current sums of the p_{ijk} probabilities for each kth variable currently equal unity (1.0), we need only find a set of weights such that they sum to unity themselves, vary between zero and unity, and reflect the relative impact of each of the kth variables on a particular type of transaction. These weights would then have the following properties and effects:

$$0 \leqslant b'_k \leqslant 1; \ \sum_{k=1}^{m} b'_k = 1; \text{and} \ \sum_{g=1}^{n} \sum_{f=1}^{n} \sum_{k=1}^{m} b'_k p_{gfk} = 1.$$

Notice that these weights may be considered to be probabilities themselves, in the sense that the kth ecosocial probability variable has *in toto* b'_k probability of affecting some type of transaction t_h. If we were to stop here, we would have the following equation:

$$P(t_{ijh}) = b'_1 p_{ij1} + b'_2 p_{ij2} + \ldots + b'_m p_{ijm} \tag{11}$$

and

$$\hat{t}_{ijh} = T \cdot P(t_{ijh}), \tag{12}$$

where $P(t_{ijh})$ is the probability of a transaction from i to j of type h, $\hat{t}_{ijh}$ is the estimated probable frequency of such transactions *given*

[12] Satosi Watanabe (1969). Watanabe's work is especially interesting because it deals with the fact that *order* of experimental treatments can change final behavioral results. As applied to possible integrative processes, differences in the order of integrating transactional subsystems may lead to different resulting integrative structures. The logical process constructed here by Watanabe formalizes such an effect so that computer programs may be written to take it into account in analyzing time-series flows.

some total volume of transactions, T. Such an equation would not permit the "climate of the times" or *Zeitgeist* to influence total volumes of transactions. We therefore need to place an additive probability, a', into (11) to represent the increase or decrease (depending upon whether a' is positive or negative) due to such conditions as depressions, periods of expansion, war, etc; thus we have:

$$P(t_{ijh}) = a' + b'_1 p_{ij1} + b'_2 p_{ij2} + \ldots + b'_m p_{ijm} \tag{13}$$

and (12) as before, but now with the probability from (13), above. That (12) is now acceptable (no longer assumes that T is the total to be distributed) can be seen by expanding (12) in terms of (13):

$$\hat{t}_{ijh} = Ta' + Tb'_1 p_{ij1} + Tb'_2 p_{ij2} + \ldots + Tb'_m p_{ijm}\,. \tag{14}$$

Notice that Tb'_1, Tb'_2, and so on, are the proportions of total trade that are distributed by the ecosocial variables, while Ta' represents the proportion of observed trade to be added to (or subtracted from) each estimate based upon the other probabilities. In this case, the sum of the $\hat{t}_{ijh}$'s may be either greater than or less than the observed total T.

For purposes of empirical investigation, we need to consider an error term, so that the a' and b'_k coefficients may be estimated, given a real transaction matrix and real ecosocial variables. "Error", in this sense, is due to two sources: unmeasured, relevant ecosocial variables, and measurement error. (We do not define "error" to include the impact of political interventions, as the *deviations* from the ecosocially probable will measure this effect. We are distinguishing between "error" in the sense of the definition of an error term in an equation, and "error" in the sense of deviations from expected values). In terms of this ecosocial model, a' should equal zero (or not significantly differ from zero), and the total of the deviations from the probability expectations should not be significant (unless there are unmeasured, relevant ecosocial variables). Thus our empirical equation is:

$$t_{ijh} = a + b_1 p_{ij1} + b_2 p_{ij2} + \ldots + b_m p_{ijm} + e \tag{15}$$

where

$$e = \sum_{k=m+1}^{M} b_k p_{ijk} \,. \tag{16}$$

Notice that we have replaced Ta' with a, Tb' with b, and so on; and the error term, e, is the set of all unmeasured ecosocial variables with significant b coefficients. Because we assume that an error term of ecosocial variables exists, the b (and derivable Tb'), as well as our *Zeitgeist* coefficient a (and derivable Ta') may be to some degree in error, i.e., not what they would be if no unmeasured ecosocial variables existed. It is important, therefore, to be more inclusive, more eclectic, than one would normally be to properly estimate these values, both as regards the variety of measurements taken and as regards the methods of analysis. Notice also, that while the model represented by Equations (15), (16) makes no assumptions about the presence of political coordination effects on behavior, it does permit an analysis of the deviations D_{ij} ($D_{ij} = t_{ij} - \hat{t}_{ij}$, where $\hat{t}_{ij} = t_{ij} - e$), *as if* all ecosocial variables were taken into account. If we make the assumption that the model, as applied, is sufficient to describe behavior, in other words, then deviations, by contradicting the model, must be measuring something else. We interpret that "something else" to be the effects of political coordination.

Relative volumes of transactions are thus made operational by taking the proportions above or below expected volumes of transactions, of actual volumes. For each type, h, of transactions, we thus have the following statistic:

$$RC_{ij} = \frac{t_{ij} - \hat{t}_{ij}}{\hat{t}_{ij}} = \frac{D_{ij}}{\hat{t}_{ij}} \tag{17}$$

where RC is relative coordination, and $\hat{t}_{ij}$ is an estimate generated from the model represented by (15), (16). In this definition, we follow the original work of Savage and Deutsch (previously cited). If the type of transaction being observed is rewarding, positive RC_{ij} indices would indicate (in conjunction with covariance, to be developed in the next section) some degree of integration between i and j.

It should be noted that the D_{ij} and RC_{ij} are both measures of deviation from ecosocially probable interaction. Both are easily interpreted, but the RC_{ij} index has the added advantage of controlling for the absolute magnitude of the expected value (note: the greater the sum of t_{ij} and $\hat{t}_{ij}$, the greater can the difference between the two be). In addition, the *clustering properties* of the two may be markedly different. Small differences can produce larger RC_{ij}'s on occasion than larger differences, depending upon the size of the $\hat{t}_{ij}$ value. Two systems with large expected values may produce a large D_{ij} but a small RC_{ij}, whereas two systems with a small difference could produce a large relative coordination index. The D_{ij} represents the size or volume of the effect; the RC_{ij} measures it relative to background ecosocial effects. Whether the actual volume of the effect is more important than the relative volume or vice versa can only be demonstrated through research. It is our contention, however, that small expected levels, since they represent small ecosocial capabilities, imply that the political system embedded within them has less to work with, to manipulate. Thus, by controlling for the ecosocial capability for generating transactions in the RC_{ij} index, we also norm for the potential effects caused through political coordination or cybernetic processes. For example, though Ireland may be highly integrated with the United Kingdom as regards their economies, the actual volume of trade may be much smaller than between the United Kingdom and the United States, simply because Ireland is far smaller.

Patterning in the RC_{ij} (or possibly the D_{ij}) values, in conjunction with reward and covariance, should indicate clusters or regions of integration. As Savage, Deutsch, Brams, Alker, and Puchala have demonstrated with trade flows, using the Savage-Deutsch model, or Goodman's variation on it, clustering of positive deviations does occur where one would expect (in the European Common Market, and so on)[13]. Regional RC_{ij} indices may be cumulated in the same manner Savage and Deutsch did (by summing the expected values and the actual values for a set of nations, and dividing by the sum of the expected values).

Covariance of Conditions. Covariance implies a change in one system's behavior (nation-states here) or attributes causal changes in other systems' behavior and attributes. Another term for this is *interdependence*. Interdependence can exist without high RC_{ij} indices. In such cases, interdependence is presumed to arise through ecosocial conditions and processes (see Figure 2 for the feedback loop from ecosocial processes to transactions and back to ecosocial processes

[13] For sources, see footnote 2, *supra*.

through attributes). Individuals, groups, and nation-states may continue to interact with each other at high volumes simply because they perceive little alternative. This could be the case, while the RC_{ij} index is negative. For example, the United Kingdom and the United States, though far from being integrated economically, still are good trading partners, as is indicated by the fact that they are in the top ranks by volume but have negative RA_{ij} indices (same as RC_{ij} but using the Savage-Deutsch method)[14].

Covariance of conditions should manifest itself by changes over time. For example, a simple type of covariance would be the RC_{ij} and RC_{ji} indices between two systems over time. This would imply obtaining correlations on time-series data. Another type of covariance would be covariance of conditions over time, as in growth rates of various types. For example, growth in production has occurred within the EEC at a faster rate than outside the EEC among European countries (Alker and Puchala in Singer, 1968). A more complicated concept of covariance is to assume that change over time in one system is a function of change over time in a set of other systems:

$$\Delta i = f(\Delta j, j = 1, n). \tag{18}$$

This concept might be applied to a region we suspect is integrated, such as the EEC, and the model might be made operational in terms of a simple linear equation for short periods of time. Thus: change in GNP of i equals a weighted sum of changes in GNP of all nations in the region, except i. With regard to transactions, we might write:

$$\Delta (i \rightarrow j) = f(\Delta (g \rightarrow h)), (g \rightarrow h) = 1, (n^2 - 1), \tag{19}$$

where $\Delta(i \rightarrow j)$ is a change in the RC_{ij} of two nations, and $(g \rightarrow h)$ is the set of all permutations of actors in the system, except the directed pair $(i \rightarrow j)$.

For example, a change in the RC_{ij} from France to Germany over some period of time is a linear function of changes in the interactions among all other members of the EEC.

---

14 *Ibid.*

Note that by taking the measurement of relationship over the RC_{ij}'s, *we in effect control for ecosocial change over time.* In addition, we may want to control for general increases in political development, which should cause the *standard deviation* of the RA_{ij}'s to change over time. Yet development itself might be an important effect of integration; hence we may want to compare both types of results.

For the purpose of analyzing political covariance, we may want to measure relative coordination in other ways. The RC_{ij} index considers only the *ij*-dyad relative to its own expected levels of transactions, given the total system analyzed. We may wish to measure the D_{ij} *relative to some total system or subsystem* so as to better measure the effects of the *concentration* of political coordination. This may be done by changing the denominator of (17) in such a way as to index *sender-relative coordination* (SRC_{ij}) as follows:

$$SRC_{ij} = \frac{t_{ij} - \hat{t}_{ij}}{\sum_{k=1}^{n} \left| t_{ik} - \hat{t}_{ik} \right|}, \tag{20}$$

where n is a relevant set of actors.

Similarly, *receiver-relative coordination* would be defined by cumulating the absolute value of the D_{ij}'s over j's inputs ($\sum_{k=1}^{n} |t_{kj} - \hat{t}_{kj}|$). Two-way or *mutual relative coordination* might be defined (MRC_{ij}) by adding these two absolute sums together and subtracting the D_{ii} so as not to include it twice. In fact, one meaningful index of political development might be the MRC_{ii} index, i.e., how much of a nation's political coordination is concentrated in its own transactions (internal interaction). Systems with relatively low MRC_{ii}'s but high SRC_{ij} and RRC_{ij}'s along some behavioral dimensions (e.g., trade and internal gross domestic product) would probably also be colonies, such as Angola and Mozambique. For this would indicate that the system's interaction pattern is controlled from without. In terms of covariance, such systems would be almost wholly determined by a few other systems, with very little autocorrelation (predicting itself over time).

Reward. High RC_{ij}'s combined with high covariance over time in transactions and attributes are not enough to indicate that two or more systems are integrated. The interaction could be *hostile*, such as wars or lesser military and diplomatic interactions. Such a condition could be used to indicate the presence of conflict or coercive systems of political interaction. The transactions themselves must be *rewarding* to the participants.

Survey and content-analysis data might be good sources to use in indicating the level of reward. But such data imply that our concept of reward is a *perceptual* one; that is, that reward at the *system* level is usefully defined as some aggregation of perceptions of individuals, be they the general population, government spokesmen or statesmen, or newspaper and professional analysts' opinions.

It is possible to depart from a perceptual concept of reward if we accept the behavioral concept of *positive or amplifying feedback*[15]. From a mathematical point of view, this is defined as the second derivative of a time-series curve being positive. Figure 7 below exemplifies such curves.

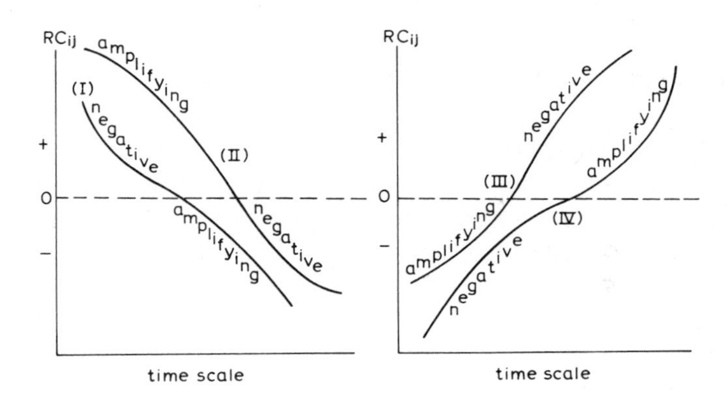

Fig. 7. – Positive (amplifying) and negative feedback

Amplifying (positive) feedback is seen as an increasing *rate* of either increase or decrease in RC_{ij}'s. If we accept this concept of reward, all conditions characterized as "amplifying" feedback in Figure 7 would imply that a system is being "rewarded" increasingly over time by such behavior. Thus, if the RC_{ij} in trade between *i* and *j* were going

[15] See Milsum for detailed development. For the earliest direct application of the concept of feedback of which I am aware, see Karl W. Deutsch (1963, pp. 182–99).

down at an increasing rate (the bottom part of curve (I) and the top part of curve (II) in Figure 7), we would assume that the decrease is "rewarding" at least in the sense of decreasing dissatisfactions stemming from the preceding relationship. The amplifying portions of curves (III) and (IV) indicate, as regards trade for example, increasing rewards from the coordination resulting in greater levels of trade, relative to total system trade capabilities.

This amplifying concept of reward at the system level has disturbing implications for what we would normally consider hostile behavior. Arms races and defense spending, if following for some period of time a curve such as the upper part of (IV), would be interpreted as rewarding for both systems (though not necessarily for the individuals who create and maintain such systems). *Purely* in terms of the growth and operation of military subsystems, such an interpretation may be quite acceptable however, even though from other perspectives such growth would constitute the severest of punishments. Which of these two concepts – perceptions of individuals or amplifying feedback – is used in substantive research may be a matter of the definition of the final product aimed at. If we are to distinguish readily between an integrated region and a conflict region, however, we need either to categorize certain types of behavior as conflictful a priori or accept a perceptual conception of reward. Otherwise, the distinction between conflict and cooperation becomes purely a matter of change over time – an interpretation we do not find heuristically useful.

Conclusion

We have defined and elaborated upon a conception of political coordination or power as the effects on transaction systems and ecosocial attributes of conscious efforts of statesmen or other individuals and groups to alter the ecosystem. Application of this concept of political coordination to the concept of political *integration* led to a simple characterization of integration as the conjunction of three conditions: greater transactions among a set of systems (nation-states) than ecosocially expected, covariance of transactional conditions among the systems integrated, and rewards perceived over time in consequence of the transactions. For any integrated region, such conditions are presumed to have a high probability of being present, and can be thought of as input conditions further enhanced by cybernetic (political) subsystems over time. Such a stable condition is further presumed to create a high probability of system maintenance under challenge, expectations of peaceful change among the population, and perhaps a sense of community (popular identification with the system). The analytic framework developed within the elaboration upon *integration* should be applicable to any type of transaction network, from groups of individuals, to metropolitan areas to nation-states and international organizations. Further theoretical development of the relationships between goals (conceived of as planned transaction and attribute distributions and levels), *probable* (in the ecosocial sense) transaction and attribute conditions, and actual conditions requires development (now in progress).

REFERENCES

Alker, Jr., H.R. "An IBM 709 Program For the Gross Analysis of Transaction Flows." *Behavioral Science* 7:498–99.

Brams, S.J. (1966a). "Transaction Flows in the International System." *The American Political Science Review* LX:880–98.

Brams, S.J. (1966b). "Trade In the North Atlantic Area: An Approach to the Analysis of Transformations in a System." *Peace Research Society: Papers VI*, Vienna Conference, pp. 143–64.

Dahl, R.A. (1957). "The Concept of Power." *Behavioral Science* 2:201–18.

Day, R.H., and Tinney, E.H. (1968). "How to Co-operate in Business Without Really Trying: A Learning Model of Decentralized Decision Making." *The Journal of Political Economy* 76:583–600.

Deutsch, K.W. (1960). "Toward an Inventory of Basic Trends and Patterns in Comparative and International Politics." *The American Political Review* LIV:24–57.

Deutsch, K.W. (1963). *The Nerves of Government.* New York: The Free Press.

Deutsch, K.W. (1966a). "Integration and Arms Control in the European Political Environment." *The American Political Science Review* LX.

Deutsch, K.W. (1966b). "Power and Communication in International Society." In *Conflict in Society*, CIBA Foundation Symposium, ed. by A.V.S. deReuck and Julie Knight, pp. 300–16. London: J. & A. Churchill, Ltd.

Deutsch, K.W.; Burrell, S.A.; Kann, R.A.; Lee, Jr., M.; Lichterman, M.; Lindgren, R.E.; Loewenheim, F.L.; and VanWagenen, R.(1957). *Political Community and the North Atlantic Area: International Organization In The Light of Historical Experience.* Princeton: Princeton University Press.

Etzioni, A. (1965). *Political Unification: A Comparative Study of Leaders and Forces.* New York: Holt, Rinehart, and Winston, Inc.

Goodman, L.A. (1963). "Statistical Methods for tne Preliminary Analysis of Transaction Flows." *Econometrica* 31:197–208.

Goodman, L.A. (1964). "A Short Computer Program for the Analysis of Transaction Flows." *Behavioral Science* 9:176–86.

Haas, E. (1964). *Beyond the Nation State: Functionalism and International Organization.* Stanford: Stanford University Press.

Harsanyi, J.C. (1962). "Measurement of Social Power: Opportunity Costs and the Theory of Two-Person Bargaining Games." *Behavioral Science* 7:67–80.

Jacob, P.E., and Toscano, J. V., eds. (1964). *The Integration of Political Communities.* Philadelphia: J. B. Lippincott Company.

Levi, W. (1965). "The Concept of Integration in Research on Peace." *International Studies Quarterly* (formerly *Background*) 9:111–26.

Linnemann, H. (1966). *An Econometric Study of International Trade Flows.* Amsterdam: North-Holland Publishing Company.

Milsum, John H. (Ed.) (1968). *Positive Feedback: A General Systems Approach to Positive/ Negative Feedback and Mutual Causality*. New York: Pergamon Press.

Minar, D.W., and Greer, S. (1969). *The Concept of Community: Readings with Interpretations.* Chicago: Aldine Publishing Company.

Nye, J.S. (1968). "Comparative Regional Integration: Concept and Measurement." *International Organization* XXII:855–80.

Puchala, D.J. (1968). "The Pattern of Contemporary Regional Integration." *International Studies Quarterly* 12:38–64.

Rummel, R.J. (1965). "A Social Field Theory of Foreign Conflict Behavior." *Peace Research Society: Papers, IV, Cracow Conference*, pp. 197–208.

Rummel, R.J. (1969). *Field Theory and Indicators of International Behavior.* Honolulu: DON Project Report No. 29.

Russett, B.M. (1967). *International Regions and the International System.* Chicago: Rand-McNally, Inc.

Savage, I.R., and Deutsch, K.W. (1960). "A Statistical Model of the Gross Analysis of Transaction Flows." *Econometrica* 28:551–72.

Singer, J.D., ed. (1968). *Quantitative International Politics: Insights and Evidence.* New York: The Free Press.

Watanabe, S. (1969). "Modified Concepts of Logic, Probability, and Information Based on Generalized Continuous Function." *Information and Control* 15:1–21.

White, H. (1963). "Cause and Effect in Social Mobility Tables." *Behavioral Science* 8.

The Vietnam War from the 1968 Tet Offensive to the 1970 Cambodian Invasion: A Quantitative Analysis

*JEFFREY S. MILSTEIN**

The Tet Offensive started at the end of January 1968, and marked a climax and turning point in the Vietnam War. The numerous coordinated attacks made throughout all of South Vietnam by the North Vietnamese and Viet Cong forces demonstrated to the Johnson administration that American policy in Vietnam had not been successful. In particular the intervention of more than a half million American troops and the massive bombing of North Vietnam had clearly failed to defeat the Communist forces.

The Tet Offensive spurred the Johnson administration to re-evaluate its Vietnam policy. The subsequent changes in American policy are common knowledge: the United States began to limit the bombing of North Vietnam; to negotiate with the North Vietnamese about halting the bombing; to convene formal negotiations among all

---

*Department of Political Science, Yale University. This chapter is an early version of a chapter in the author's book *Dynamics of the Vietnam War* (1973). This work has been supported by the World Data Analysis Program of Yale University under Grant 2635 from the National Science Foundation. I wish to express my deepest appreciation to Lloyd Etheredge for his assistance in making computer runs, and to Jackie Berman, Janet Seymour, Mary Huang, Ann Morris, Nancy Nager, Michelle Press, May Sanzone, and Robin Nadel for the great amount of assistance they have given me in preparing this manuscript. I am also indebted to Paul Berman and Joseph B. Kadane for their statistical advice. The responsibility for the execution, conclusions, and any failing in this work is, of course, my own.

the parties to the conflict, including the United States, the South Vietnamese government, the North Vietnamese government, and the Viet Cong; and to de-Americanize the war. The Nixon Administration continued this new policy under the name "Vietnamization," gradually withdrawing a major part of the American troops from Vietnam, reducing American participation in ground combat, and at the same time attempting to strengthen the South Vietnamese forces and have them assume the main effort in the ground fighting.

Neither the Paris peace talks, nor the halt in bombing, nor the scaling down of American combat involvement in the war produced peace, however. Indeed, the Cambodian invasion of May 1970 marked another milestone in the war – the overt spread of the war throughout Indochina. It is thus important to look back over this two-and-a-quarter-year period following the Tet Offensive to see what the pattern of relationships was in order to discover why the turn to de-escalation of American involvement did not produce peace. This analysis of the empirical relationships in the Vietnam War during this period will help us evaluate the policies initiated during this period and continued beyond it.

Methods

The methods used in this study are common statistical methods: correlational analysis, cross-lagged correlation, and bivariate and multiple regression analysis.[1]

In a multiple regression equation of the form $Y_i = a_i + b_1X_1 + b_2X_2 \ldots + b_nX_n + U_i$, the regression coefficient, b_i, indicates the change in the dependent variable, Y, for each unit change in each independent variable, X_i. The U term stands for all other sources of variation in Y not specified in the model.

The standard error of the regression coefficient is used in com-

[1] Standard tests of statistical significance of correlation coefficients and regression coefficients have not been used. They are inappropriate since the monthly observations on different variables, such as casualties, troops, and armed attacks, are not a randomly drawn probability sample of some larger universe of observations, but are in fact the entire population of observations for the period under study. Even with a probability sample, the level of statistical significance varies with the sample size; therefore, statistical significance will not be emphasized. The correlation coefficients reported are, thus, to be considered as estimates of the strength of association between variables.

parison with the size of the regression coefficient to evaluate the explanatory power of that variable. The t ratio of the value of the regression coefficient to its standard error is not given because the coefficients were not derived from a random probability sample. The statistical significance of the regression coefficient depends upon the sample size; therefore, calculating a precise probability of observing a sample t ratio at least as high as that observed, if the true t ratio were zero (the statistical significance level), is uninformative since we know that the probability is close to zero (Friedheim, *et al.*, 1970). A criterion for evaluating the regression coefficient is that the t ratio be greater than 2.1. This criterion would indicate statistical significance at the 95 percent confidence level if these data were a randomly drawn sample of this size (27 months).

The structure of relationships set forth in all of the regression equations in this study can be used to estimate the consequences of given actions or conditions. The regression coefficients (b) state (within some stated standard error [SE]) the magnitude of the effect of an independent variable on a dependent variable. These equations can be used to predict the value of a dependent variable given the value of an independent variable, assuming that the value of the independent variable stays within the range of the values it has had in the past and from which these regression equations were derived. The proportional reduction in the error of the prediction of a dependent variable, as compared with the error associated with using the mean value as the predicted value of the dependent variable, is measured by the square of the multiple correlation coefficient, or R^2.

Data

The data collected are monthly values of variables that indicate seven major concepts relevant to the war policies of the belligerents during the period from the Tet Offensive to the Cambodian invasion. The data are corrected for the number of days in a month where such correction is appropriate. These concepts and variables are:

1. *'Vietnamization'*
   a) South Vietnamese ground operations of battalion size or larger

b) $\left(\frac{\text{South Vietnamese ground operations}}{\text{U.S. ground operations}}\right)$

c) $\left(\frac{\text{U.S. troops killed}}{\text{South Vietnamese troops killed}}\right)$

2. *U.S. Actions*
   a) Bombing missions in North Vietnam
   b) Bombing attack sorties in South Vietnam
   c) Helicopter attacks
   d) U.S. troop levels and monthly changes
   e) U.S. ground operations of battalion size or larger

3. *'Pacification' or Security from North Vietnamese and Viet Cong Attack*
   a) Viet Cong abductions of civilians
   b) Viet Cong killings of civilians
   c) Viet Cong terrorist incidents
   d) Viet Cong and North Vietnamese armed attacks

4. *Military Outcomes*
   a) U.S. troops killed
   b) South Vietnamese troops killed
   c) North Vietnamese and Viet Cong troops killed

5. *South Vietnamese Political and Economic Stability (Popular Confidence)*
   Black market piastre value in Saigon

6. *Viet Cong Political Support*
   Military and political defectors from the Viet Cong

7. *U.S. Public Opinion*
   Percentage approving Johnson's handling of his job as president and President Nixon's handling of the Vietnam War (from the Gallup Poll)

Except for the black market piastre value and the public opinion data, all data come from "Unclassified Statistics from Southeast Asia," a table prepared monthly by the Directorate for Information

Operations of the U.S. Department of Defense. The public opinion data come from the Gallup Poll (the American Institute of Public Opinion in Princeton, New Jersey). The monthly data on the black market value of the South Vietnamese piastre come from dealers in Saigon, Hong Kong, and San Francisco.[2]

Findings

American policy since the Tet Offensive – decreasing U.S. military operations and withdrawing American troops – has depended for its success upon the achievement of three conditions: (1) *Vietnamization*, i.e., the South Vietnamese government's assumption of the major military efforts in the war; (2) *pacification*, i.e., the South Vietnamese government's securing the population from North Vietnamese and Viet Cong attacks; and (3) the *confidence* of the South Vietnamese people in the stability of the South Vietnamese government (Johnson, 1970; Committee on Foreign Relations, 1970). We will here explore the relationships of these three conditions to each other and to U.S. actions, military casualties, and political effects in the U.S. and among the Viet Cong.

Vietnamization

President Nixon stated that the withdrawal of U.S. troops from Vietnam required Vietnamization. To evaluate this policy, therefore, it is important to determine the extent to which the South Vietnamese forces took over the combat burden as the Americans withdrew. In addition, we must determine how the South Vietnamese Government forces reacted to North Vietnamese and Viet Cong actions.

In this study Vietnamization is measured in two ways. The first is simply the number of battalion-size or larger ground operations[3]

---

[2] U.S. Department of Defense data were used because they are the most complete available anywhere. They may be inaccurate or biased, but they do represent the Department of Defense's view of what has happened in the Vietnam War. My use of these data is in no way an endorsement of the activities they report.

[3] All ground operations used as measures in this study are those of battalion size or larger.

initiated by the South Vietnamese forces. When measured in this way, Vietnamization was independent of North Vietnamese and Viet Cong armed attacks of the previous month, and independent of U.S. ground operations as well. However, South Vietnamese ground operations increased with Viet Cong terrorist incidents within the same month.[4]

$$\text{South Vietnamese ground operations} = 570 + \underset{(0.9)}{2.0}\ \text{V.C. Terrorist incidents} \quad (R = -0.40) \tag{1}$$

The second operational measure of Vietnamization is the ratio of South Vietnamese ground operations to U.S. ground operations. This measure incorporates the concept of the relative combat efforts made by the South Vietnamese as compared to the Americans. One could reasonably hypothesize that the South Vietnamese government reacted with its own military operations to recent Viet Cong abductions of civilians, Viet Cong killings of civilians, other Viet Cong terrorist incidents, North Vietnamese and Viet Cong armed attacks, and to the amount of popular confidence and stability it enjoyed. One could also hypothesize that Vietnamization increased as the rate of U.S. troop withdrawals increased. The regression equations show that the ratio of South Vietnamese ground operations to those of the U.S., i.e., Vietnamization, appears to have been dependent upon each of these above-mentioned independent variables, except civilians killed by the Viet Cong in the previous month.

$$\left(\frac{\text{S.V. ground operations}}{\text{U.S. ground operations}} \; (R = -0.45)\right) = 12 - \underset{(0.001)}{0.004}\ \text{Civilians abducted by V.C.}_{t-1} \tag{2}$$

Among these relationships this is particularly true of the rate of U.S. troop withdrawals and the past month's value of the piastre. The greater the rate of U.S. troops withdrawn, the less Vietnamization.

$$\left(\frac{\text{S.V. ground operations}}{\text{U.S. ground operations}} \; (R = -0.61)\right) = 8.8 - \underset{(0.00005)}{0.00021}\ \text{monthly change in number of U.S. troops} \tag{3}$$

The faster the piastre fell in value (indicating an increasing loss of confidence by the South Vietnamese in their government), the more South Vietnamese forces, as compared to U.S. forces, engaged in

[4]Values for all variables in the regression equations are monthly. Values are within the same month except those marked t–1, which are of the previous month.

large scale military operations. This finding may mean that pressure resulting from decreasing popular confidence led the South Vietnamese government to increase its combat efforts in an attempt to focus attention on its enemy and divert negative popular attitudes and behavior from itself.

$$\left(\frac{\text{S.V. ground operations}}{\text{U.S. ground operations}} \atop (R = -0.82)\right) = \underset{}{24} - \underset{(400)}{3000}\ \text{Piastre value}_{t-1} \tag{4}$$

When the effects of Viet Cong terrorist incidents and North Vietnamese and Viet Cong armed attacks are considered together, both of these factors are found to be important determinants of Vietnamization. The Vietnamization program was slowed down when the North Vietnamese and Viet Cong launched more attacks in the previous month, and increased by increased Viet Cong terrorism.

$$\left(\frac{\text{S.V. ground operations}}{\text{U.S. ground operations}} \atop (R = 0.79)\right) = 7.2 + \underset{(0.01)}{0.05}\ \text{V.C. terrorist incidents} - \underset{(0.003)}{0.01}\ \text{N.V.} + \text{V.C. armed attacks}_{t-1} \tag{5}$$

U.S. Troops Killed/South Vietnamese Troops Killed: A Measure of Vietnamization

The ratio of U.S. troops killed to South Vietnamese troops killed is an indicator of Vietnamization. It measures the relative amount of combat with the North Vietnamese and Viet Cong. As Vietnamization increases, this ratio decreases.

The bivariate regressions show that as the rate of U.S. troop withdrawals increased, the casualty ratio declined. As one would expect, the ratio also decreased with more South Vietnamese ground operations and with fewer U.S. ground operations and air attacks in the South.

$$\left(\frac{\text{U.S. troops killed}}{\text{S.V. troops killed}} \atop (R = 0.57)\right) = 0.49 + \underset{(0.000002)}{0.000007}\ \text{monthly change in number of U.S. troops} \tag{6}$$

$$\left(\frac{\text{U.S. troops killed}}{\text{S.V. troops killed}} \atop (R = -0.46)\right) = 0.71 - \underset{(0.0001)}{0.0003}\ \text{S.V. ground operations} \tag{7}$$

$$\left(\frac{\text{U.S. troops killed}}{\text{S.V. troops killed}} \atop (R = 0.40)\right) = 0.23 + \underset{(0.001)}{0.003}\ \text{U.S. ground operations} \tag{8}$$

$$\left(\frac{\text{U.S. troops killed}}{\text{S.V. troops killed}}\right) = \underset{}{0.11} + \underset{(0.000004)}{0.00002} \text{ U.S. bombing attack sorties in S.V.} \qquad (9)$$
$(R = 0.78)$

U.S. Actions

U.S. disengagement from Vietnam was initiated by the Johnson administration's realization that its past policy of escalating American commitments to South Vietnam, increasing U.S. combat operations, and bombing North Vietnam had been unsuccessful in achieving the American military objective of defeating the North Vietnamese and Viet Cong armed forces. When General Westmoreland requested more than two hundred thousand additional American troops after the 1968 Tet Offensive, a complete re-evaluation of American policy was made because the request for more troops asked for more of the same measures that had been shown to be unsuccessful (Clifford, 1969; Kenworthy in Sheehan, Chap. 10, 1971).

U.S. Troops in South Vietnam

What were the determinants of the number and the change in the number of U.S. Troops in Vietnam from the Tet Offensive to the Cambodian invasion? One could hypothesize that U.S. public opinion influenced the number of U.S. troops and the rate of their withdrawal. President Nixon stated that Vietnamization also affected the rate of U.S. troop withdrawals, as did North Vietnamese and Viet Cong hostile actions.

Bivariate regressions of operational indicators of the above variables with monthly changes in the number of U.S. troops (i.e., the *rate of change*) in Vietnam show that increased numbers of South Vietnamese ground operations, indicating greater Vietnamization, increased the rate of U.S. troop withdrawals.

$$\text{Monthly change in number of U.S. troops} = 19{,}000 - \underset{(0.8)}{3.} \text{ S.V. ground operations} \qquad (10)$$
$(R = -0.54)$

Viet Cong killing of civilians in South Vietnam and other Viet Cong terrorist incidents, indicating the degree of pacification, were independent of the rate of U.S. troop withdrawals, as was the monthly percentage of the U.S. public that approved of the way the president handled his job. The latter finding indicates that troop withdrawal decisions were not continually influenced by U.S. public opinion on a monthly basis, although they might have been from a longer time perspective. The decisions themselves covered troop withdrawals implemented over a number of months.

When the ratio of U.S. troops killed to South Vietnamese troops killed declined (an indicator of the decreasing fraction of combat engaged in by the U.S. as compared to the South Vietnamese), the monthly rate of U.S. troop withdrawals increased.

$$\text{Monthly change in number of U.S. troops} = -19{,}000 + \underset{(14{,}000)}{34{,}000}\left(\frac{\text{U.S. troops killed}}{\text{S.V. troops killed}}\right) \quad (R = 0.44) \tag{11}$$

U.S. Troop Levels

U.S. troop levels were independent of the number of South Vietnamese ground operations, Viet Cong killing of civilians, and other Viet Cong terrorist incidents. Thus, the statement of the Nixon administration that important factors determining U.S. troop levels would be North Vietnamese and Viet Cong activities and the progress of Vietnamization was not true systematically month after month.

U.S. troop levels did decrease as the ratio of U.S. troops killed to South Vietnamese troops killed in the previous month decreased. Since the ratio of troop casualties is a good indicator of the actual combat engaged in by U.S. as compared to South Vietnamese forces, it is apparent that South Vietnamese forces took over more and more of the combat as U.S. troops withdrew.

$$\text{Number of U.S. troops} = 420{,}000 + \underset{(36{,}000)}{190{,}000}\left(\frac{\text{U.S. troops killed}}{\text{S.V. troops killed}}\right)_{t-1} \quad (R = 0.73) \tag{12}$$

Large U.S. Ground Operations

Even as U.S. forces withdrew from Vietnam, the remaining forces continued to engage in large ground operations of battalion size or larger. Because of the Vietnamization program, one would expect that these U.S. ground operations would have decreased as the number of South Vietnamese ground operations increased. This was not the case however. Empirically, U.S. ground operations were generally independent of those of the South Vietnamese.

One would expect that U.S. ground operations would have increased as North Vietnamese and Viet Cong attacks increased, and decrease after they decreased. The regression equations show that this was the case, even when controlling for the number of South

Vietnamese ground operations. This finding is consistent with a pattern of action and reaction: the U.S. engaged in fewer major ground operations in response to fewer North Vietnamese and Viet Cong armed attacks.

$$\text{U.S. ground operations} = 67 + \underset{(0.03)}{0.07}\ \text{N.V.} + \text{V.C. armed attacks}_{t-1} \quad (R = 0.49) \qquad (13)$$

The number of U.S. ground operations was entirely independent of U.S. public opinion, thus indicating that war operations were carried out more in response to the battlefield situation than to the homefront during the period following the Tet Offensive.

U.S. Bombing in South Vietnam

U.S. air attacks in South Vietnam were made primarily to provide close air support for allied troops engaged in combat. The number of U.S. bombing attacks in South Vietnam declined after the Tet Offensive, although the Vietnamization policy of the U.S. Government included continued American air support for the South Vietnamese forces.

One might hypothesize that as the bombing of North Vietnam was reduced and then halted, more airplanes were available for use in South Vietnam, and, therefore, there would be more attacks in South Vietnam. This was not the case, however. U.S. bombing in the North and in the South were independent of each other. This independence reflects the different military objectives of bombing the North and bombing the South, as well as different weather patterns in Vietnam.

Bombing attacks were made in support of South Vietnamese as well as American troops; however, the bivariate regressions show that U.S. bombing decreased as South Vietnamese ground operations increased.

$$\text{U.S. bombing attack sorties in S.V.} = 25{,}000 - \underset{(3.4)}{13.}\ \text{S.V. ground operations} \quad (R = -0.61) \qquad (14)$$

U.S. bombing was independent of the number of large U.S. ground operations and of the number of North Vietnamese and Viet Cong armed attacks of the previous month. The faster the monthly rate of U.S. troop withdrawals, however, the fewer air attacks there were in South Vietnam.

$$\text{U.S. bombing attack sorties in S.V.} = 16{,}000 + \underset{(0.07)}{0.27} \text{ monthly change in number of U.S. troops} \quad (R = 0.63) \qquad (15)$$

It is thus significant that the American air war in South Vietnam was scaled down as U.S. troops were being withdrawn, generally irrespective of large U.S., South Vietnamese, or Communist ground combat operations.

U.S. Helicopter Attack Sorties in South Vietnam

According to the policy of Vietnamization, U.S. helicopter attack sorties in South Vietnam, like U.S. bombing missions, might continue to support the South Vietnamese after U.S. troops are withdrawn. Only Viet Cong terror is found to be associated with increased numbers of helicopter attack sorties, while North Vietnamese and Viet Cong armed attacks, South Vietnamese ground operations, and U.S. ground operations are found to be independent of helicopter attack sorties.

$$\text{U.S. helicopter attack sorties in S.V.} = 68{,}000 + \underset{(26)}{61} \text{ V.C. terrorist incidents} \quad (R = 0.43) \qquad (16)$$

'Pacification': North Vietnamese and Viet Cong Actions

'Pacification' in South Vietnam above all means the security of the people from attack by the North Vietnamese and Viet Cong. The success of Vietnamization and of American withdrawal was dependent upon the North Vietnamese and Viet Cong's willingness to scale down their own actions as the Americans disengaged or on their inability to continue their hostile actions at a high rate as the South Vietnamese forces were strengthened. Thus, it is important to see to what extent North Vietnamese and Viet Cong actions were affected by U.S. and South Vietnamese actions.

North Vietnamese and Viet Cong Armed Attacks

In the post-Tet period, North Vietnamese and Viet Cong armed attacks declined with the decline of U.S. ground operations in the same month.

$$\text{N.V.} + \text{V.C. armed attacks} = 56 + \underset{(1.3)}{2.9} \text{ U.S. ground operations} \quad (R = 0.42) \qquad (17)$$

Communist armed attacks were systematically independent of

these other variables that were thought to be related: South Vietnamese ground operations, the proportion of South Vietnamese to total U.S. and South Vietnamese ground operations, the total of U.S. and South Vietnamese ground operations, the rate of U.S. troop withdrawals, the number of U.S. troops in Vietnam, and the number of bombing attacks in South or North Vietnam. Thus the North Vietnamese and Viet Cong did seem to de-escalate their main force armed attacks as the U.S. de-escalated its own major ground combat operations. This remarkable reciprocal de-escalation could be interpreted as support for the dovish idea that hostilities can be reduced through mutual example: each side's reduction of hostilities rewards the other side's reduction. It could also be argued, however, that in the aftermath of the unprecedented fighting and losses during the Tet Offensive and the following few months, both sides were forced, at least temporarily, to reduce their major ground combat. For the American forces, this reduction was formalized and continued in the Vietnamization policy.

Viet Cong Terrorist Incidents

Viet Cong terrorist incidents were increased by increases in South Vietnamese ground operations in the previous month and decreases in U.S. bombing attack sorties in South Vietnam in the previous month. The Viet Cong apparently reacted to the increased number of South Vietnamese ground operations – the indigenous escalation inherent in the policy of Vietnamization – especially when they were given more freedom to carry out their terrorist attacks as the harrassment of U.S. bombing attacks in South Vietnam was reduced.

$$\text{V.C. terrorist incidents} = 52 + \underset{(0.03)}{0.07}\ \text{S.V. ground operations}_{t-1} \quad (R = 0.40) \qquad (18)$$

$$\text{V.C. terrorist incidents} = 210 - \underset{(0.001)}{0.007}\ \text{U.S. bombing attack sorties in S.V.}_{t-1} \quad (R = -.68) \qquad (19)$$

Viet Cong Killing of Civilians

Both the Viet Cong and the South Vietnamese government have over the years sought to eliminate each other's political and administrative leadership. If one hypothesized that Viet Cong political or military defectors were evidence of loss of Viet Cong support, then it might follow that as they lost more political support, the Viet Cong would try to eliminate more Saigon government leaders in an attempt to regain control. This was not the case however: Viet Cong killing of civilians was independent of Viet Cong defectors. It was also independent of U.S. or South Vietnamese ground operations in the previous month.

Viet Cong Abductions of Civilians

The Viet Cong abducted civilians to impress them into service in the Viet Cong army or into temporary local labor for the Viet Cong. These abductions were independent of U.S. or South Vietnamese ground operations in the previous month, and of total Viet Cong defectors.

Summary of Findings on Pacification

In summing up the main findings concerning pacification, it appears that as U.S. ground operations declined, North Vietnamese and Viet Cong armed attacks also declined. Since in the post-Tet period, North Vietnamese and Viet Cong armed attacks were carried out primarily by regular North Vietnamese units, it appears that the U.S. de-escalation was reciprocated by the North Vietnamese and Viet Cong. Viet Cong terrorist incidents, however, increased in the post-Tet period, facilitated by a decrease in U.S. bombing attack sorties in South Vietnam, and to some extent stimulated by the increasing strength and 'pacification' efforts of the South Vietnamese government forces. Terrorism appears to have been the major coercive means used by the Viet Cong in the struggle for political control while trying to rebuild military units and political cadres decimated during the Tet and spring offensives of 1968.

Military Outcomes

The number of troops killed is an indicator of the overall intensity of fighting in an armed conflict (Rummel, 1969). Moreover, the United States fought the Vietnam War as a war of attrition, in which one of the strategic objectives was to kill as many Viet Cong and North Vietnamese troops as possible in order to so weaken the Communists' military capabilities that they would be unable to achieve their political objectives of overthrowing the South Vietnamese government by force. The North Vietnamese also adopted a policy aimed at increasing the number of Americans killed in order to affect public opinion in the United States (Szulc, 1970).

There has been some argument as to what affected casualties. The U.S. military command, for example, has argued that North Vietnamese and Viet Cong attacks, rather than their own military operations were the primary determinants of U.S. casualties. Domestic critics of the war in the United States asserted that one way the U.S. could decrease the number of Americans killed in Vietnam was to stop the large "search and destroy" operations. Others have argued that large operations merely send many men out to "beat the bush" and that relatively few Viet Cong or North Vietnamese are killed in such operations. Others have somewhat cynically asserted that large South Vietnamese ground operations are not really aimed at engaging the Communist forces, but at satisfying their American advisors that ARVN forces are making some effort to defend their own country. Contact with the Communist forces would be evidenced by South Vietnamese casualties.

Empirically, North Vietnamese and Viet Cong armed attacks increased South Vietnamese casualties. Surprisingly, the greater the number of South Vietnamese ground operations, the fewer South Vietnamese soldiers were killed. One might infer from this finding that the majority of South Vietnamese casualties were not suffered by the ARVN in large ground operations, but by the Regional Forces and Popular Forces who made contact with the Viet Cong in small unit actions.

$$\begin{aligned} \text{S.V. troops killed} &= 2{,}300 - \underset{(0.6)}{2.0}\ \text{S.V. ground operations} \\ (R = 0.81)\qquad & \quad + \underset{(0.8)}{3.5}\ \text{N.V.} + \text{V.C. armed attacks} \end{aligned} \tag{20}$$

U.S. Troops Killed

Bivariate regressions show that fewer troops were killed as the rate of troop withdrawal increased, and North Vietnamese and Viet Cong armed attacks and large U.S. ground operations decreased. In a multiple regression including all three factors, North Vietnamese and Viet Cong armed attacks and the rate of U.S. troop withdrawals remain significant causes of U.S. troops killed. U.S. ground operations, however, do not remain a significant factor. Thus, there is some support for the statement that U.S. casualties were primarily determined by Communist attacks rather than U.S. ground operations; of course, casualties were also reduced as U.S. forces were withdrawn.

$$\text{U.S. troops killed} = 52 + \underset{(3.6)}{3.4}\ \text{U.S. ground operations} + \underset{(0.5)}{1.9}\ \text{N.V.} + \text{V.C. armed attacks} + \underset{(0.007)}{0.019}\ \text{monthly change in number of U.S. troops} \quad (R = 0.80) \tag{21}$$

North Vietnamese and Viet Cong Troops Killed

The bivariate regressions show that Communist casualties were increased by North Vietnamese and Viet Cong armed attacks. Communist casualties were systematically independent of U.S. ground operations, South Vietnamese ground operations, and U.S. bombing attacks in South Vietnam. Thus, North Vietnamese and Viet Cong armed attacks were the primary determinant of casualties on both sides during this post-Tet period. From this we can infer that the Communists generally controlled the intensity of the fighting during this period.

$$\text{N.V.} + \text{V.C. killed} = 960 + \underset{(7)}{39}\ \text{N.V.} + \text{V.C. armed attacks} \quad (R = 0.77) \tag{22}$$

Popular Confidence in and Potential Stability of the South Vietnamese Government

In this study the black market value (sell in Saigon price) of the piastre, the currency unit of the South Vietnamese government, is used as an indicator of confidence the people in the market economy in Saigon and in the other major cities of South Vietnam have in the government. The more people are willing to risk holding the currency of the government that the Communists are threatening to overthrow, the greater the value of the piastre on the black market. In addition, the black market value of the piastre is an indicator of the economic soundness of the South Vietnamese government. To the extent that the stability of the South Vietnamese government depends upon a sound economic base, the black market value of the piastre is an indicator of the government's potential stability. Although the U.S. uses various means to support the piastre, those attempts only reduce the variation in value. The black market value is still an indicator of increased or decreased demand for U.S. dollars as compared to piastres, and this relative demand indicates the confidence of the people. During the period under study, the piastre was worth an average of about one fourth of one cent on the black market.

After the Tet Offensive the primary influence on confidence in the South Vietnamese government was various aspects of U.S. troop withdrawals from South Vietnam. The greater the rate of troop withdrawals and the smaller the number of remaining troops, the lower the value of the piastre. Thus, confidence in the regime was highly dependent upon the presence of U.S. forces, and that confidence was shaken as the rate of withdrawal increased.

$$\text{Piastre value in U.S. \$} = 0.0044 + \underset{(0.0000000003)}{0.0000000027} \text{ Number of U.S. troops} \quad (R = 0.90) \tag{23}$$

$$\text{Piastre value in U.S. \$} = 0.0049 + \underset{(0.000000014)}{0.000000068} \text{ monthly change in number of U.S. troops} \quad (R = 0.69) \tag{24}$$

The degree of Vietnamization was related to U.S. troop withdrawals and also affected the value of the piastre. The smaller the ratio of U.S. troops to South Vietnamese troops killed, and the fewer South Vietnamese troops killed, the lower was the value of the piastre in the following month.

$$\text{Piastre value in U.S. \$} = 0.0019 + \underset{(0.00010)}{0.00061} \left(\frac{\text{U.S. troops killed}}{\text{S.V. troops killed}}\right)_{t-1} \quad (R = 0.77) \tag{25}$$

$$\text{Piastre value in U.S. \$} = 0.0039 + \underset{(0.00000021)}{0.00000045} \text{ S.V. troops killed}_{t-1} \quad (R = 0.40) \tag{26}$$

U.S. troops killed can be taken as another indicator of the intensity of fighting assumed by the U.S. forces. As the number of U.S. troops killed declined, so did the piastre value in the following month. The confidence of the South Vietnamese in their government depended not only on the presence of U.S. forces, but also on the part these forces took in combat.

$$\text{Piastre value in U.S. \$} = 0.0035 + \underset{(0.0000003)}{0.0000014} \text{ U.S. troops killed}_{t-1} \quad (R = 0.68) \tag{27}$$

Viet Cong terrorist incidents also affected popular confidence. As Viet Cong terror increased, the piastre value declined the following month.

$$\text{Piastre value in U.S. \$} = 0.0063 - \underset{(0.000006)}{0.000015} \text{ V.C. terrorist incidents}_{t-1} \quad (R = -0.48 \tag{28}$$

However the piastre value appeared to be independent of the number of North Vietnamese and Viet Cong armed attacks and the number of civilians killed or abducted by the Viet Cong in the previous month.

Thus we may conclude that as U.S. troops withdrew and Vietnamization increased – and Viet Cong terrorist incidents increased – popular confidence in the Saigon regime declined, and its potential stability was reduced as its economic foundation was weakened.

These findings indicate that one of the major policy objectives of the Vietnamization program was not being achieved between the Tet Offensive and the Cambodian invasion: popular confidence in and potential stability of the South Vietnamese government. These findings, thus, have important significance both for the American and for the South Vietnamese governments: the Vietnamization program and U.S. disengagement weakened the regime politically rather than strengthened it.

Viet Cong Political Support: Defectors

If fighting weakened the political position of the South Vietnamese regime, what was its effect on the political support for the Viet Cong? An indicator of *lack* of popular support for the Viet Cong is the number of political and military defectors. Defecting can be viewed as "voting with one's feet," although the behavior of defection may not follow the desire because of mitigating circumstances. Likewise, actual defection may not be politically motivated, but simply be an attempt to survive by giving oneself up to government forces who locally or temporarily have military superiority. Defection may often be motivated by the desire to return to one's family or home at harvest time. Past studies have shown that the longer a soldier remains with the Viet Cong, the less likely he is to defect. Most of the defectors did so within a few months of their joining or impressment into the Viet Cong (Berman, 1970).

A plausible hypothesis is that as the South Vietnamese regime gained support, the Viet Cong would lose support, and vice versa. Empirically, however, in the two and a quarter years following the Tet Offensive, the piastre value declined while the number of political defectors from the Viet Cong increased. It thus appears that the South Vietnamese regime and the Viet Cong both lost political support after the Tet Offensive.

The number of defectors was independent of the number of North Vietnamese and Viet Cong troops killed. This finding presents clear evidence that simply "killing Viet Cong" did not change the allegiance of the South Vietnamese people in this war.

The fewer civilians the Viet Cong abducted, the more Viet Cong defectors there were. This finding suggests that when the Viet Cong was less coercive, people took the opportunity and defected more readily.

$$\text{Total V.C. defectors} = 3300 - \underset{(0.5)}{1.3} \text{ civilians abducted by V.C.} \quad (R = -0.46) \tag{29}$$

After the Tet Offensive, U.S. bombing attack sorties in South Vietnam declined as the total number of Viet Cong defectors increased. As the intensity of the fighting decreased (thus requiring less U.S. air support), more Viet Cong had the opportunity to defect because they were less frequently engaged in combat.

$$\text{Total V.C. defectors} = 4600 - \underset{(0.04)}{0.15} \text{ U.S. bombing attack sorties in S.V.} \quad (R = -0.55) \tag{30}$$

The Viet Cong's loss of support as the Americans withdrew offers some supporting evidence to the contention that the Viet Cong gained political support by emphasizing their nationalism, representing themselves as the protectors of the Vietnamese people against the foreign invaders who wrought destruction on their country. As the Americans disengaged, this argument was less relevant, and therefore support for the Viet Cong declined. As voluntary support declined, the Viet Cong increasingly used terror in their attempt to control the population.

Most strongly associated with the total number of Viet Cong defectors is the number of South Vietnamese ground operations.

$$\text{Total V.C. defectors} = 1500 + \underset{(0.6)}{5.0} \text{ S.V. ground operations} \quad (R = 0.86) \tag{31}$$

As these large ground operations increased, Viet Cong defected in greater numbers, probably to survive when and where government forces showed military superiority. Thus, paradoxically, between the time of the Tet Offensive and the Cambodian invasion, *both* the Saigon regime and the Viet Cong lost political support as a result of the opposing side's coercive actions.

U.S. Public Opinion: Domestic Political Effects of the War

Almost every month the American Institute for Public Opinion (the Gallup Poll) has measured the percentage of the U.S. public who approves and disapproves of the way the president (Johnson or Nixon) had been handling the war, as well as his job as president. The responses to those two questions have been highly correlated, especially during the Johnson administraticn. Since it is translated into votes, public opinion has important consequences, as Lyndon Jonhson found out when his public approval was so low that he could not realistically seek re-election. Public approval of President Johnson did increase, however, as the number of bombing missions over North Vietnam the previous month declined. This increased approval near the end of his administration was no doubt related to the implication that peace would finally be achieved.

$$\underset{(R = -0.63)}{\text{Percentage U.S. public approval}} = 52 - \underset{(0.0003)}{0.001}\ \text{U.S. bombing missions in N.V.}_{t-1} \qquad (32)$$

The more South Vietnamese ground operations in the previous month, the greater was public approval for the president and his Vietnam policy.

$$\underset{(R = 0.57)}{\text{Percentage U.S. public approval}} = 31 + \underset{(0.006)}{0.02}\ \text{S.V. ground operations}_{t-1} \qquad (33)$$

This finding shows that the U.S. public responded positively to the Vietnamization program and to the South Vietnamese assuming more ground combat. The regression analysis supports this conclusion, for the greater the Vietnamization (as measured by the ratio of U.S. to South Vietnamese troops killed), the greater was the public approval for the president's Vietnam policy.

$$\underset{(R = -0.52)}{\text{Percentage U.S. public approval}} = 65 - \underset{(11)}{34} \left(\frac{\text{U.S. troops killed}}{\text{S.V. troops killed}}\right)_{t-1} \qquad (34)$$

The domestic political implications of these findings are clear: since (1) greater public approval for the president and his Vietnam policy depended upon fewer U.S. casualties relative to those of the South Vietnamese; (2) fewer U.S. casualties depended upon fewer North Vietnamese and Viet Cong armed attacks; and (3) fewer North Vietnamese and Viet Cong armed attacks depended upon fewer large

U.S. ground operations, then President Nixon's policy of decreasing U.S. involvement in the war was a correct one for his purpose of keeping the popular support necessary for his possible re-election.

However, the analysis above has shown that the policy of U.S. troop withdrawals and Vietnamization that strengthened the political position of the president in the U.S. by reducing American involvement and casualties in South Vietnam, weakened the political position of the South Vietnamese government. These findings posed a continuing dilemma for the president of the United States. President Johnson faced this dilemma in 1965: whether to intervene in South Vietnam with massive U.S. military power and save the South Vietnamese government from collapse and overthrow by the Viet Cong at the risk of losing popular support in the U.S. He intervened, and the subsequent escalation of the war and the massive participation by United States forces that was required to save the South Vietnamese government from overthrow led directly to large numbers of American casualties and other war costs that badly reduced the president's support.

President Nixon apparently faced a similar dilemma. His Vietnamization policy required that there be fewer U.S. troops and fewer U.S. casualties in Vietnam. As this was done, he maintained U.S. public support. However, this very withdrawal of U.S. troops led to a severe loss of popular confidence in and potential stability of the South Vietnamese regime. Moreover, even though a stronger and more active South Vietnamese military force weakened Viet Cong support, at least temporarily, increased South Vietnamese government military activity stimulated the Viet Cong to respond with increased terrorist activity, which itself contributed to a decline in popular confidence in the Saigon regime. Thus, both presidents Johnson and Nixon have faced the same dilemma: whether to achieve domestic political objectives in the U.S. or international political objectives in Vietnam. Although both presidents obviously preferred to have it both ways, both have had to choose because of the very structure of reality analyzed here. Each president made a fundamentally different choice. President Nixon's choice was no doubt informed by his predecessor's early retirement.

A Simplified Model of the Vietnam War from the Tet Offensive to the Cambodian Invasion

Figure 1 is a simplified model in flow diagram form, i.e., a chain of relationships among the variables. Regression analysis has been used to reveal the simplified structure of relationships that are in reality interwoven into a complex whole.

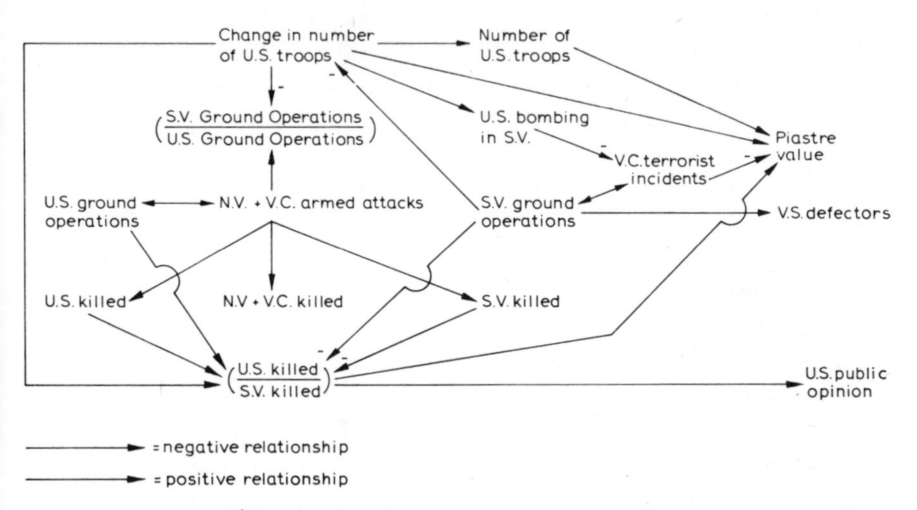

Fig. 1. – Major relationships in the Vietnam war from the Tet Offensive to the Cambodian invasion

This structure of relationships and the regression equations upon which this structure is based can be used to trace what would have been the probable consequences of any particular action engaged in by either side during the period from the Tet Offensive to the Cambodian invasion. The policy implications of this structure of relationships are clear: one can see the necessary actions or conditions that are linked to certain policy objectives. For example, if the U.S. president was concerned about increasing his popular support, he would find that if he decreased the number of U.S. ground operations, this would lead to decreases in North Vietnamese and Viet Cong armed attacks and to decreases in U.S. troops killed, which in turn would lead to an increase in U.S. public support for the president and his policy.

Since the structure of relationships represented in the regression equations and in the flow diagram is partly based on time-lagged relationships, the entire structure can be used to forecast likely outcomes resulting from specified actions taken in the present. With a complex structure, this forecasting can be done by means of computer simulation in which the predicted value of each dependent variable is used as the value for that variable when it appears as an independent variable in another regression equation farther along the chain of relationships. As long as there is at least one time-lagged relationship, one can reiterate this procedure to make month-by-month predictions of each variable by boot-strapping from only the initial values of each variable. If the predictions from such a computer simulation prove to be close to the actual values for the period from which these regression equations were derived, then one has more confidence in the predictions of the value of each variable in the months beyond the last real data point (Milstein and Mitchell, 1969).

Once such a simulation model proves to make valid predictions, one could exercise the model to see what the likely outcome in a number of dependent variable would be when one changes the values of manipulable independent variables. For example, one could estimate the magnitude of the likely effect on public approval of the president's Vietnam policy if large U.S. ground operations in Vietnam were increased or decreased by given amounts. Or one could find the likely effect of increasing or decreasing the rate of U.S. troop withdrawals from Vietnam on such variables as South Vietnamese political stability, political support for the Viet Cong, or U.S. public opinion.

A simple example of how one can predict the value of a variable (with or without a computer) is as follows: for every additional ten thousand U.S. troops withdrawn from Vietnam each month, the ratio of U.S. to South Vietnamese troops killed would be reduced by approximately seven one-hundredths (*See* Equation 6). For every additional monthly reduction of approximately seven one-hundredths in the ratio of U.S. to South Vietnamese troops killed, there would be an increase of about two and four-tenths percent in U.S. public approval of the president (*See* Equation 33). Following through this chain of relationships, one can thus forecast the probable consequences, measured in numerical terms, of a number of possible actions that a policy-maker is considering and among which he must choose.

This ability to predict consequences of alternative actions is one of the purposes of scientific and quantitative analysis of international relations. Such analysis strengthens our capability for critical evaluation of existing policies, and potentially could enlighten policy-making so that future tragedies can be avoided.

REFERENCES

Berman, Paul (1970). "The Liberation Armed Forces of the NLF: Compliance and Cohesion in a Revolutionary Army." Unpublished doctoral dissertation, Department of Political Science, Massachusetts Institute of Technology, Chap. 4.

Clifford, Clark M. (1969). "A Vietnam Reappraisal: The Personal History of One Man's View and How It Evolved." *Foreign Affairs* 47:601-22.

Committee on Foreign Relations, United States Senate (1970). "Vietnam: December 1969." A Staff Report, Committee Print, 91st Congress, 2nd Session, Washington D.C., Feb. 2, Sec. 7, p. 18.

Friedheim, R.L., Kadane, J.B., and Gamble, Jr., J.K. (1970). "Quantitative Content Analysis of the United Nations Seabed Debates: Methodology in a Continental Shelf Case Study." *International Organization* 24:479–502.

Johnson, Robert H. (1970). "Vietnamization: Can It Work? " *Foreign Affairs* 48:629–47.

Milstein, Jeffrey S. (1973). *Dynamics of the Vietnam War.* Colombus, Ohio: The Ohio State University Press.

Milstein, Jeffrey S. and Mitchell, William Charles (1969). "Computer Simulation of International Processes: The Vietnam War and the Pre-World War I Naval Race." *Peace Research Society (International) Papers* XII.

Rummel, Rudolph J. (1969). "Indicators of Cross-National and International Patterns." *American Political Science Review* LXIII:134.

Sheehan, Neil, *et al.* (1971). *The Pentagon Papers.* New York: Bantam Books, Inc., Chap. 10.

Szulc, Tad (1970). "Hanoi Calls for the Infliction of Heavier Combat Losses on U.S." *The New York Times*, April 21, p. 13.

Twenty Years of Representative Democracy in Brazil, 1945-1964

*SIMON SCHWARTZMAN**

Introduction: Background

A central issue in Brazilian politics today is the possibility of reopening the political system, which was partially closed after the fall of João Goulart in 1964, and further restricted by the so-called "Institutional Act No. 5" of December 1968. The political regime until 1964 was presidentialist and multi-party, with direct balloting for the executive at the national, state, and local levels, and proportional representation in the legislative bodies, also at three levels. Suffrage was open and mandatory to all literates over eighteen. After

---

*Escola Brasileira de Administração Pública, Fundação Getúlio Vargas. This paper was presented at the VIII World Congress of the International Political Science Association, Munich, Aug. 30 to Sept. 6, 1970. The author is personally responsible for its contents, and the ideas and interpretations expressed here may not be taken as representing the opinion of the Fundação Getúlio Vargas or the Escola Brasileira de Administração Pública. The author is indebted, however, to the Fundação Getúlio Vargas for the opportunity of presenting the paper to the Congress. Revised in May 1971. This paper is part of a broader study of the Brazilian political system which the author is undertaking. A more comprehensive theoretical framework and an historical overview going from the end of the Colonial period in 1808 to the end of the "First Republic" in 1930 can be found in Simon Schwartzman (1970). In the same place (*Dados* 7) can also be found several articles dealing with particular periods and aspects of Brazilian politics and society, within the same general framework. The author is indebted to David Nasatir for helpful criticism on form and content.

1964, there was no change in the extension of suffrage, however the political parties were dissolved and replaced by a two-party system, and hundreds of politicians lost their political rights and mandates. Elections for the presidency became indirect, and this pattern was also extended to the state level. The new arrangement could have meant an increase in power for the legislature, if it were not for the strict control exercised by the central military government upon its majority party, combined with the transfer of much of the formal decision-making power from the Congress to the Executive. The reopening of the political system is an explicit goal of the government and of almost all sectors of the country's public opinion, but the extension and meaning of this opening are generally unclear; they can go from a minimum of ending the discretionary powers which the central government assumed in December 1968, to the reintroduction of political rules similar to those which existed from 1945 to 1964.

The 1945–64 period, which is also known as the "Third Republic," was the time of greatest political openness and enfranchisement in Brazilian history, and a coherent view of what happened in this twenty-year period is still to be produced. Interpretations of this recent history are at the roots of the contemporary debate on political openness in Brazil, since this is the fullest and most recent experience of political openness in the country's memory. A central question is to decide whether the 1964 movement is reversible or not. Was it an historical accident which could be reversed, or did it come as a consequence of an irreversible process of change in the political system, thus preventing the re-establishment of the previous constitutional framework. [1] The thesis in this paper is that the latter formulation is more correct, and that the debate on political openness will not be fruitful unless it brings to bear new conceptions of political participation which are still unknown in Brazilian history and experience.

It is a further contention of this paper that Brazilian politics should be studied less in terms of a continuum of left-right orientations, or a continuum from traditional to modern life, attitudes, values and participation, than in terms of a line of cleavage which I call "representation vs. cooptation." This cleavage has to do with the

[1] For a theoretical discussion of problems related to political openness in Brazil, cf. Simon Schwartzman (1969).

relative independence of the economy vs. the relative independence of the state apparatus *vis-à-vis* the rest of the society. It is peculiar to Brazil that this division separates the state of São Paulo, which is the most modern and industrialized section of the country, from the rest of the political system. São Paulo is also the largest state in the country, and we shall compare it systematically with two other states: Minas Gerais, which is the second largest state and typifies the "cooptation" system, and the state of Guanabara, which includes the city of Rio de Janeiro and was the country's capital until 1960 when Brasilia was inaugurated. Table 1 gives some general figures which help to show the differences between these states, compared to the rest of the country. Data on urbanization, income and industrialization are, as usual, correlated with the standard measures of modernity, in terms of education, exposure to mass media, and welfare.

TABLE 1

DEMOGRAPHIC AND INCOME CHARACTERISTICS OF THREE BRAZILIAN STATES, 1960

	São Paulo	*Minas Gerais*	*Guanabara*	*Brazil*
Total population	18.3%	13.8%	4.7%	100% (70, 967, 185)
Percent of population in urban centers	92.9%	40.2%	97.4%	
Percent of Gross Internal Product (GIP) in the State	34.7%	10.0%	12.0%	100%
Percent of GIP of the state by sectors				
primary	18.2%	38.3%	1.2%	27.6%
secondary	33.7%	12.9%	17.3%	21.5%
tertiary	48.1%	48.8%	81.5%	50.9%
TOTAL	100%	100%	100%	100%
Governmental sector as percent of GIP	5.3%	6.0%	20.1%	8.0%

SOURCE: Instituto Brasileiro de Geografia e Estatística, 1960 Census, and *Anuário Estatístico do Brasil*, 1969.

Political Cooptation and Political Representation in Brazil

I do not intend to make the concepts of "representation" and "cooptation" follow from the data I shall present, but rather to show how this conceptualization could help to understand their otherwise unrecognizable patterns. It is necessary, therefore, to give a short summary of what I mean by these terms and what I see as their usefulness for the analysis of the Brazilian political system[2].

There are many roads leading to these concepts. One possibility is to start from the attempt of S.M. Lipset and S. Rokkan to use Parsons' functional categories for the analysis of European political systems[3]. Talcott Parsons, as is well known, proposes an analytical division of social systems into four general functions, which make up the *A-G-I-L* framework (adaptation, goal achievement, integration, and pattern maintenance, or latency). Another Parsonian generalization is the proposition that when social systems tend to increase in size and complexity the four analytical functions tend to become four empirically differentiated subsystems: the economic (for adaptive functions), the political (for the attainment of social goals), the social and political participation (for the integrative functions), and the educational and family subsystem (for the pattern maintenance functions). Lipset and Rokkan are concerned in their study with the internal structure of the subsystem of social and political participation, in terms of its internal cleavages. They show how this analysis leads to the study of two main axes of political cleavages, one along the adaptation–integration poles (the cross-local, functional cleavage) and the other along the goal-achievement-latency poles (the center–periphery axis).

Another analytical road, which is suggested here, is to think about the four subsystems as the locus of four processes of social change, and the main problem in the analysis of systems of political participation becomes to evaluate how much of what happens in the sub-

---

[2] A detailed analysis of this framework in the context of a broader historical spectrum is found in the articles of *Dados* 7, above.

[3] Cf. S.M. Lipset and S. Rokkan (1967). Another road is suggested by Reinhard Bendix in "Social Stratification and the Political Community" (1966). Although more arduous, it is not impossible to derive these categories from the Marxian tradition, where the discovery of Marx's "Grundrisse" led to a revival of the concept of "Asiatic mode of production," and gave new legitimacy to the analysis of the state structure as a relatively autonomous variable.

system of political participation is a function of interactions among the other three.

Changes in A can be considered to be changes in the process of economic development, changes in G to be a process of transformation and growth of the state structure, changes in L to be transformations in society's values and motivations (which are usually measured in terms of changes in rates of urbanization and education, and are analyzed as a process of "modernization"), and finally, changes in I to be essentially those related to transformations in the structure of social and political participation.

This means essentially that the structure of political participation is seen as an intervening variable between the state and the processes of economic development and modernization; this gives us four types of participation according to the dominant process:

TABLE 2

POLITICAL COOPTATION AND REPRESENTATION: A CONCEPTUAL FRAMEWORK

Dominant Process (A, G, L)	*Dependent Process (A, G, L)*	*Intervening Political Structure (I)*
Economic growth (A)	Growth and differentiation of the state (G)	Political representation: party systems of the European kind (I)
Growth and differentiation of the state (G)	Economic growth (A)	Political cooptation: governmental political parties and one-party systems (I)
Modernization and secularization of values (L)	Growth and differentiation of the state (G)	Collective movements through autonomous mobilization: charismatic populism (I)
Growth and differentiation of the state (G)	Modernization and secularization of values (L)	Collective movements through induced mobilization: nationalism and paternalistic populism (I)

It is necessary to say a few words about how Brazilian political parties and movements can be described in terms of this cleavage. The consideration of the state structure as an independent variable seems to be necessary in the analysis of Brazilian politics but is often disregarded. I have argued for this need in another place, and I shall only list here some very general features of Brazilian history which support this assertion. It is important to know that the Brazilian political structure is the historical heir of the Portuguese colonial administration, and that this structure was accentuated by the arrival of Portuguese families in Brazil in 1808, following Bonaparte's occupation of Portugal. Formal independence in 1822 was a consequence of the Portuguese attempt to bring Brazil back to colonial status, and the new Brazilian government was headed by the son of Portugal's king. Political cleavage in early independent Brazil consisted of the Portuguese vs. "criollo" aristocracy and was expressed in terms of centralization vs. decentralization of the political system. The final outcome was the dominance of centralization tendencies; the existence of a huge and well-installed government structure helps to explain both the political stability and the geographical integrity of Brazil in the nineteenth century. The peculiarity of this situation becomes very clear when we compare Brazil with Argentina, and see how the separation from Peru freed Argentina from the costs and benefits of a huge and expensive governmental bureaucracy. The push of the Argentinian "generation of the 80's" towards economic growth was paralleled in Brazil by the efforts of the São Paulo coffee growers to bring in European immigrants, to introduce modern patterns of labor to the plantations, and to start, in the beginning of the twentieth century, an aggressive policy of valorization of international prices for coffee. In Argentina the emerging social and economic forces were able to organize and direct the state according to their interests, but in Brazil the pre-existing governmental structure was, from their point of view, a dead weight against which they had to fight.[4] The beginning of the Republic meant a relatively high

[4]For a short English summary of the Paulista expansion in the late nineties, *see* Richard M. Morse (1958). For a very detailed and old-fashioned account, cf., Alfredo Ellis, Jr. (1937). For Argentina in the same period, *see* Oscar Cornblit, *et al.* (1965).

There is a widespread – but often naive – belief that the process of industrialization in late-developing countries tends to be opposed by their rural sectors. Ezequiel Gallo (1970) shows that industry and agriculture developed in Argentina at the same time and in mutual reinforcement. The main obstacle to Argentinian development seems to have been urban politics, since "it was precisely the representatives in congress of the new popular parties, radicals and socialists, who opposed most actively any attempt to raise tariff barriers" (p. 57). A similar reasoning can be applied to Brazil, if we think that industry and export agriculture also developed by mutual reinforcement in the east and south of the country. The main obstacle to it seemed to be the over-centralized government in the late nineteenth century, which led to the end of the Empire. This is more important than the fact that the governmental sector recruited its members mostly from the decaying agriculture of the northeast. *See* Lucia Maria Gomes Klein and Olavo Brasil de Lima, Jr. (1970).

degree of decentralization and local autonomy for the states. In 1930, a new, strong government was installed, and in 1932, São Paulo was the site of a popular revolt against federal intervention, which was defeated. From that time on the great paradox of Brazilian politics becomes progressively clearer. São Paulo was the beneficiary of an industrial expansion which started in Brazil after the world crisis of 1929, but this occurred along with a growing alienation of that region from the center of political life.

The Vargas regime, which lasted from 1930 to 1945, arose from a split in the entente among the state oligarchies (shattered by rebellions of young officers), from unrest in the urban centers, and from the rigidity of aging leaders. With the new regime the young military men came to power, but as leaders of a civilian government. Vargas never showed his origins as the political son of Borges de Medeiros (oligarchic leader in the south), but the dependence of local oligarchies on the central government became stronger as a result of his ascendancy. The new regime was concerned with the rationalization of the state, industrialization and modernization, and felt the need to create the conditions to coopt the emerging urban working class to the welfare and trade-union systems which were created and directed by the government. The Vargas regime fell in 1945 in the wake of democratic movements which swept Latin America after World War II. At that moment everything was prepared for a political resurrection which, indeed, occurred as soon as the political game was declared open.

It seems proper to characterize the two political parties created by Vargas in terms of "cooptation." The first of these parties was called the Social Democratic Party (PSD). It was formed by the state and local leaders who had been on good terms with the dictatorship. The term "coronelismo" is used in the Brazilian political literature to characterize a type of rural boss who derives his local strength from his access to patronage at the governmental level, and can bring the local votes to his party[5]. The "coronel" cannot survive without access to government, and it is, therefore, not surprising that the

[5]The classic analysis of the "coronelismo" system in Brazilian politics is in Victor Nunes Leal (1948). His main contention is that this system is not so much an expression of the strength of traditional leadership based on local, familial and patrimonial ties, as it is of its weakness. The "coronel," as a local boss, has little power in a stagnant economy without access to the government.

party which joined these leaders together became the biggest party in the country. A similar structure of cooptation was developed in the urban areas, through the Labor Party (PTB), to which Vargas affiliated himself. Its instrument of political control was the Ministry of Labor and the trade unions which were politically and financially dependent on it; thus, the ministry became a powerful instrument for political patronage.

In both political parties, electoral power derived from access to governmental positions and decision centers. Ideological issues were obviously secondary, and the major interests political leaders showed were those relating to more positions, facilities, and sinecures from the government. It would be, of course, too simplistic to say that these were the only goals and purposes of the parties. At the policy-making level, more-or-less well-defined goals of economic development, administrative efficiency, and welfare existed. But these goals had little (if not contradictory) relation to the structures created to coopt and handle electoral support. What these two levels of the political system did have in common was the fact that both operated in almost purely distributionist terms[6].

Opposition to this system came from different sources. There was a liberal opposition to Vargas which combined urban middle classes with members of local rural leadership who had lost their access to the centers of decision-making in the "coronelismo" system[7]. There were members of the army who were impatient and intolerant of the price the government was paying for its maintenance in terms of political patronage. There were members of the working class who sought more militance and ideological involvement from the trade unions and more pro-labor policies from the central government. There were military, intellectual, and working-class groups which

---

[6] The contrast between distributionist political "arenas," on the one hand, and regulatory and redistributive arenas on the other, is developed for the United States by Theodore J. Lowi (1964). Although it was developed through a close scrutiny of decision-making processes in the United States, there is little doubt that this framework could be very useful in a broader political spectrum. In the case of Brazil, it seems clear that this framework can lead to a significant step further in the study of the repercussions of a system of political patrimonialism and cooptation at the decision-making level.

[7] For an analysis and updating of the study on Brazilian local politics, *see* José Murilo de Carvalho (1965); Bolivar Lamounier (1969); and especially Antônio Octávio Cintra (1971).

sought to direct the country towards a more nationalistic foreign policy.

It is possible to summarize all this in terms of how access to government was obtained or sought for. The cooptation system was considered either adequate, or in need of expansion, or in need of restrictions. What all groups had in common, roughly speaking, was that their political influence derived either from control of governmental agencies, or from access to the government for political patronage, or, finally, from their demands for more access for some groups and sectors.

This is not, however, what participation politics is all about. When an economic system is dynamic and social groups are organized and structured, these groups get together politically to influence political decisions that have some bearing on their share of society's goods, goods which are not owned patrimonially by the government or its bureaucracy. This kind of politics is what I call "politics of representation," and it is probable that the liberal regimes of the Western world are the best known, but not necessarily the only conceivable, arrangement for its manifestation.[8] Its essential condition is economic and/or organizational autonomy and self-reliance. In Brazil it developed most in the São Paulo area. It appeared often as liberal ideologies which defined governmental intervention in politics, economics, and welfare as absolute evil; or as trade union movements based more on autonomous organization than on access to the Ministry of Labor, and which had wage issues as a central concern.[9] Finally, it developed as populist movements which included elements of personal charisma corresponding to less structure and autonomy at the grass roots, but also to less direct control of patronage in the

---

[8]David E. Apter showed a clear perception of the limitations of the Western model of political representation, but I am a little uncertain on his ideas about the forms of participation which should correspond to his "hierarchical systems." *See* D. Apter (1968).

[9]It is easy to see that the cleavage in terms of representation *vs.* cooptation cuts across the class cleavage. Phillipe Schmitter, in his work on interest groups in Brazil, shows very clearly that representation politics in Brazil was surprisingly inconspicuous even in periods of open politics, and was almost restricted to the area of Sao Paulo. The explanation for this cannot be found in soeme peculiarities of the Brazilian political culture, but rather through theoretical means. Helio Jaguaribe, many years before, called the attention to the cleavage between the "cartorial" and other autonomous sectors of the Brazilian social strata. *See* Helio Jaguaribe (1962) and P. Schmitter (1971).

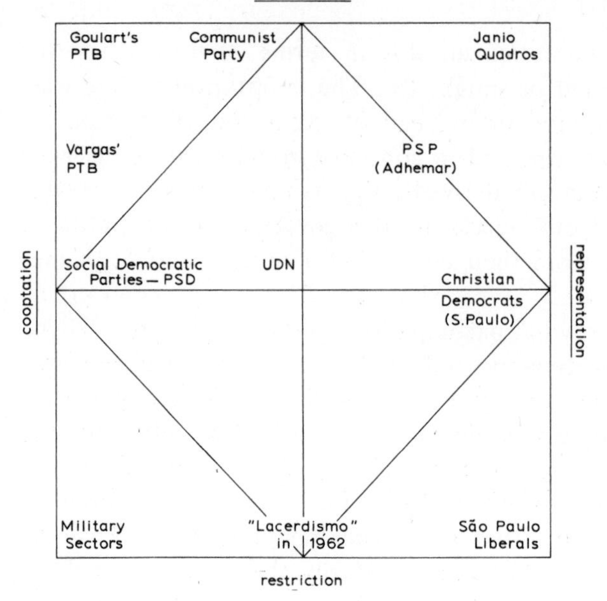

Fig. 1. Political parties and groups in Brazil: Cooptation and Mobilization

central government.[10] Figure 1 gives a general picture of the party system in the Third Republic.

The Changing Voting Patterns: Participation[11]

The first outstanding characteristic of the Second Republic was the substantial increase in voting turnout in comparison with the period before 1930. Presidential elections before 1930 tended to have single candidates, and the introduction of competition did not

[10] The best known studies of Brazilian populism, which are probably those of Francisco Weffort, do not seem to arrive at a satisfactory distinction between induced populism, which is personified in São Paulo by Adhemar de Barros, and the more typically charismatic populism of Jânio Quadros. *Cf.* Francisco Weffort (1965a, b; 1966).

[11] What follows is a first approximation to the systematic analysis of Brazilian electoral politics in terms of regional differentiation. This analysis is limited here to the biggest states of the country, São Paulo and Minas Gerais, and the city-state of Rio de Janeiro, which is the former capital of the country. Data on these states are compared with data for the country as a whole. An analysis for all 21 states is being done. The methodology is similar in intent, although not in technique, to the model developed by Donald E. Stokes (1965, 1967).

alter the low turnout, as can be seen by the figures in table 3. These data are still incomplete, and any conclusion is tentative, but the general pattern is clear.

TABLE 3

COMPETITIVE PRESIDENTIAL ELECTIONS IN THE FIRST REPUBLIC (INCOMPLETE FIGURES)

	1910	*1914*	*1930*
States of the opposition	São Paulo Bahia, Rio de Janeiro	Bahia	Minas, Paraíba, Rio Grande do Sul
Average percentage of votes for candidates winning the presidential elections in the states where they won	89.5% (16 states)	95.6% (10 states)	85.4% (9 states)
Average percentage of votes for candidates losing the presidential elections in the states where they won	73.7% (Bahia and São Paulo)	62.1% (Bahia)	84.8%
Percentage of voters out of the total population	1.64%	2.14%	5.1%

SOURCE: *see* Franco, *et al.* (1970).

The year 1910 witnessed the first competitive election in the Republic with a turnout of about 1.6 percent of the total population; in 1914 it was 2.14 percent; but in 1926, not shown in the table, there was a single candidate, and the turnout figure fell to 2.06 percent. Only in 1930, on the brink of the Vargas revolution, did turnout rise to above 5 percent. This was the first emergence of intrastate competition and in the city of Rio de Janeiro the winning candidate received only 51 percent of the votes. The general rule, however, was that the states had single-party systems, and political cleavages, if any, did not cross state borders. By 1945, however, the number of actual voters had risen to 13.4 percent of the total population and continued to grow steadily up to 20 percent by the early sixties[12].

[12] Data gathered by Celina Moreira Franco, *et al.* (1970).

TABLE 4

BRAZIL, TURNOUT FIGURES FOR 1945–66: ELECTIONS FOR THE PRESIDENCY AND CHAMBER OF DEPUTIES

Year	*Total Population (1,000)**	*Percentage of Registered Voters/ Population*	*Percentage of Actual Voters/ Population*	*Percentage of Actual/ Registered Voters*	*Percentage of Blank and Null Votes/Votes*	
					Presidential Elections	*Chamber of Deputies*
1945	46,069	16.2%	13.3%	83.1%	2.3%	3.2%
1950	48,227	16.0	11.3	72.1	4.4	7.0
1954	57,226	26.4	15.9	65.5		6.6
1955	58,663	25.9	15.5	59.7	10.7	
1958	63,102	21.8†	20.1	92.0†		9.2
1960	69,720	22.1	18.0	81.0	7.2	
1962	74,096	25.0	19.9	79.6		17.8
1966	83,890	26.6	20.6	77.4		21.1

SOURCE: Brasil, Tribunal Superior Eleitoral, *Dados Estatísticos*, 6 Vols., 1964. Data for 1966 are taken from Brazil, IBGE, *Anuário Estatístico*, 1969.

*Population figures are from the Brazilian census for 1950 and 1960, and projections for other years.

†The decrease in registration and increase of the actual/registered voters for this year are due to a renewal of the official enrollment lists.

These figures on turnout must be considered in light of the disfranchisement of the illiterate (about 50 percent of the population) and the population's age structure (about 50 percent under 18). Since to register and to vote is mandatory, abstention or lack of registration can create all sorts of difficulties in legal and bureaucratic procedures. It is expected, therefore, that turnout grows with increasing urbanization and education, and the number of actual over registered voters is little more than a reflection of the updating of the electoral lists. The same is not true, however, for blank and null votes, which are a clear indication of political disaffection. The increase from 2.3 percent to 21.1 percent of these invalid votes is a clear indication of the progressive failure of the political system to correspond to the constituent's values and aspirations.

The picture becomes still clearer if we begin to compare the states of São Paulo, Minas Gerais, and Guanabara with the global figures for Brazil, as in tables 5, 6, and 7.

Table 5 shows large variations in relative turnout, both between

TABLE 5

BRAZIL, ACTUAL VOTERS AS PERCENTAGE OF TOTAL POPULATION (BRAZIL = 100).

Year	*São Paulo*	*Guanabara (City of Rio)*	*Minas Gerais*	*Brazil (100)*
1945	128%	175%	105%	13.4%
1950	103	161	108	15.9
1954	121	170	120	15.9
1955	122	162	102	15.5
1958	121	152	108	20.1
1960	132	172	99	18.0
1962	122	149	103	19.4
1966	153	187	135	20.6

SOURCE: *see* Table 4.

states and through time. Differences between states are not really surprising, if we bear in mind their different levels of literacy.[13] Time variations, however, are much more interesting. The general tendency is towards a relatively higher increase of turnout in states where the levels of economic development and literacy are higher. The exception to this rule is the state of Minas Gerais, which had in 1966 a level of turnout which was 35 percent above the country's level. The meaning of this deviation will be seen below.

Data on null and blank votes show an increase through time which is steeper than the increase of voters. This relationship between increase in turnout and in blank and null votes is expected, and is very often understood in terms of the relative socio-economic marginality of newly enfranchised groups[14]. In the Brazilian case, however, where electoral enrollment is mandatory, this interpretation can be misleading. The increase in the electorate can be explained by an increase in the enforcement procedures, and the increase in blank and null votes can be interpreted as a manifestation of political

[13]Data on literacy are particularly inaccessible in Brazil. Figures for 1960 were never published, and estimates for 1970 exist only for the country as a whole. in 1950, however, the city of Rio de Janeiro had 71.2 percent literate population, followed by São Paulo (50.6 percent) and Minas Gerais (31.2 percent). The figure for Brazil was 35.6 percent, and there is no reason to suppose that this ordering was altered. This sequence corresponds exactly to the ordering of the correlations of the three states with Brazil in Table 9.

[14]*See*, for the United States, Angus Campbell (1960).

disaffection, which does not come necessarily from the lower end of the social structure. It is probably more apt to suppose that these blank and null votes measure the disaffection of the more modern and well-educated sectors of the society regarding a political system which is based in the cooptation of local chieftains in the country-side, urban paternalism, and patronage.

TABLE 6

INVALID (BLANK AND NULL) VOTES, PRESIDENTIAL ELECTIONS (BRAZIL = 100)

Year	*São Paulo*	*Guanabara (City of Rio)*	*Minas Gerais*	*Brazil (100)*
1945	130%	57%	57%	2.3%
1950	95	104	105	4.4
1955	117	35	107	10.7
1960	71	61	139	7.2

SOURCE: *see* Table 4.

TABLE 7

INVALID (BLANK AND NULL) VOTES, CONGRESSIONAL ELECTIONS (BRAZIL = 100)

Year	*São Paulo*	*Guanabara (city of Rio)*	*Minas Gerais*	*Brazil (100)*
1945	122%	47%	63%	3.2%
1950	134	77	103	7.0
1954	115	70	103	6.6
1958	189	75	103	9.2
1962	168	88	85	17.8
1966	168	82	82	21.1

SOURCE: *see* Table 4.

A look at the product–moment correlations among the data on blank and null votes for the presidential and congressional elections through these 20 years gives a deeper perception of the picture.

TABLE 8

INVALID (NULL AND BLANK) VOTES, PRESIDENTIAL ELECTIONS, 1945–60 (PRODUCT-MOMENT CORRELATIONS, $N = 4$)

	Guanabara	*Minas Gerais*	*Brazil*
São Paulo	–.36	–.89	–.21
Guanabara		.06	–.56
Minas Gerais			.62

The results of this table[15] are very consistent with the line of thought which is being suggested. The national variance is obviously very dependent upon the variance of São Paulo, since it contains more than 22 percent of the total electorate. (Minas, which is the second largest state, has around 14 percent, and Rio de Janeiro, the fourth largest, 7 percent. The third largest state, Rio Grande do Sul, which was not included in the analysis, contains 9 percent. These figures are for 1960.) In spite of that, the correlation between Paulista and national figures is negative. Minas gives the pattern which is dominant for the country as a whole, and the correlation between Minas and São Paulo is negative and very high. Minas typifies the national politics of cooptation, and this leads to political disaffection in São Paulo. Conversely, when in 1960 a candidate from São Paulo won, Minas retracted.

The correlations with Guanabara (the city of Rio de Janeiro) are somehow unexpected. Since it does not follow the national pattern, Guanabara should follow the pattern of São Paulo – but it does not. The former capital, in spite of being a purely urban and relatively rich state, shares with the rural Minas Gerais adherence to the same system of political cooptation, which has its head in Rio and its base in Minas. Socio-economic variables are not strong enough to place Guanabara in opposition to Minas Gerais, although they do differentiate it from the country as a whole.

In other words, there seems to be another factor which can explain the correlations with Rio de Janeiro, a factor which has to do with urbanization and modernization as such. This is seen very clearly when we look into the intercorrelations for the national Chamber of Deputies.

[15] The correlation coefficients in tables 8 and 9 should be taken with care. The correlations between the states and the country as a whole express a relationship between a relative index and a percentage.

TABLE 9

INVALID (NULL AND BLANK) VOTES, CHAMBER OF DEPUTIES, 1945–66 (PRODUCT-MOMENT CORRELATIONS, $N = 6$) (From Table 7)

	Guanabara	*Minas Gerais*	*Brazil*
São Paulo	.60	.15	.64
Guanabara		.53	.78
Minas Gerais			–.06

The figures are almost exactly opposite. Now Rio de Janeiro fits the national pattern, and Minas Gerais is unrelated. It is as if the cleavage between the cooptation and representation systems operated only on the level of the presidency, but not of the legislature. Null and blank votes for the Congress seem to be related not to the relative marginality of a given region towards the national politics, but to the impact of modernization and development upon a conservative and rural-based Congress. (A dominant feature of Brazilian politics in the early sixties was precisely the deep conflict between the Congress and the Excutive, which was clearly understandable due to their different electoral bases.)

Here again the correlations between Minas and Guanabara are higher than what might be expected in a single-factor model, and here again the explanation seems to be the same. The two most and least urban states, respectively, are brought together by what they have in common, the system of political cooptation. But they are separated by the progressive asymmetry in their development, which is inherent in this type of political arrangement. It is possible to interpret the correlations in Tables 8 and 9 as functions of two factors, one that ties Minas and Guanabara and isolates São Paulo, and the other that ties São Paulo and Guanabara and isolates Minas Gerais. These two factors correspond to two cleavages: one, which operates on a regional basis and at the executive level, corresponds to the cooptation vs. representation systems of participation; the other, which seems to be more cross-local, appears at the legislative level, and is related to contrasts between city and country, mobilization and demobilization. Or, in terms of the model suggested at the beginning, one has to do with the *A-I-G* and the other has to do with the *L-I-G* interactions. It was on the interplay between these cleavages that the fate of the Third Republic depended.

The Changing Voting Patterns and Party Orientations

Table 10 gives a first picture of the political cleavages at the presidential level. The alliance between the two Vargas parties, PSD–PTB, won all the elections except in 1960. Only in 1950 was there a split in the alliance, due to a personal move by Vargas who imposed himself and was not accepted by the political leadership of the PSD (the figures in parentheses for 1950 correspond to the votes given to Cristiano Machado, the PSD candidate). Vargas' victory in 1950 is an indication not only of his personal charisma, but also of his direct command of the political clientele over and above the leadership of his major party. His major source of support was

TABLE 10

BRAZIL, PRESIDENTIAL ELECTIONS, 1945–60: PERCENTAGES OF VALID BALLOTS

	Votes for PSD–PTB Candidates	*Votes for UDN Candidates*	*Votes for PSP Candidates*	*Others*
Brazil				
1945 (Gen. Dutra)	55.3%	34.7%	–	9.9%
1950 (G. Vargas)	70.3 (21.5)	29.6	–	–
1955 (Kubitscheck)	35.8	30.3	25.7%	8.2
1960 (J. Quadros)	32.9	48.2	18.8	–
São Paulo				
1945	57.7%	27.9%	–	14.4%
1950	65.0 (10.6)	25.0	–	–
1955	12.7	33.0	45.8%	8.4
1960	15.3	55.0	29.6	–
Minas Gerais				
1945	57.3%	40.6%	–	2.1%
1950	65.2 (32.3)	34.8	–	–
1955	58.6	23.3	11.5%	6.5
1960	43.7	44.5	11.8	–
Guanabara				
1945	33.9%	37.5%	–	28.6%
1950	60.5 (5.1)	29.5	–	–
1955	29.5	25.9	39.4%	5.2
1960	28.3	47.2	24.5	–

SOURCE: Calculated from Brazil, Tribunal Superior Eleitoral, *Dados Estatísticos*, 1964.

however, urban and popular. The split within the PSD in Minas Gerais gave 32 percent of the votes to Vargas and is a reflection of the predominantly rural society and political structure in that state. It was quite clear that the PSD allegiance to Vargas was due less to ideological preferences than to the need to remain close to the source of power.

The participation of São Paulo in the alliance was through Adhemar de Barros, formerly Vargas' caretaker in the state. In 1950, Barros felt strong enough to create his own political party, the PSP, and in 1955 and 1960, he was an independent candidate for the presidency, carrying Rio and São Paulo in 1955 but getting only about 25 percent of the national vote. It is very clear that Barros was always a regional candidate who did not fill the national cleavage between PSD–PTB and UDN.

The election of 1960 was the first and only victory of São Paulo, with Jânio Quadros. Quadros emerged without the support of a party structure, and climbed step by step from the local government of the city of São Paulo to the presidency. His appeal was personal, his issues were honesty and sincerity, and his personal appearance was unkempt, in contradiction with the broomstick which was his electoral symbol. To pass from local to national politics he had to be absorbed by the UDN ticket, even though he had little in common with this party. He was able, when in government, to attract the opposition of almost everybody, and resigned from office after eight months, leaving the country in a crisis from which it would not recover.

The election of Quadros did not mean that the cleavage between the cooptation and the representation systems was bridged by São Paulo, but rather that it had been superseded by a new cleavage between tendencies toward expansion vs. tendencies toward restriction of the political system. Balloting for the Vice-President was done independently, and João Goulart, the V-P candidate from the PSD–PTB coalition, defeated his opponent, who was well identified as a man from UDN. The PSD–PTB presidential candidate was a General identified with left-nationalistic groups, and his acceptance by the PSD was an indication of the party's inability to articlulate a winning candidate of its own. General Lott was a loser on many accounts. His surprisingly high position in the state of Minas Gerais is really an indication of the PSD's difficulty in acting independently from official determinations emanating from the central government.

The erosion of the PSD–PTB hegomony can be better analyzed through table 11, where data for congressional elections are displayed. The PSD never ceased to be the biggest party, but its relative size fell progressively as time passed. Alliances and coalitions of all kinds tended to absorb up to 50 percent of the congressional vote. An analysis of these coalitions is still to be made, but table 12 presents both the data on coalitions and an attempt to place them under the major dominant party for the three states of São Paulo, Minas Gerais, and Guanabara. This attempt is, of course, provisional and should be backed up by a detailed analysis of the political processess in each state, which would be out of place here. It is enough to note how the three parties of the cooptation system disappeared completely from São Paulo in 1962 as independent political entities.

TABLE 11

CONGRESSIONAL ELECTIONS, PARTY VOTES AND VOTES FOR COALITIONS 1945–62: PERCENTAGES OF VALID VOTES

	PSD	*PTB*	*UDN*	*PSP*	*Others*	*Alliances and Coalitions*
1945	44.0%	10.5%	27.4%	–	22.1%	–
1950	27.0	16.4	17.0	7.3%	12.1	20.2%
1954	23.1	15.6	14.3	9.3	10.7	27.0
1958	19.0	15.9	14.3	2.5	11.5	35.9
1962	18.3	14.2	13.2	1.0	5.0	48.3

SOURCE: Calculated from Brazil, Tribunal Superior Eleitoral, *Dados Estatísticos*, Vol. 6, 1964.

The disappearance of the big national parties in São Paulo was followed not by an increase in political regionalism, but, paradoxically, by a progressive nationalization of state politics. If we look at the congressional alliances in the state, we notice that in the 1958 election the PSP entered into an alliance with the PSD, even though the former was clearly dominant (it had 411,510 votes for the state Congress, as against 181,700 for the PSD). In 1962, the PSD–PSP alliance again came in second to an alliance of two regional parties

(Christian Democrats and MTR). The alliance also benefited from the political inheritance of Jânio Quadros in the state. In Rio the Labor Party entered into an alliance with the Socialists, and received the support of the illegal but active Communist Party. Only in Minas Gerais did the party configuration remain remarkably stable, as a coalition of the small PTB with the still smaller PSP in the state.

TABLE 12

CONGRESSIONAL ELECTIONS, PARTY VOTES: THREE STATES, 1945–1962: PERCENTAGES OF VALID VOTES

	PSD	*PTB*	*UDN*	*PSP*	*Others*	*Alliances and Coalitions*
Guanabara (City of Rio de Janeiro)						
1945	17.5%	26.9%	23.1%	2.3%	30.2%	–
1950	14.0	39.8	17.9	7.2	21.1	–
1954	10.3	29.5	(32.9)*	11.1	16.2	35.0%
1958	(14.8)*	28.7	33.8	20.6	2.1	14.8
1962	(13.9)*	(49.8)*	30.0	–	6.3	63.7
Minas Gerais						
1945	47.0%	7.2%	22.2%	–	23.6%	–
1950	38.7	12.9	29.3	3.1%	16.0	–
1954	44.9	12.5	25.1	4.5	13.0	–
1958	43.0	12.3	19.9	3.6	12.2	–
1962	42.6	(15.4)*	31.3	–	10.7	15.4%
São Paulo						
1945	36.0%	17.9%	21.5%	5.5%	19.1%	–
1950	15.3	20.9	13.1	29.2	21.5	–
1954	29.4	17.2	8.7	24.5	20.2	–
1958	–	10.7	9.7	(38.5)*	41.1	62.0%
1962	–	(15.1)*	–	(28.2)*	56.7	89.3

SOURCE: Calculated from Brazil, Tribunal Superior Eleitoral, *Dados Estatísticos*, Vol. 6, 1964.

***Figures in parentheses correspond to votes given to alliances (See the text for additional explanation).**

The 1962 congressional election was characterized both in Rio and São Paulo by the presence of strong candidates who concentrated the votes. Leonel Brizola, from the PTB–PSB alliance, received 62.8

percent of the votes of his constituency, while Amaral Netto, from the UDN, got 47.5 percent of his party's votes. Emilio Carlos, in São Paulo, got 44 percent of the votes of his PTN–MTR alliance. In Minas Gerais, however, the most popular candidate, Sebastião Pais de Almeida of the PSD, got only 80,000 votes (as against 269,000 for Brizola, 123,000 for Amaral Netto, and 154,000 for Emilio Carlos), comprising only 10.6 percent of his party's votes. The concentration of votes in legislative elections was a sign of ideological polarization which took place in the urban centers but was characteristically absent in Minas Gerais. During this period, congressional representation was proportional to a state's population, but enfranchisement was limited to the literate. This added strength to states such as Minas Gerais, which were little affected by the increase in mobilization politics which became characteristic of Rio, São Paulo, and a few other big centers, like Recife and Porto Alegre. A gap started to develop between politics leading to the executive posts and politics leading to the elections for Congress. The latter process remained stable and absorbed much of the mobilization effects, while the former was much more exposed to these effects. The PSD–PTB coalition was palatable to the army and conservative sectors while the PSD had the lead, but when Goulart had to replace Quadros, the crisis broke. The first solution, characteristically, was to force through a parliamentary system which could take away the powers of the President. This was done in 1961, but Goulart was strong enough, in 1963, to call a national plebiscite which restored his full constitutional powers. After this, the crisis was irreversible and led to his overthrow in 1964.

Conclusions

If one wants to summarize the changing voting paterns from 1945 to 1964, the following traits seem to be most relevant:

a) Two lines of cleavage defined the political system in 1945. One was regionally marked, and corresponded to the cooptation vs. representation system. The other existed within each of these systems, and went roughly from left (the PTB) to right (the UDN) on the cooptation side. In the São Paulo area, the left was represented in 1945 by the Communist Party (it got almost 20 percent of the congressional vote in this state, but only 8.2 percent of the national votes, and was declared illegal in 1947). The center right never acquired a defined party configuration in the state.

b) As time passed and the levels of education, urbanization, and industrialization rose, the cooptation system started to falter. Political alienation, as indicated by invalid votes, increased, and this was particularly acute in the São Paulo area.

c) The entrance of São Paulo as an independent political agent in national politics was at first in terms of representational politics of a stabilizing or restrictive character, but acquired almost immediately a mobilizing connotation. Analysis of interest groups, the trade unions, and even the educational system in the São Paulo area points to a base for representational politics, but the state's alienation from national politics meant that it never shaped articulated political parties. The PSP started from the beginning using mobilizational appeals and used as much political cooptation as was possible at the state level.

d) The victory of Jânio Quadros (UDN–São Paulo) and Goulart (PTB) for the presidency and vice-presidency in 1960 had two essential consequences. First, it meant that politics became national, and the political isolation of São Paulo had come to an end. Second, and perhaps more importantly, it meant that the route toward nationalization of politics was via the increase in political mobilization and the emergence of clearly ideological cleavages at the national level. Minas Gerais, which had the same political profile as the whole country for presidential and congressional elections up until 1954, lost its place to Guanabara, which set the pattern for the 1960 presidential election.

If the balance of forces was adequate for a political system based on limited suffrage, cooptation of political leaders, and electoral isolation of the economic centers, it could not hold when mobilization increased and politics became national. Political cooptation through mobilization of the urban centers demanded a kind of mobilization system which lacked organizational support, as well as economic, military, and international backing. The alternative was to restrict the levels of political participation and to force the reintroduction of restrictive cooptation. The new arrangement after 1964 was to increase the power of the Executive, but at the same time, to channel political participation through a two-party system in the Legislature. It is worth noting that this formula was acceptable to the PSD, which could continue the politics of patronage at the local level while counting on a strong executive to restrict attempts at political mobilization.

TABLE 13

CONGRESSIONAL ELECTIONS, 1966

	São Paulo	*Minas*	*Guanabara*	*Brazil*
ARENA (government)	34.6%	63.6%	20.4%	50.5%
MDB (opposition)	30.0	19.0	54.2	28.4
Blank and Null	35.4	17.4	25.4	21.1
Totals	100%	100%	100%	100%

SOURCE: IBGE, *Anuário Estatístico do Brazil*, 1969.

Regional politics apparently disappeared with the two-party system. However, the high level of participation shown in the election of Quadros in São Paulo also faded, and the same thing happened in Guanabara. With the restriction of mobilization, political alienation increased, and Congress began a downhill slide which ended in its complete subordination to the Executive. A new kind of cooptation system was installed, based on a military and technical mandate, and the political system came to a position of almost complete closure.

If the analysis so far is correct, some conclusions seem to follow necessarily. It becomes clear that the political process in an underdeveloped country like Brazil cannot be understood in terms of more or less explicit variables such as "modern" and "traditional," or "rural-urban." Brazil shares with the rest of Latin America an outstanding lack of agrarian parties, and this is a strong indication that political cleavage does not cut along the rural-urban line. The closest thing to a rural-party in Brazil was the PSD, but its strength lay not in the countryside, but in the control and exploitation of a huge and complex governmental structure. It would be misleading to think that this structure was "traditional." Since imperial times in the nineteenth century, Brazil's central government has been an agent of modernization. Even after 1930, it had a very explicit policy of economic growth and bureaucratic rationalization, which it did not relinquish afterwards. Efficiency tended to be low, certainly, but this was never the only goal of a strongly patrimonialistic and status oriented state.

Another conclusion which follows is that the Brazilian internal political process cannot be simply explained away in terms of its insertion in an international context of dependence. External factors are obviously very important, in the sense that they place limits on the alternatives which are open for the country, but they are not sufficient to explain the developments that led to the present political configuration of the country.

We can now return to the question we asked at the beginning: what kind of political reopening is possible in Brazil? We can certainly say that cooptation politics with limited participation seems no longer possible in a noncoercive regime. As the state rationalizes to cope with the pressures of underdevelopment in a context of demographic explosion and rising aspirations, piecemeal patronage becomes unsatisfactory and politically inefficient.[16] What was formerly a sound political approach based on administrative advocacy becomes political corruption. Brazil is now witnessing the death of its old "political class."[17] Much of this process is in the hands of the government and manifested through direct and indirect sanctions. In addition, the process is hampered by its lack of function in a context polarized by administrative and economic efficiency vs. political mobilization.

The prospects for representation with limited participation are still dimmer. The 1932 revolution in São Paulo was probably the peak of the attempts to establish an autonomous political force in the country *vis-à-vis* the cooptation system. After 1945, this kind of politics in São Paulo led more to political withdrawal than to party structure and organization, and when São Paulo emerged again on the national political scene, it was on terms of charismatic mobilization and expanded participation. As the government has extended its

[16]The logic of this process was well characterized by Peter Heintz (1964).

[17]The concept of "political class" belongs to Brazilian political jargon, and expresses very well the existence of a system of political leadership which does not depend as much on the exercise of representation of other classes, as on a special social position which is defined by a relationship of dependence on the state.

control of the economic system and increased its role as an entrepreneur, as well as its participation in all sectors of the country's life, it is indeed difficult to see the possibility of an open political system based on representational politics in the foreseeable future.

The three remaining possibilities are that a political opening will not occur, or that it will occur with expanded participation in either the representation or cooptation mode. There is no reason to assume that the political system cannot remain closed or highly restricted for a long period, with some oscillations. Scattered empirical evidence seems to indicate that the urban middle-class sectors are willing to accept and support a closed military-backed regime if the economic crisis is not too overwhelming, and the demographic explosion does not lead to crisis in the countryside. The social costs of this alternative are, of course, an entirely different matter.

Expanded participation in terms of representation is difficult to conceive, since it would require the dismantling of the present governmental organization. The final possibility is mobilization with and through the governmental structure, with or without the present leadership. This alternative has been intensely discussed in terms of the Peruvian experience, and it is not beyond the range of possibilities.[18]

The future is, of course, unknown, and each of the possible alternatives must be ultimately tested by its efficiency in coping with the tensions of underdevelopment. One of the main difficulties which will certainly arise in any attempt at political openness will be the almost total lack of a new civilian leadership. The system of the 1945–64 period did not leave heirs, just orphans. The major political problem for Brazil in the years to come will be its ability to establish forms of autonomous and legitimate representation within a governmental structure which seems to become progressively more centralized and overhelming. This is not a problem which can be easily solved – and it is not a purely Brazilian problem either.

---

[18]It is interesting to note that the "Peruvian way" attracts the attention of Brazilians much more than the political process in Argentina, which seems, however, much closer to the restoration of representative democracy than other military-backed governments in Latin America. It is possible to speculate that the differences between Peru and Argentina might be traced back to the historical split which freed Argentina from the Spanish colonial administration in Lima (I am indebted to Roberto Cortes-Conde for calling my attention to the parallel between São Paulo – Rio and Buenos Aires – Lima).

REFERENCES

Apter, David E. (1968). "Notes for a Theory of Non-Democratic Representation." In *Some Conceptual Approaches to the Study of Modernization*. New York: Prentice-Hall, Inc.

Bendix, Reinhard, and Lipset, S.M. (1966). *Class, Status and Power*. 2nd Ed. New York: Free Press.

Campbell, Angus (1960). "Surge and Decline: A Study of Electoral Change." *Public Opinion Quarterly*: Fall.

Carvalho, José Murilo de (1965). "Estudos de Poder Local no Brasil." *Revista Brasileira de Estudos Politicos*.

Cintra, Antônio Octávio (1971), "A Integraçao do Processo Político no Brasil: algumas hipóteses inspiradas na literatura", *Revista de Administração Pública*, vol. 5, 2.

Cornblit, Oscar; Gallo, Ezequiel; and O'Connell, Alfredo A. (1965) "La generación del 80 y su proyecto: antecedentes y consecuencias." In Torcuato S. Di Tella, *et al., Argentina, Sociedad de Masas*. Buenos Aires: Eudeba.

Ellis, Jr., Alfredo (1937). A Evolução da Economia Paulista e suas Causas. *Brasiliana*, Vol. 90.

Franco, Celina Moreira; Oliveira, Lucia Lippi; and Hime, Maria Aparecida (1970). "Comunidade Política às Vésperas da Revolução de 30." *Dados* 7.

Gallo, Ezequiel (1970). "Agrarian Expansion and Industrial Development in Argentina, 1930." In Raymond Carr, Ed., *Latin American Affairs*. Oxford University Press.

Heintz, Peter (1964). "El Problema de la Indecisión Social en el Desarollo Económico." *Anales de la Facultad Latinoamericana de Ciencias Sociales*. Santiago.

Jaguaribe, Helio (1962). *Desenvolvimento Econômico e Desenvolvimento Político*. Ed. Fundo de Cultura, Rio de Janeiro (There is a new and rev. English version of this book).

Klein, Lucia Maria Gomes and Lima, Jr., Olavo Brasil de (1970). "Atôres Políticos do Império." *Dados* 7.

Lamounier, Bolivar (1969). "Ideologias Conservadoras e Mudanças Estruturais." Rio de Janeiro, *Dados* 5.

Leal, Victor Nunes (1948). *Coronelismo, Enxada e Voto*. Rio de Janeiro.

Lipset, S.M., and Rokkan, S. (1967). "Cleavage Structures, Party Systems and Voter Alignments." *Party Systems and Voter Alignments*. New York: Free Press.

Lowi, Theodore J. (1964). "American Business, Public Policy, Case Studies and Political Theory." *World Politics* XVI, 4.

Morse, Richard M. (1958). *From Community to Metropolis, A Biography of São Paulo, Brasil*. Gainsville: University of Florida Press, Chap. 14.

Schmitter, Philippe C. (1971), *Interest Conflict and Political Change in Brazil*, Stanford: Stanford University Press.

Schwartzman, Simon (1969). "Political Participation and Political Openness." *Dados* 6 (in Portuguese). Also in the *Proceedings* of the First Round Table of the International Political Science Association in Rio de Janeiro.

Schwartzman, Simon (1970). "Representação e Cooptação Política no Brasil." *Dados* 7. (IUPERJ, Rio de Janeiro.)

Stokes, Donald E. (1965). "A Variance Components Model of Political Effects." In The Arnold Foundation, *Mathematical Applications in Political Science*. Dallas, Texas.

Stokes, Donald E. (1967). "The Nationalization of Political Forces." In W.N. Chambers and W.D. Burnham, *The American Party Systems*. New York: Oxford University Press.

Weffort, Francisco (1965*a*). "Raizes Sociais do Populismo em São Paulo." *Revista Civilização Brasileira* 1, 2.

Weffort, Francisco (1965*b*). "Política de Massas." In Octavio Ianni, *et al., Política e Revolução Social no Brasil*. São Paulo.

Weffort, Francisco (1966). "Estado e Massas no Brasil." *Revista Civilização Brasileira* 1, 7.

Part Two:

Rational Choice Theories

Introduction

The papers in this section have a different character from that of the others in this volume.

The papers in part one use established data analysis methodologies to address specific substantive problems defined within various, usually well-defined areas of research. They are founded, and firmly grounded, on empirical data, and are mostly written by a single political scientist using established statistical techniques. The object of their study is, for most of them, a precise, quite definite and recognized problem in a single or small group of countries.

Like those in the next section as well, the following three papers, on the other hand, are much more global in their aims, more mathematical in their means, and may be slightly more controversial, if definitely stimulating and pathbreaking. They share a rationalistic orientation, are frequently coauthored and are infused with ideas from economic and psychological theories of decision-making. Statistical data, concepts, and methods complement primarily deductive, analytical, theory-building concerns.

Thus in "Campaign Strategies for Alternative Election Systems," the authors, P.H. Aranson, M.J. Hinich and P.C. Ordeshook, are placing their analysis in the Western hemisphere political framework, and draw the majority of their examples from the American recent experience. But the general outlook adopted and the conclusions arrived at go well beyond the scope of any specific country and may be taken as general in nature.[1] "Threat Games: A Comparison of Performance of Danish and American Subjects," by A. Rapoport, M. Guyer and D. Gordon is actually the first approximation of a test which might lead to the study of the basic behavior and psychological attitudes of the citizens of any country; it represents part of a much larger project on decision-making in game-like situations. And "The Problem of Salience in the Theory of Collective Decision-Making" by M. Taylor is, in the author's own words, "a model of collective decision-making by any voting body choosing multi-attribute, or multi-dimensional alternatives." The level of abstraction is undoubtedly very high.

Furthermore, like the papers of the next section, every one of these papers rests on an elaborate, deductive mathematical structure, itself embedded in advance mathematical theories, which constitutes the core of the paper, even if (as in Rapoport, Guyer, and Gordon's paper) the mathematical theory is sometimes left, so to speak, in the background. And here again, we see clearly a differentiating element from the papers of the first section, where the mathematical apparatus tends more to be a statistical accessory.

One can say also that these papers are almost pre-paradigmatic in nature, in the sense that they stem from very restricted groups of pioneering scholars, share a number of key assumptions, results and puzzles about the appropriate meaning of rational behavior, but have not received yet the full understanding and agreement of classical political scientists. Yet the increasing number of similar papers in the past few years, the rapid progress of rationalistic theories, the dedication of teams of pluri-disciplinary scientists, combining their efforts often for several years, are already seen by many as testimonies of a fruitful path, which seems to broaden in scope and become ever more relevant for political science.

It is probably useful to acknowledge here the vision of those few social scientists who, in the fifties, foresaw this development. Von Neuman and Morgenstern provided a firm foundation for a rational theory of competitive behavior by solving the problem of infinite

---

[1] However it is to be regretted that the French two-run election system has not been considered.

regress in researches for appropriate strategies vis-à-vis other rational actors. They used and modified classical economic equilibrium ideas. Kenneth Arrow's work on the voters paradox, a problem going back at least to Condorcet, was in part resolved by Duncan Black's proof that single-peaked preference curves along shared ideological continua obviate Arrow's problem. Rapoport's empirical work on the Prisoner's Dilemma has helped provoke analogous theoretical responses by Harsanyi, Howard, and others in ways reminiscent of earlier developments in public finance and public goods theory by Samuelson and others.

In "Threat Games: A Comparison of Performance of Danish and American Subjects," the authors show, in a quite theoretical way, how, confronted with certain problems of rational choice, a certain attitude of passivity leads surprisingly to better results. Perhaps the most exciting feature of this paper, is that A. Rapoport, M. Guyer, and D. Gordon have designed in a very clever and astute way a new psychological test in terms of how subjects respond to a threat-choice situation. Surely the real goal pursued in the experiment must have escaped the subjects: it looks like a game of skill, where one either wins or loses. Ultimately, however, the authors' intention is quite different: they want to detect and assess the patterns of behavior and character which differentiate various nations. It is a stimulating device, which leaves an open path for further research on how political identities affect competitive choices.

However, the statistical significance of the results remains dubious. The authors mention this problem several times, and it is surely to their credit that they draw the attention of the reader to a question which one will be led to ask more and more frequently as the sophistication and the precision of the techniques made up increase.

But if all three papers in this chapter are equally concerned with the meaning of rational choices in problematic situations, a still greater similarity, a stronger *air de famille* may be felt by the alert reader between the last two of them, and for no accidental reason. Both "The problem of salience in the theory of collective decision-making" and "Campaign strategies for alternative election systems" are closely related from a paradigmatic point of view. They belong to the latest development of the economic theory and democracy as developed by a number of authors, among whom Downs, Buchanan and Tullock, Davis, Hinich, Sen, well deserve to be cited here, besides Arrow and Black already mentioned.

This is precisely the case for "Campaign strategies for alternative election systems." This paper comes after a series of contributions by varied combinations of names within a group which includes those of Aranson, Davis, Hinich, Ledyard, Ordeshook, Riker. The Taylor paper, however, well illustrates the fact that this list is not inclusive. Be it said parenthetically, Kramer and Plott would be two other instances of the same general trend, whereas the Savage school of mathematical analysis on utility theory may yet converge to further progress in the field of political science. But undoubtedly, more is to be expected and we are already referred in a footnote to a forthcoming article by Shepsle.

P.H. Aranson, M.J. Hinich and P.C. Ordeshook appear to be primarily inspired by a deductive economic theory, but also by probabilistic statistics. Here, we find a strong predisposition in favor of rational modelling and interpretation leading to definite conclusions in the field of political science. It is worth noting that, "Campaign strategies" is another example of the deductive applicability of theorems of general character although revised, adapted, and altogether quite general.

The basic query of the paper is the sofar unsolved question of the influence of the alternative election systems (single-member district system, and proportional representation formula) upon the public policies of the bodies elected under such systems. As the reader will find in the last pages, there is no unambiguous answer to this question, because there are a number of conditions which may induce contestant candidates in both systems to adopt identical objectives; and should they adopt different objectives, supposedly better adapted to this or that system, the conditions of equivalence and non-equivalence of the objective functions chosen, depend on exogenous election and contestant characteristics.

Thus, the candidate objectives appear as an intervening variable, the discussion of which constitutes the hard core of the paper. The public policies supported by a candidate when elected are, one may assume, closely linked with the strategies adopted by him before the election. But the wish to maximize the vote, the plurality of the vote, and the proportion of the vote, usually lumped together in the loose phrase of "election goals", which in turn might depend on various election systems, do not necessarily elicit identical strategies, nor do they necessarily produce different strategies: there are for it specific conditions, which the paper discloses by a recourse to the utility function. In this connexion, it should be noted that gain (or utility) need not simply be expressed in terms of money, but can be estimated in a great number of other dimensions. On a specific point, the authors have therefore resolved an ambiguity and clarified a very loose notion by explicating the Bentham's intuition of the "arithmetic of pleasure". The concept of utility gain, so prominent in the economic field, finds a direct application in political science, and the same kind of gain-maximization reasoning used in econometrics, leads to similar conclusions in political science.

M. Taylor's paper, "The Problem of Salience in the Theory of Collective Decision-Making", relies on the basic assumption that individuals of a committee engaged in choices between issues have a salience ranking of the policy dimensions, although this salience ranking may not be the same for all the individuals. As in economics, theorems are proved pertaining to how many equilibrium points can be expected, to their stability, and to when a unique equilibrium point or a unique stable decision will be reached. Several voting procedures are considered, among which unanimity and simple majority may appear as the most important. But the relevance of the theory and results go well beyond the initial assumptions. The basic theorems are still valid for the two-stage decision process: dominance, then lexicography. Even if the human mind does not exactly follow such a decision process, M. Taylor's paper is indeed a major contribution to a developing tradition of increasingly more powerful analysis.

Threat Games: A Comparison of Performance of Danish and American Subjects*

ANATOL RAPOPORT, MELVIN GUYER, and DAVID GORDON

The type of game used in the experiments to be described is represented by the following payoff matrices. It is listed as Game 19 in Rapoport and Guyer (1967).

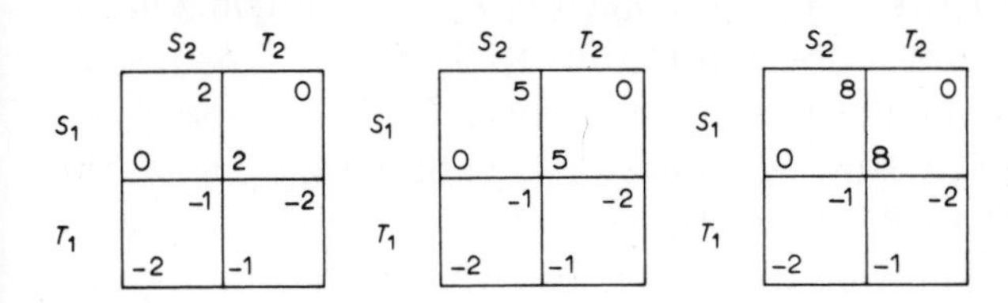

Fig. 1.

Player 1, called Row, and Player 2, called Column, choose simultaneously one of two strategies, S or T, represented by the horizontal rows and the vertical columns of the matrices. The outcome of a play of the game is one of the four boxes of a matrix. The number at lower left is the payoff to Row; at upper right, to Column.

Strategy S is the dominating strategy for both players. That is, each player gets a larger payoff if he chooses S rather than T, *regard-*

*The research work on which this paper is based was supported in part by National Institutes of Health, Grant NIH-MH 15942, and the Mental Health Research Institute, University of Michigan.

less of how the other player chooses. One can therefore expect that, if the game is played only once, the outcome $(S_1 S_2)$ will obtain. It will be called the *natural outcome*. The game is not symmetric. The natural outcome favors Column, who gets the largest possible payoff. Row, on the other hand, gets zero. The object of the experiments is to investigate the behavior of the players if the games are played many times in succession without explicit communication.

We can expect that in such iterated plays Row will not be satisfied with the repetition of the natural outcome, which awards him zero, while Column gets two, five, or eight. Column can, if he chooses, share a portion of the largest payoff with Row by occasionally switching to T_2, while Row continues choosing S_1. The amount so shared is entirely up to Column. By playing T_2 a certain fraction of the time, Column will share with Row that fraction of the largest payoff. In this sense, we say that Column *exercises power* in this game, namely the power to share at his discretion.

What recourse has Row if he is not satisfied with his share, which may well be zero? The only alternative open to Row is to shift from strategy S_1 to T_1. Coupled with Column's S_2, the shift results in the outcome $(T_1 S_2)$, in which both players suffer a loss. In fact, Row suffers a larger loss than Column. If, following $(T_1 S_2)$, Column shifts to T_2 while Row persists in T_1, outcome $(T_1 T_2)$ will obtain. On the face of it, Column is not motivated to shift to T_2 *from* $(T_1 S_2)$, since he will get even less in the resulting outcome $(T_1 T_2)$, namely -2 instead of -1 in $(T_1 S_2)$. However, once $(T_1 T_2)$ obtains, Row has the opportunity to shift to S_1, thus effecting $(S_1 T_2)$, which gives Row the largest payoff. Following that outcome, Column has the opportunity to restore the natural outcome $(S_1 S_2)$.

In a way, therefore, the shift by Row from the natural outcome to T_1 can be regarded as a "message" to Column that Row is not satisfied with the repeated occurrence of $(S_1 S_2)$. If Column "gets the message," he will shift to T_2, giving Row the opportunity to effect Row's preferred outcome $(S_1 T_2)$. If Column does not shift to T_2 from $(T_1 S_2)$, Row can continue to play T_1, "punishing" both himself and Column in the expectation that Column will eventually "yield" (shift to T_2), because only in this way can he induce Row to return to S_1, which is better than T_1 for *both* players.

In summary, the situation is as follows. Column has full control of how much of the largest payoff will accrue to each, as long as Row stays with S_1. Column exercises this control by choosing either his "selfish" strategy S_2 (giving nothing to Row) or his "thoughtful" strategy T_2 (giving everything to Row). Row, on the other hand, chooses between the "submissive" strategy S_1 and the "threat" strategy T_1. The latter may force Column to share. If Column shares "voluntarily," i.e., while Row still plays S_1, we shall call Column's behavior *fair* or *appeasing*. If Column shares only in response to Row's threat (T), we shall call Column's behavior *yielding*. Row's behavior in the face of Column's choice of S_2 will be called *submissive* if Row chooses S_1, and *threatening* if he chooses T_1. Frequencies of choices of the two players under various conditions, to be described, will be interpreted as quantitative measures of corresponding propensities.

Experiment 1

The subjects in this experiment were 42 male students at the Technical University of Denmark and 40 male students at the University of Michigan. All subjects were paid volunteers. The games were played for money: in Denmark at two öre (about 1/4¢) per point, in the U.S. at 1/5¢ per point. In Denmark, additional compensation was provided, if necessary, to comply with the Danish minimum wage laws. In the U.S., the subjects were paid a rate of $ 1.35 per hour, to which winnings were added or from which losses were subtracted. An *experimental run*, involving a pair of subjects, lasted about two–three hours.

Subjects were assigned randomly to pairs. After the game was explained, instructions given, and questions answered, each pair

TABLE 1

	Natural (S_1S_2)	*Sharing* (S_1T_2)	*Threat* (T_1S_2)	*Concession* (T_1T_2)
Game 1	3094	699	348	59
Game 2	2923	615	543	119
Game 3	2781	803	521	95
Total	8798	2117	1412	273
Percent	70%	17%	11%	2%

played six sequences of 100 plays each. Thus an experimental run consisted of 600 plays. Each subject participated in only one experimental run, alternating between the role of Row and that of Column. In each experimental run all three matrices were used in different sequences. Consequently, each subject played each of the three games 100 times as Row and 100 times as Column, 600 plays in all.

The Outcome Frequencies

Table 1 shows the distribution of the four outcomes in the performance of Danish subjects: 21 pairs times 600 plays or 12,600 choices.

Table 2 shows the same data from American subjects: 20 pairs times 600 plays or 12,000 choices.

TABLE 2

	Natural (S_1S_2)	*Sharing* (S_1T_2)	*Threat* (T_1S_2)	*Concession* (T_1T_2)
Game 1	1938	845	1019	198
Game 2	1956	576	1257	211
Game 3	1742	693	1365	200
Total	5636	2114	3641	609
Percent	47%	18%	30%	5%

In what follows, comparisons will be made without reference to the statistical significance of differences. In some cases, differences will be so slight as to be almost certainly insignificant. In other cases, they will be so large as to be almost certainly significant. We shall rely on these "naked eye" estimates, and our conjectures and conclusions are to be understood as contingent on the significance or insignificance of observed differences. Our feeling is that if a difference is of sufficient interest, *additional* experiments should be performed to establish it beyond reasonable doubt. In view of certain errors in design, to be noted in the discussion below, the present experiments are to be viewed as a "conjecture-generating pilot study."

We first examine the differences in the distributions of outcome attributable to the differences between the payoff matrices of the three games.

The a priori expectation was that, as the discrepancy between Row's and Column's payoffs in the natural outcome increases from two to five to eight points, there should be a decrease in the frequency of this outcome ($S_1 S_2$) because of Row's increasing dissatisfaction with it. Further, outcomes ($S_1 T_2$) and ($T_1 S_2$) should increase in frequency from Game 1 to Game 2 to Game 3; the former because Column might be more inclined to share, the latter because Row, being more dissatisfied, might be more inclined to threaten as the discrepancy increases.

From Tables 1 and 2, we see that there is a slight decrease in the frequency of ($S_1 S_2$) from Game 1 to Game 3 in both populations. The decrease is monotone in the Danish population (Game 2 being intermediate), but not in the American population. There is also an increase in the frequency of ($T_1 S_2$) in both populations, which is monotone in the American but not in the Danish population. A consistent trend in the frequency of ($S_1 T_2$) is not observable.

On the whole, the differences in the outcome distribution associated with the different games are slight. If we combine the two populations, we get a monotone decrease in ($S_1 S_2$) frequencies and a monotone increase in ($T_1 S_2$) frequencies from Game 1 to Game 3, as shown in Table 3, indicating, perhaps, and increasing dissatisfaction of Row with the natural outcome as the discrepancy between his and Column's payoffs increases. However, since the changes are not systematic in each population separately, we make no conjecture about the effect of the game matrix on the frequencies of choices. We shall ignore the difference and at times will combine the outcome frequencies from all three games for each population. The combined frequencies are shown in the "Total" rows of Tables 1 and 2.

TABLE 3

	$(S_1 S_2)$	$(T_1 S_2)$
Game 1	5032	1367
Game 2	4879	1800
Game 3	4523	1886

Comparing combined relative frequencies of the four outcomes in the two populations, we immediately see apparent differences. The frequency of $(S_1 S_2)$ is markedly smaller in the American population; that of $(T_1 S_2)$ is correspondingly larger. We state our first conjecture:

C_1: American Row players resort to the threat strategy more frequently than Danish Row players.

We note in this connection that there is no apparent difference between the tendency of Danish and American players to share the largest payoff with Row, as is evidenced by very nearly equal frequencies of the $(S_1 T_2)$ outcome. A straightforward calculation reveals that the mean payoff of the Danish Column players was 3.26 points per play, while the mean payoff of the Danish Row players was 0.62 points per play. Hence the overall Danish Column (top-dog) player got 84 percent of the joint payoff, while the overall Danish Row (underdog) player got 16 percent. Thus the ratio of top-dog to underdog payoffs was approximately 5:1. The mean payoff of the American Column player was 1.89 points per play, while the mean payoff of the American Row player was 0.19 points per play. Consequently the American top-dog/underdog split was 91 percent–9 percent, or ten to one. American underdogs rebelled more and got considerably less of top-dog/underdog split than their Danish counterparts.

However, as will appear below, if we look at just those 100 play sequences in which Row (underdog) never carried out the threat, the American top-dog/underdog split was 68 percent–32 percent and the Danish split, 79 percent–21 percent. The smaller overall earnings of the Americans are attributable primarily to the considerably larger "rebelliousness" of the underdog.

The Propensities

The analysis of data can be refined somewhat by introducing the conditional probabilities of choice. A conditional probability of a choice is defined with respect to the outcome occurring immediately prior to the choice. There being four outcomes, four such conditional probabilities are defined for Row and four for Column. Each has, of course, a complementary probability (of the other choice). We shall call these probabilities *propensities* and will give them psychologically suggestive names. The propensities will be estimated by the corresponding conditional frequencies. The names we give them are not, of course, meant to imply that the frequencies are reliable measures of character traits or anything of the kind. The names have been chosen merely for their suggestiveness, as will appear in the discussion below.

Row's Propensities:

CONDITIONAL PROBABILITY	NAME	SYMBOL
$P(T_1 \mid S_1 S_2)$:	"Revolt"	$\tilde{x}_1$
$P(T_1 \mid S_1 T_2)$:	"Dissatisfaction"	$\tilde{y}_1$
$P(T_1 \mid T_1 S_2)$:	"Persistence"	$\tilde{z}_1$
$P(T_1 \mid T_1 T_2)$:	"Distrust"	$\tilde{w}_1$

Explanation

In shifting to T_1 after a natural outcome, Row "revolts" against Column's advantageous position in the game. Following $(S_1 T_2)$, Column has the opportunity to re-establish the natural outcome by shifting to S_2, provided Row stays with S_1, i.e., provided Row has been satisfied by receiving the largest payoff. $P(T_1 \mid S_1 T_2)$ is the probability that Row will *not* allow the natural outcome to be established, hence is a measure of his "dissatisfaction" even after receiving the largest payoff. Following $(T_1 S_2)$ Row shows his "persistence" by repeating the threat strategy. (Had he shifted to S_1, he would have given up his "revolt.") Following $(T_1 T_2)$, Row has the opportunity to get the largest payoff in $(S_1 T_2)$ by shifting to S_1. However, this will happen only if Column will permit it by staying with T_2. If Row supposes that Column will "doublecross" him by shifting simultaneously to S_2, so as to re-establish the natural outcome, Row manifests his "distrust" by staying with T_1, so that if Column does shift, $(T_1 S_2)$ will result, and Column will receive the threat immediately instead of on the next play.

Column's Propensities:

CONDITIONAL PROBABILITY	NAME	SYMBOL
$P(T_2 \mid S_1 S_2)$:	"Fairness" or "Appeasement"	$\tilde{x}_2$
$P(T_2 \mid S_1 T_2)$:	"Generosity"	$\tilde{y}_2$
$P(S_2 \mid T_1 S_2)$:	"Adamance"	z_2
$P(S_2 \mid T_1 T_2)$:	"Doublecross"	w_2

Explanation

By shifting to T_2 from the natural outcome, Column seeks to forestall the use of threat by Row; hence he is "appeasing" Row. Alternately, he may be sharing the largest payoff with Row in the interest of "fairness." If Column *repeats* T_2 after $(S_1 T_2)$, he is giving Row the largest payoff *again*, hence is acting "generously." If Column persists in S_2 after Row has "revolted," he is being "adamant." Finally, shifting to S_2 after $(T_1 T_2)$ prevents Row from reaping the reward of his "revolt." Hence Column has "double-crossed" Row. We shall on occasion examine also $P(T_2 | T_1 S_2)$, the complement of "adamance," which we shall call "yielding."

Figure 2 shows the mean values of the propensities in percentages (averaged over individual propensities in each game) of the two populations of Danish and American players. The notation $\tilde{x}_1, \tilde{x}_2$, etc., is used in the interest of consistency. The letters without the "tilde" always refer to conditional choices of S; those with the "tilde," the complementary conditional choices of T.

		$\tilde{x}_1$	$\tilde{y}_1$	$\tilde{z}_1$	$\tilde{w}_1$
Game 1	DK	07	02	49	28
	US	15	12	74	40
Game 2	DK	09	06	59	39
	US	16	15	75	58
Game 3	DK	09	05	60	19
	US	20	13	75	54

		$\tilde{x}_2$	$\tilde{y}_2$	z_2	w_2
Game 1	DK	22	05	88	83
	US	29	31	84	74
Game 2	DK	18	11	81	76
	US	25	08	83	81
Game 3	DK	27	06	82	78
	US	32	10	85	73

Fig. 2.

The clearest differences between the Danish and the American populations are seen in the performances of the Row players. The propensities are all Row's tendencies to play the threat strategy, following each of the four outcomes. All of these propensities without exception are larger in American Row players. They lead us to make the following conjectures:

C_2: Americans as underdogs tend to "revolt" more frequently than do Danes ($\tilde{x}_1$).

C_3: Americans as underdogs tend to prevent the restoration of the natural outcome more frequently than do Danes.

C_4: Americans as underdogs tend to persist in the threat posture more than do Danes ($\tilde{z}_1$).

C_5: Americans as underdogs tend to "distrust" the top-dog more frequently than do Danes.

Examination of Column's propensities reveals no consistent differences among the Column players of the two populations, except possibly in $\tilde{x}_2$, which would imply:

C_6: Americans as top-dogs tend to share more frequently with underdogs than do Danes.

However, the very large value of American $\tilde{y}_2$ in Game 1 seems anomalous.

The value of z_2 indicates that Americans and Danes as top-dogs are about equally "adamant" (do not yield to threat).

The most striking and quite unexpected result is the very high value of w_2 in both populations. We expected that following a threat by Row and yielding by Column, leading to outcome $(T_1 T_2)$, Column would allow Row to get the largest payoff. To do this, Column would have to repeat T_2 so as to allow $(S_1 T_2)$ to obtain. Instead, Column quite frequently "doublecrosses" Row by shifting to S_2 after $(T_1 T_2)$, as is evidenced by the high values of w_2. The reason for the high values of w_1 (Row's distrust of Column) is now evident. Referring back to Figure 2, we see that Danes and Americans "doublecross" with about equal frequency, but Americans manifest distrust considerably more frequently than Danes, as we have already noted (C_5).

In the light of the above results, the following general picture emerges. As underdogs, Danes are more submissive than Americans. They seem to "defer to power." As top-dogs, Americans are somewhat (but only slightly) more "fair" or more "generous" than Danes.

It is interesting to compare the tendencies to "appease" and to "yield." The index of the former is $\tilde{x}_2$; of the latter, in our notation, $\tilde{z}_2 = 1 - z_2$. The comparison is shown in Figure 3.

	'Appeasement'	'Yielding'
DK	22	16
US	29	16

Fig. 3.

American subjects seem to "appease" more frequently than Danish subjects. The difference, however, is slight. On the other hand, the difference between "appeasement" and "yielding" is marked in both populations. Voluntary sharing occurs about one and one-half times as frequently as yielding under threat, in spite of the fact that in shifting from $(S_1 S_2)$ to $(S_1 T_2)$, Column reduces his payoff by two, five, or eight points, whereas in shifting from $(T_1 S_2)$ to $(T_1 T_2)$, he reduces his payoff by only one point. However, it must be kept in mind that a pattern of equal sharing $(S_2 T_2 S_2 T_2 \ldots)$ established by several Column players contributes to $\tilde{x}_2$.

The Four Types of Players

The last conjecture regarding "underdog" and "top-dog" behavior can be further tested. Consider four types of players, designated as follows.

$S_1 S_2$: These players predominantly *submit* to power when they are underdogs (play S as Row) and *wield* power when they are top-dog (play S as Column). Call them "authoritarian."

$S_1 T_2$: These players predominantly submit to power when they are underdogs (play S as Row) but do *not* abuse power when they do have it (play T as Column). Call them "trusting and generous."

$T_1 S_2$: These players do not submit to power when they are underdogs (play T as Row), but wield power when they have it (play S as Column). Call them "aggressive."

$T_1 T_2$: These players do not submit to power (play T as Row) and do not abuse power when they have it (play T as Column). Call them "fair-minded."

These designations (without parentheses), referring to *players* in their two roles, should not be confused with the similar designations (with parentheses), referring to *outcomes.*

We now combine the two populations into one (82 subjects). Each subject has an S_1 score (the overall frequency of his S choices as Row) and S_2 score (the overall frequency of S choices when he is Column). We determine the median S_1 and the median S_2 score of the entire population. Individuals whose S_1 and S_2 scores are both above median are assigned to the $S_1 S_2$ category. Those with S_1 scores above median and S_2 below (scores exactly at the median are considered to be below) are assigned to the $S_1 T_2$ category; those with S_1 scores below and S_2 scores above median are assigned to the $T_1 S_2$ category; those with both scores below median are assigned to the $T_1 T_2$ category. Figure 4 shows the distribution of the Danish and American populations among the four categories.

	DK	US	
$S_1 S_2$ ("authoritarian")	16	4	20
$S_1 T_2$ ("trusting and generous")	11	10	21
$T_1 S_2$ ("aggressive")	7	14	21
$T_1 T_2$ ("fair-minded")	8	12	20
	42	40	

Fig. 4. – The median S_1 score is 248.5; the median S_2 score is 238.5 out of 300 plays.

From Figure 4 we see that "authoritarian" players predominate among our sample of Danish subjects, while "aggressive" players predominate among American subjects. "Trusting and generous" players occur with equal frequencies; "fair-minded" players, with somewhat larger frequency in the American population.

The difference between the population profiles is interesting. A rough estimate of its significance by the Chi-square test reveals that a difference so large or larger would occur by chance with probability of less than 0.02 (x^2 = 10.35; df = 3). The appropriateness of the Chi-square test, however, can be questioned because the subjects were paired, so that the performance of one subject may well have depended on the performance of the other, contrary to the assumption of independence.

Nevertheless we can investigate the question of whether how a subject behaved as Row influenced how he behaved as Column. The contingency tables are shown in Figure 5.

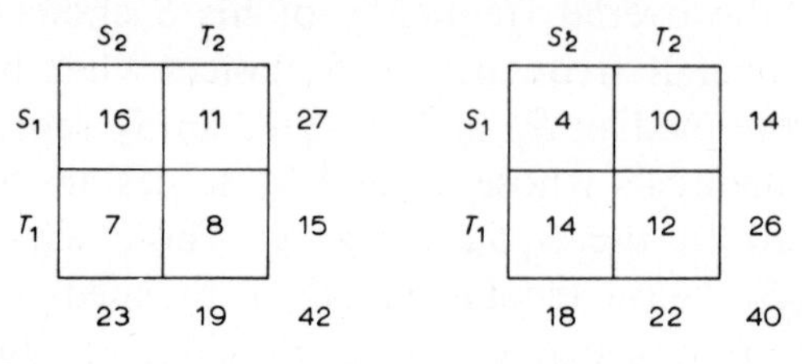

	S_2	T_2	
S_1	16	11	27
T_1	7	8	15
	23	19	42

DK: $X^2 = 0.214$, not significant.

	S_2	T_2	
S_1	4	10	14
T_1	14	12	26
	18	22	40

US: $X^2 = 1.439$, not significant

Fig. 5.

From Figure 5 we see that how the subject behaved as Row was not significantly correlated with the way he behaved as Column. Therefore, on this score at least, the use of the Chi-square test in comparing the population profiles was justified.

We can also investigate the population profiles for just those subjects who started as Row or as Column. This separates pairs eliminating any dependence of a subject's response upon the response of any other player in the same profile.

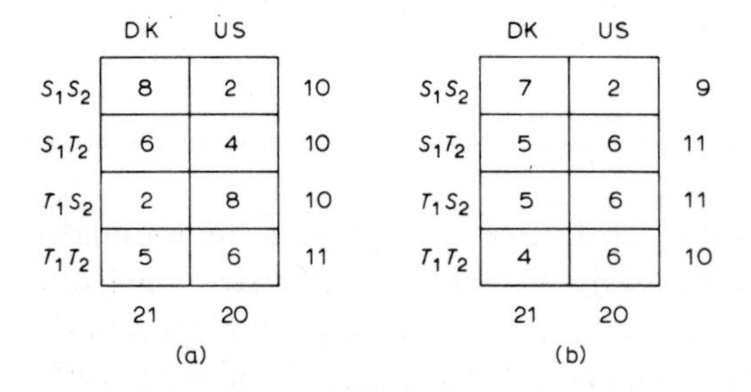

(a)

	DK	US	
S_1S_2	8	2	10
S_1T_2	6	4	10
T_1S_2	2	8	10
T_1T_2	5	6	11
	21	20	

(b)

	DK	US	
S_1S_2	7	2	9
S_1T_2	5	6	11
T_1S_2	5	6	11
T_1T_2	4	6	10
	21	20	

Fig. 6. – The median S_1 scores are 234 in (*a*) and 253 in (*b*); S_2 scores are 244 and 238, respectively, out of 300 plays.

Figure 6 (*a*) above exhibits profiles similar to those found in Figure 4. The Chi-square test reveals that a difference this large or larger would occur with a probability of less than 0.06 ($X^2 = 7.67$, $df = 3$). The expected frequency in cells S_1S_2, S_1T_2 and T_1S_2 for the U.S. data is 4.88. We assume this is sufficiently close to a frequency of 5 for Chi-square to be applicable. The differences in Figure 6 (*b*) above are not significant. It stands to reason that the population profiles exhibiting both the similarities and the differences of the two populations could be more firmly established by a larger experiment.

Experiment 2

The subjects in this experiment were 60 male students at the Technical University of Denmark and 60 male students at the University of Michigan. Each subject played 6 sequences of 100 plays each against a programmed player (a computer), hereafter called *stooge*. In three of the sequences the subject played as Row; in three, as Column. The matrices were the same as those in Experiment 1. The computer was programmed with six different strategies, three as Row and three as Column. All three games were used in each experimental run; that is, all three were played by each subject. The games were combined with the programmed strategies in various ways so that all combinations occurred.

The programmed Row strategies were as follows.

Y ("yielding"): the stooge as Row always chooses S.

M ("modest"): the stooge chooses S so long as Column (the bona fide player) chooses S no more than twice in succession. Following the third successive choice of S by Column, the stooge invariably shifts to T_1 and remains with T_1 until Column "yields" (switches to T_2), whereupon Row (the stooge) returns to S_1 and remains with it until Column once again has chosen S_2 three times in succession.

D ("demanding"): here Row is satisfied with nothing less than the entire positive payoff. Consequently, the stooge plays S_1 only after Column has played T_2. He always plays T_1 after Column has played S_2.

The programmed Column strategies are as follows.

A ("adamant"): stooge as Column always chooses S.

T ("tight"): as long as Row chooses S, Column (the stooge) plays the pattern $SSSTSSST$ . . ., thus giving Row 1/4 of the total gain. If Row resorts to threat, stooge never yields.

O ("opportunistic"): as long as Row "submits" (chooses S), stooge plays S_2; but stooge always yields to Row's threat, i.e., plays T_2 following Row's T_1. This also permits Row to get the largest payoff after (T_1 T_2).

Since the stooge's strategy is fixed, the bona fide player is essentially playing a "game against nature." Corresponding to any fixed strategy of the stooge, there is an optimum counter-strategy, which we shall calculate in each case.

Note that a calculation of an "optimum strategy of iterated play" in the case of two bona fide players is not possible. To be sure, since *S* dominates *T*, *S* is the rational choice for both players in a single play of the game. In an iterated game, however, it is quite possible that Row can get more than zero per play (which he gets in the natural outcome) by an "adroit" use of the threat strategy. However, what an "adroit" use is depends on the psychological characteristics of his opponent, the particular Column player. Nor can these characteristics be assumed to be fixed and so conceivably estimated by various probing strategies (as one could do in estimating, say, the payoff characteristics of a slot machine). For the probing stategies *themselves* can conceivably change the predispositions of the other player.

These difficulties vanish if the other player is programmed by a fixed strategy. If this strategy is known, it remains to calculate the optimal (payoff maximizing) counter-strategy. If the stooge's strategy is not known, but it is known that the opposing player *is* a stooge with a fixed strategy, the bona fide player faces the preliminary problem of estimating this fixed strategy before he can optimize his own. If the bona fide player does not even know that he is playing against a fixed strategy, the problem he faces depends on whether he *poses the question* of whether the opposing player is a stooge. If he does pose this question, he faces the problem of first determining whether the opposing player is indeed a stooge; next, if so, the bona fide player's problem is to determine the stooge's fixed strategy, and only then can he tackle the problem of optimizing his own strategy. If the bona fide player does not even pose the question of whether the opposing player is a stooge, then the bona fide player does not face a well-defined problem. He can only proceed by more or less haphazard trial and error.

We assume that our subjects had varying degrees of knowledge as to (1) whether the opposing player was a stooge; (2) if so, what his fixed strategy was, and (3) what counter-strategy was optimal. We shall simply compare the performance of our subjects with *the* corresponding optimal performance against each fixed strategy in each of the games.

The basis of our comparison will be the number of points won by the subjects compared with the maximum gain that could have been won playing against each of the strategies in each of the games. The optimal counter-strategies against our six fixed strategies are the following:

Fixed Strategy	*Optimal Counter-Strategy*
Row's *Y*	Always *S*
Row's *M*	In Games 1 and 2, the pattern *SSTSST*.....; in Game 3, the pattern *SSSTSSST*.....
Row's *D*	The pattern *STST*.....
Column's *A*	Always *S*
Column's *T*	Always *S*
Column's *O*	In Game 1, either always *S* or the pattern *TSTS*....; in Games 2 and 3, the pattern *TSTS*....

Explanation

The counter-strategies against *Y, A*, and *T* are obvious. The counter-strategy *SSTSST* . . . . against *M* forestalls the use of threat by Row and so gets Column 2, 2, 0, 2, 2, 0 . . . ., i.e., 4/3 points per play in Game 1, and 5, 5, 0, 5, 5, 0 . . . ., i.e., 10/3 per play in Game 3. The pattern *SSSTSSST* . . . . does not pay in Games 1 and 2, since it gets Column 2, 2, 2, −2 . . . . in Game 1, i.e., 1 point per play, and 5, 5, −2 . . . . in Game 2, i.e., $13/4 < 10/3$ points per play. It is easy to see that all the other strategies are worse.

Against *D*, the pattern *STST* . . . . gets Column 2 − 2 = 0, 5 − 2 =

TABLE 4

Points per play gained by subjects playing against fixed strategies. The last row shows points per play that can be gained using the optimal counter-strategy.

Fixed Strategy Played Against	*Row's*			*Column's*		
	Y	*M*	*D*	*A*	*T*	*O*
DK	4.09	2.23	0.92	−0.75	0.19	0.79
US	4.07	2.23	0.84	−0.53	0.40	0.90
Optimal	5.00	3.39	1.50	0.00	1.25	1.50

3, and 8 – 2 = 6 points per two plays in the three games respectively. Column can do no better. Against Column's *O*, the pattern *TSTS* .... results in the alternation $[(T_1 S_2), (S_1 T_2)]$, which gets Row –2 + 5 = 3 in Game 2 and –2 + 8 = 6 in Game 3 per two plays, the best he can do. In Game 1, this pattern gets Row –2 + 2 = 0, so that "always *S*" is equally good.

The performance involving fixed strategies is shown in Tables 4 and 5. All three games are combined in these data.

On the whole, it seems that American subjects playing against fixed strategies gain as much as, or somewhat more than, Danish subjects. However, the reversal in playing vs. Row's "demanding" strategy (*D*), and the rather small differences, indicate that the performances probably do not differ significantly.

TABLE 5

Points per play gained by the stooge, playing the fixed strategies. The last row shows the points per play that would have been gained by the stooge if the subject had played corresponding optimal counter-strategies.

Fixed Strategy		*Row's*			*Column's*	
	Y	*M*	*D*	*A*	*T*	*O*
DK	0.91	0.42	0.76	2.75	2.45	1.56
US	0.93	0.61	–0.55	3.46	2.76	1.03
Optimal	0.00	0.69	–0.50	5.00	3.75	–0.50

Table 5 suggests a comparison of the "effectiveness' of each of the six fixed strategies in playing against Danish and American subjects. Thus Row's "yielding" strategy seems to be about equally effective; that is, Danish and American Column players share the same amount with a "yielding" Row. Strategies *M,D,A*, and *T* seem to be more effective against American than against Danish subjects. Column's "opportunistic" strategy seems to be more effective against Danish subjects.

However, there is another way of interpreting these data. As has been said, a rational player, playing against a known fixed strategy, can be expected to play an optimal counter-strategy. Under this interpretation, American subjects seem to be playing closer to the optimal counter-strategy than Danish subjects, as is seen in comparing the stooge's gains per play with those he would have obtained playing against a player who optimized his counter-strategy. This is so even in the case of Column's strategy O, where, we note, the gain per play against an optimizing player is negative.

Bona Fide "Yielding" and "Adamant" Strategies

The interpretation of the data from Experiment 2 may be obscured by the fact that the behavior of the subjects may be partly "psychological," partly purely strategic (optimizing). To eliminate the possible effects of the subjects' knowledge that they are playing against a stooge, we return to the data of Experiment 1. We select those sequences of 100 plays in which either Row always played S_1 or Column always played S_2. Thus, we shall be examining sequences in which a *bona fide* player played a "yielding" or an "adamant" strategy. Since these extreme strategies were played only occasionally during a complete experimental run (600 plays) by bona fide subjects, we can assume that their partners did not get the (false) impression that they were playing against a stooge.

Table 6 shows the fractions of 100 play sequences where a subject used each of the two extreme strategies, and the fractions of subjects who played an extreme strategy at least once.

TABLE 6

F_y: fraction of 100 play sequences in which Row played the "yielding" strategy; f_y: fraction of subjects who, as Row, used the "yielding" strategy at least once. F_a and f_a refer analogously to Column's "adamant" strategy.

	F_y	f_y	F_a	f_a
DK	0.22	0.52	0.33	0.45
US	0.21	0.35	0.18	0.35

The fractions in the two populations are comparable. The incidence of extreme strategies is, perhaps, somewhat higher in the Danish subjects.

Table 7 shows performances in 100 play sequences in which a bona fide Row played the "yielding" strategy.

TABLE 7

	Column's Gain Per Play	*"Yielding" Row's Gain Per Play*	*Row's Share (%)*
DK	4.02	1.09	21
US	2.98	1.41	32

Table 8 shows the bona fide "adamant" Column player's gain per play – the maximum he could have gained against a "yielding" Row – and Row's gain per play.

TABLE 8

	"Adamant" Column's Gain Per Play	*Maximum*	*% of Maximum Taken by Column*	*Row's Gain Per Play*
DK	4.58	4.85	94	−0.11
US	3.03	5.00	61	−0.63

Here we have the clearest evidence of the difference noted earlier between the two populations. Danish "underdogs" tend to yield more than American "underdogs" to an "adamant top-dog." On the other hand, Danish "top-dogs" tend to exploit a "yielding underdog" more than do American "top-dogs." These results were not observed in Experiment 2, where subjects played against fixed strategies throughout. Our conjecture is that, to the extent that subjects became aware of the rigidity of their opponent (possibly inferring that he may be a stooge), they may have turned to simple optimizing strategies. On the whole, as noted, American subjects tended to play closer to optimal strategies than did Danish subjects in Experiment 2. Consequently Americans shared less with a *Y*-playing stooge and yielded more to an *A*-playing stooge than did Danish subjects. It is in the interaction with a bona fide opponent that the differences in "top-dog" and "underdog" behavior were manifested.

Comparison of Gains Per Play

In comparing the gains per play by bona fide players of both populations (Experiment 1), we shall also compare these gains with those prescribed by the Nash solution of the corresponding cooperative games; that is, with what each player would have got had the players been able to *negotiate* the division of the largest payoff according to the procedure described by Nash (1953). The comparison is shown in Figure 7.

	Game 1		Game 2		Game 3		Mean	
	Row	Col.	Row	Col.	Row	Col.	Row	Col.
DK	0.15	1.36	0.45	3.29	1.26	5.13	0.62	3.26
US	-0.14	0.62	0.04	2.03	0.65	3.04	0.19	1.89
Nash	0.50	1.50	2.00	3.00	3.50	4.50	2.00	3.00

Fig. 7.

The gains per play of American players are smaller throughout than those of Danish players. Both are, of course, smaller than those prescribed by the Nash solution, because, in negotiating the game, the "threat strategy," although it is one of the factors in the negotiation that determine Row's claim to a share of the total payoff, need not be actually carried out. Thus the greater "rebelliousness" of the American Row player impairs the mean gain of both players. We note also that the American Row player comes off relatively worse than the more submissive Danish Row player. The former gets only 9 percent of the total payoff, while the Danish Row player gets 16 percent. Both get considerably less than 40 percent, the share allotted to Row by the Nash solution.

We have already seen that in *playing against the stooge* the gains of the two populations are much more nearly equal. The overall means are shown in Figure 8.

	Mean Gain Per Play			Share (%)	
	Row's	Column's	Total	Row's	Column's
DK	0.08	2.41	2.49	3.2	96.8
US	0.26	2.38	2.64	9.8	90.2
Opt.	0.92	3.30	4.22	21.8	78.2

Fig. 8.

Here the American Row player comes off better than the Danish. As has been noted, Americans playing against fixed strategies tend to play more closely to the optimal counter-strategies than the Danes. Still, the Row players in both populations come off relatively worse than the Column players, getting less than the share they would have got by optimal play. Apparently the "underdog" departs more from optimal play than the "top-dog."

Our last comparison will be between the sharing patterns in the two populations when the threat strategies are *not* used; that is, the way the *positive* payoffs are apportioned among Row and Column. The results are shown in Table 9. The entries are Row's shares of the positive payoffs, in percentages.

TABLE 9

	Game 1	*Game 2*	*Game 3*
DK	22%	10%	31%
US	41	27	43
Nash	25	40	44

We see that, on the whole, American Column players share greater portions of the positive payoff, and (except in Game 1) the Danish Column players share considerably less than is prescribed by the Nash solution. Also, the increase of Row's prescribed share, related to increasing discrepancy in Games 1, 2, and 3, is not reflected in the performance.

Discussion

The absence of systematic differences in performance attributable to the matrices may have been the result of a contagion effect. As stated earlier, each of our subjects played all three games in the several 100-play sequences in the experimental run. Since the structure of the three games is identical, a subject in the course of the experimental run may have established a certain way of playing: e.g., "unyielding" or "fair," or "yielding under pressure," as Column; "yielding up to a point," as Row, etc.; and this pattern may have persisted with the given subject throughout the experimental run, thus erasing differences between games.

In previous experiments with the Prisoner's Dilemma Game

(Rapoport and Chammah, 1965), evidence of such a contagion effect was actually found. Seven game matrices were used in those experiments, in which the payoff parameters were systematically varied. It was found that, when each group of subjects played only one of the games, the frequencies of the "cooperative" response (*C*) varied systematically in the expected direction with the corresponding payoff parameter, so that the frequency of that response ranged from 77 percent in the "mildest" dilemma game to 27 percent in the most "severe." However, when all seven games were combined in blocks of 50 in single experimental runs, the variation was reduced to range from 70 percent for the mildest games to 40 percent for the most severe. This was also the range when the seven games were *completely* mixed in an experimental run, so that the game for each play was chosen randomly.

To ferret out the effect of the payoff parameters in the threat game, it is probably advisable to assign a single game to each group of subjects. Thereby one loses the advantage of having subjects serve as their own controls, but one avoids the contagion effect. The population of performances on each game becomes truly a random sample.

The use of fixed strategies with regular, easily discernible patterns was probably an error. There is evidence that many subjects easily discovered these patterns and adjusted their counter-strategies accordingly. As a result, the variance attributable to "psychological" instead of to purely strategic considerations was reduced. This error can be easily corrected by making fixed strategies probabilistic. For instance, Column's "tight" strategy might be designed as one in which Column plays *S* with probability of 0.75 (as long as Row plays *S*) in a randomized fashion, instead of in the *SSST* pattern. The introduction of uncertainty in the stooge's choices will most likely prevent the immediate recognition of the fixed strategy and will bring the "psychological" component of performance back into play.

Caution should be exercised in attributing whatever differences were observed to differences in the nationality of the subjects. The subjects in Denmark were all engineering students. Those in the United States were recruited from all sectors of a university. The comparison would be more convincing if students were more accurately matched in respects other than nationality.

REFERENCES

Nash, J.F., Two-person cooperative games. *Econometrica*, 21 (1953), 128–140.

Rapoport, Anatol and Chammah, Albert M., *Prisoner's Dilemma*, Ann Arbor: The University of Michigan Press, 1965.

Rapoport, Anatol and Guyer, Melvin, A taxonomy of 2 × 2 games. *General Systems*, 11 (1966), 203–214.

Campaign Strategies for Alternative Election Systems: Candidate Objectives as an Intervening Variable[1]

PETER H. ARANSON, MELVIN J. HINICH and PETER C. ORDESHOOK

I. Introduction

Even before John Stuart Mill called proportional representation "the very greatest improvement yet in the theory and practice of government," scholars had long argued the virtues and vices of alternative forms of constitutions and regimes.[2] Today, many people, especially those who live in the Western Hemisphere, agree on some form of popular control of government. Yet this agreement is terribly insubstantial: there appear to be an infinity of ways to arrange election and representation laws for even the most rudimentary democracies and republics. These arrangements include many forms of single-member district systems, proportional representation for-

[1] This study develops some implications from an earlier study's findings about equivalence and non-equivalence of election objectives. See Peter H. Aranson, Melvin J. Hinich, and Peter C. Ordeshook, "Election Goals and Strategies: Equivalent and Non-Equivalent Candidate Objectives," prepared for delivery at the Annual Meeting of the American Political Science Association, Washington, D.C., September 5–9, 1972. The present paper presents a number of theorems whose proofs are included in an appendix to the earlier study. This research is supported by a grant from the National Science Foundation to Carnegie-Mellon University.

[2] As quoted in Carl J. Friedrich, *Constitutional Government and Democracy* (ed. rev.; Boston: Ginn and Company, 1950), p. 277.

mulae, run-off elections, alternative *Sperrklausel* levels, and various requirements for nomination and slate and list making.[3] Of course, there is much disagreement on the best set of rules for an election system to follow.

These disagreements usually fall into one of three broad categories. First, there is little consensus on the policy implications of a given set of election laws or procedures. We do not know, for example, if two legislatures, one drawn from single-member districts and the other drawn from proportional representation lists, are likely to adopt substantially different or similar public policies. Needless to say, there are innumerable complicating factors; yet, even the most stringent set of *ceteris paribus* conditions does not now permit us to utter reliable theoretical sentences about the public policy implications of alternative election rules.

Second, and subsidiarily, even if it were possible to utter such sentences, there is little or no agreement on the public policies that legislatures ought to adopt. Suppose, for example, that we can array the members of a legislature on some left–right continuum. Suppose, further, that there are strong theoretical reasons to believe that legislatures drawn from single-member districts adopt public policy positions at the relative center of the continuum, while legislatures drawn from proportional representation lists adopt public policy positions at some distance from the relative center of the continuum. Certainly, a protagonist for either system will advocate the appropriate set of election rules, according to his own policy predispositions.[4] And, just as certainly, even if we are fortunate enough to understand the policy implications of a given election law, there is likely to be little or no agreement on the policy itself.

---

[3] For a discussion of these representation formulae see Douglas Rae, *The Political Consequences of Electoral Laws* (New Haven: Yale University Press, 1967). The classic work, of course, is Maurice Duverger, *Political Parties*, transl. Barbara and Robert North (New York: John Wiley and Sons, 1954), pp. 206, *passim*. For an attempt to explore systematically the effects of a family of representation formulae, see Henri Theil, "The Desired Political Entropy," *American Political Science Review*, 63, 2 (June, 1969), pp. 521–525.

[4] This was demonstrated most forcefully at the 1972 Democratic National Convention. Party reform leaders, most of them McGovern supporters, had ruled for the allocation of convention delegates by proportional representation. When California continued to use the plurality system, thus giving all of its 270 delegates to McGovern, the reformers voted down the objections of Humphrey supporters to the Credential Committee report. The objections, of course, called for delegate allocation by proportional representation. Cf. footnote 36.

Third, and perhaps of less importance, there is considerable disagreement on election rules and procedures, independent of their policy implications. This disagreement generally centers on the notion of procedural justice or rightness, with little or no regard for the policy consequences of the alternative procedures. Perhaps because of their ephemeral nature, it is difficult to imagine concrete examples of such disputes. Many people advocate a given set of election procedures, nevertheless, for reasons that define the procedures themselves. The single-member district system, for example, "represents only large segments of the electorate." More impressively, pure proportional representation "represents everyone."[5]

This paper ignores the second and third categories of disagreement: our concern is with the partial explanation and prediction of variations in public policy with variations of election rules. Specifically, we present here a number of findings about the effects a contestant's election objectives have on his choice of election strategies. And, viewing generally the dynamic of elections we argue that the selection of an objective depends mightily on the rules under which an election occurs, as well as on the contestant's strategic environment.

This argument needs elaboration. Suppose we wish to predict the public policies that legislatures and elected executives might adopt. That is, suppose we seek reliable theoretical sentences about the first category of disagreement we described earlier. Surely, there are many reasons for the adoption of a given public policy. Nevertheless, a minimal theoretical accounting of these reasons must include, at the very least, a specification of five basic relationships.

First, we must understand the relationship between a contestant's environment and his election objectives. Environment, in this sense, includes such traditionally cited matters as constituency characteristics (e.g. policy preferences), opponent capabilities, chances of success, and information. Candidates who expect to lose an election (e.g. Stevenson, 1952, 1956; Goldwater, 1964), might adopt election objectives to "educate the electorate." Candidates who expect to win, though, might adopt election objectives to "learn from the elec-

[5] See, for example, the initial arguments in Clarence Gilbert Hoag and George Henry Hallet, Jr., *Proportional Representation* (New York: Macmillan Company, 1926), and in F.A. Hermens, *Democracy or Anarchy? A Study of Proportional Representation* (Notre Dame, Indiana: The Review of Politics, 1941).

torate." Similarly, candidates who have absolutely no information about their opponents' electoral fortunes might adopt as their election objective the maximization of their own vote totals. Candidates with more reliable sources of information, though, might adopt as their election objective the maximization of plurality.

Second, we must understand the relationship between election laws, rules, and institutions, and a contestant's election objectives. This is a relationship that political scientists, for the most part, have ignored.[6] Hence, rather than depend upon *revealed* or *derived* election objectives, we must rely on *postulated* objectives as they relate to given election rules. Suppose, for example, a small party competes in a proportional representation system election with a 1% *Sperrklausel*, as in Israel.[7] We set as the party members' election objective to maximize the probability that their proportion of the vote exceeds 1%. If the *Sperrklausel* level is 5%, as in Germany, we set as the party members' objective to maximize the probability that their proportion of the vote exceeds 5%.[8] Later, we postulate several such objectives, and link them informally to alternative election rules and laws.[9]

Third, we must understand the relationship between a contestant's election objectives and his election strategies. Suppose, as in the previous example, the German Bundestag adopts a 1% *Sperrklausel*, while the Israeli Knesset adopts a 5% *Sperrklausel*. Will the corresponding variations in election objectives cause the party members in question to change their election strategies? Further, for *any* level of *Sperrklausel*, do these corresponding election objectives create strategic incentives that differ from those of a party whose members seek as their objective to win a parliamentary majority? A theoretical specification of this third relationship answers these questions.

[6] There are, of course, a number of quasi-formal explications of the idea that plurality system (two-party) candidates converge on public policy matters while proportional representation system (multi-party) candidates do not converge. See, Anthony Downs, *An Economic Theory of Democracy* (New York: Harper and Row, 1957), chap. viii.

[7] Leonard J. Fein, *Politics in Israel* (Boston: Little, Brown and Company, 1967), p. 97.

[8] For a discussion of the changing applications of the *Sperrklausel* in Germany see, Uwe Kitzinger, *German Electoral Politics: A Study of the 1957 Campaign* (London: Oxford University Press, 1960), pp. 17–37.

[9] Cf. Sections II and IV of this study.

Stated differently, we ascertain some partial relationships by finding conditions for equivalence among alternative election objectives as functions of election strategies.

Fourth, we must understand the relationship between the election strategies a candidate adopts and the public policy measures he sponsors if he is elected. Such relationships as may exist fall usually under the rubric of "constituency influence."[10] It is apparent if we spell out all of these requisite theoretical relationships, though, that the specification of a relationship between constituency preferences and legislative voting patterns is not simple. Indeed, the intervention of candidate (e.g. incumbent) objectives alone could modify the usual patterns of legislative voting we expect, but which the literature on constituency influence does not support unambiguously.[11] The point is that campaign platforms and promises constitute a subset of election strategies. How these election strategies enter into the office holder's legislative decision making is a matter about which we know very little, though it is one of the more important relationships we must understand to explain and predict public policy choice in democracies and republics.

Fifth, and finally, we must understand the relationship between the public policy that an office holder espouses in the legislature and the public policy that the legislature, or elected exectutive adopts. Here, of course, we enter the world of legislative coalition formation, bargaining, and logrolling, which are under the influence of various institutions and rules (e.g. seniority).[12] Yet, strategic – sophisticated – roll call voting can greatly affect the configuration of legislator responses on any number of public policy dimensions.[13]

---

[10] A recent attempt to examine constituency influence formally is, Morris P. Fiorina, "Representatives and Their Constituencies: A Decision Theoretic Analysis," prepared for delivery at the Annual Meeting of the American Political Science Association, Washington, D.C., September 5–9, 1972. Fiorina's study maps constituency preferences directly into legislative voting, without the intervention of campaign strategies.

[11] See for example, Donald Stokes and Warren Miller, "Party Government and the Saliency of Congress," *Public Opinion Quarterly*, 26 (1962), pp. 531–546.

[12] For recent work on these subjects see, Richard A. Niemi and Herbert F. Weisberg, eds., *Probability Models of Collective Decision Making* (Columbus, Ohio: Charles E. Merrill Pub. Co., 1972), chaps. i–viii.

[13] William H. Riker, "The Paradox of Voting and Congressional Rules for Voting on Amendments," *American Political Science Review*, 52 (1958), pp. 349–366; Robin Farquharson, *Theory of Voting* (New Haven: Yale University Press, 1969).

A complete theoretical specification of all five relationships constitutes a minimal theory of public choice in democracies and republics. Our intention here is not to provide that theory. Rather, we investigate some elements of the first three relationships. First, we postulate differences in election objectives with differences in candidate environment and election rules, laws, and institutions. Second, we examine these objectives as functions of campaign strategies, to ascertain conditions for which these objectives are equivalent or non-equivalent.

A brief example, which we expand later, should suffice to demonstrate this procedure. Suppose that in a single-member district election we postulate that a candidate chooses strategies to maximize his expected plurality. Suppose, also, that in a proportional representation system election we postulate that party leaders choose strategies to maximize the party list's proportion of the expected vote. Here are two election objectives: maximization of expected plurality and maximization of proportion of the expected vote. *Ceteris paribus*, are these objectives equivalent? If they are, then we cannot attribute variations in campaign strategy (which might lead to variations in legislative policy decisions) to variations in campaign objectives, which, in turn, we postulate to be derivatives of election rules, laws, and procedures.

Section II offers notations, definitions, and discussions of the central analytical concepts: strategies; campaign objectives; equilibrium; equivalence; and symmetry. Section III presents five equivalence theorems and, by implication, several corollary equivalences deriving from the basic theorems. Section IV returns to our initial questions about the policy implications of a given set of election laws and procedures, and places special emphasis on the significance of our results for ascertaining the nature of these implications.

II. Definitions and Notation

A. Strategies

A campaign strategy, broadly defined, is anything a contestant might vary in pursuit of an election goal. Our consideration of such strategies is extremely general. Yet, to emphasize the political and policy implications of our research, we describe here several of the forms that contestants' strategies might take.

Issue Strategies

Position The most obvious campaign strategy is a contestant's positions on public policy issues. Many scholars consider these strategies to be of secondary importance, while others view them as being at the center of election campaigns.[14] The argument is whether issues are window dressing, or whether citizens respond intelligently to issue positions. But the objective importance of issue position strategies is not in question. What does matter is the contestants' subjective beliefs about the importance of issues in a campaign, both to themselves and to their opponents and constituents.

We assume only that such issue positions exist. It might be the Hotelling variety, in that we can place it on some spatial continuum (e.g., taxation levels, expenditure levels of specific public programs, or other proposals about income or wealth redistribution).[15] Similarly, an issue might be the kind Stokes identifies, a "valence" issue, in that it is an either/or proposition.[16] There are no real continua along which it makes sense to array specific strategy positions (e.g., the proposed appointment of a particular jurist, or even a declaration of war).[17]

---

[14] See the recent exchange by Gerald M. Pomper, Richard W. Boyd, Richard A. Brody, Benjamin I. Page, and John H. Kessel, entitled, "Issue Voting," *American Political Science Review*, 66, 2 (June, 1972), pp. 415–470.

[15] Harold Hotelling, "Stability in Competition," *The Economic Journal*, 39 (1929), pp. 41–57. See also Downs, *loc.cit.*

[16] Donald Stokes, "Spatial Models of Party Competition," *American Political Science Review*, 57, 2 (June, 1963), pp. 368–377.

[17] It is useful here to anticipate a possible objection to our discussion. Earlier, we argue that it is reasonable to postulate objectives for contestants as a result of various election laws and institutions. Furthermore, we assert that these objectives affect campaign strategy decisions, which, in turn, map into sets of legislative policy objectives and, ultimately, into sets of public policies. Here, though, we plumb only the relationship between election objectives and campaign strategies. The reader might well object that our findings are not useful for predicting the public policy effects of election procedures since we do not account for these latter relationships. We respond, simply, that we wish only to find reasons for public policy variations as functions of campaign strategies. And, campaign strategies derive partially from the election objectives that we postulate from election laws and procedures.

Salience An equally obvious campaign strategy is the variation of emphasis, or salience, of issues. In the 1972 campaign, for example, President Nixon emphasized his personal diplomacy in China and Russia. Senator McGovern, though, emphasized Nixon's failure to remove American military forces from Southeast Asia. Each strategy, of course, seeks to increase the citizen's attention to those issue positions on which the respective candidate believes he has an advantage.

Ambiguity A third strategic consideration about public policy issues is the degree of certainty or uncertainty the contestant generates about his issue position. Political scientists have long known that the "strategy of ambiquity" is an important attribute of most election campaigns.[18] This strategy serves not only to hold together a coalition of heterogeneous supporters, but also to gain support among those citizens who accept risk in their voting decisions. Hence, contestants might refuse to divulge their exact positions on issues, hoping not to significant numbers of citizens.

Personal Attribute Strategies: The Salience of Personal Attributes A contestant has little or no immediate control over personal attributes like age, race, sex, religion, geographical origin, party identification, and physical appearance. Yet important strategic variation is possible. Though the contestant cannot vary significantly the objective existence of these attributes, citizens often consider them in their voting decisions. The basic strategic possibility here is to vary the salience of a personal attribute.

Some research suggests, for example, that in the 1960 campaign, Senator Kennedy, having lost as many anti-Catholic votes as possible, made an issue of his religion – increased its salience – to mobilize support among Catholic American citizens.[19] Campaign posters afford a second example of this phenomenon as it applies to party identification. We have come to expect in heavily Democratic American constituencies, that the Democratic candidate's signs read, "John

---

[18] See, Kenneth A. Shepsle, "The Strategy of Ambiguity: Uncertainty and Electoral Competition," *American Political Science Review*, 66, 2(June, 1972), pp. 555–568.

[19] Ithiel de Sola Pool, Robert Abelson, and Samuel Popkin, *Candidates, Issues, and Strategies* (Cambridge: MIT Press, 1965).

Smith, DEMOCRAT," while the Republican candidate's signs read, "JOHN SMITH, Republican." Similarly, contestants often take advantage of the coattails of popular figures on the ticket, by emphasizing the equivalent party identification.

Campaign Allocation Strategies

The final class of strategies concern those in which a contestant must allocate a scarce campaign resource. Clearly, contestants and their supporters have real resource constraints. In federal systems, for example, the contestant must decide how much time and money to spend campaigning in each district. Even in unitary systems, the contestant must decide in what areas the election outcome – the sum of individual citizen decisions – is a foregone conclusion, and in what areas he can mobilize support. The candidate must decide, in either case, how much money to spend on billboards, television time, and even on personal transportation. As these are variables whose values affect the election outcome, they are campaign strategies.[20]

Notation for Strategies

We let θ_i be a vector denoting contestant i's strategies. If there are m possible things a candidate can vary in pursuit of an election objective, then,

$$\theta_i = (\theta_{i1}, \theta_{i2}, \ldots, \theta_{im}).$$[21]

Similarly, we define,

$$\theta = (\theta_1, \theta_2, \ldots, \theta_n),$$

as a vector denoting the strategies of all contestants in an election of n contestants.

[20] A discussion of the allocation problem is, Gerald Kramer, "A Decision-Theoretic Analysis of a Problem in Political Campaigning," in Joseph Bernd, ed., *Mathematical Applications in Political Science, II* (Dallas: Southern Methodist University Press, 1966), pp. 137–160. See also John C. Blydenburgh, "A Controlled Experiment to Measure the Effects of Personal Contact Campaigning," *Midwest Journal of Political Science*, 15, 2(May, 1971), pp. 365–381.

[21] θ_{ij}, for example, might be contestant i's position on public school expenditures.

B. Expressions of Votes

We wish to indicate that the electoral success of any given contestant may be a function of the strategies all n contestants adopt. Stated differently, each citizen's decision to vote for one of the contestants or to abstain may be a function of the strategies of all n contestants. Hence, we let $V_i(\theta)$ denote the proportion of citizens that votes for contestant i. Similarly, since the contestant might not know $V_i(\theta)$ with certainty, we let $v_i(\theta)$ denote the expected value of $V_i(\theta)$.

C. Campaign Objectives: Objective Functions

Contestants pursue a diverse set of objectives in their campaigns for elective office. These objectives may be bizarre, Freudian, the result of personal beliefs, or the desire to "educate the electorate." Our analysis, though, concerns only contestant objectives that are some function of vote. This apparent disregard of objectives such as the public display of personal ideology is not as "heroic" as it may seem. Recall that our discussion is about the strategic incentives of certain objectives, which we postulate to be a function of electoral laws, institutions, and competitive environments. It is difficult to imagine how such laws, institutions, and environments might affect a contestant's personal ideological or pedagogical objectives. Clearly, the effects of institutional variations, e.g. proportional representations or single-member district constituencies, are strongest on the objectives that relate to vote distributions, and not on the contestant's personal ideologies. While such things as a satisfaction of personal ideologies are doubtlessly important objectives, they appear unrelated to institutional and legal election qualities: they do not enter into the kinds of objective variations we investigate. Hence, we ignore them.

This reduction to goals as functions of votes, though, does not produce too much simplification. First, even scholars who concentrate on votes as election objectives are remarkably vague and overly general. Many writers lead us to believe that all candidates who maximize votes, plurality, or vote proportion, are pursuing roughly equivalent objectives.[22] We disprove this notion later. Second, and more importantly, what "winning" means in terms of votes may depend largely on electoral law, representations formulae, and post-election coalition processes.[23] Third, even controlling for electoral law might not be tantamount to specifying a particular objective, since information, expectations, and attitudes toward future elections may affect the contestant's choice of campaign objective.

Thus, we must proceed carefully in defining what it is that contestants seek in their campaigns, even if it is only a function of vote, which, in turn, is a function of strategy. To this end, we denote $\phi_i(\theta)$ as contestant i's objective function, postulating thereby that ϕ_i depends on θ, the vector of all n contestants' strategies. We assume, further, that a contestant prefers θ' to θ'' if $\phi_i(\theta') > (\theta'')$. Thus, the contestant acts as if he has an election objective. This goal is a standard for evaluating alternative strategy sets. The function $\phi_i(\theta)$ measures this evaluation.

Table I lists the six objective functions we consider here, in terms

TABLE I

CANDIDATE OBJECTIVE FUNCTIONS

		Interpretation; Maximizing:
0_1	$\phi_i = v_i(\theta) - \max_{j \neq i} \{v_j(\theta)\}$	Expected Plurality
0_2	$\phi_i = v_i(\theta) / \sum_{j=1}^{n} v_j(\theta)$	Proportion of the Expected Vote
0_3	$\phi_i = v_i(\theta)$	Expected Vote
0_4	$\phi_i = Pr[V_i(\theta) - \max_{j \neq i} \{V_j(\theta)\} \geqslant \lambda_i]$	Probability that Plurality Exceeds Some Level
0_5	$\phi_i = Pr[V_i(\theta) / \sum_{j=1}^{n} V_j(\theta) \geqslant \lambda_i]$	Probability that Proportion Exceeds Some Level
0_6	$\phi_i = Pr[V_i(\theta) \geqslant \lambda_i]$	Probability that Vote Exceeds Some Level

[22] See Melvin J. Hinich and Peter C. Ordeshook, "Plurality Maximization vs. Vote Maximization: A Spatial Analysis with Variable Participation," *American Political Science Review*, 64, 3(September, 1970), pp. 772–791. Hinich and Ordeshook cite many examples of this ambiguity.

[23] For a detailing of these possibilities, see Peter H. Aranson, *Political Participation in Alternative Election Systems*, prepared for delivery at the Annual Meeting of the American Political Science Association, Chicago, Illinios, September 7–11, 1971. See also Peter H. Aranson, *A Theory of the Calculus of Voting for Alternative Three-Contestant Election Systems*, Unpublished Ph.D. dissertation, Rochester, N.Y.: The University of Rochester, 1972, chap. iii.

of their formal statements and verbal interpretations. The discussion that follows details briefly the nature and sources of these functions. Section IV includes some dynamic possibilities for postulating these objectives. We postpone a fuller discussion of these objectives to that Section, so that we can present possibilities for equivalences and non-equivalences.

1. Maximizing Expected Plurality, 0_1

The first objective function we consider is 0_1, the maximization of expected plurality. For simple two-candidate, single-member district systems elections, this objective function postulates that the candidate adopts some set of campaign strategies to maximize the difference between his expected vote and his opponent's expected vote, or,

$$\phi_i(\theta) = v_i(\theta) - v_j(\theta).$$

It is not immediately clear, though, what expected plurality maximization means in the context of n-candidate elections, since for any single candidate there are $n-1$ pairwise comparisons from which to denote plurality. To tailor this expression to meet some "first-past-the-post" idea of winning, we postulate for the n-candidate case that the candidate calculates expected plurality in relation to the opponent with the greatest number of votes, or,

$$\phi_i(\theta) = v_i(\theta) - \max_{j \neq i}\{ v_j(\theta)\}$$

($\max_{j \neq 1} \{v_j(\theta)\}$ reads, "the maximum $v_j(\theta)$, j not equal to i.") Of course, if there are only two candidates, then this expression reduces to the previous one.

2. Maximizing Proportion of the Expected Vote, 0_2

While it seems intuitively obvious to postulate 0_1, the maximization of expected plurality, for candidates in single-member district systems, it is not immediately apparent what kind of objective function to postulate for party strategists in proportional representation systems, We can insure with the appropriate set of post-election coalition formation rules, for example, that the party with the greatest number of votes cast will not be in the cabinet.[24] This possibility illustrates the difficulty of defining "winning" for proportional representation systems.

This difficulty aside, we postulate 0_2, the maximization of proportion of the expected vote, as a possible objective function for party strategists in proportional representation systems. Thus,

$$\phi_i(\theta) = v_i(\theta)/\sum_{j=1}^{n} v_j(\theta)$$

As we show later, moreover, 0_2, also may be an appropriate goal for candidates in some plurality elections.

3. Maximizing Expected Vote, 0_3

Previous spatial theories of election competition frequently use 0_3, maximizing expected vote, as an alternative to 0_1 and 0_2. The probable cause of this usage is Downs's political translation of the earlier economic studies of Smithies and Hotelling.[25] Firms might maximize profit, not caring to compare their profits with those of their competitors. Unfortunately, Downs's translation is incomplete, as he continues with vote maximization, rather than a more politically oriented plurality maximization. Nevertheless, we can imagine some circumstances, e.g. of limited information, in which candidates might maximize expected votes, or,

$$\phi_i(\theta) = v_i(\theta).$$

Thus, we include 0_3 in our analysis as a possible objective function.

4. Maximizing the Probability that Plurality Exceeds Some Level, 0_4

The functional form of 0_4 is,

---

[24] E.g. if $n = 3$, $V_1(\theta) \neq V_2(\theta) \neq V_3(\theta)$, and only minimum winning coalitions form, then the largest party (max $\{V_i(\theta)\}$) can be automatically excluded from the cabinet. For this coalition formation rule see William H. Riker, *The Theory of Political Coalitions* (New Haven: Yale University Press, 1962).

[25] That is, the firm might maximize profits without regard to the profits of its competitors, or its "share of the market." Such objectives in politics create defeat in many plurality system elections. See Hinich and Ordeshook, *loc.cit.*

$$\phi_i = Pr\,[V_i(\theta) - \max_{j \neq i}\{V_j(\theta)\} \geqslant \lambda_i]$$

(*Pr* reads, "the probability that.") A useful illustration of 0_4 is as follows. Assume a two-candidate election in which $\lambda_i = 0$. 0_4 then reduces to,

$$\phi_i = Pr\,[V_i(\theta) \geqslant V_j(\theta)],$$

which, in a plurality election, is the probability that candidate *i* does no worse than tie his opponent. If ties are not likely (e.g. if there are many voters), then the expression represents the probability that candidate *i* wins the election. If $\lambda_i = 0$, but there are more than two candidates, then 0_4 is the probability that no opponent receives more expected votes than candidate *i*. Thus, if $\lambda_i = 0$, 0_4 is the formal statement of the assumption that the candidate adopts election strategies to maximize his probability of winning in single-member district elections.

Our analysis generalizes the level of λ_i, though, so that we can ascertain the effects of expected plurality or other quotas on candidate strategies. These quotas might be a function of expectations of future elections, or even quotas that superiors set in a party hierarchy.

5. Maximizing the Probability that Proportion of the Vote Exceeds Some Level, 0_5

The formal statement of 0_5 is,

$$\phi_i(\theta) = Pr[V_i(\theta)/\sum_{j=1}^{n} V_j(\theta) \geqslant \lambda_i].$$

There is an analogy, of course, between 0_1 and 0_4 for single-member district systems, and 0_2 and 0_5 for proportional representation systems. Thus, 0_2, maximizing proportion of the expected vote, and 0_5, maximizing the probability that proportion of the vote exceeds some level, might represent alternative proportional representation system election goals. As we suggest later, 0_5 might also represent a candidate's primary election objective, should a minimum probability insure his viability over a series of sequential (e.g. presidential) primary contests.

6. Maximizing the Probability that Vote Exceeds Some Level, 0_6

As with 0_4 and 0_5, 0_6, maximizing the probability that vote exceeds some level, is an alternative objective to 0_3, maximizing expected vote. As with 0_4 and 0_5, so with 0_6: we do not constrain λ_i to any given level. Formally, 0_6 is,

$$\phi_i(\theta) = Pr\,[V_i(\theta) \geqslant \lambda_i].$$

Similarly, 0_6 also may find its origin in quotas or expectations for future elections.

D. Equilibrium

The previous discussion of strategies, votes, and objectives, postulates that a contestant's payoff, $\phi_i(\theta)$, depends not only on his strategy, θ_i, but also on his opponents' strategies. Hence, it is useful to conceptualize the election contest as an *n*-person game, which we assume to be non-cooperative.[26] Following this conceptualization, we define $\theta^* = (\theta_1^*, \theta_2^*, \ldots \theta_n^*)$ as an equilibrium strategy set with respect to the set of objectives $(\phi_1, \phi_2, \ldots, \phi_n)$, if

$$\phi_i(\theta^*) \geqslant \phi_i(\theta_1^*, \theta_2^*, \ldots, \theta_i, \ldots, \theta_n^*),$$

for all i and $\theta_i \neq \theta_i^*$.

This notion asserts that θ^* is an equilibrium strategy set if no contestant has an incentive to alter his strategy unilaterally once all n contestants arrive at their respective equilibrium strategies.

There are two important observations about this definition of equilibrium. First, the subsequent analysis does not require that all n contestants arrive at their respective equilibrium strategies, but only that they are capable of doing so. That is, in terms of most payoffs in competitive election situations, the worst that can happen to a contestant is that his opponents arrive at their respective equilibrium strategies. Hence, he should be prudent enough to expect that they

[26] Non-cooperative games, formally, are games without communication among the players. See R. Duncan Luce and Howard Raiffa, *Games and Decisions: Introduction and Critical Survey* (New York: John Wiley and Sons, Inc., 1957), p. 89. We need not rely on this stipulation. The sense of "non-cooperative" we use here requires only that election coalitions are impossible, or that such coalitions represent a single party.

will do so, and to adopt his own equilibrium strategy accordingly.[27]

Second, since some of these strategies involve public policy, we can restate the definition of equilibrium with a limited game theoretic example, showing the correspondence between the spatial and gaming conceptualizations, as they apply to public policy. Spatial analysis ascertains the existence and location of θ^*.[28] Typically, spatial theories of election competition ask if two expected plurality maximizing candidates converge to the electorate's median preference on matters of public policy. In game theoretic terms, we ask if $n = 2$, and if ϕ_i denotes candidate i's expected plurality, $i = 1,2$, then does a unique equilibrium strategy pair (θ_1^*, θ_2^*) exist, such that $\theta_1^* = \theta_2^*$ = the median preference? In this sense, convergent strategies would imply identical public policy advocacy.

E. Equivalent Objective Functions

The definition of equivalent objective functions follows the sense of equilibrium:

> ϕ' and ϕ'' are equivalent objective functions for contestant i if, given his opponents' objective functions, θ^* is an equilibrium strategy set for $\phi_i' \Leftrightarrow \theta^*$ is an equilibrium strategy set for ϕ_i''.[29]

---

[27] Stated differently, the contestant acts as if he expects his opponents to adopt their equilibrium strategies, hence, his response is a minimax-like consideration.

[28] For the correspondence between spatial analysis and the theory of games, see: James L. Barr and Otto A. Davis, "An Elementary Political and Economic Theory of the Expenditures of Local Governments, *The Southern Economic Journal*, 33 (October, 1966), pp. 149–165; Martin Shubik, "A Two-Party System, General Equilibrium, and the Voters' Paradox," *Zeitschrift fur Nationalökonomie*, 38 (1968), pp. 341–354; Melvin J. Hinich, John O. Ledyard, and Peter C. Ordeshook, "A Theory of Electoral Equilibrium: A Spatial Analysis Based on the Theory of Games," *The Journal of Politics*, forthcoming; Peter C. Ordeshook, "Pareto Optimality and Election Competition," *American Political Science Review*, 65, 4 (December, 1971), pp. 1141–1145; John M. Kessel, "A Game Theoretic Analysis of Campaign Strategies," in M. Kent Jennings and L. Harmon Zeigler, eds., *The Electoral Process* (Englewood Cliffs, New Jersey: Prentice Hall, 1966), pp. 290–304.

[29] We can usefully restate the definition of equivalence thus: if θ^* satisfies the definition of an equilibrium strategy set for all contestants $j \neq i$ (*i.e.*, $\phi_j(\theta^*) \geqslant \phi_j(\theta_j^*, \ldots, \theta_j, \ldots, \theta_i^*, \ldots, \theta_n^*)$) then ϕ' and ϕ'' are equivalent for contestant i if and only if $\phi_i(\theta^*)_1 \geqslant \phi_i(\theta_1^*, \ldots, \theta_i, \ldots, \theta_n^*) \Leftrightarrow \phi_i''(\theta^*) \geqslant \phi_i''(\theta_1^*, \ldots, \theta_i, \ldots, \theta_n^*)$ for all such θ^*.

Two objective functions are equivalent, then, if a candidate can substitute one for the other with no incentive to disrupt the electoral equilibrium being generated. If, for example, two elections are identical except that in one a candidate maximizes expected plurality, while in the other he maximizes his probability of winning, then the equilibrium strategy sets are identical if the two objectives satisfy the definition of equivalence just stated.[30]

F. Symmetric Elections

We denote an election as symmetric with respect to $(\phi_1, \phi_2, \ldots, \phi_n)$ if, for all i and j, $v_i(\theta^*) = v_j(\theta^*)$, such that θ^* is an equilibrium set under $(\phi_1, \phi_2, \ldots, \phi_n)$, and, with respect to contestant i, $v_j(\theta_1^*, \ldots, \theta_i, \ldots, \theta_n^*) = v_k(\theta_1^*, \ldots, \theta_i, \ldots, \theta_n^*)$, for all j and $k \neq i$.

These two conditions insure, first, that at equilibrium all candidates receive the same number of expected votes, and second, that if contestant i moves from his equilibrium strategy, he affects all of his opponents equally. Illustrating this definition, a two-candidate election is symmetric if: (1) both candidates employ the same objective function; (2) the candidates choose from identical strategy sets (e.g. we do not restrict one candidate to "liberal" positions and his opponent to "conservative" positions); and (3) citizens are not predisposed to vote for one candidate or the other: all voting corresponds strictly to the candidates' strategy sets.

---

[30] A simple lemma illustrates further the notion of equivalence. Lemma: if ϕ' and ϕ'' are equivalent for contestant i and for contestant k and if θ^* is an equilibrium for any of

$$(\phi_1, \ldots, \phi_i', \ldots, \phi_k', \ldots, \phi_n),$$
$$(\phi_1, \ldots, \phi_i'', \ldots, \phi_k', \ldots, \phi_n),$$
$$(\phi_1, \ldots, \phi_i', \ldots, \phi_k'', \ldots, \phi_n),$$
$$(\phi_1, \ldots, \phi_i'', \ldots, \phi_k'', \ldots, \phi_n),$$

then θ^* is an equilibrium for all four. Suppose, for example that ϕ' is maximizing expected plurality, while ϕ'' is maximizing probability of winning (i.e. 0_1 and 0_4). Suppose, also, that $\theta^* = (\theta_1^*, \theta_2^*)$ is an equilibrium for two contestants who maximize their respective probabilities of winning. To demonstrate that θ^* is also an equilibrium if the two contestant maximize their respective expected pluralities, or if one contestant maximizes expected plurality while the other maximizes the probability of winning, it is sufficient to show that maximizing expected plurality and probability of winning satisfy the definition of equivalence for each contestant.

We can offer three examples of non-symmetric elections. First, if the electorate's preference are distributed bimodally, if there are three candidates, and if an equilibrium strategy set entails a candidate at each mode and a candidate at the median, then the election is not symmetric for two reasons: (1) the candidate at the median generally does not receive the same number of votes as the other two candidates; (2) if the candidate at the median departs from his equilibrium strategy, and moves his policy position toward one or the other modal candidates, then, generally, he affects the two modal candidates' expected votes differently. Second, if an electorate is biased in favor of a candidate, so that even in equilibrium his opponents are likely to lose, then the election is not symmetric because $\nu_i(\theta^*) \neq \nu_j(\theta^*)$. Third, even if the candidates have no strategic constraints and the electorate has no non-strategic biases, if $n-1$ candidates maximize their proportion of the expected vote, and the nth candidate maximizes his expected vote, then the election is not symmetric if there is no reason to suppose that all candidates receive the same expected vote in equilibrium.

It is fairly obvious that it is simpler to guarantee symmetry for two-contestant elections than for n-contestant elections. All we need guarantee in two-contestant elections is that no electorate biases exist and that the contestants have no strategic constraints and adopt identical objectives. We must guarantee in n-contestant elections some configuration of preferences such that any movement from an equilibrium by one contestant will affect all candidates equally. We can insure this, of course, if equilibrium entails strategic convergence, but other examples are *ad hoc* in the extreme.

G. Assumptions and Conditions

The reader should interpret the preceding definitions and conditions with care. In earlier formal theories of political processes, the purpose of assumptions is to ease the deduction of parsimonious statements about several varieties of political decisions. But, the central concepts and definitions we offer are not assumptions about election competition or about the conditions under which it occurs. Indeed, many of our results do not employ them. Certain objective function equivalences hold, though, if we assume that elections are symmetric. Hence, these results not only reveal some conditions for which certain election goals are equivalent; they also suggest a set of equally important conditions for which these goals are not generally equivalent.

III. Equivalence and Non-equivalence

We offer here five theorems that give sufficient conditions for certain equivalences among the six objective functions we listed earlier. Our procedure is to state each theorem, and to follow the statement with a discussion to interpret and to illustrate the results.

A. Theorem One

Statement of Theorem One

Let $\theta^* = (\theta_1, \theta_2, \ldots, \theta_i' \ldots, \theta_n)$ *and* $\theta'' =$
$(\theta_1, \theta_2, \ldots, \theta_i'' \ldots, \theta_n)$; *if for all* $j \neq i$, *and*
for all θ,
(*a*) $v_i(\theta') < v_i(\theta'') \Rightarrow v_j(\theta') \geqslant v_j(\theta'')$,
(*b*) $v_i(\theta') = v_i(\theta'') \Longleftrightarrow v_j(\theta') = v_j(\theta'')$,
(*c*) $v_i(\theta') > v_i(\theta'') \Leftarrow v_j(\theta') < v_j(\theta'')$,
then 0_1, 0_2, *and* 0_3 *are equivalent for candidate i.*

Discussion of Theorem One

The thrust of Theorem One is that if an election is zero-sum-like in expected vote, then maximizing expected plurality, proportion of the expected vote, or expected vote, are equivalent objective functions, which is to say that if a contestant substitutes one of these three for another, then he has no incentive to change his strategy and, therefore, he creates no incentive for his opponents to change their strategies. We can state these conditions in relation to the three conditions of the theorem: (a) if candidate i changes his strategy from θ_i' to θ_i'', intending thereby to increase his expected vote, then his opponent's(') expected vote(s) must either decrease or remain unchanged; (b) if he changes his strategy from θ_i' to θ_i'', and his expected vote remains unchanged, then his opponent's(') expected vote(s) also must remain unchanged; (c) if he adopts a strategy to increase his opponent's(') expected vote(s), then his expected vote must decrease. The election game is highly competitive, much like the zero-sum game that it would be were the possible equality of condition (a) removed, and the payoffs stated exactly in expected vote.

Examples of Theorem One

Consider two examples for which Theorem One holds. First, assume a simple two-candidate, plurality system election with constant turnout: $v_i(\theta) + v_j(\theta) = c$. This election meets all three conditions of Theorem One: (a) if $v_i(\theta)$ increases, then $v_j(\theta)$ must decrease (b) if a change in θ_i produces no change in $v_i(\theta)$, then no change of $v_j(\theta)$ occurs; (c) if candidate i adopts a strategy that increases $v_j(\theta)$, then $v_i(\theta)$ must decrease. The logic of the example is sufficiently clear to demonstrate equivalence among 0_1, 0_2, and 0_3. If candidate i adopts an expected vote maximizing strategy, then necessarily his additional votes are at candidate j's expense, hence such a strategy also maximizes expected plurality, 0_1, and proportion of the expected vote, 0_2.

Second, assume an election like the previous one, except that turnout is a variable (sensitive to strategic variation), and $v_j(\theta)$ is insensitive to variations in θ_i: one candidate's strategy cannot affect the other's expected vote. This election meets two conditions of Theorem One: (a) if $v_i(\theta)$ increases, then $v_j(\theta)$ remains the same; (b) if a change in candidate i's strategy does not change $v_i(\theta)$, then obviously it does not change $v_j(\theta)$; condition (c) is irrelevant, as the implication is unnecessary for this example. Similarly, the logic of the example is clear. If candidate i adopts a strategy to maximize his expected plurality, 0_1, it must be a vote maximizing strategy, 0_3, since $v_j(\theta)$ remains invariant. Similarly candidate i maximizes proportion of the expected vote, 0_2, with 0_3 (assuming $v_j(\theta) > 0$).

To clarify further the three conditions of Theorem One, we offer two elections as illustrations that fail to satisfy the three conditions, and for which equivalence does not hold. These examples have the additional importance of refuting the intuitive belief that, at least for two-candidate elections, 0_1, maximizing expected plurality, and 0_2, maximizing proportion of the expected vote, are always equivalent.

Assume, for the first example, that one candidate's expected vote is a constant proportion of the other candidate's expected vote.

Hence, let,

$$v_j(\theta) = cv_i(\theta),\ c \geqslant 0.$$

This example violates conditions (a) and (c) of Theorem One: (a) if $c > 0$, an increase in $v_i(\theta)$ increases (rather than decreases) $v_j(\theta)$; (c) if $c \geqslant 0$, a decrease in $v_j(\theta)$ at best leaves $v_i(\theta)$ unchanged (rather than increasing it).

To show non-equivalence formally, observe that candidate i's expected vote is simply $v_i(\theta)$; his expected plurality is,

$$v_i(\theta) - v_j(\theta) = (1 - c)v_i(\theta);$$

his proportion of the expected vote is,

$$v_i(\theta)/[v_i(\theta) + v_j(\theta)] = v_i(\theta)/[v_i(\theta) + cv_i(\theta)] = 1/[1 + c].$$

Clearly, proportion of the expected vote is constant for all θ, but expected vote and expected plurality are not constant for all θ (except for the degenerate case in which $v_i(\theta)$ is constant for all θ and $c = 1$). Thus, the candidate is indifferent among all θ for 0_2; he is not indifferent among all θ for 0_1 and 0_3.

The implication of this result is that all θ can be equilibria for 0_2, but not for 0_1 and 0_3. Indeed, if the set of all strategies is compact and convex, and if $v_i(\theta)$ is a concave-convex function of θ_i and θ_j respectively, then a unique equilibrium exists for 0_1 and 0_3. Thus equilibria exist for 0_2 that are not equilibria for 0_1 and 0_3, which is to say that 0_2 is equivalent neither to 0_1 nor to 0_3.[31]

Comparing 0_1 and 0_3, if $c = 1$, expected plurality is a constant but expected vote is not. Thus, 0_1 and 0_3 are not equivalent. If $c > 1$, an increase in $v_i(\theta)$ decrease candidate i's expected plurality $(1 - c < 0)$, hence candidate i's expected plurality becomes more negative as $v_i(\theta)$, his expected vote, increases. Again, therefore, 0_1 and 0_3 are not equivalent.[32]

---

[31] See Hinich, Ledyard, and Ordeshook, *loc.cit.*

[32] If $c < 1$, candidate i's plurality is a monotonically increasing function of $v_i(\theta)$ and candidate j's plurality is a monotonically decreasing function of $v_j(\theta)$. This example is interesting because if 0_1 and 0_3 are equivalent for candidate i, then they cannot be equivalent for candidate j, and vice versa.

Assume, for the second example, that expected plurality is a constant. Hence, let,

$$v_i(\theta) - v_j(\theta) = -c, \ c > 0.$$

This example violates conditions (a) and (c) of Theorem One: (a) since $v_i(\theta) = v_j(\theta) - c$, an increase in $v_i(\theta)$ increases (rather than decreases or leaves unchanged) $v_j(\theta)$; (c) a decrease in $v_i(\theta)$ decreases (rather than increases) $v_j(\theta)$.

Candidate i's proportion of the expected vote is,

$$v_i(\theta)/[v_i(\theta) + v_j(\theta)] = v_i(\theta)/[2v_i(\theta) + c],$$

which is monotonically increasing with $v_i(\theta)$. Observe, now, that 0_1, expected plurality, is constant for all θ, but 0_2, proportion of the expected vote, and 0_3, expected vote, are not constant for all θ (except for the degenerate case of $v_i(\theta)$ constant for all θ). Thus, paralleling the previous example, all strategies can be equilibria for 0_1, but not for 0_2 or 0_3. 0_1, then, is equivalent neither to 0_2 nor to 0_3.[33]

B. Theorem Two

Statement of Theorem Two

If an election is symmetric with respect to contestant i, then 0_1 and 0_2 are equivalent for contestant i.

Discussion and Examples of Theorem Two

To illustrate the implications of Theorem Two, consider two examples for which it holds. First, suppose that an electorate's preferences are distributed symmetrically and unimodally, and that two candidates vie with neither electorate biases nor spatial constraints. We know that for such conditions, plurality maximizing candidates converge to the electorate's median preference. Since this election

[33] Observe, though, that 0_2 and 0_3 can be equivalent. This emphasizes that Theorem One presents a sufficient condition for equivalence, and not a necessary one.

conforms to one of our examples of symmetry, it follows from the lemma in note 30 and from Theorem Two that two candidates who maximize their proportion of the expected vote converge also to the median preference. Similarly, if two plurality maximizing candidates fail to converge because preferences are distributed bimodally, then two candidates who maximize their respective proportions of the expected vote fail to converge also.

Second, suppose that an election is symmetric, that more than two candidates vie, and that if each candidate maximizes his proportion of the expected vote, all candidates converge to the median policy preference; then plurality maximizing candidates converge to the median (i.e. the election is strongly symmetric, since if one candidate moves off the median he affects all other candidates equally).

To show that 0_1 and 0_2 are not equivalent universally, we offer a two-candidate illustration that demonstrates the logic of the symmetry condition. Suppose that $v_i(\theta)$ and $v_j(\theta)$ are continuously differentiable in θ. Thus, $\theta^* = (\theta_1^*, \theta_2^*)$ is an equilibrium strategy pair for 0_1, expected plurality maximization, only if

$$\frac{\partial}{\partial\theta_i}[v_i(\theta) - v_j(\theta)] = \frac{\partial v_i(\theta)}{\partial\theta_i} - \frac{\partial v_j(\theta)}{\partial\theta_i} = 0, \qquad (1)$$

for $\theta = \theta^*$. Similarly, θ^* is an equilibrium strategy pair for 0_2, maximizing proportion of the expected vote, only if,

$$\frac{\partial}{\partial\theta_i}\left[\frac{v_i(\theta)}{v_j(\theta) + v_j(\theta)}\right] = v_j(\theta)\frac{\partial v_i(\theta)}{\partial\theta_i} - v_i(\theta)\frac{\partial v_j(\theta)}{\partial\theta_i} = 0; \qquad (2)$$

for $\theta = \theta^*$. Suppose that θ^* satisfies (1) but that the election is not symmetric, i.e., $v_i(\theta^*) \neq v_j(\theta^*)$. Clearly, (2) cannot be satisfied. A strategy pair that satisfies (1), consequently, cannot satisfy (2), and vice-versa. Hence $0_1 \not\Leftrightarrow 0_2$.

To illustrate further the implications of Theorem Two, recall the two examples we offer earlier, which violate the conditions of Theorem One, and which do not yield equivalence among 0_1, 0_2, and 0_3. Since Theorem Two presents a sufficient condition for equivalence, it must be the case that these examples fail to satisfy the symmetry condition also.

First, with respect to the example for which $v_j(\theta) = cv_i(\theta)$, $c \geqslant 0$, $v_i(\theta^*) \neq v_j(\theta^*)$ (except for the degenerate cases of $v_i(\theta^*) = 0$, $c = 0$, *or* $c = 1$). Hence, the election is not symmetric. (If $c = 1$, of course,

0_1 and 0_2 are equivalent since expected plurality and proportion of the expected vote are both constant for all θ.)

Second, with respect to the example for which $v_i(\theta) - v_j(\theta) = -c$, $c > 0$, since $v_j(\theta) = v_i(\theta) + c$, *if* $c \neq 0$, $v_j(\theta^*) \neq v_i(\theta^*)$. Hence, again the election is not symmetric.

C. Theorems Three, Four, and Five

Theorems Three, Four, and Five require an additional condition which we do not include previously in Section II. Specifically, these theorems concern equivalences between the ordinary maximization objectives (expected plurality, proportion of the expected vote, and expected vote) and the corresponding objectives of the probability that these measures exceed some level. An analysis of these probabilistic objective functions requires that we can specify the relationship between θ and the respective probabilities. This implies that we know the characteristics of the contestant's error in ascertaining the function $V_i(\theta)$. Suppose, then, that the contestant estimates $V_i(\theta)$ in accordance with the usual stochastic assumptions of linear models. That is, let $V_i(\theta) = v_i(\theta) + \epsilon_i$, $i = 1,2, \ldots ,n$, and,

Condition C: $E(\epsilon_i) = 0$ and ϵ_i is distributed independently of θ.

Thus, for example, condition C requires that the variance of ϵ_i does not depend on $v_i(\theta)$. We can now state Theorems Three, Four, and Five, as well as a Corollary to Theorem Three.

Statement of Theorems Three, Four, and Five

Theorem Three: If C holds, maximizing expected plurality and maximizing the probability that plurality exceeds some level, λ_i, are equivalent for contestant i.

Corollary to Theorem Three: If C holds, maximizing expected plurality and maximizing the probability of winning in a plurality system are equivalent for contestant i.

Theorem Four: If C holds, maximizing proportion of the expected vote and maximizing the probability that proportion of the vote exceeds some level λ_i, are equivalent for contestant i.[34]

[34] The correspondence between 0_2 and 0_5 in Theorem Four requires a slight restatement of our stochastic model, namely, that the candidate estimates proportion of the vote directly rather than that he computes proportion from estimates of each $v_i(\theta)$.

Theorem Five: If condition C holds, then maximizing expected vote and maximizing the probability that vote exceeds some level, λ_i, are equivalent for contestant i.

Discussion of Theorems Three, Four, Five, and the Corollary

Maximizing expected plurality 0_1, and maximizing the probability that plurality exceeds some level, 0_4, as well as the special case of maximizing the probability of winning in plurality system elections, appear to be intuitive and distinct election objectives. If condition C holds, however, by Theorem Three and its Corollary they are equivalent.

Similarly, Theorem Three, its Corollary, and Theorems Four and Five impose no conditions on the context of election competition. Unlike the equivalences among 0_1, 0_2, and 0_3, which Theorem One identifies, there is no zero-sum-like condition. Unlike the equivalence between 0_1 and 0_2, which Theorem Two identifies, there is no symmetry condition. Theorems Three, Four, and Five, as well as the Corollary to Theorem Three, depend only on the properties of the contestant's forecast error.

Additional Corollaries

We can deduce several additional corollaries from the equivalences that the five theorems identify. Suppose, for example, that an election is symmetric. Hence, 0_1, maximizing expected plurality, and 0_2, maximizing proportion of the expected vote, are equivalent. Suppose, further, that condition C holds. Hence O_2 and O_5, maximizing the probability that proportions exceeds some level, are equivalent. Therefore we assert that for this election, O_1 and O_5 are equivalent. Rather than state these corollaries formally, we summarize them in Table II.

TABLE II

SUMMARY OF THE CONDITIONS UNDER WHICH CANDIDATE OBJECTIVE FUNCTIONS ARE EQUIVALENT

Objective Function

	0_1	0_2	0_3	0_4	0_5	0_6
0_1	–	1 or 2	1	3	3, 1 or 2	3, 1
0_2		–	1	3, 1 or 2	3	3, 1
0_3			–	1, 3	1, 3	3
0_4				–	3, 1 or 2	3, 1
0_5					–	3, 1
0_6						–

Key: 1: Conditions of Theorem One
2: Symmetry
3: Condition C.

IV. Implications of the Theorems for the Construction of Election Laws, Institutions, and Procedures

We limit ourselves in the introduction of this study to a discussion of conditional ought statements. In the context of election systems and their effects on public policy decisions, this limitation implies that if we are *given* a policy goal, we can state with some confidence what election laws or procedures we ought to adopt to achieve that goal. First, though, we must find the relationship between election institutions and campaign objectives. Second, we must find a relationship between campaign objectives and campaign strategies, gainsay a relationship between campaign strategies and legislative performance as measured by the given public policy goal.

Since the previous discussion begins only by postulation to connect institutions with objectives, and election objectives with election strategies, we leave the other relationships undefined. But if we show equivalence between two election objectives, then we must account for systematic legislative public policy differences, or even elected executive policy differences, by reference to other than differences in election procedures.

We direct our inquiry into the implications of our analysis to three areas. First, we consider proposals to modify the plurality (single-member district) system with primaries and caucuses, as it now operates in the United States. Second, we consider proposals to modify the proportional representation system as it now operates in some developing nations and Western European democracies. Third, we consider proposals to adopt a proportional representation system in present plurality systems, and a plurality system in present proportional representation systems. In each instance, we postulate differences in objective functions within and between each system, and discuss the imperatives of election strategies in terms of public policy.

A. Objective Function Variations in Plurality Systems

We assert previously, and somewhat casually, that maximizing expected plurality, O_1, is a reasonable and intuitively plausible objective for plurality system election candidates. Yet, we can imagine a diverse set of circumstances in plurality systems for which this objective may not be proper. Some of these circumstances relate to information, some to sequential contests, and some to quotas.

1. Variations in Objectives with Variations of Information

We begin with the observations, pedestrian though they are, that information is not free, and that at various times and in various circumstances, no two candidates have equivalent levels of information. In the context of election campaigns, this information might include a candidate's expected vote, his opponents' expected votes, and the contestants' respective strategy sets. It is patent that information can affect a candidate's objective function: if you do not know how well your opponent is doing, you cannot very well maximize expected plurality. These information inequalities aside, it is possible to imagine three very broad categories of information levels for which we can postulate corresponding campaign objective functions.[35]

[35] For discussious of campaign information for candidates, see John W. Kingdon, *Candidates for Office: Beliefs and Strategies* (New York: Random House, 1968), pp. 90–93. See also a series of articles on the use of campaign polls in, *Public Opinion Quarterly*, 27 (1963).

Low level campaigns. Some campaigns are not sufficiently important to receive the attention of professional polling organizations, like Gallup and Harris, and are for offices whose payoffs to the winners are not great enough to warrant the candidate conducting his own poll. Such candidates have some information, though: they can estimate how well they are doing by the number of people that recognize them, the level of campaign contributions they receive, and the number of people who turn out to hear them speak. It is reasonable to postulate for these candidates 0_3, maximizing expected vote, as a campaign objective function.

Intermediate level campaigns. At some point in the hierarchy of public offices, it becomes important enough for newspapers to poll the constituency on its voting intentions. This occurs usually at the mayorality level, though it may depend upon the degree of urbanization, as well as the constituency size. But, newspapers report the result of their polls in proportion of the expected vote for each candidate. Hence, 0_2, maximizing proportion of the expected vote, is a reasonable goal to postulate in these circumstances.

"Important" campaigns. Eventually, the significance of the contested office and the value of that office to the candidate will evoke a desire for sophisticated private polls on turnout, both for the candidate and his opponents. This kind of contest is likely to be fought over plurality. Hence, we postulate 0_1, maximizing expected plurality, as a reasonable campaign objective for battles over national presidencies.

2. Variations in Objectives for Sequential Contests

Variations of information do not exhaust the possible environmental descriptions for candidates in plurality systems. We can also imagine situations in which candidates must face at least three stages of campaigning, corresponding to three different sequential election problems.

Pre-primary campaign phase. Before the candidate announces his availability for nomination, he probably spends some time, overtly or otherwise, gaining initial support. This support takes the form of campaign contributions, promises of endorsements, and promises of support in particular districts. It is reasonable to suspect that in this situation the candidate adopts strategies to maximize expected votes, which is to say that he adopts 0_3.

Primary campaign phase. As the candidate enters the primaries, the major press reports are not in raw vote or plurality, but in vote proportion. Similarly, as there are large numbers of candidates in these primaries, plurality is relatively meaningless, and those who look for a viable candidate look for trends in vote proportion. To these considerations we add a third: the Democratic Party in the United States has indicated its desire to elect convention delegates by proportional representation. Hence, 0_2, maximizing proportion of the expected vote, is a reasonable objective to postulate for the primary campaign phase of the contest.

General election phase. As each party completes its nomination phase, we are left with a general election operating in a winner-take-all plurality system. At this point, 0_1, maximizing expected plurality, becomes a reasonable campaign objective, and we can expect the candidates to adopt strategies to this end.

3. Variations in Quotas

Even in plurality system elections, the oft referred to "fifty-percent-plus-one" rule does not always pertain, especially if the campaign decision-maker is not directly responsible for the election results, or if the immediate election results serve only to portend trends for the future. Often, campaign decision-makers set quotas for themselves or for others. That is, they seek to maximize the probability that a given function of votes exceeds some level. Here are three examples.

Future election orientations. Suppose a Republican mayorality candidate campaigns in a Democratic city with absolutely no chance of winning. But, his motivation is to receive the Republican nomination for governor at the next primary. If state-wide elections are closely contested, his party will want a candidate who can get votes from Democrats. Hence, he might campaign to "do better" than any previous Republican mayorality candidate. Finally, suppose that the smallest Democratic plurality in the mayorality contest is 50,000 votes of an electorate of 1,000,000. Thus, the Republican candidate might seek to maximize,

$$\phi_i(\theta) = Pr[V_i(\theta) - V_j(\theta) \geqslant \frac{50,000}{1,000,000}].$$

which is a variant of O_4, maximizing the probability that plurality exceeds some level, λ_i.

Primary election quotas. Primary election candidates infrequently win all of their contests, especially if they take on opponents in the latters' home territories, or areas of traditional strength. In these situations, they set quotas for themselves and often publicize them widely, e.g., "If I get 35% of the vote in New Hampshire, my campaign will continue to the White House." Candidates who take such quotas seriously, in effect, adopt strategies to maximize the probability that proportion of the vote exceeds some level, O_5.

External quotas. Sometimes, campaign leaders and strategists receive quotas from the candidates that demand particular kinds of allocation strategies, unlike the public policy strategies the previous examples imply. (Of course, policy strategies may also be important.) These kinds of quotas might take the form of statements like a governor telling a precinct captain, "You must do your part: we have to come out of New York City with one and a half million votes if the Senator is to be reelected." This example postulates as a campaign objective, O_6, maximizing the probability that vote exceeds some level.

B. Implications for Reform Proposals in Plurality Systems

1. Proposal One: Allocate Convention Delegates by Proportional Representation

The Democratic party in the United States has adopted the procedure of allocating its convention delegates to the National Convention by proportional representation. Given that the general election is by plurality (with the electoral college modification), it is reasonable to ask if this nomination has policy consequences for the Democratic candidate and, if he is successful, for the Democratic

President-elect.[36] Comparing the possible objective functions, we can imagine that the nomination candidate might adopt 0_2, maximizing proportion of the expected vote in the primary phase of the campaign, and 0_1, maximizing expected plurality, in the general election phase of the campaign. Recall that by Theorems One and Two, if the election is either zero-sum-like or symmetric, then the strategic imperatives of the objective functions create no strategic differences. That is, the candidate maintains consistent policy positions between the primary and general elections. Similarly, if the conditions of Theorems One and Two hold, then the change from plurality to proportional representation primaries should, in itself, have no policy consequences.

If the conditions of neither Theorem One nor Theorem Two hold, however, then the strategic imperatives of the two situations might be different. That is, the Democratic candidate might espouse one set of public policies in the primaries and quite another set of public policies in the general election.[37] Similarly, we should expect Democratic Presidential nomination aspirants to espouse public policy that differs from that of the plurality system primary days.

An additional complication could occur. It is possible that as the primaries progress, a nomination candidate might begin to calculate "how many delegates" he needs in the following primaries to insure himself the nomination. This raises the possibility that in the earlier primaries the candidate adopts strategies – public policy positions – to maximize proportion of the expected vote, 0_2, while in the later primaries he adopts strategies to maximize the probability that vote proportion exceeds some level, O_5. If the conditions of condition C, the nature of the candidate's forecast error, do not hold, then the difference in objective functions could result in different strategies, which is to say that the would-be nominee might alter the public policy he espouses.

In any case, the proponents of proportional representation allot-

[36] We refer here, of course, not to the alleged "quota" system of ethnically balanced delegations, but to the idea that if a candidate receives 10% of the vote in a primary he should receive 10% S, of the state's convention delegates.

[37] We have reason to believe that 0_1 and 0_2 will not be equivalent for the general and primary election precisely because a party identification bias is present in the former, though it is not present in the latter. Thus, at least by Theorem Two, 0_1 and 0_2 cannot be equivalent.

ments of convention delegates can claim no policy implications for this reform, which are independent of the candidates' competitive environments, information, and stage of the campaign. Indeed, they are in the unenviable position that if the conditions of the respective theorems hold, their reforms create no policy differences. If the conditions of the theorems do not hold, then their reforms may create strategic incentives for their candidates to be inconsistent at best, and liars at worst.

2. Proposal Two: Eliminate the Electoral College

We need not document the vast literature advocating the elimination or alteration of the Electoral College in American Presidential Elections. Similarly, we cannot list all of the alleged effects of this electoral institution. We can speak, though, to one of these alleged effects. The Electoral College seems to generate a differentiated appeal by Presidential candidates to those states whose electoral votes appear to be pivotal in the contest. That is, the candidate identifies those states in his column, those states in his opponent's column, and those states in which the election outcome is in doubt.[38] Since winning by one vote is as good as winning by 1,000,000 votes, we postulate that the candidate goes to the marginal states and therein acts as if he maximizes his probability of winning, a variant of 0_4, maximizing the probability that his plurality exceeds some level. If we assume, for sake of argument, that marginal states do not differ significantly from non-marginal states in constituency characteristics and preferences (a ridiculous assumption), and if we postulate that in a straight popular vote national election the candidate acts as if he maximizes expected plurality, 0_1, then we might ask if these two election institutions imply different policy positions as election strategies.[39]

[38] A continuous representation is also possible, such that the candidate can calculate the return of the last "dollar" spent in a given campaign. Thus, if x_j is the allocation of x dollars or hours campaigning in state $j (j=1, \ldots, 50)$, the first order optimality condition (subject to a budget or time constraint) is

$$\frac{\partial \phi_i}{\partial x_1} = \ldots = \frac{\partial \phi_i}{\partial x_j} = \ldots = \frac{\partial \phi_i}{\partial x_{50}} .$$

[39] From this perspective, the assumption of identical constituency characteristics is not so ridiculous, as we seek to ascertain the effects of the Electoral College *per se*, quite independent of constituency characteristics.

If condition C holds, then by Theorem Three, the two objective functions are equivalent. If it does not hold, then the two objective functions are not generally equivalent, and the candidate might espouse different policy positions, which is to say that the Electoral College has implications for policy as it dictates equivalent or non-equivalent objective functions.

C. Objective Function Variations in Proportional Representation Systems

It is obvious that many of the same influences on the selection of objective functions that operate in plurality systems, also operate in proportional representation systems. That is, it is reasonable to suspect that variations in information, nomination and election sequences, and quota levels can generate as diverse a set of party election objectives as we find in the plurality systems. This can be even more pronounced if party strategists in the proportional representation systems seek to exploit geographical strengths. Thus, it is not necessary to recapitulate the list of possible objectives for proportional representation systems, as we do for single-member district plurality systems. And, since all six objective functions are possible for proportional representation system parties, we cannot say that, "plurality system candidates do this and proportional representation system candidates do that."

Nevertheless, proportional representation systems present some additional possibilities that we do not find in the single-member district system, winner-take-all, elections.

1. Formal and Informal Rules as Sources of Campaign Objectives

Sperrklausel levels. A minor rule that is present in most proportional representation systems is the *Sperrklausel* (exclusion clause).[40] This law sets a proportion of the vote each party must win to receive parliamentary representation. Hence, the *Sperrklausel* is a formal requirement. Clearly, major parties need not consider the

[40] Cf. footnotes 7–8. We note that the *Sperrklausel* might reduce the number of competing parties because of anticipations of electoral failure. Thus, the *Sperrklausel* can affect policy even though O_2 and O_5 might be equivalent. *Ex post*, however, this is a modest limitation. *Ex ante*, it is quite serious.

threshold percentage (though they act as if they do, *ceteris paribus*, if 0_2, maximizing proportion of the expected vote, and 0_5, maximizing the probability that proportion of the vote exceeds some (the legal) level are equivalent). Of course, these thresholds can have an important effect on the number of parties that compete, because they may limit the likelihood that any one party can gain parliamentary representation. Minor parties close to the threshold proportion, though, must be cognizant of their precarious situation. Hence, an application of the objective that the legal requirement implies can tell us whether or not the threshold level in itself (i.e., holding constant the number of competing parties) has strategic policy consequences. If condition C holds, by Theorem Four the *Sperrklausel* has no strategic policy consequences and, *ceteris paribus*, we cannot distinguish the parties by virtue of their size alone; should the condition not hold, though, such a distinction is possible.

Coalition formation rules. A second and more important variation in the adoption of campaign objectives derives from the nature of extra-legal coalition formation rules. If, for example, government coalitions contain traditionally the party with the greatest number of legislative seats, we can expect the major parties to seek strategies that maximize expected plurality.[41]

Alternatively, if the plurality party coalition advantage does not operate, then it is reasonable to suspect that the goals of party members in proportional representation systems focus on proportion of the expected vote, 0_2, rather than on expected plurality, 0_1. Similarly, we can offer an illustration of 0_5 operating: the party strategists seek to espouse policy to maximize the probability that their proportion of the vote exceeds some level. Suppose that a government consists of a majority coalition of legislative parties and that an undistorted proportional representation formula operates, mapping directly from proportion of the vote to proportion of the legislative seats. A party might then adopt 0_5, the probability that proportion of the vote exceeds some level. Specifically, if the party leaders seek to govern alone, then they set the level, λ_i, at one-half. Such an objective might be especially appealing if some variant of the Italian

[41] This seems to be the case in Israel and Chile. See Aranson, *loc.cit.*

"swindle law" operates, giving more than a majority to such a party.[42]

Satisficing objectives. The previous example illustrates that 0_5 can represent the goal of maximizing the probability of maintaining (or achieving) a parliamentary majority. Additionally, a party whose leaders believe that it has no chance to capture a legislative majority might satisfice by adopting policy positions to maximize the probability that the party retains as many seats as it holds currently. If s_i is the number of seats party i commands, and if S is the total number of parliamentary seats, then, for the satisficing party, 0_5 is the appropriate objective function, and $\lambda_i = s_i/S$.

Paralleling our discussion of the strategic effects of the *Sperrklausel*, if condition C holds, then 0_2 and 0_5 are equivalent objective functions, independent of λ_i. Hence, parties whose leaders seek to maximize the probability of a legislative majority and satisficing parties can be strategically indistinguishable. If condition C does not hold, then we might anticipate real strategic differences between the "satisficing" and the "maximizing" parties.

D. Implications for Reform Proposals in Proportional Representation Systems

The general problems scholars cite for proportional representation systems revolve around the stipulation that there might be no clear "winner", and that coalition governments resulting from this condition might be unstable.[43] The concommitant proposals for reform range all the way from abolishing proportional representation to adopting some complex representation formula.

The first proposal we speak of later. Because they are difficult to conceptualize, we ignore the representation formulae proposals. Now, though, we can examine some simple proposals about minority parties.

---

[42] For a discussion of the "swindle law" see Giorgio Galli and Alfonso Prandi, *Patterns of Political Participation in Italy* (New Haven: Yale University Press, 1970); 258–259.

[43] Cf. e.g. Hermins, *loc. cit.*

1. Proposal One: Set High *Sperrklausel* Levels to Eliminate Minor Parties
2. Proposal Two: Set no *Sperrklausel* Levels to Insure Everyone "Fair" Representation

These two proposals have opposite motivations.[44] Nevertheless, we can ask again if the *Sperrklausel* level has any effects on policy. The answer, for proportional representation systems, depends upon the nature of the contestants' forecast errors. If they have mean zero and are distributed independently from $v_i(\theta)$, which is to say that condition C holds, then by Theorem Three, *ceteris paribus*, we can attribute no policy implications to the exclusion clause, its existence, or its actual level. If, on the other hand, Theorem Three does not hold because condition C is not met and 0_2 and 0_5 are not equivalent, then we can expect major and minor parties to adopt different strategies as a function of their relative strengths and electoral expectations.

E. Proportional Representation Versus Plurality System Elections

We conclude with a venerable set of reform proposals. These proposals assert either that a proportional representation election system should be changed to a plurality system, or that a plurality election system should be changed to a proportional representation system. The operant question, in either case, is: what variations in campaign objectives can we attribute to one system or the other, even as we do previously, by postulation? Additionally, we must ask if these different objective functions lead to different strategic incentives for the contestants: will the candidates espouse different kinds of public policy because of their strategic incentives which, in turn, are derivatives of the election system?

We can standardize this question thus: assume that the preferences of two electorates are identical, but that one elects by plurality and the other proportional representation; can we expect the contestants in the two systems to advocate different public policy? Our answer must be ambiguous even if we assume that the substitution of one

[44] They also represent a trade-off between "stability" and minority representation.

system for the other does not affect the number of parties that compete.

First, there are a number of conditions relating to information, sequential election stages, quotas, and *Sperrklausel* levels for which the answer is trivial: the contestants in both systems adopt *identical* objective functions. Hence, candidates in plurality system elections and party strategists in proportional representation system elections may both adopt any of the six objective functions we describe earlier.

Second, if the proportional representation and plurality candidate do not adopt identical objective functions, but e.g. the first maximizes proportion of the expected vote while the second maximizes expected plurality, then no answer is universal. All of the findings of equivalence and non-equivalence depend on exogenous election and contestant characteristics. The differences in election institutions may imply differences in objective functions, but the equivalence or non-equivalence of those objective functions depends upon symmetry, zero-sum-like competitive conditions, and forecast error characteristics: matters that are quite separate from the election systems themselves.

The Problem of Salience in the Theory of Collective Decision-Making

*MICHAEL TAYLOR**

A city council of fifteen members is making a decision on a new park. The possible alternatives are seen by the members as varying in just two respects, the budget and the location. Simplifying further, let us suppose that the budget is seen merely as a single sum, and the location is defined as a distance from the urban core. (Both assumptions are apt to be over-simple, but the addition of more dimensions would only serve as a further illustration of the need for a theoretical model.) Suppose further that the members of the council (*A*, *B*, . . ., *O*) have the "first choices" or "optima" shown in Table 1. Do these preferences define an expected outcome? If so, what is it? It is impossible to see that any policy is substantially more apt to be adopted than any other. The first of the models to be presented below, however, would offer a quite exact prediction, if the council were using simple majority rule: a park costing 1.5 millions and located three miles from the core city should be the policy outcome.

In this first model, it is assumed that, in the estimation of every single council member, the two policy dimensions (location, budget) are ranked in the same order of importance. This will often be

---

***University of Essex, England.** **I am grateful to the Social Science Research Council (U.K.) for a grant in support of some experimental work on collective decision-making, from which, in part, this paper has grown.**

unrealistic. In our second model below, we shall relax this assumption, and examine the consequences of the existence of two different "salience groups" on the council, location being the salient dimension for one group, the budget being salient for the other.

After some preliminary definitions and an explanation of the lexicographic principle (which underlies the members' preference orderings in both models), we consider, in our first model, the special case of an odd number of individuals using simple majority rule, following with a general result for a committee of any size using any decision rule. We then turn to a discussion of lexicographic preference orderings and their plausibility in political decision-making. In our second model, we admit the possibility of different "salience rankings" of the policy dimensions, and prove a theorem for the case when the policy space is two-dimensional and the simple majority decision rule is being used.

Definitions and Assumptions

A voting body with m members is to decide on a "public policy" or "collective choice," from a set of alternatives which are assumed to vary on n dimensions $(x_1, x_2, \ldots, x_n)$. We shall use the word "committee" to describe any such voting body. It might be deciding between alternatives which possess several "attributes"; for example, it might be choosing between candidates on the basis of several abilities relevant to the office in question. On the other hand, it might have to make a single decision on several things at once; for example, when a given sum is available to be spent on two items, with no restriction that all of it be spent, it is often necessary or desirable to decide the two amounts simultaneously (which might in practice be accomplished by first deciding the total amount to be spent, then the proportion of this to be spent on one of the items).

We assume that, for each individual there is a point in the n-dimensional policy space which he would most prefer the committee's decision to be; we call this his *optimum* policy. The further away from his optimum an alternative is, the more dissatisfied he is with it. Various assumptions have been made in the past about this relationship between distance and dissatisfaction, that is, about each individual's preference ordering of the alternatives in the policy

TABLE 1

HYPOTHETICAL PREFERENCES FOR PARK CONSTRUCTION POLICY

Member	*Most Preferred Location (as Distance from Core City)*	*Most Preferred Budget Amount (in Millions)*
A	0.0 miles	2.0
B	0.0	1.5
C	0.0	1.0
D	1.0	1.0
E	1.0	0.5
F	2.0	0.5
G	2.5	2.0
H	3.0	2.0
I	4.0	0.75
J	4.0	1.5
K	4.0	2.0
L	5.0	2.0
M	5.0	1.5
N	5.0	1.0
O	5.0	0.5

space. We shall return to these later. The assumption made here is radically different from all of these; it supposes, in effect, a far greater simplification of his choice problem by the individual decision-maker faced with a set of complex, multidimensional alternatives.

Suppose a committee is deciding between alternatives which differ in two respects (x_1, x_2) and which can therefore be represented as points in a two-dimensional space. We shall assume that an individual simplifies his decision problem by first paying attention to only one of the dimensions, and choosing, out of any two alternatives, the one which comes closest to his ideal (his optimum point) on this dimension alone, no matter what positions these two alternatives have on the second dimension. Only if they are equal on the first dimension will he use the second, again choosing the alternative which is closest to his optimum.

More generally, the points of an n-dimensional policy space are said to be *ordered lexicographically* by the ith individual, whose optimum is at $(x_1{}^i, x_2{}^i, \ldots, x_n{}^i)$ when the dimensions can be labelled (ranked, in effect) so that he prefers the alternative P whose components are $(x_1{}^P, x_2{}^P, \ldots, x_n{}^P)$ to the alternative Q at $(x_1{}^Q, x_2{}^Q, \ldots, x_n{}^Q)$ if and only if

$$|x_j{}^i - x_j{}^P| < |x_j{}^i - x_j{}^Q|$$

and

$$|x_k{}^i - x_k{}^P| = |x_k{}^i - x_k{}^Q|$$

for all $k < j$, for some value of j. In other words, he prefers P to Q if P's first component is closer than Q's to the first component of his optimum; if they are equal then he prefers the one with the closer second component and so on. Only if the two alternatives have all components identical is he indifferent between them.

The lexicographic principle, in effect, supposes that an individual has a "salience ranking" of the policy dimensions – he ranks them in order of importance. We do not, of course, believe that this will be the case for all individuals in all areas of collective decision-making. But in many important areas, the lexicographic principle would seem to be a highly plausible basis for individual choice.

It is important to note that, in defining the lexicographical principle, we have made no assumptions about the precise form of the relationship between the distance of an alternative from an individual's optimum point and its "utility" for him. All we have assumed is that, of two alternatives, he prefers the one which is closer on the most important dimension (and so on, for successive dimensions, if the alternatives are tied on the earlier ones). Thus, he can be thought of as possessing a separate utility function in each dimension, independently of the other dimensions. All we have assumed is that each individual behaves as though he has a utility function $U_j(x_1, x_2, \ldots, x_n)$ in the jth dimension which is an increasing function of x_j in $x_j < x_j{}^i$ and a decreasing function of x_j in $x_j > x_j{}^i$. A great advantage of the present model is its generality in that we do not need to specify these functions in any greater detail. We need not assume that they are linear, quadratic, etc. Thus, any individual's utility functions $(U_1, U_2, \ldots, U_n)$ do not have to be the same in all dimensions. Further, the function U_j can vary between individuals.

Although each individual can be thought of as possessing n utility functions, one for each policy dimension, he does not combine these utilities in any way to form a single total or overall utility. Indeed, if he uses the lexicographic principle, he cannot. The lexicographic ordering is in fact the standard example of a preference ordering which cannot be represented by a single utility indicator. (More precisely, it is a complete quasi-ordering – based on the preference-or-indifference relation – which cannot be represented by a real-valued function.) Thus, there are no indifference curves associated with an individual's preferences.

Finally, we define an *equilibrium point* to be a point P in the policy space such that there is no other point which k individuals prefer to P, where k is the decision rule – the number of individuals who must agree on a proposal before it is adopted by the committee. In practice, k is typically a simple majority of the m voters. In principle, k can be any number from 1 to m. "Equilibrium point" is really shorthand for "a point of stable equilibrium," since a sequence of committee votes – where a proposal is rejected by the committee if there is some other point which k members prefer – must either go on forever or terminate at an equilibrium point. Once an equilibrium point is proposed the process must terminate because no other point can be introduced which can obtain a simple majority over it. The set of all equilibrium points we call the *equilibrium set*.

If there is a unique equilibrium point, and if certain assumptions are made about the committee's voting procedure, then it will be the policy outcome, the committee's decision. If the equilibrium set contains more than one point, then we can use the model to predict only that the policy outcome will be one of the points in the set. In fact, it will be proved that, if the decision rule is simple majority rule, as it most often is in practice, then there is only one equilibriun point.

Simple Majority Rule

In this section and the next, we shall assume that the salience ranking of the policy dimensions is the same for each individual. We adopt the convention throughout that $x_1, x_2, \ldots, x_n$ is the labelling of the dimensions when they are ranked in order of importance for the purposes of using the lexicographic principle. In this section, we consider the case when the number of individuals is odd and simple majority rule is being used. For simplicity of exposition, we present the theorems and proofs for two-dimensional policy spaces; but they will later be generalized to any number of dimensions.

Let $x_1 = x_{1a}$ be the (vertical) line such that there are less than a simple majority of individuals in the space $x_1 < x_{1a}$ and less than a simple majority in $x_1 > x_{1a}$. Similarly, let $x_2 = x_{2a}$ be the (horizontal) line such that there are less than a simple majority in $x_2 < x_{2a}$ and less than a simple majority in $x_2 > x_{2a}$. Thus, these are the lines through the median individual optima in each dimension. We call them the *median lines*. They are indicated in the example given by Figure 1 (where $m = 5$). Then we can prove the following

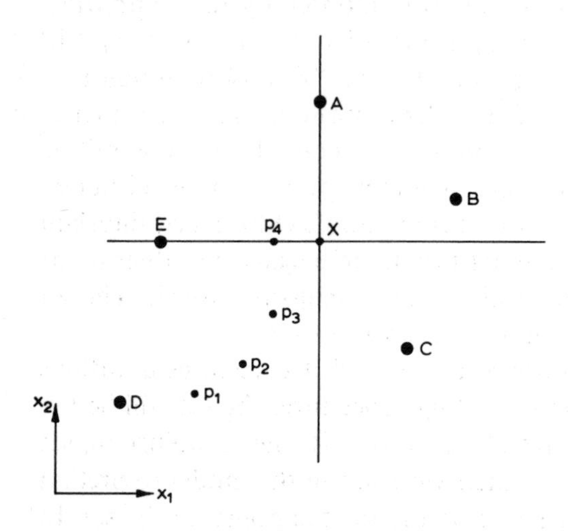

Fig. 1.

Theorem

When the committee has an odd number of members and simple majority rule is being used, the intersection (X) of the two median lines is the unique equilibrium point.

Proof

Consider any point with coordinates (x_{1p}, x_{2p}). If it is in the half-plane $x_1 > x_{1a}$, then any point whose x_1 coordinate is less than x_{1p} but greater than or equal to x_{1a} is preferred to P by a simple majority of the individuals – all those on and to the left of the vertical median line – simply because its x_1 coordinate is closer to theirs, and therefore, using the lexicographic principle, they are not interested in its x_2 coordinate. On the other hand, if P is in the half-plane $x_1 < x_{1a}$, then any point whose x_1 coordinate is such that $x_{1p} < x_1 \leqslant x_{1a}$ is preferred to P, for the same reason, by the simple majority on or to the right of the vertical median line. Hence, if there are any equilibrium points, they must lie on the line $x_1 = x_{1a}$. But consider any point P *on* the line $x_1 = x_{1a}$. If it is above the point X (i.e., $x_{2p} > x_{2a}$), then any point (say Q) on $x_1 = x_{1a}$ between P and X (more precisely, any point whose x_2 coordinate is such that $x_{2a} \leqslant x_2 < x_{2p}$) is preferred to P by the simple majority of individuals on or below $x_2 = x_{2a}$. Similarly, any point Q on $x_1 = x_{1a}$ whose x_2 coordinate is such that $x_{2p} < x_2 \leqslant x_{2a}$ is preferred to P by the simple majority in the half-plane $x_2 \geqslant x_{2a}$. Both of these statements follow from the fact that, since P and Q have identical x_1 coordinates, each individual chooses between them on the basis of their x_2 coordinates, and in each case Q's is the closer.

Thus, X is the only possible equilibrium point; but we must show that it *is* an equilibrium point – by showing that any move away from X would not gain the support of a simple majority of the voters.

An alternative which represents a move away from X in any direction with a positive x_1 component will be rejected in favour of X by the simple majority in the half-plane $x_1 \leqslant x_{1a}$. Similarly, a move in a direction with a negative x_1 component will be rejected. Finally, no alternative which represents a move from X along the line $x_1 = x_{1a}$ will be preferred to X by a simple majority, since it will be as good as X on the first dimension but worse on the second – for the simple majority in $x_2 \leqslant x_{2a}$ if it is above $x_2 = x_{2a}$, for the simple majority in $x_2 \geqslant x_{2a}$ if it is below $x_2 = x_{2a}$.

Thus, *X is the unique equilibrium point under simple majority rule* – the only point in the policy space which is such that no other point is preferred to it by a simple majority of the individuals.

Notice that all the statements in the proof about preferences between pairs of points are contingent only upon the assumption that each member has a separate utility function in each dimension which is a decreasing function of distance from his optimum. The proof does not require these functions to be the same in each dimension and for each individual.

Consider an example (Figure 1) of a possible sequence of proposals. Suppose that the point P_1 is proposed (by the individual at D). Then a simple majority (the individuals whose optima are at A, B and C) prefer the point P_2, for example, since it is closer to their optima on the x_1 dimension. But P_2 can be "defeated" by P_3, since A, B and C all prefer P_3, again as it is closer to their optima on the x_1 dimension. In turn, P_4 is preferred to P_3 by a simple majority, this time composed of the individuals at E, A and B, since P_4 and P_3 are equal on the first dimension, but closer to these three on the second.

The proof given above was for the two-dimensional case; but the generalization to any number of dimensions is immediate. The median lines are, of course, replaced by "median hyperplanes," which are always orthogonal and therefore intersect in a single point.

When the number of individuals is even, instead of a unique equilibrium point there are several equilibrium points. Rather than treat this case separately – having treated the odd case of simple majority rule as an important illustration, and because, as we shall see, it is unique in possessing a unique equilibrium point – we now prove a general theorem of which the simple majority results are special cases. The general theorem specifies the equilibrium points for each decision rule $k = 1, 2, \ldots, m$. Again, we present the argument in two dimensions (so that it can be followed easily on a diagram), although the theorem holds for any number of dimensions.

Other Decision Rules

In the example shown as Figure 2, there are seven individuals. Suppose, first, that the decision rule is $k = 5$. Moving in the positive x_1 direction, we count off individual optima and draw a vertical line ($x_1 = x_{1b}$) through "the fifth." Of course, there might be several optima on this line, so that it is rather loose to speak of "the fifth." In general, we define this line to be such that there are at most $k - 1 = 4$ individuals in the space $x_1 < x_{1b}$ and at most $m - k = 2$ individuals in $x_1 > x_{1b}$. Similarly, $x_1 = x_{1a}$ is the line such that there are at most 4 individuals in $x_1 > x_{1a}$ and at most $m - k = 2$ individuals in $x_1 < x_{1a}$. In the x_2 dimension $x_2 = x_{2b}$ and $x_2 = x_{2a}$ are the analogous (horizontal) lines through "the fifth" optimum in each direction. These four lines are shown as dotted lines in Figure 2, where they bound a rectangle labelled k = 5. We show that this rectangle is the set of equilibrium points when the decision rule is k = 5.

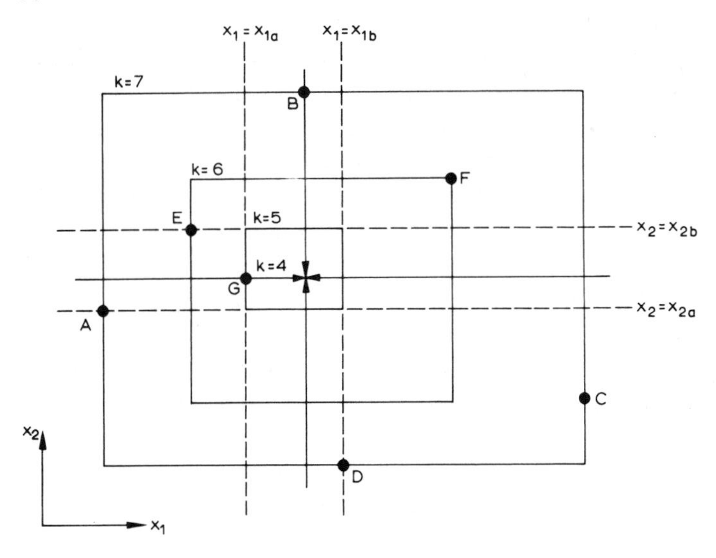

Fig. 2. Salience in collective decision-making.

Proof

The argument parallels that given above for simple majority rule. Consider any point P at (x_{1p}, x_{2p}). If it is in the half-plane $x_1 < x_{1a}$, then any point whose x_1 coordinate is such that $x_{1p} < x_1 \leqslant x_{1a}$ is preferred to P by the five individuals in the space $x_1 \geqslant x_{1a}$, because its x_1 coordinate is closer to their optima than P's, and they will therefore ignore the x_2 coordinate. If P is in $x_1 > x_{1b}$, then any point with $x_{1b} \leqslant x_1 < x_{1p}$ is preferred to P by the five in $x_1 \leqslant x_{1b}$. Thus, if there are any equilibrium points, they must lie in between or on the two lines $x_1 = x_{1a}$ and $x_1 = x_{1b}$. But consider any point P, at (x_{1p}, x_{2p}), inside this strip (i.e., $x_{1a} \leqslant x_1 \leqslant x_{1b}$) but below the line $x_2 = x_{2a}$ (i.e., with $x_2 < x_{2a}$). Such a point cannot be an equilibrium point, since any point Q with the same x_1 coordinate but whose x coordinate is such that $x_{2p} < x_2 \leqslant x_{2a}$ is preferred to P by the five individuals in $x_2 \geqslant x_{2a}$, because for them, P and Q are equal as far as the most important dimension, x_1, is concerned, but Q is better than

P on the second dimension. Similarly, any point P in the strip $x_{1a} \leqslant x_1 \leqslant x_{1b}$ with $x_2 > x_{2b}$ cannot be an equilibrium point. Thus, if there are any equilibrium points, they lie in or on the rectangle. The proof that these *are* equilibrium points is similar to that given for simple majority decision.

Analogous results hold for the decision rule $k = 6$. The equilibrium set consists of all points in and on a rectangle which is bounded by the lines drawn through the sixth optimum from "the left," from "the right," from "below," and from "above." The case $k = 7 = m$ corresponds to the unanimity rule, the equilibrium set being what is usually called the Pareto optimal set. The equilibrium sets for $k = 4$ (a single point), $k = 5$, $k = 6$ and $k = 7$ are shown in Figure 2. The equilibrium set increases monotonically in size as k increases from the simple majority value to the unanimity value; below the simple majority value, it is empty. Note that for simple majority rule when m is *even*, an equilibrium set exists, but does not in general consist of a single point, as it does when m is odd.

These results may be summarized in a single theorem (for two dimensional policy spaces).

Theorem

The equilibrium set is the intersection of the four regions $x_1 \geqslant x_{1a}, x_1 \leqslant x_{1b}, x_2 \geqslant x_{2a}, x_2 \leqslant x_{2b}$.

This intersection or overlap is empty when the decision rule is below the simple majority value.

This result can be generalized to any number of policy dimensions. $2n$ lines (hyperplanes) $x_i = x_{ia}$ and $x_i = x_{ib}$ for each dimension $i = 1, 2, \ldots, n$ can be defined: $x_1 = x_{1a}$ is the line (hyperplane) such that there are at most $k - 1$ individuals in the half-space $x_1 > x_{1a}$ and at most $m - k$ individuals in the half-space $x_1 < x_{1a}$, etc. The equilibrium set is always identical with the common points, if there are any, of the $2n$ spaces $x_1 \geqslant x_{1a}, x_1 \leqslant x_{1b}, x_2 \geqslant x_{2a}, x_2 \leqslant x_{2b}$, etc.

When equilibrium points exist, we might say that the decision-making process possesses *stability*: a sequence of proposals (points in the policy space) being put against the status quo (the last proposal accepted) and requiring k positive votes before being accepted as the new status quo is likely to terminate at a point in the equilibrium set, since no other point is preferred to an equilibrium point by k individuals. Thus, decision-making procedures with values of k below simple majority have no stability. But if the equilibrium set is large, we might say that the process is *indeterminate*, since the outcome could be *any* of the equilibrium points. Because simple majority rule has the smallest non-empty equilibrium set, it could be said to be the least indeterminate of the stable decision rules.

The Lexicographic Principle and the Problem of Salience

The recent interest in lexicographic orderings, chiefly amongst mathematical economists, has stemmed from criticisms of one of the postulates upon which von Neumann and Morgenstern founded their index of cardinal utility. Von Neumann and Morgenstern showed that if a man can give a complete weak ordering not only of all the basic alternatives but also of all the probability combinations of the alternatives, and if he makes choices so as to maximize expected utility, then a cardinal measure of utility can be constructed for him. A thorough survey of von Neumann and Morgenstern's work and the considerable volume of discussion which has followed it, together with an extensive bibliography, is given by Rothenberg (1961, Chaps. 9 and 10). A number of axiomatizations of the expected utility hypothesis have been developed (Rothenberg, 1961, p. 217 ff.). Here, we are interested in only one of the postulates of these axiom systems – the so-called Continuity or Archimedean postulate, which states:

> If f is strictly preferred to g and g is strictly preferred to h (where f, g and h are any three prospects),[1] then there is a probability p $(0 < p < 1)$ such that g is indifferent to the probability mixture $pf + (1 - p)h$, which is a gamble such that f is the outcome with probability p and h is the outcome with probability $(1 - p)$.

It has been said that this postulate will be violated in choices in which the utility difference between f and g is "incomparably smaller" than the difference between g and h, as in Thrall's (1954)

[1] If the basic alternatives or "events" or "outcomes" are, $e_1, e_2, \ldots, e_N$, then a *prospect* f is a probability distribution $(f_1, f_2, \ldots, f_N)$ over the e_is, with $\Sigma_{i=1}^{N} f_i = 1$.

example: let f = be given two common pins, g = be given one common pin, and h = be hanged at sundown. Clearly (for most people) f is preferred to g and g is preferred to h, yet it is reasonable to suppose that for some people the number p of the postulate will not exist, that they would prefer the certainty of receiving one pin to any risk involving even the remotest possibility of death.[2]

If this criticism is allowed, the theory must be modified so as to admit the possibility of choices between alternatives of noncomparable subjective value. This has been done in Hausner and Wendel (1952), Hausner (1954), Thrall (1954), and Debreu (1954). The key result (Hausner, 1954) is that if a set of preferences satisfies all of the axioms for von Neumann and Morgenstern utility except for the Archimedean axiom, then those preferences can be represented, not by a single number, but by *vectors*; and that if the vectors have a finite number of components, then they can be chosen so that the ordering of the alternatives is *lexicographic* – i.e., so that an alternative represented by the vector $(x_1^P, x_2^P, \ldots, x_n^P)$ is preferred to one represented by $(x_1^Q, x_2^Q, \ldots, x_n^Q)$ if and only if $x_i^P > x_i^Q$ and $x_j^P = x_j^Q$ for all $j < i$, for some value of i. This is of course the definition of the lexicographic principle introduced earlier.

A strong case has been made out for lexicographic utility, especially by Georgescu-Roegen (1954) and Chipman (1960). Utility, says Chipman

> "*in its most general form* (italics mine) is a lexicographic ordering, represented by a finite or infinite dimensional vector with real components, . . . and these vectors . . . are ordered lexicographically . . ."

Georgescu-Roegen argues his Principle of the Irreducibility of Wants that "human needs and wants are hierarchized"; they cannot all be reduced to a common basis; there is not a unique want to which all others can be reduced. And in support of it, he refers to

---

[2] Against this criticism, Rothenberg (1961, pp. 234–5) has argued that people do habitually choose risky prospects containing a non-zero probability of an unpleasant premature death – they cross city streets, smoke cigarettes, travel in airplanes, etc. Decision theorists themselves seem particularly attracted to such gambles: Edwards and Tversky (1967, p. 9) note five airplane pilots and one paratrooper among the contributors to their reader on decision-making!

"the isolated farmer whose uses for corn are arranged in the well-known order of importance: food, seeds for next season, alcoholic beverages, fodder, growing parrots"; to "many everyday facts: that bread cannot save someone from dying of thirst, that living in a luxurious palace does not constitute a substitute for food, etc."; and to many other examples. In similar vein, Chipman asks, "If you are a 'security risk', is there some level of competence and intelligence high enough to induce the State Department to employ you nevertheless? " and quotes Mill, "It is better to be a human being dissatisfied than a pig satisfied," in the same breath as Orwell's famous "All animals are equal, but some animals are more equal than others."

But even if we agree with Georgescu-Roegen (1954, p. 517) that:

> (1) The hierarchy of wants seem to be for all men identical up to a certain rank. One may be almost sure that this refers at least to: thirst, hunger, leisure, shelter. (2) Individuals belonging to the same culture are likely to have in common still a greater number of wants at the top of the hierarchy than those common to all men,

there still remains the question of whether such hierarchically ordered wants ever underlie the (multidimensional) alternatives which are the subject of actual decision-making in politics.

Of course, all the dimensions ($x_1, x_2, \ldots, x_n$), which describe the alternatives between which a committee (using the word in the general sense introduced earlier) must choose, may be in the same "want-category," that is they may be all at the same rank in the lexicographical hierarchy. In this case, it will be possible to describe preferences by a single utility number. If our theory of collective decision-making will be applied only to committees whose members always have preferences of this kind, then we have no need of the lexicographic model.

Usually, however, there will be complications. First, the dimensions of the policy space (which may be distinct "decision variables") and the hierarchical wants may be interwoven in a complicated way, rather than being in a one-to-one correspondence (Georgescu-Roegen, 1954, p. 517). Even if the lexicographical ordering is the same for every member of the committee in the decision situation in question, and even if they all perceive the connection between the hierarchy of wants and the dimensions of the policy space in the same way, nonetheless some complex problems are posed for a theory of collective decisions. We shall not attempt to treat them here.

It seems to us, however, that whether or not men order their *wants* hierarchically, and no matter what the connection between their wants (in Georgescu-Roegen's sense) and the dimensions of the policy-space, nevertheless *they will, as decision-makers, sometimes choose lexicographically between alternatives on the basis of a hierarchy of the policy dimensions themselves.* It is to this situation that the equilibrium theorems above, and the one which follows, are intended to apply. The following are examples.

1) A committee has to choose between several alternative proposals for a new public building. The alternatives cost roughly the same amount but vary chiefly with respect to site and design. One member (at least) is concerned above all with one of those dimensions – the site; he is supremely anxious that the building should be in his locality, and at first directs all his efforts on the committee to securing a favorable outcome on this dimension. Only when he sees that he has failed to secure a decision to build in his locality, does he begin to think about the other dimension involved. As far as he is concerned, all sites other than the local one are equally undesirable on this first dimension, so that in choosing between any two other alternatives, he has recourse to the second dimension, the design.

2) An electoral district is choosing a representative. The candidates (to simplify somewhat) vary with respect to their opinions on national domestic affairs, on foreign affairs, and on a local affair that is currently of concern to some of the electors. Just about every one of the possible hierarchical rankings of these dimensions (issue-areas) is a feasible basis for a lexicographical ordering of the candidates. Some voters may be overwhelmingly concerned with the local issue, perhaps because they are personally affected by it. Only if they must choose between two candidates who take the same stand on this issue will they have recourse to the dimension which is second in importance for them. The issue second in importance might plausibly be national domestic affairs, perhaps because immediate welfare and race questions loom so large in their lives that foreign policy issues seem irrelevant.

In the first example, it is quite possible that all the committee's members think that the question of the site is supremely important

– they may come from different localities – and that they all order the alternatives using the resulting lexicographic basis. It is equally possible that this is not so. In the second example, it is unlikely that all the voters have the same salience ordering of the three issue-areas; and among those who have a definite ranking of the three, there nevertheless will be many who do not order the alternatives lexicographically.

A case in which we might expect fo find most, if not all, the members of a collectivity choosing lexicographically is that of a committee whose members represent various interests, especially when these interests have very strong views on the issue being decided. (The first example above might be an instance of this, the interests being geographical.) For this reason, such representatives may often have *different* rankings of the dimensions.

An interesting question is whether or not the theorems proved above are still true when not all the committee members rank the dimensions of the policy space in the same order of importance as a basis for their lexicographic orderings of the alternatives. The answer, in general, is that they are not. Is it still possible, nevertheless, to prove any general results about equilibrium points? Restricting ourselves to a two-dimensional policy space and to simple majority rule, we now prove such a theorem, which specifies the equilibrium set for any number of individuals and any configuration of their optima.

Suppose that the committee is composed of two groups, not necessarily of the same size. The members of one group (let us call them Group One) order the alternatives lexicographically using the first dimension, which we now call x, as the most important (the most salient), and use the other dimension, y, to choose between two alternatives which have the same x value. The members of the second group (Group Two) also order the alternatives lexicographically, but the order of importance (salience) of the policy dimensions is for them the reverse of that for the first group, that is, y followed by x. We shall call these groups *salience groups*. As before, each individual is assumed to have an optimum point in the policy space.

Consider the members of Group One. Define for them the same four median lines, two in each dimension, which were defined for the ordinary lexicographic model in the simple majority case. These are the lines bounding the equilibrium set (degenerating into one line in each dimension when the number of individuals is odd) which would result if this group by itself were using simple majority rule. Let us suppose that they are at $x = a$, $x = b$, and $y = c$, $y = d$. Let the same four lines for the members of Group Two be $x = e$, $x = f$, and $y = g$, $y = h$. Figure 3 shows an example: there are eight individuals altogether; four of these are in Group One, who consider the x dimension to be the most important, and their optima are labelled X; the other four form Group Two and their optima are labelled Y; the median lines corresponding to the use of simple majority rule by Group One alone (three out of four required for agreement) are indicated by bold lines; the same median lines for Group Two alone (whose simple majority rule happens to be three out of four also) are indicated by broken lines; the two equilibrium sets are shaded.

Finally, let the four median lines of *the whole committee* (simple majority rule being five out of eight) be $x = s$, $x = t$, $y = u$, $y = v$. These are the lines bounding the equilibrium set which would result if *all* the committee members used the same lexicographic ranking of the policy dimensions. Some of these lines might coincide with some of the median lines for the separate groups, as they do in the example of Figure 3, where $s = a$, $t = f$, $u = g$, and $v = d$.

We now state and prove a theorem for this two-dimensional, simple majority case, and give an interpretation. The equilibrium set

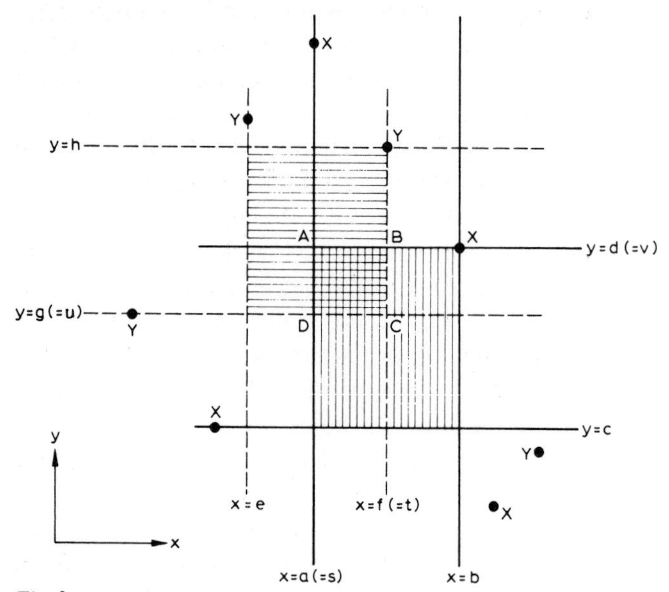

Fig. 3.

(under simple majority rule) is defined here as before: a point P is in the equilibrium set if and only if there is no point which a simple majority strictly prefers to P.

Theorem

If a committee, all of whose members order the alternatives (x, y) of a two-dimensional policy space lexigraphically, is composed of two different salience groups as defined above, then the equilibrium set under simple majority rule is the intersection of: (i) the area bounded by Group One's vertical *median lines $(x = a, x = b)$ and Group Two's* horizontal *median lines $(y = g, y = h)$; and (ii) the area bounded by the four median lines of the whole committee; that is, the lines $x = s, x = t, y = u, y = v$.*

The intersection of these two areas is shown (cross-hatched) in Figure 3; in this example it happens to coincide with the second of the two areas.

Proof

Throughout, K will denote a simple majority of the entire committee; that is, $K = (m + 1)/2$ when m is odd, and $K = m/2 + 1$ when m is even. Thus, $m - K + 1 = \mathbf{K}$ individuals are required to block a majority of the whole committee. Let k_1 be a simple majority of Group One, and let κ_1 be the number required to block it (the number of individuals in the Group minus k_1 plus one). Similarly, k_2 and κ_2 for Group Two. Note that $k_1 + \kappa_2 \geqslant K$ and $\kappa_1 + k_2 \geqslant K$. The proof is in three stages. First we prove that, if there are any equilibrium points, they must lie in the area specified in (*i*) of the theorem; second, that any equilibrium points must lie in the area in (*ii*); third, that any point in the intersection of these two areas is in fact an equilibrium point.

1)[3] Consider any point P in the area $x < a$ as a candidate for an equilibrium point. If P is in $y < g$, then any other point Q above and

[3] This section might be more easily followed if reference is made to Figure 4, or an example together with a Figure 4 in which the ks are replaced by actual numbers. In this figure (and in Figure 5) the arrow marked κ_1 to the right of the line $x = b$ means that there are κ_1 optima in the area $x \geqslant b$, and so on.

to the right of it (i.e., with larger x and y coordinates) but in $x \geqslant a$ is preferred to P by the k_1 individuals whose optima are in $x \geqslant a$ (since Q is closer than P along the x dimension to k_1 members of Group One) and by the κ_2 individuals in $y > g$ (since Q is closer to P along the y dimension to these k_2 members of Group Two). Since $k_1 + \kappa_2$ is at least a simple majority of the whole committee, P cannot be an equilibrium point. If P is in $y > f$, then any point Q *below* and to the right of it (but still in $x \leqslant a$) is preferred to P by the simple majority comprising the k_1 members in $x > a$ and the κ_2 in $y < f$, so that such a P cannot be an equilibrium point. Thus any point in the area $x < a$ cannot be an equilibrium point. Entirely similar considerations (Figure 4) rule out the areas $x > b$, $y < f$ and $y > g$. Hence, if there are equilibrium points, they must lie in or on the area bounded by $x = a$, $x = b$, $y = f$, and $y = g$.

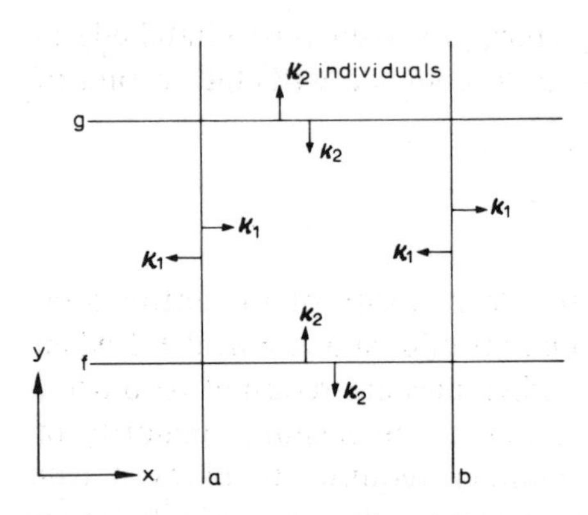

Fig. 4.

2) Consider next any point P lying in $x < s$. In $x \geqslant s$ there are, according to the definition of this median line, K individuals. Any point Q which is in $x < s$ to the right of P (i.e., which has the same y coordinate, but a larger x coordinate) must be preferred to P by all K individuals in $x \geqslant s$, since for those of them who are members of Group One, Q has an x coordinate closer to their optima than P's (which is all they want), while for those of them who are in Group Two, Q is identical with P on the y dimension, so that they must choose between them on the basis of their x coordinates, and thus prefer Q to P as Q is closer on this dimension, For any P in $x < s$, there is always such a point Q. Thus, points in $x < s$ cannot be

equilibrium points. Similarly, the areas $x > t$, $y < u$ and $y > v$ are ruled out. Hence, if there are any equilibrium points, they must lie in or on the area bounded by $x = s$, $x = t$, $y = u$ and $y = v$ (the median lines for the whole committee).

3) We have shown that any equilibrium points must lie both in the area specified in (*i*) and in the area specified in (*ii*). Combining these two results, we now have that any equilibrium points must lie in the (possibly empty) intersection of these two. We must show that such points are in fact equilibrium points. This area of overlap (if it exists) is, by its definition, bounded by four lines (Figure 5) all of which

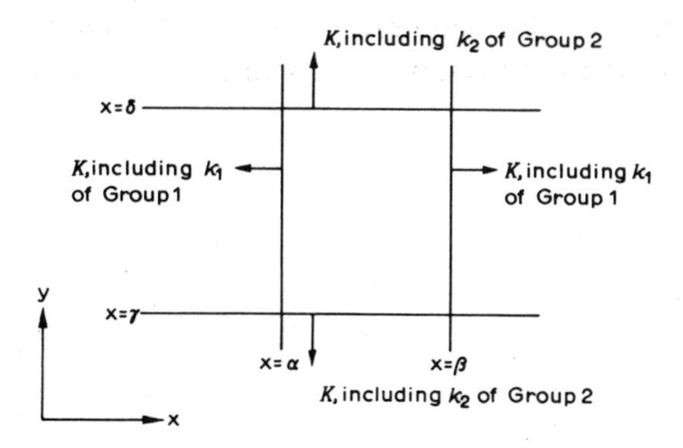

Fig. 5.

coincide in various possible ways with some of the lines already labelled. But let us re-label them $x = \alpha, x = \beta, y = \gamma, y = \delta$. Since this area is the intersection of the areas defined in (1) and (2), there must be $\boldsymbol{K}$ optima (including κ_1 from Group One) in $x \leqslant \alpha$ and in $x \geqslant \beta$, and there must be $\boldsymbol{K}$ optima (including κ_2 from Group Two) in $y \leqslant \gamma$ and in $y \geqslant \delta$. Consider any point P in or on this overlap area. No other point Q with the same x coordinate is preferred to P by a simple majority since, if Q is below P, the $\boldsymbol{K}$ individuals in $y \geqslant \delta$ prefer P to Q, and if Q is above P, the $\boldsymbol{K}$ individuals in $y \leqslant \gamma$ prefer P to Q. Similarly, for points Q with the same y coordinate as P. Consider any point Q above and to the right of P: it will be rejected in P's favor by κ_1 individuals in $x \leqslant \alpha$ *and* the κ_2 individuals in $y \leqslant \gamma$; since $\kappa_1 + \kappa_2 \geqslant K$, Q cannot get a simple majority over P. Similarly for points Q in the other three quadrants at P. In sum, no other point is strictly preferred by a simple majority of the whole committee to any point P in the overlapping area. Thus, points in this area are equilibrium points.

This completes the proof of the theorem.

The first thing to notice about this result is that there are always some equilibrium points for the whole committee if the separate equilibrium sets of the two groups overlap; in fact, in this case, this overlap *is* the equilibrium set for the whole committee for it is also necessarily the area specified in (*ii*) in the theorem. In Figure 3, it can be checked that the overlap of the two Groups' equilibrium sets, the rectangle labelled $ABCD$, is also the equilibrium set which would result if all the committee members used the same lexicographic principle, and is therefore also the equilibrium set for the whole committee. Figure 6 shows another example. A committee of seven

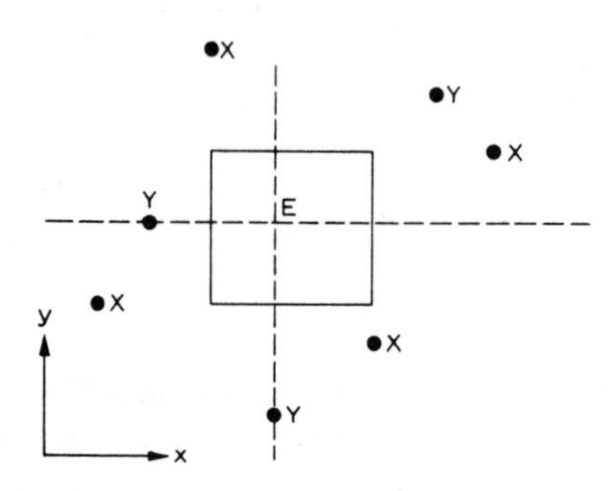

Fig. 6.

(simple majority rule requiring the agreement of four) is divided into two groups, one of four members (the Xs) who rank the policy dimensions in the order (x, y) of importance, the other of three members (the Ys) who rank the dimensions (y, x). The equilibrium set for Group One is the rectangle shown; the equilibrium set for Group Two is a single point, E. The point E is thus also the equilibrium point for the whole committee.

When the two Groups' equilibrium sets do not have an intersection, there will often not be any equilibrium points at all; if, in this case, the equilibrium set is non-empty, then it can be shown that it contains only one point. An example is shown in Figure 7. A committee of eight divided into two groups (marked Ys and Xs) whose separate equilibrium sets are bounded respectively by the four dotted median lines and the four continuous median lines. Thus the area defined in (*i*) of the theorem is the rectangle labelled *ABCD*. The area defined in (*ii*) of the theorem is shown shaded. The equilibrium set for the whole committee – the intersection of these two areas – is therefore the single point labelled *D*. If the whole committee has an odd number of members, the equilibrium set will always contain one point or be empty.

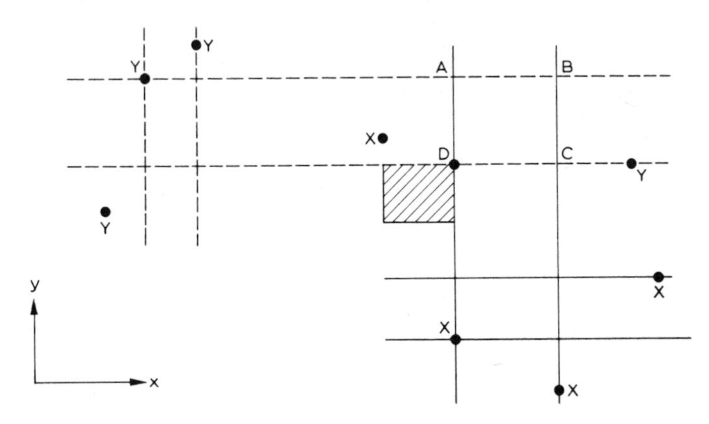

Fig. 7.

If actual bargaining and collective decision-making are approximated by this model – if a policy is proposed, and rejected by a majority because there is another policy which they all prefer to the first, and so on in a sequence of proposals until a policy is reached which cannot be supplanted by another preferred to it by a simple majority – then the outcome, the final undefeated policy, will be a point in the equilibrium set. Looking carefully at the statement of the theorem, it is seen that this outcome, if it occurs (that is, if there are any equilibrium points), will always be a compromise between the two groups. Consider the case when the two groups' separate equilibrium sets intersect. If Group One were to make a collective decision by itself, the outcome would be in its equilibrium set; similarly for Group Two. Each group might reasonably be satisfied, then, if the outcome of decision-making in the whole committee were a point in its own equilibrium set. This is precisely what happens. The equilibrium set for the whole committee consists in this case of the points common to both of the separate equilibrium sets.

Consider the case when the groups' separate equilibrium sets do not intersect (Figure 7). If Group One cannot secure an overall decision in its own equilibrium set, it will be most concerned to get its way at least with respect to the dimension x which is of overriding importance (lexicographically) to it – that is, to secure a decision inside its median lines in that dimension. Similarly for Group Two in the y dimension. Thus, a compromise overall decision would be a point in the area bounded by Group One's median lines in the x dimension and by Group Two's median lines in the y dimension (the area $ABCD$ in Figure 7). This is guaranteed by the theorem in (*i*).

In both cases, *the theorem in (i) says that, if there is an outcome (if the equilibrium set is non-empty), then it is such that each group gets its way (in the sense described above) on the dimension which is most important to it. And each group gets its way by horse-trading – by conceding on the dimension which is relatively unimportant to it. But the theorem in part (ii) also says that there can be no equilibrium unless this compromise area, in which each group gets its own way, has some points in common with the equilibrium set which would result if all members of the committee used the same type of lexicographic ordering.*

Discussion

Our first theorem showed that there is always a unique equilibrium point in a policy space of any number of dimensions when the committee has an odd number of members and uses simple majority rule, no matter how the individual optima are distributed in the space. This contrasts with previous results due to Black and Newing (1951) and Plott (1967), who assume that each individual has a single utility function defined on the policy space, which is differentiable and leads to continuous, strictly convex indifference curves. Plott's more general result shows that, under this assumption about utility functions, equilibrium points (under simple majority rule) exist only in very special circumstances – for highly unusual indifference curves combined with particular distributions of optima.

Another approach (Taylor and Rae, 1969), however, has used city-block utility functions: the disutility of a point $(x_1, x_2, \ldots, x_n)$ in the policy space for an individual with an optimum at $(x_1{}^i, x_2{}^i, \ldots,$

$x_n{}^i$) is assumed to be $\Sigma_{j=1}^{n} \mid x_j{}^i - x_j \mid$, that is, the sum of the differences in each dimension. If all individuals have exactly the same city-block utility function, then the first two equilibrium theorems proved above (for the case when all individuals have the same salience ranking of the dimensions) are valid here also. Unfortunately, if any of the utility functions depart slightly from the city-block form, the equilibrium theorems are no longer true. And, although the theorems still hold when the dimensions are weighted differently (the disutility functions becoming $\Sigma_{j=1}^{n} c_j \mid x_j{}^i - x_j \mid$, where c_1, c_2, . . ., c_n are positive constants), they hold only if the same set of weights c_i is used by every individual. If this very strict requirement is relaxed – if the members are allowed to vary with respect to the importance they attach to the various dimensions – then no general results about equilibrium policies can be proved in the city-block model. In the last section, however, we were still able to prove a fairly general theorem for the lexicographic model after dropping the assumption of a uniform hierarchy of policy dimensions. This theorem showed that, even though a committee is divided into two groups which attach great importance to different components of the choice alternatives, nevertheless a collective decision can often be reached, depending on the particular configuration of optima in the policy space.

But the present model has nevertheless assumed a certain amount of homogeneity amongst the committee members: for it has assumed that they all use the lexicographic principle. In practice, *some* committees deciding *some* issues will use the principle. There will be some situations in which each member uses a single overall utility indicator, such as the city-block utility function or approximations to it (which would usually satisfy the Black-Newing and Plott assumptions). *Mixed* committees will be equally common. Some members will use the lexicographic principle, others a single utility indicator. Furthermore, two or more of these simple methods of evaluating the policy alternatives may be combined in a single individual's choices, as when he *phases* his decision-making. Suppose there is one dimension which is overwhelmingly important to him, but he does not rank the other dimensions. Thus, he chooses between two alternatives on the basis of this dimension only, ignoring the others, as in the lexicographic model, unless the alternatives are equal on the first dimension. If so, he uses them, but he does not use them lexicographically. He may use them by combining them additively, as in the city-block model.

Finally, we suggest that the lexicographic principle is a more plausible basis for a voter's choice amongst candidates in a general election than the quadratic loss criterion which is the basis of several recent mathematical treatments of the Downsian theory of party competition (Davis and Hinich, 1966, 1967, 1968; Davis, Hinich and Ordeshook, 1970). Sen (1969) has in fact suggested that voters might use the three-stage decision criterion, proposed by MacCrimmon (1968), which consists of the successive application of the principles of satisficing, dominance, and lexicography. In the first stage, the voter checks to see if any candidates are too far from his optimum point (beyond his tolerance limit). If all the candidates are, he does not vote; if only one is inside it, he votes for him; if two or more are inside it, he moves to the second stage (dominance) of his decision-making procedure. If one of the candidates is closest to his optimum on all dimensions (issues), he votes for him. If not, then he enters the third stage, in which he applies the lexicographic principle used throughout this paper (the candidates are the alternatives, the campaign issues are the policy dimensions).

The first stage of this three-stage decision criterion is not usually relevant to the kinds of collective decision-making with which we have been concerned, namely situations where all the individual decision-makers are face-to-face. But the principles of dominance and lexicography seem to form a very plausible *two-stage decision criterion* for committee decision-making. And it can be proved that the first two theorems proved above (the first, simple majority rule result being a special case of the second) still hold when it is assumed that each individual uses such a two-stage decision criterion in choosing between pairs of policy alternatives. This is simply because, if an individual prefers P to Q according to the dominance criterion, then he necessarily prefers P to Q according to the lexicographic criterion, whatever his ranking of the policy dimensions. Let us state this in the form of the following

Theorem

If the preferences of all members of a committee are based on the two-stage decision criterion (the successive application of the

principles of dominance and lexicography), then the equilibrium set for any decision rule k is identical with the equilibrium set which results when all members use only the lexicographic principle.

We have indicated a number of ways in which the basic lexicographic model can be extended. These consist chiefly of admitting mixed decision criteria for the individual (such as the use of lexicographic and city-block principles in phase, or of dominance and lexicography in phase) and mixed committees (decision criteria differing from person to person). But the limitations of most individuals' rational decision-making capabilities should give us some confidence in the simpler models, such as the basic lexicographic model presented here.

REFERENCES

Black, D., and Newing, R.A. (1951). *Committee Decisions with Complementary Valuation.* London: William Hodge & Co.

Chipman, J.S. (1960). "The Foundations of Utility." *Econometrica* 28: 193–224.

Davis, O.A., and Hinich, M. (1966). "A Mathematical Model of Policy Formation in a Democratic Society." In *Mathematical Applications in Political Science, II.* Ed. by J.L. Bernd. Dallas: Southern Methodist University Press, pp. 175–208.

Davis, O.A., and Hinich, M. (1967). "Some Results Related to a Mathematical Model of Policy Formation in a Democratic Society." In *Mathematical Applications in Political Science, III.* Ed. by J.L. Bernd. Charlottesville: University Press of Virginia, pp. 14–38.

Davis, O.A., and Hinich, M. (1968). "On the Power and Importance of the Mean Preference in a Mathematical Model of Democratic Choice." *Public Choice* 5: 59–72.

Davis, O.A., and Hinich, M., and Ordeshook, P.C. (1970). "An Expository Development of a Mathematical Model of the Electoral Process." *American Political Science Review* 64.

Debreu, G. (1954). "Representation of a Preference Ordering by a Numerical Function." In *Decision Processes.* Ed. by R.M. Thrall, C.H. Coombs, and R.L. Davis. New York: Wiley.

Edwards, W., and Tversky, A., Eds. (1967). *Decision Making.* Harmondsworth, Middlesex: Penguin Books, Ltd.

Georgescu-Roegen, N. (1954). "Choice, Expectations and Measurability." *Quarterly Journal of Economics* 68: 503–34.

Hausner, M. (1954). "Multidimensional Utilities. In *Decision Processes.* Ed. by R.M. Thrall, C.H. Coombs, and R.L. Davis. New York: Wiley.

Hausner, M., and Wendel, J.G. (1952). "Ordered Vector Spaces." *Proceedings of the American Mathematics Society* 3: 977–82.

MacCrimmon, K.R. (1968). *Decision Making Among Multi-Attribute Alternatives.* Santa Monica: Rand Corporation Memorandum RM–4823.

Plott, C.R. (1967). "A Notion of Equilibrium and Its Possibility Under Majority Rule." *American Economic Review* 57: 788–806.
Rothenberg, J. (1961). *The Measurement of Social Welfare.* Englewood Cliffs: Prentice Hall.
Sen, S. (1969). "Models of Political Campaign Strategies." Paper read at the 65th Annual Meeting of the American Political Science Association.
Taylor, M.J., and Rae, D.W. (1969). "A Spatial Model of Policy Outcomes in Voting Bodies." Paper read at the 65th Annual Meeting of the American Political Science Association.
Thrall, R.M. (1954). "Applications of Multidimensional Utility Theory." In *Decision Processes.* Ed. by R.M. Thrall, C.H. Coombs, and R.L. Davis. New York: Wiley.
Thrall, R.M., Coombs, C.H., and Davis, R.L., Eds. (1954). *Decision Processes.* New York: Wiley.

Part Three:

Structural Theories

Introduction

The two papers in this chapter are, explicitly or implicitly, developments of structural analogies. In "Everyday Life in Stochastic Networks," H. White takes advantage of Kleinrock's theorems on nets of physical facilities to bring some insight into human networks and social systems, to clarify the understanding of human relations. In "Toward the System Theory of Dependence: Further General Theoretical Remarks," F. Charvát, J. Kučera, and M. Soukup present some classical elements of information theory, although from a completely new standpoint, giving new insight into how various structural relations of dependency can be considered and interpreted in these terms.

In "Everyday Life in Stochastic Networks," H. White redefines "messages in human networks" to include wide varieties of exchanges among people, not only "official messages, rumors, and gossip," but also "moods and sentiments" and their meaning is even extended to include such activities as "lining up contacts for an acquaintance to achieve a substantial introduction to some remote person of importance." Human beings are, of course, not machines. However, Professor White's analysis seems quite far-reaching. Although the analogy between human networks and telecommunication systems is not straightforward (one problem being that human networks evolve, i.e., links between people are created, then disappear), Kleinrock's results on the analysis of nets of physical facilities explain many observable types of human behavior. And new developments in network theory are beginning to allow formal analysis of self-changing systems.

White presents numerous important conclusions in his paper concerning very general topics, such as the order of priority in which messages are treated. Messages of similar character tend to be treated in immediate succession when this is possible; moreover, in a human network humans must necessarily have free time if the net is to function at all. Provocatively, White demonstrates why social systems based on a formal table of organization cannot function in this way. However, since the connected net is the most efficient structure, according to Kleinrock, such a structure may have to remain necessary.

In the same way that H. White had to redefine the meaning of messages, F. Charvát, J. Kučera, and M. Soukup present us with a complete series of new definitions. The authors may, therefore, rightly claim that their main objective is to present us with a basic taxonomy for the study of dependence relations. Their interpretation of the quantity of "mutual information between two channels," a well-known concept in information theory, as a notion of dependence between two systems, is full of insight. But are their remarks fully developed? The model remains quite abstract and general, but with a little imagination, one could apply the consequences of the theory of these Czechs to the relationship between a dominant national system and a subordinated one. A fanciful example might be the relations between Lilliput and Blefuscu, after the seizure of the Blefuscu fleet, if Gulliver had dutifully carried out the orders of His Imperial Majesty of Lilliput to help enslave Blefuscu. More realistic cases might be classical imperialisms or externally driven regional integration systems, as modeled in Alker's paper below.

Their other concepts are also immediately derived from information theory. The reader familiar with that theory will recognize in "dependence capacity" the usual notion of "capacity of a channel," in the concept of "entropy of behavior of the systems S_1," the entropy of the measure $N({}^1 b_i)$, where $N({}^1 b_i)$ can even be viewed as a probability from a mathematical standpoint once it has been standardized. These equivalences complete the link with information theory. However, the authors introduce further notions in a quite original way. For example, they give a perfectly logical definition of the concept of power, the equivalent of which does not exist directly in information theory. One benefit of this reconceptualization is the demonstration that whenever the varieties of power or dependence reach an extreme position, a situation is attained such that a new game must be defined and a change in the data basis of the dependence must be anticipated. Another possibility is a reconciliation of the Czech approach with the related cybernetic concepts used in Chadwick's treatment of systems theory, but we shall not pursue that here.

Both papers, therefore, are suggestive transfers of works undertaken for a specific scientific area to a further understanding in political science. If they excite sufficient interest, they may help define new paradigms that would become the basis for cumulative sustained bodies of scientific research. But even before such a development takes place, it is worth emphasizing the highly provocative insights which different branches of mathematics can bring to social scientific understanding. Conventional statistical models have some of their origins in the study of states and are now widely accepted. Rational game-theoretic models developed by von Neumann and others are increasingly being used as tools for political analysis. When a general body of formal, manipulatable, and testible theory develops in political science to the point where a distinct "politicometrics" label is appropriate, it will certainly be a richer body of theory if it is not limited to any one school or type of formal analysis.

Human nature is nothing abstract, inherent to the individual. In fact, it is the sum-total of social relations.

Karl Marx

We, as human beings, are not isolated systems. We take in food, which generates energy, from the outside, and are, as a result, parts of that larger world which contains those sources of our vitality. But even more important is the fact that we take in information through our sense organs, and we act on information received.

Norbert Wiener

Toward the System Theory of Dependence: Further General Theoretical Remarks

FRANTIŠEK CHARVÁT, JAROSLAV KUČERA, and MIROSLAV SOUKUP

The present paper forms another part of a long-term project, inspired by the authors' aim to contribute to a more precise delimitation of a conceptual framework which would rationally reproduce the main dimensions of the global system and help in elaborating the program of empirical research into the dynamic structure of this system. The authors believe that the theory of dependence has a significant place within the framework of reference of both Marxian sociology and methodology. The aim of this paper is not to call attention to the model of the global system, but only to suggest the basic taxonomy, the minimum set of conceptual tools, to formulate some propositions and to present some methodical impulses for working out possible cybernetic expressions conveying some of these concepts and relations.

First of all, let us briefly recapitulate some ideas which have already been discussed elsewhere (Soukup, *et al.*, 1968).

The general theory of dependence proceeds from the hypothesis that dependence represents a basic property of all relations existing among both living and nonliving systems. The physicists in their inquiries into mechanical systems, e.g. into the solar system, were troubled by the question of how to explain inertia: What leads the bodies to remember the direction and the speed of motion and to choose their trajectory in a specific way? Why do they move along curved trajectories and with varying speed? In classical physics, these problems were explained by the operation of a certain force. But no satisfactory answer was found as to the nature of either gravitational force or inertia. In contrast to this, modern relativistic physics demonstrates that bodies have a tendency to move along the shortest world-lines, and that it is irrelevant whether these world-lines figure in Minkowski's diagram as straight or as curved lines. If the actual world-line deviates from the shortest world-line, a "force" appears the intensity of which is given by the extent of the respective deviation. The processes operating in social systems are, of course, substantially more complex, due to the fact that here – at least in the light of knowledge attained so far – the element of chance and the element of freedom play a substantially more significant role. Conceived of as a complex of roles constituting a social system, a human group has characteristics, such as expectations, beliefs, values, perception, and knowledge; all these affect its decision-making, its behavior. Social systems are at a substantially higher level of complexity than nonsocial living systems: e.g., only the location of the idea between the input and the output of the system essentially increases the difficulty of a correct prediction of the system's behavior, of its future states. The search for the limits within which it is possible to predict the behavior of these complex stochastic systems and for the probability of these predictions belongs to the standard tasks of the social sciences. However, in spite of the substantial differences between social systems and the other living and nonliving systems existing within social systems, the system of filters represented by the structure of roles and by the structure of norms is relatively stable in a given time and space. This is not at all affected by the fact that these structures may differ to a relatively great extent both in time and space. The statement that the components of a social system tend to assume the shortest trajectory along a particular "social world-line" forms the basic proposition of the social system theory of dependence. By creating an abstract theoretical model of dependence relations, we hope to improve our understanding of what factors compel social systems and the components of these systems – the individual, the group, the organization, the state, the coalition of states – to perform a certain role, or to give up this role and to assume another role. The theory of dependence proceeds from the postulate that the relative stability or change in the behavior of social systems, such as the long-term performance of a certain role or its abandonment by a component of the system, is caused not by some social inertia, but by the relative stability of a certain structure of dependence relations within the system, as well as among the systems, or by their change.

Introductory Remarks to the System – Theoretical Approach

There exist three levels of communication problems: How accurately can the symbols of communication be transmitted? (Shannon's technical problem). How precisely do the transmitted symbols convey the desired meaning? (The semantic problem). How effectively does the received meaning affect the conduct in the desired way? (The behavioral problem). This last-mentioned level, involving social change, will be at the center of our concern, but let us first introduce some remarks on the concept of system. We conceive a system as an abstraction facilitating gnoseological application in all the dimensions of the cognitive process. From the purely gnoseological viewpoint, it is a relational category of both the subject and the object. The "formal character" of the system concept or of its delimitation is, in this respect, in conformity with the laws, due to the fact that – from the ontological viewpoint – it covers the entire materially unambiguous reality of the world. It is an abstraction of a degree facilitating the gnoseological application in all the dimensions of the cognitive procedures.

For explicating the system concept, only the concept of the set, i.e., of so-called general space, is needed. By general space we understand the ordered pair of a certain set A and a subset of the Cartesian product, $A \times A$, denoted as ρ. Symbolically represented:

$I = (A, \rho)$,

where I is the general space.

By a system S we then mean the ordered pair of general spaces I and E, symbolically represented:

$S = (I, E)$, where $I = (A, \rho)$, $E = (B, \sigma)$

I is the sign for the internal structure of the system S, E for the external structure of the system S, A for the set of internal elements of the system S (the set of elements of the internal structure of the system S), ρ for the set of relations of the internal elements of the system S (the links of the internal structure of the system S). Analogically, the same definitions apply to the sets B and σ with the respective substitution of the term "external" for "internal." The inclusion of the formal concept of the system, explained in this way, into the sphere of cognitive procedures takes place by means of its semantic fulfilment, e.g., by means of a semantic interpretation of the separate constitutive components of the concept explained above. In terms of cognitive procedure, we view the examined object as a system and determine – by an interpretation on the object of cognition – what is the set of internal elements, what is the set of couplings in the internal structure, etc. The system category thus semantically fulfilled may be called the concrete system, while the preceding delimitation would, in this sense, refer to the so-called formal or abstract system.

From the philosophical viewpoint, we are concerned with the basic problem whether it is possible to realize the semantic interpretation of the formal system in each segment of concrete totality, in other words, whether it is possible gnoseologically to apply the system category on any object of cognition. A positive answer to the problem presented is the basic philosophical starting-point of the system-theoretical approach in contemporary thinking. From the viewpoint of Marxian philosophy, this fundamental thesis is a direct consequence of the principle of the material unity of the world. We may come across the verification of this thesis as a methodological hypothesis of contemporary scientific knowledge in all the modern gnoseological procedures – either in a manifest or in a latent form.

The system-theoretical approach offers the possibility of creating a system of properties in any research subject in the endeavor to discover the way in which these properties emerge from the laws governing the system components and their interaction. We should like to emphasize that the inquiry might prove to be more useful after an understanding of the basic properties of the system as a whole has been arrived at. In this context, Marx's sociology is an ideal example of the system-theoretical approach to social sciences.

At first sight, the impression may rightfully arise that the contribution of the system-theoretical approach has an expressively a posteriori significance, being a mere instrument for effectively perfecting a record which has been already known before, while there is no increase whatsoever in cognitive potencies. Disregarding the fact that a perfect, logically consistent view of the system of the ascertained pieces of knowledge indubitably represents an expressive positive asset, it is necessary to emphasize just this "transfer" function of system categories in the mathematical, logical, and cybernetic findings of other scientific disciplines. And here, most certainly, the task of the system concept does not correspond to a mere instrument of an a posteriori perfection.

From the viewpoint of political science, the application of the system-theoretical approach means systems categories are introduced for all the object phenomena of political knowledge. In order to prevent in advance the measure of vagueness of such categories, when applied to the concrete political system, let us here emphasize that the concrete political system thus conceived, has a broader significance than is often intuitively ascribed to it in traditional political literature.

In this sense, the system-theoretical approach is related to cognition of all kinds, and its application is the internal methodological component of every scientific discipline. In the social sciences, it is characterized by the fact that the semantic interpretation of formal systems categories is realized in terms of the objects and phenomena of social reality. Within the scope of the differentiation of social knowledge, it is necessary, however, to find objective criteria for the classification of such phenomena.

As our definition implies, a system may also be conceived of as a concept having two parts: a set of components in mutual interaction and a boundary. The component is a system unit which, interacting with other units, functions in a way enabling it to process inputs in order to produce outputs. The boundary of the system is the area separating one system from another; its function is to filter or select inputs or outputs. Boundaries are filters of both the quality and the velocity of input and output flows between the system and its environment. One can also distinguish relations among the components within boundaries from those reaching across a boundary.

Inputs are the energies absorbed by the system. The maintenance inputs are those which prepare or maintain the functioning of the system; the process inputs are those elaborated by the system. Outputs are the energies representing the results of the system operation and differing, in some significant way, from the inputs. For the purposes of this discussion, let us also assume that all the systems are open, that the universe is conceived as a system of systems, that the functions of a system are dependent upon its structure, and that a critical proximity is the precondition for the interaction of the components.

Let us mention some further propositions. The state of the system is one of the determinants of the output. Both maintenance input and process input are necessary for the long-term survival of a system. The outputs may be either useful or useless, these criteria being determined by the supra-system. The supra-system selects those outputs of its subsystems which are useful and, on the contrary, rejects the useless outputs. The viable systems are those in which the useful outputs exceed the useless ones.

The outputs are limited not only by the character of the system's components, but also by the extent to which the outputs serve as the maintenance inputs of another system, on the supposition that there is a reciprocity of maintenance inputs between both systems.

Systems have outputs of two kinds: performance outputs measured in terms of the extent to which the system is fulfilling the tasks expected of it by a supra-system; and system and components needs satisfaction (*SCNS*), which outputs are analogical to maintenance inputs. A supra-system reveals a tendency to control the lower boundary of its subsystem's performance output and the upper limit of the output of its subsystem's *SCNS* while, on the contrary, a subsystem has a tendency to control the lower boundary of its own *SCNS* output and the upper boundary of its performance output[1].

---

[1] The outputs of open systems are probabilistic outputs. This is due to the fact that, on the one hand, open systems are in interaction with other systems which, by themselves, have a probabilistic character, and, on the other hand, that no system may be observed without a certain influence being exerted by the observer on the observed system (Heisenberg's principle of indeterminacy). The variability or the limits of the output are controlled by the structure of the component system and by the boundaries, as well as by the ultimate number of states the system may have with regard to the given structure and boundaries. The capacity of the system is the range of its variability. By organization we understand the

A system develops relations of two kinds: on the one hand, coupling with other equal-level systems, and, on the other hand, subordination-dominance relation with its supra-system[2].

Selected Taxonomy and Formalization

Basic Concepts

The goal-directed activity (in the following, only "activity") is designed to satisfy a specific need of the system. Activity is the only primary means of satisfying the need, whereas the secondary means of need satisfaction is the means of realization which is the result of a certain activity[3]. In social systems it is possible, in a great number of cases, to replace the category of need by the category of interest, which is a social category corresponding to the projection of the phenomena and relations of the system's environment into the space of the system's needs. It is possible to define *SNCS* by a utility function, i.e., one of the central concepts of the theory of utility.

If we conceive information as every communication or signal influencing our behavior, then we must ascribe informative significance to the communication spread by dependence channels. The ascription of informative significance must not necessarily have a conscious character.

---

coupling of real systems, e.g., if symbiotic couplings are established between two coupled systems, or if feedback relations are developing among complex systems consisting of more than two components. The organization of the system develops in the direction of greater complexity and new characteristics. Adaptations are modifications of the behavior and structures in the life of the system or in generations widening the possibilities of its survival. They consist in the blocking or neutralization of potentially detrimental maintenance inputs. Growth may be regarded as a structural modification facilitating the acceptance of maintenance inputs. New characteristics of the system and potential modifications of the structure are the inevitable consequences of growth. The growth modifications may also be considered as adaptations since they enable the system to increase its vitality. Growth is circumscribed by the limits of adaptation and memory. Learning is regarded as a structural modification arising as a consequence of process inputs.

---

[2] In the case of the first type, there is a mutual reciprocity of inputs and outputs, while the capacity of the channels among these systems imposes limitations to the extent of exchange. Thus the coupling among systems represents one of the possibilities of intersystem structural organization. This symbiotic coupling is not to be confused with feedback.

[3] For a discussion concerning the concept of need, *see* Richta (1969).

The dependence relation of two systems is thus defined as a relation in which one system affects – by specific means (rewards and punishments) – the *SCNS* of another system. The dependence relation is not determined by what has happened, but by what might have happened if the behavior of another system would not, in certain respects, have corresponded to the selective demands of the first system. The dependence coupling is the set of dependence relations between two systems.

The dependence space is the set of dependence relations among three or more systems. More generally, a system S_1 is dependent upon all the systems influencing its *SCNS*. The dominant dependence relation refers to the dominant need. By a hegemonous system of dependence $S_2 \rightarrow S_1$ we understand the system affecting the possibility of satisfying the substantial needs of the set of *SCNS*'s of another system.

The compatibility of two systems depends on their capability of mutually satisfying the system needs, on their complementarity and on their similarity as to the extent of required exchange with other systems in all the areas of need.

In this conception, the dependence operating among social systems has a formal function, apparently similar to that of the force operating among inanimate systems. The relative independence of the internal structure of the system may be a source of an anti-dependence activity.

It is for two basic reasons that the supra-system of the process of growth has a tendency to reinforce the hegemonous dependence: on the one hand, it is the growth of specialization of the subsystem which is the product of the demand of the supra-system made on the maximum output of the subsystem – i.e., the ability of the subsystem to survive independently decreases with growing specialization; on the other hand, the role the supra-system performs as a source of maintenance inputs for the subsystem is increasing. In case this process does not develop properly, if the organizational input and output couplings are deformed, the result is a sub-optimum degree of integration. A dialectical relation of contradiction and unity exists between the requirements of the supra-system and the requirements of the subsystem's continuous identity. This relation may even result in a latent or open conflict.

The Need Relations Among the Elements Constituting the External Structure of Systems.

The set of elements of the external structure of system S_1, i.e., the set B_1, will be called the set of activities of the system S_1. It will now be our aim to specify the set σ_1 from the viewpoint of the needs of this system, or, in other words, the so-called need relations among the activities of the system S_1.

Let us designate as X a certain set which we shall call the set of needs (and possibilities) of the activities of the system S_1, supposing that an equivalence relation χ operates on this set. The mapping of the set B_1 into the set X, designated as N, will be called the system of needs of the activities of the system S_1.

The relation σ_1 operated on B_1, defined by the following

$$[{}^1b_r, {}^1b_r] \in \tau_1 \Leftrightarrow [N({}^1b_r), N({}^1b_s)] \in \chi$$

will be called the need relations among the activities of the system S_1. And finally, we shall denote as N the set of all ${}^1b_r$ – such that ${}^1b_r \in B_1$.

This formal construction corresponds to concrete methodological procedures; it means that with each activity of the system S_1 we determine its need which represents an element of a certain set of all potentially possible needs (and possibilities) X which, as we presume, are organized by a certain equivalence relation χ. We concretely assume that the activities of the system S_1, i.e., the projection N, is determined exclusively by the internal structure of the given system S_1. Thus the need relations of the elements of the system's external structure are a certain mapping of the internal relations of the system into its external relations.

The need relations among the activities of the system S_1 are that sort of relations in which we abstract from the environment of the given system under examination, conceived for the given moment as a system "by itself."

In the above, we have mentioned that the set X represents the space of needs and possibilities of the activities of the system S_1. We shall now endeavor to determine with more precision, what is meant by the so-called system of possibilities of the activities of the system S_1 with respect to the activities of the system S_2, the system S_2, the set of which is denoted by B_2.

The system of possibilities of the activities of the system S_1 with regard to the activity ${}^2b_p$ of the system S_2 will be called the mapping of the set B_1 into the set X which will be designated as $P_{{}^2b_p}$. The set of all $P_{{}^2b_p}({}^1b_r)$ in which ${}^1b_r \in B_1$ will be designated as $P_{{}^2b_p}$. Formally, there is no difference between the system of needs of the activities of the system S_1 and the system of possibilities of the activities of this system as regards the activity ${}^2b_p$ of the system S_2.

There is a substantial difference, however, in the content interpretation of these concepts, since the system of possibility relations represents the expression of the system's relation to its environment, in our case to the system S_2.

Let us globally call the set of all $P_{{}^2b_p}$, in which ${}^2b_p \in B_2$, the set of possibility relations of the system S_1 to the system S_2 and designate it as P. For the sake of completeness, let us introduce the concept of all the possibilities of the activities of the system S_1 as regards the system S_2 as the set

$$P = \{ P_{{}^2b_p} \mid {}^2b_p \in B_2 \}.$$

From what has been mentioned above, it is evident that the equivalence relation χ operating on the set of needs and possibilities of the system S_1 generates relations among the elements of the external structure of the system S_1 in consideration of the mappings $P_{{}^2b_p}$, where ${}^2b_p \in B_2$. We could introduce the relation $\sigma^*_{{}^2b_p}$ on the set of activities in the following way:

$$[{}^1b_r, {}^1b_s] \in \sigma^*_{{}^2b_p} \Leftrightarrow [P_{{}^2b_p}({}^1b_r), P_{{}^2b_p}({}^1b_s)] \in \chi.$$

Moreover, the fact that both $N \subset X$ and $P_{{}^2b_p} \subset X$ for each ${}^2b_p \in B_2$ allows the possibility of introducing the relation between the needs and possibilities of the activities of the system S_1. This brings us to a further relevant concept.

Dependence Relations Among Systems

We shall now define unambiguously the dependence relation of the systems as a category expressing the contradiction between the needs and possibilities, between the internal structure of the so-called dependent system and its environment, i.e., of the so-called hegemonic system S_2.

Definition: Let us say that the system S_1 is dependent upon the system S_2, if there exists at least one pair ${}^1b_r$ and ${}^2b_s$ of elements constituting the external structures of the systems S_1 and S_2, for which the following is valid:

$$[N({}^1b_r), P_{{}^2b_s}({}^1b_r)] \notin \chi \tag{1}$$

Expressed in simple words, this means that the need of activity ${}^1b_r$ "is different" from the possibility of this activity with respect to the activity ${}^2b_s$, while the difference means that the two are not in an equivalent relation operating on the set of needs and possibilities of the system S_1.

For the sake of presenting a didactic illustration, let us express the concept of dependence by the following diagram:

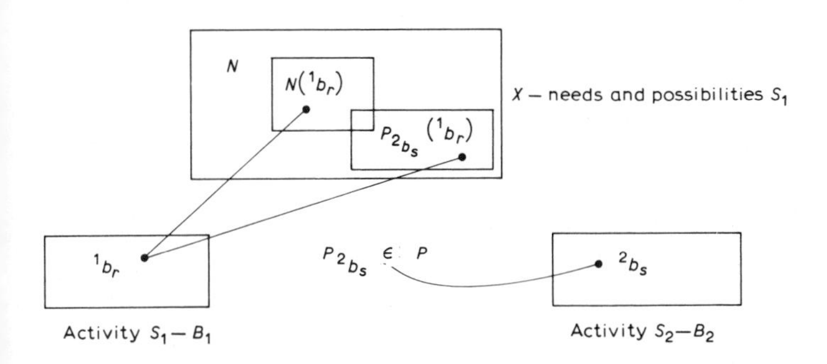

Fig. 1.

The relation χ is expressed in the diagram by the relation of the incidence of points illustrating activities on the one hand, and the needs and possibilities of these activities on the other.

As a natural consequence of defining the dependence of the systems S_1 and S_2, it is possible unambiguously to delimit the fact that the system S_1 is independent of the system S_2: this is the case if, for arbitrary

$^1b_r \in B_1$ and $^2b_s \in B_2$, then

$$[N(^1b_r), P_{^2b_s}(^1b_r)] \in \chi.$$

In other words: all the needs of the activities of the system S_1 are in an equivalence relation with the possibilities of these activities with respect to the system S_2.

The independence of the system S_1 on the system S_2 is a singular case of dependence of the system S_1 upon the system S_2, in the sense that it is a zero-dependence.

In case that (1) takes place, we write $S_2 \rightarrow S_1$ (*see* Soukup, *et al.*, 1968) or $[S_2, S_1] \in D$, where D is the so-called dependence relation on the set of all the systems. It is not uninteresting to examine the properties of the dependence relation on the set of all the systems – this, however, exceeds the scope of our contribution. From the complex of problems included in this area, we shall deal with the question of the construction of a reasonable and natural relation on the dependence relation, in other words, with the ways of comparing the separate dependencies. For this purpose, let us concisely reproduce some of the basic results of the cited study by Soukup, Charvát, Kučera (1968).

Quantification of the Needs and Possibilities of the Activities of Systems

By the quantification of the needs and activities of the system S_1 we mean a situation in which the set of needs and activities represents a certain set of real numbers, in our case a closed interval $< 0, 1 >$.It stands to reason that this is a rather simplified specification. We might proceed analogically as in traditional econometric constructions, e.g., in the theories of utility and social choice (K.J. Arrow, 1963), while we might be able, in general, easily to adapt these considerations for the purposes of politometric considerations. In this case, the projection of the set of needs and activities of the given system on a certain numerical set would be such as to reproduce the mentioned equivalence relation on the relation of equality of real numbers. If our method reduces this twofold way of projecting, it is, as a matter of fact, not to the detriment of generality, since – from the formal viewpoint – the non-numerically conceived space of needs and possibilities of the activities of the system S_1 is superfluous; not, however, from the viewpoint of desirability, which we must always be aware of in interpreting our procedures.

For our further considerations it will be natural to assume that the sets of activities of the systems S_1 and S_2 are finite; the numbers of their elements are designated as $|B_1|$, $|B_2|$.

The result of the quantification of the needs of the system S_1 is the sequence of numbers

$N(^1b_1), \ldots, N(^1b_i), \ldots, N(^1b_{|B_1|})$, satisfying the condition: $N(^1b_i) \geqslant 0$, for $i = 1, \ldots, |B_1|$, and further the so-called norm-setting condition

$$\sum_{i=1}^{|B_1|} N(^1b_i) = 1$$

Here, the relation of equality of the real numbers plays the role of the relation χ. The need relations among the elements of the external structure of the system S_1 are, in this case, expressed quantitatively.

On the set of the quantified needs of the activities of the system S_1, it is possible to introduce the category of the so-called entropy of behavior of the system S_1 as the variable:

$$\epsilon(S_1) = -\sum_{i=1}^{|B_1|} N(^1b_i) \cdot \log_2 N(^1b_i), \tag{2}$$

possessing certain useful features: it expresses the homogeneity of the needs of the activities of the systems in the sense that it attains its maximum if all the needs of the activities are equal, and that it attains its minimum if one need of activity is maximum and the others are minimum. The axiomatic construction of this variable is a traditional matter of the nowadays already classical information theory (Faddejev, 1956)[4].

Similarly, also the set of quantified possibilities of the activities of the system S_1 as regards the activity $^2b_r \in B_2$ of the system S_2 may be introduced. It is the following sequence of numbers:

---

[4] Let us note here that, in a certain sense, the category of the entropy of behavior may be introduced even when the quantified needs of the activities of the system S_1 are not considered – this, however, is not the subject of our interest.

$$P_{^2b_r}(^1b_1), \ldots, P_{^2b_r}(^1b_i), \ldots, P_{^2b_r}(^1b_{|B_1|}),$$

which fulfills the conditions:

$$P_{^2b_r}(^1b_i) \geqq 0, i = 1, \ldots, |B_1|$$

and further the so-called norm-setting condition:

$$\sum_{i=1}^{|B_1|} P_{^2b_r}(^1b_i) = 1$$

Again, even here, the role of the relation χ is played by the relation of equality among the real numbers.

The possibilities of the activities of the system S_1 as regards the activity ^2b_r of the system S_2 are expressed quantitatively for each $^2b_r \in B_2$.

These facts of quantitatively expressing the needs and possibilities of the activities of the system-S_1 naturally lead to a quantitative expression of the dependences of the system S_1 upon the system S_2.

Quantification of the Dependence of the System S_1 on the System S_2.

With the quantified needs and possibilities of the system S_1, the relation (1) is modified in the following way: The system S_1 is dependent upon the system S_2 when there exists at least one pair ^1b_r, ^2b_s of the elements of the external structures of the systems S_1 and S_2, for which the following holds true:

$$N(^1b_r) \neq P_{^2b_s}(^1b_r) \qquad (1^*)$$

On the contrary, the independence of the system S_1 upon the system S_2 (a zero, singular dependence) appears wherever for an arbitrary

$$^1b_r \in B_1 \text{ and } ^2b_s \in B_2$$

the relation:

$$N(^1b_r) = P_{^2b_s}(^1b_r)$$

holds true.

In quantifying the needs of the activities of the system, we have introduced – as a higher quantitative characterization – the entropy of behavior of the system S_1. Similarly, on the set of needs and possibilities of the system S_1 we introduce a quantitative characterization which, in a natural way, expresses the dependence of the system; in other words, it is a certain possible measure of the system dependence.

As a measure of the dependence $S_2 \rightarrow S_1$ we introduce the following quantity:

$$d(S_2 \rightarrow S_1) = -\sum_{i=1}^{|B_2|} N(^2b_i) \cdot \log_2 N(^2b_i) +$$

$$\sum_{K=1}^{|B_1|} \sum_{i=1}^{|B_2|} N(^2b_i) \cdot P_{^2b_i}(^1b_K) \cdot \log_2 \frac{N(^2b_i) \cdot P_{^2b_i}(^1b_K)}{\sum_{s=1}^{|B_2|} N(^2b_s) \cdot P_{^2b_s}(^1b_K)} \qquad (3)$$

where the first member in the relation (3) is denoted as $\epsilon(S_2)$ and the second addend $\epsilon(S_2 \mid S_1)$, so that the relation (3) may be simplified to the form

$$d(S_2 \rightarrow S_1) = \epsilon(S_2) - \epsilon(S_2 \mid S_1) \qquad (3^*)$$

The quantity $\epsilon(S_2)$ is the entropy of the behavior of the system S_2. It is determined in the same way as the entropy of the behavior of the system S_1, with which it is, moreover, coupled – in view of the dependence relation – by the natural relation:

$$N(^1b_K) = \sum_{s=1}^{|B_2|} N(^2b_s) \cdot P_{^2b_s}(^1b_K)$$

This measure of dependence has natural properties: it is zero when and only when, for arbitrary $^1b_r \in B_1$ and $^2b_s \in B_2$,

$$N(^1b_r) = P_{^2b_s}(^1b_r)$$

and it is maximum, if the arbitrary activity of the system S_1 is determined by a certain activity of the systems S_2. The validity of $0 \leqslant d(S_2 \rightarrow S_1) \leqslant \epsilon(S_2)$, may be easily demonstrated. It means that the maximum dependence of the system S_1 upon the system S_2 may be found when $\epsilon (S_2 \mid S_1) = 0$ and the measure of dependence of the system S_2 upon the system S_1 is equal to the entropy of the hegemonous system S_1.

For technical reasons, it appears useful to define the so-called standard measure of the dependence of the system S_1 upon the system S_2 as a quantity determined by the relation:

$$d^*(S_2 \rightarrow S_1) = \frac{d(S_2 \rightarrow S_1)}{\epsilon(S_2)}$$

This attains its maximum, i.e., it equals 1, if the dependence of S_2 upon S_1 is maximum, and it attains its minimum, i.e., it equals 0, if S_2 is independent of S_1. The significance of the measure of the standard measure of dependence is primarily that this functional on the dependence field enables us to compare the dependencies in a natural way, since the relation "τ" generates the relation "τ" on the dependence field in the following way:

$$[S_p, S_q], [S_r, S_u] \in \tau \Leftrightarrow d(S_p \rightarrow S_q) \leqq d(S_r \rightarrow S_u),$$

conceivably $[S_p, S_q] \in D$, $[S_r, S_u] \in D$.

This is a particularly important characteristic, advantageous especially for politometric procedures.

Dependence Capacity

From what has been said above, it is evident that the dependence relation is determined by the following system of politometric data:

$$N(^1b_r),\ ^1b_r \in B_1, P_{^2b_s}(^1b_r),\ ^2b_s \in B_2,$$

or equivalently by the system:

$$N(^2b_s),\ ^2b_s \in B_2, P_{^2b_s}(^1b_r),\ ^2b_s \in B_2,\ ^1b_r \in B_1.$$

The following subsystem is common to these systems of politometric data:

$$P_{^2b_s}(^1b_r),\ ^2b_s \in B_2,\ ^1b_r \in B_1.$$

We call it the data basis of the dependence $S_2 \rightarrow S_1$ and denote it as

$b(S_2 \rightarrow S_1)$. This data basis represents the quantification of the dependence relation which "abstracts" from the separate systems constituting the dependence relation. (Let us note that the data basis may be formally expressed by means of a matrix of the type $|B_2| x |B_1|$.)

In analyzing the quantity $d(S_2 \rightarrow S_1)$, we find that, besides the elements of the data basis, it contains the data $N(^2b_s)$, $.^2b_s \in B_2$, or the entropy of the behavior of the hegemonous system S_2.

It seems natural to ask – with regard to the given data basis of the dependence $S_2 \rightarrow S_1$ – in what way the hegemonous or the dependent system is going to "control" its behavior.

Intuitively, the conception seems acceptable that the hegemonous system S_2 will strive to maximize the dependence relation. This intuitive consideration leads to the introduction of a further significant category of the system-dependence theory, i.e., the concept of the so-called *dependence capacity*.

Definition: The dependence capacity of the relation $S_2 \rightarrow S_1$ is the maximum of the function $d(S_2 \rightarrow S_1)$, while the data basis of the dependence $S_2 \rightarrow S_1$ is given (fixed). Let us denote this quantity as $c(S_2 \rightarrow S_1)$.

For the purposes of a numerically technical illustration, let us present a simple model example:

Let us assume that $|B_2| = 3$, $|B_1| = 2$, where the data basis $b(S_2 \rightarrow S_1)$ is given as follows:

$$P_{^2b_1}(^1b_1) = 1 \qquad P_{^2b_1}(^1b_2) = 0$$

$$P_{^2b_2}(^1b_1) = 0 \qquad P_{^2b_2}(^1b_2) = 1$$

$$P_{^2b_3}(^1b_1) = 0 \qquad P_{^2b_3}(^1b_2) = 1$$

It is very easy to demonstrate that in this case $c(S_2 \rightarrow S_1) = 1$; $d(S_2 \rightarrow S_1)$ attains this value when the needs of the activities of the hegemonous system S_2 are quantified by the values:

$$N(^2b_1) = \frac{1}{2}, N(^2b_2) + N(^2b_3) = \frac{1}{2}.$$

(*See* A. Feinstein, 1958.)

Even if we have defined the capacity of the dependence $S_2 \to S_1$ "quantitatively" (as an extreme of the function), its sense (as well as the potentially possible modified variants of its more precise delimitation) is primarily qualitative: for it represents an instrument for finding such a sort of behavior of the hegemonous system S_2 which would maximize the dependence relation $S_2 \to S_1$.

On the other hand, as has already been mentioned, the dependent system S_1 will tend to a situation in which the dependence relation $S_2 \to S_1$ would be minimized, naturally for the known data basis $b(S_2 \to S_1)$. For this reason, it is natural to introduce the so-called *dependence boundaries* of the dependence $S_2 \to S_1$. They are the minimum of the function $d(S_2 \to S_1)$ where the data basis given is $b(S_2 \to S_1)$ and denoted as $h(S_2 \to S_1)$. Thus it is evident that the following is valid:

$$h(S_2 \to S_1) \leqq d(S_2 \to S_1) \leqq c(S_2 \to S_1)$$

where $b(S_2 \to S_1)$ is given.

The interval $< h(S_2 \to S_1), c(S_2 \to S_1) >$ is here called *the variety of the dependence relation* $S_2 \to S_1$.

We may easily make sure that, in the above example, the interval $< 0, 1 >$ is the variety of the dependence relation $S_2 \to S_1$.

It should be noted that the mentioned definition-constructions carried out in this section were characteristic due to our assumption that the data basis of the dependence $S_2 \to S_1$ is constant – and on this assumption we have further analyzed the dependence relation. It may be taken for granted that, in real situations, there exist also other, higher developmental forms of the dependence relations in which the development of the data basis of dependence takes place. However, the change in the data basis of dependence represents a qualitative turnover in the dependence relation; this takes place after a certain time period characterized just by the constant data basis of dependence which it has developed within the space given by the variety of the dependence relation, and is conceivably, not rigid in time.

The Trend Generalization of Dependence

All our considerations presented hitherto have not explicitly reckoned with the time factor which, undoubtedly, is of decisive significance. This shortcoming, however, may be easily eliminated by generalizing all the categories we have introduced until now to what can be called "trend categories."

The substance of this procedure lies in that we do not conceive all the concepts (needs, possibilities, dependences, etc.) as elements of the respective spaces, but as abstract functions with values in the respective spaces. If the respective space is numerical, we get, instead of numbers, functions, numerical progressions, sequences, etc. This conception allows our categories to be variable in time or continually developing.

It is, however, necessary to point out that some categories need not be conceived in terms of trends. For example, activities in general and the data bases of dependence in a certain period of time may not vary without reducing the applicability of our dependence model. The trend character of the activities is indirectly expressed by the trend character of the needs of these activities, and the data bases of dependence represent, in a certain period of time, a constant norm in the relations among systems.

Hereafter, we shall conceive these categories or quantities in terms of trends; this trend character will be denoted by the right lower index (subscript):

Needs of activities $N_t\,({}^1b_r), N_t\,({}^2b_s)$,

Entropy of the system's behavior: $\epsilon_t\,(S_1), \epsilon_t\,(S_2)$

The measure, of dependence: $d_t(S_2 \to S_1)$, or the standard measure of dependence: $d^*_t(S_2 \to S_1)$.

We shall further assume that the trend index possesses a value within a certain time interval I.

As for the other quantities defined above, we assume that they are invariable in the interval I, for example, the data bases of dependence, the capacity, and the boundaries of dependence.

Dependence and Power

The category of dependence is useful methodologically for precisely defining the main politological category of power, the semantics of which is characterized, in politological literature, by a considerable measure of vagueness and subjectivity.

The category of power – analogically, the category of dependence – must be conceived as referring to the systems of social totality. Moreover, it is possible to define the category of power of the system S_2 over the system S_1 as a derivate of the category of dependence of the system S_1 upon system S_2.

Definition: System S_2 has power over system S_1, if the system S_1 is dependent upon system S_2 and the dependence coupling $S_2 \rightarrow S_1$ influences the behavior of the hegemonous system S_2 in the direction of the growth of this dependence relation (or at least of its constancy) within the framework of the variety of the dependence relation $S_2 \rightarrow S_1$.

Thus, it is evident that the category of power is a polar category of the previously defined concept of dependence. In the same way we may – in the special case of "dynamic" dependence – refer to the capacity of power, the limits of power, the measure of power, the variety of power relations, etc.

The specificity of the power relation is given by the fact that the systems figuring in this specific dependence relation dispose of information concerning this dependence relation as a basis for controlling their behavior in order to maximize or to minimize the dependence relation.

This fact also leads to the analysis of the dependence relation, or of power and information. Information may here be conceived as a change in the dependence relation, i.e., as an increase or decrease of the dependence relation. Information represents a system of knowledge concerning the dependence or power relation on the basis of which the development of the dependence relation takes place.

From a descriptive viewpoint, we may consider the development of the dependence or power relation of the systems as a game situation in which the role of gain is played by the measure of dependence (or power) $d_t(S_2 \rightarrow S_1)$ acquiring values in the interval

$$< h(S_2 \rightarrow S_1), c(S_2 \rightarrow S_1) >.$$

Here the choices of the needs of activities, i.e., the successions

$$N_t({}^2b_s), {}^2b_s \in B_2$$

(in the system S_2) or the successions

$$N_t\,({}^1b_r),\ {}^1b_r \in B_1$$

(in the system S_1) represent the strategies of the separate elements of the dependence relation.

The "move" in such a dependence or power game is conceived as the possibility of either a hegemonous or a dependent system adjusting its behavior within the scope of the chosen strategy. The difference between the measure of dependence after and before the move is an aid for measuring the information disposed of by the given system of the dependence relation in which the game takes place. For the sake of illustration, we shall demonstrate the situation of one move in the dependence or power structure in the scheme:

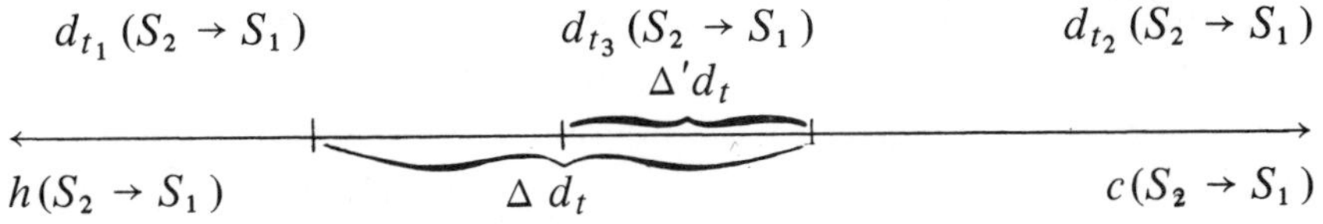

$d_{t_1}(S_2 \to S_1)$ $d_{t_3}(S_2 \to S_1)$ $d_{t_2}(S_2 \to S_1)$

$\Delta' d_t$

$h(S_2 \to S_1)$ $\Delta\, d_t$ $c(S_2 \to S_1)$

At the moment t_1, system S_2 has chosen a strategy leading to an increase of dependence by Δd_t (measuring the amount of information the hegemonous system had on the dependence relation) and, on the contrary, the system S_1 has chosen, at the moment t_2, a strategy which decreased the dependence relation by $\Delta' d_t$, etc.

In the given period of time, the hegemonous system tends to acquire the capacity of the dependence relation, whereas the dependent systems aims at making the measure of dependence acquire its minimum, i.e. the limit of dependence.

We may take for granted that the attainment of one of the extreme positions of the variety of the dependence or power relation results in the close of the game, since in this situation, it is natural to anticipate a change in the data basis of the dependence $S_2 \to S_1$.

Dependence Data

It should be noted that, in contrast to a great number of other politometric indices, the data appropriate for this model of systemic dependence and power must be generated in terms of this general theory.

It should also be noted that a stochastic conception of quantities figuring in this theory is both possible and of substantive interest. Thus, the quantified needs of activities may be thought of as probabilities of the realization of these activities which are determined by the internal structure of the given systems. In this case, the mentioned dependence model is, in substance, isomorphic with the cybernetic model of a discrete information channel without memory. This correspondence, among others, is a sure guarantee of its pragmatical significance.

The sense of this briefly outlined theory of dependence lies, however, not only in the possibility of generating dependence or power data and of modelling the dependence or power game, but, to a decisive extent, in its contribution of an unambiguous construction within the category system of contemporary political science.

The analysis of these further serious politological problems immediately implied by the theory of systemic dependence and power is, however, not within the scope of this contribution.

We hope that, in spite of the high level of abstraction and of an insufficient amount of data supporting our propositions, the hypothetical-deductive conclusions will have some heuristic value for further inquiries into the theory of modelling the guidance systems of social processes.

REFERENCES

Alker, Jr., Hayward R. (1965). *Mathematics and Politics*. New York: The Macmillan Co.

Arab-Ogly, Eduard; Kolman Arnošt; Zeman, Jiří (1965). *Kybernetika ve společenských vědách* [Cybernetics in Social Sciences]. Prague: Nakladatelství Československé akademie věd.

Arrow, Kenneth J., 1963 (1951). *Social Choice and Individual Values*. New Haven: Yale University Press.

Ashby, W. Ross (1961). *Design for a Brain*. New York.

Bartos, Otomar J. (1967). *Simple Models of Group Behaviour*. New York and London: Columbia University Press.

Berg, A.I., Ed. (1967). *Informacija i kibernetika* [Information and Cybernetics]. Moscow: Sovetskoje radio.

Bertalanffy, L. von (1962). "General System Theory, a Critical Review." *General Systems* 7.

Blauberg, I.V., Ed., *et al.* (1969). *Problemy metodologii sistemnogo issledovanija* [The Problems of the Methodology of the System Research]. Moscow: Mysl.

Blauberg, I.V.; Sadovskij, V.N.; Judin, E.G. (1969). *Sistemnyj podchod: predposylki, problemy, trudnosti* [The System Approach: Prerequisites, Problems, Difficulties]. Moscow: Znanie.

Borodkin, F.M.; Dončeva, S.; Penkov, D. (1970). Ob izmerenii vlijanija v sisteme parametrov [*On the Measurement of the Influence in the System of Parameters*]. Paper presented at the 7th World Congress of Sociology, Varna.
Brillouin, L. (1949). "Life, Thermodynamics, and Cybernetics." *American Scientist* 36.
Buckley, Walter (1967). *Sociology and Modern Systems Theory*. Englewood Cliffs, New Jersey: Prentice-Hall, Inc.
Deutsch, Karl W. (1963). *The Nerves of Government*. New York: The Free Press. London: Collier-Macmillan Ltd.
Deutsch, Karl W.; Kochen, Manfred (1969). Toward a Rational Theory of Decentralization: Some Implications of a Mathematical Approach. Paper at the National Conference of the American Political Science Association, New York.
Dobrov, G.M., Ed. (1970). *Naukovedenije, Prognozirovanije, Informatika* [Methodology of Science, Prognostics, Informatics]. Kiev: Naukova Dumka.
Fadděјev, D.K. (1956). "K pojatiju entropii konečnej věrojatnostnoj schemy" [On the Concept of Entropy of the Finite Probability Scheme]. *Uspechy mat.nauk*, No. 1.
Feinstein, Amiel. (1956). Foundations of information theory. New York.
Galtung, J. (1968). "Entropy and the General Theory of Peace." *Proceedings of the International Peace Research Association*. Paper presented at the 2nd Conference. Assen: Van Gorcum & Co.
Gluškov, V.M. (1964). *Vvedenije v kibernetiku* [Introduction to Cybernetics]. Kiev: Izdatelstvo Akademii nauk Ukrainskoj SSR.
Harsanyi, John C. (1962). "Measurement of Social Power in n-Person Reciprocal Power Situations." *Behavioral Science* 7, No. 1.
Klaus, S. (1964). *Kybernetik und Gesellschaft*. Berlin: VEB Deutscher Verlag der Wissenschaften.
Kravec, A.S. (1970). *Verojatnost i sistemy* [Probability and Systems]. Voroněž: Izdatelstvo voroněžskogo universiteta.
Krejči, Jar. (1970). On Sociological Aspects of the Development of Science as an Information System. Paper presented at the 7th World Congress of Sociology, Varna.
Kulikowski, R. (1968). Synthesis and Optimum Control of Organization in Large-Scale Cybernetic Systems. Paper presented at the 5th International Congress on Cybernetics, Namur.
Kundrjavcev, V.N., Ed. (1970). *Pravovaja Kibernetika* [Cybernetics of Law]. Moscow: Izdatelstvo "Nauka."
Lamb, George G. (1969). Basic Concepts in Subjective Information Theory, Thermodynamics, and Cybernetics of Open Adaptive Societal Systems. Presented at the International Congress of Cybernetics, London.
Lange, Oskar (1966). *Celek a vývoj ve světle kybernetiky* [The Whole and the Development in the Light of Cybernetics]. Prague: Svoboda.
Platt, John R. (1966). *The Step to Man*. New York, London, Sydney: John Wiley and Sons, Inc.
Rapoport, Anatol (1966). "Mathematical Aspects of General Systems Analysis." *General Systems* XI.
Richta, Radovan (1969). *Civilisace na vozcesti*. (English version: *Civilisation at the Cross-Roads*.) Prague.
Sadovskij, V.A., and Judin, E.G. (1969). "Zadači, metody i priloženija obščej teorii sistem" [Tasks, Methods and Assumptions of the General System Theory]. In *Issledovanija po obščej teorii sistem*. Moscow: Izdatelstvo Progress.
Shannon, C.E., and Weaver, W. (1949). *The Mathematical Theory of Communication*. Urbana, Ill.: University of Illinois Press.

Singer, J. David (1969). *Feedback in International Conflict: Self-Correcting and Otherwise*. Ann Arbor: Mental Health Research Institute, The University of Michigan.
Sistemnyje issledovanija. *Obščaja teorija sistem: Zadači i metody. Priloženija sistemnogo podchoda* [Systems Research. Tasks and Methods. Propositions of Systems Approach] (1969). Moscow: Nauka.
Soukup, M.; Charvát, F.; Kučera, J. (1968). "Toward a General Social Systems Theory of Dependence: Introduction of Entropy of Behavior." *Proceedings of the International Peace Research Association, 2nd Congress, Vol. 1, Studies in Conflicts.* Assen: Van Gorcum and Co.
Stinchcombe, Arthur L., and Harris, Robert T. (1969). "Interdependence and Inequality: A Specification of the Davis-Moore Theory." *Sociometry*, March.
Szilard, L. (1924). "Ueber die Entropieverminderung in einem thermodynamischen System bei Eingriffen intelligenter Wesen." *Zeitschrift für Physik* I, 53.
Ujemov, A.I. (1969). "Logičeskij analiz sistemnogo podchoda k objektam i jego mesto sredi drugich metodov issledovanija" [The Logical Analysis of the System Approach of the Objects and its Place among other Research Methods]. In *Sistemnyje issledovanija – 1969*. Moscow: Nauka.
Ujemov, A.I., and Sadovskij, V.N., Eds. (1968). *Problemy formalnogo Analiza Sistem* [The Problems of the Formal System Analysis]. Moscow: Vysšaja škola.
Whitehead, A.N. (1948). *Science and the Modern World*. New York: Pelican Mentor Books.
Wiener, N. (1948). *Cybernetics*. New York: John Wiley and Sons.

Everyday Life in Stochastic Networks

*HARRISON WHITE**

Four pairs of theses in tension mark this paper. Results derived for stochastic flows in prescribed technological networks will be used to guide investigation of informal social networks. Persons in everyday life are imbedded as nodes in social networks, but their participation can only partly be understood in terms of the topology of flows in particular networks. The reader is asked recurrently to view the same phenomena separately as a social analyst and as an everyday person. The manifest topic is delays and congestion in networks, but a major emphasis is the hidden benefits of congestion.

Both the attributes of humans as nodes in networks and the special topology of – the intercalations of links in – human networks will be crucial. Attention will be directed to the way humans allocate their time, and to the way networks concatenate into social structures, and to how organizations relate to informal networks. Concrete examples of flows in social networks to which congestion models may be applicable are paper flows in organizations, gossip in

*Professor of Sociology, Harvard University. Financial support from the U.S. National Science Foundation under Grant GS. 2648 is gratefully acknowledged. This paper is based in part on a talk given at the first plenary session of the 1970 World Congress of Political Science at Munich. Karl W. Deutsch has long urged the relevance of queuing models to social phenomena. I am indebted to him for stimulation and to Scott A. Boorman for criticism of an earlier draft.

communities, and cases in judicial systems. First, results on telecommunications systems are surveyed, and then the paper turns to social networks.

Machine Networks

Waiting lines[1] result from the difficulty of matching demands to facilities, in real time, where either arrival times are unpredictable (a large world phenomenon)[2] or service times vary a lot, or both.[3] The central fact is, that the server will often be idle even though on the average there are as many customers per day as he can handle working all the time. The idle time is lost forever. Hence one can minimize queue length and delays to customers only by investing in more facilities than one needs on the average (White, 1963, p. 88).[4]

The world is a network of congestion points. One's plane may have had to circle waiting for a clear runway, because an earlier plane had had to wait for a fuel truck. . . . In the hotel to which one goes,

---

[1] The best short introduction to queuing I know is Cox and Smith (1961); it has a marvelous real world flavor.

[2] By definition, arrivals are from an unbounded region outside the system proper and so have sources too diverse to be analyzable. This can be called the large world phenomenon because it presupposes the existence of a large, complex society. Stanley Milgram's (1969) "Small World" is this same large world wherein he shows that the topology of social networks is such as to link any arbitrary two nodes by remarkably short chains of acquaintances (and *see* White, 1970). The properties of rumor depend essentially on these Janus faces of social organization.

[3] Think of your favorite pub on a Wednesday afternoon. So many different individuals of different kinds might choose to enter the pub, singly or in groups of various sizes, that the best approximation may be to say the lag between one arrival and the next is randomly distributed. In technical terms, the lag may follow a negative exponential distribution so that a new arrival is just as likely to come in during the next instant, whether the previous arrival had come but a second ago or an hour ago. A bartender – there may be several "parallel" servers behind the bar – may take but ten seconds to draw a beer, or four minutes to make a planter's punch depending on the whim of the customer.

[4] Concretely, in the classic case of a single server and individual arrivals, with both service and inter-arrival times distributed exponentially, there will be four customers at the bar on the average even when the mean rate of arrivals is only 80 percent of the mean service rate. Furthermore, the chances are nearly one in three that there will be more than four customers at the bar. The reason is that on the average the bartender will stand idle with no customers before him one-fifth of the time.

are not only bars and restaurants, but a registration desk, phone booths, elevators, and so on. It has proved hard enough to analyze single congestion points: there is now a huge literature of models dealing with the infinite variety of arrival patterns, service facilities, waiting disciplines, and feedback possibilities, such as disgruntled customers leaving the system. Only recently has there been substantial progress in analyzing networks of queuing points, and then only by the clever use of computers for simulation experiments to supplement mathematical analysis.

Kleinrock (1964) has written a most insightful analysis of nets of physical facilities. He models networks of transmitters for forwarding messages around the world. First we must describe how he conceives of a network. The topology (in the electrical engineering sense of the term) is arbitrary: the designer can perhaps choose *how many nodes to have* and certainly can decide on *which nodes are linked* and *what capacity is assigned* to each channel, as long as there is some path from any node to any other node. The message traffic is treated as exogenous, independent of his control and of the arrangement of physical facilities. He breaks this traffic into its *total absolute volume* plus a *structural matrix* which tells the relative densities of flows according to the pairs of nodes at which the message enters and is to leave the network.

The operator of the system has two important controls. He decides how a message is to be *routed* – perhaps a fixed rule for each origin-destination pair, or with a set of options at each intermediate node depending on actual or anticipated traffic conditions. He can also assign messages in different *priority classes*, according to their intrinsic importance, or the demands they put on the facilities, or the current state of the network traffic. In addition, the operator might be able to reassign capacity from one link to another as he sees better where the main demands are. Kleinrock views the total of the transmission capacities distributed throughout the network as the fundamental cost – the capital required in the network. Kleinrock's criterion is *minimizing time of transit* for messages for given cost. He thereby also minimizes implicitly the sizes of queues of messages in the system, which in reality require expensive inventory facilities.

One feature of the network interacts with another in its impact on transit time; enormous numbers of simulations are required to get stable results, and a great many combinations of parameters must be simulated. Simply describing Kleinrock's results would require prolonged exposition and the use of complex series of graphs. The flavor of his results can, however, be conveyed. At a naive level, allocating total channel capacity (roughly) in proportion to the square roots of the total traffic expected in the various links is optimal, but the gain over other schemes is important only when the traffic pattern is very non-uniform.

The designer of the net must heed a more general finding: delay may be minimized by concentrating as much of the capacity and traffic as possible into as few links as possible, subject of course, to keeping at least one route between each node and each other node. This latter finding is, however, conditional upon the total volume of traffic: when the load gets very high the gain from concentration of traffic into a few links is more than offset by the longer path a message must follow on the average to get from a given origin to a given destination.[5] As in the case of a queue at a single server, system performance is very sensitive to average load, the delay typically increasing in even a small net of fourteen nodes by a factor of ten when average traffic rises from a tenth to a half of average transmittal capacity.

All these results assume the use of a fixed routing procedure, which is indeed superior to simple alternate routing when traffic structure is well known, even though it may seem irrational to hold a message waiting for a channel to clear when there is a channel free to an alternate route to the destination. The real importance of alternate routing is that it does shift actual traffic more nearly into line with maximum capacity links when the network layout is ill-adapted to traffic structure, either through ignorance or because the latter has changed. And in real networks traffic structure often shifts.

Priority assignments have been left to one side. Kleinrock has proved an interesting theorem: the overall average delay at a physical service facility is not affected by any of a very wide class of priority

---

[5]This type of effect is not incorporated into the standard turnpike models of economic growth (*see*, Koopmans, 1964), of which these particular results of Kleinrock are otherwise strongly reminiscent. Phrasing Kleinrock's result in terms familiar in pure economic theory, it is clear that we are here encountering a kind of diminishing return to scale. In terms of the standard economic interpretation of turnpike models, we might suggest that turnpike type growth strategies would no longer be optimal if not one, but several, underdeveloped economies in competition for limited resources were being simultaneously considered.

disciplines on the messages[6] – both disciplines intrinsic to the messages, as when an urgent alarm pre-empts facilities from all other messages in a military network; and those dependent on the state of the system, as when messages are repeatedly processed for fixed time lengths on a round-robin basis, a common practice in time-sharing disciplines on computers. To a first approximation, it seems that a network designer can leave priority assignment to one side as an operational matter not heavily implicated in overall performance of a network design.

The most important ideas gained from Kleinrock's work are at a more general level. Interdependencies between events at different nodes are so intractable – even for the simplest network structure and the easiest arrival and service characteristics at nodes – that mathematical analysts have sheered off from networks. Instead they have built up the enormous repertoire of variants on single-node models. Kleinrock, an engineer, obtained his results on specific networks by a clever simulation program on a very high-speed computer. He uses fourteen nodes, enough to investigate the basic kinds of topologies. Kleinrock then took a leap. After showing that the core of the intractable interdependencies is the assumption that each message has a fixed individual length during its stay in the system, Kleinrock proposes an independence assumption: the network functions *as if* each message was randomly assigned a new length from some distribution of service times at each new node on its route through the system. Note the implausibility of this assumption on its face: it is true that the whole concept of service time deserves meticulous examination and is likely to be the product of interaction between server attributes as well as the customer's properties, but in a physical network it seems unreasonable that a message looks quite different to different transmitter machines on its route. But, Kleinrock had the nerve to propose this assumption and to investigate it with a second simulation program, which duplicates each run of the first one, but with messages indeed assigned new lengths (from the same overall distribution) at each node. The results are breathtaking: in graphs of average delay time – for various network topologies, routing disciplines, capacity assignments, and traffic matrices – it is

---

[6] Welfare economists and social stratification theorists should be able to exploit this theorem.

hard to distinguish the curves obtained with and without the assumption. Most of Kleinrock's mathematical analyses of further topics (not described here) are based on the independence assumption.

One way to look at the astounding success of this unreasonable *assumption of independence* is that the interdependencies are so complex that in effect they cancel each other out. Let us now turn the assumption upside down. It obviously is enormously difficult to maintain the individual identity of messages in their routes through a network, and the centralized control of operations and records required is very expensive. A reasonable speculation is that the real physical systems which have evolved throughout our economies – whatever the official statements on forms say, and with the possible exception of new systems run wholly by computers – in actual operation do not bother to maintain message identity. At most, a few broad classes of messages – say in a priority scheme – can be kept separable in treatment. Then Kleinrock's simulation with the independence assumption is the veridical one, and the model with complex interdependencies is the approximation insisted on by the tidy minds of analysts.

Human Networks

Turn now to networks of humans. Both as social scientists and as everyday people we tend in talking about social organization to adopt very quickly some particular abstract cultural perspective in which people are replaced by actors in a role frame. Instead, consider the activities of concrete persons in real time – let these be the nodes.

Human Beings as Nodes

In the past decade it has become common to accept networks as the natural metaphor for describing how people fit together in social organization. The meaning of this metaphor depends on the nature of humans as nodes. Focus on their nature as receivers, processors, and transmitters of messages to close contacts and thence indirectly to distant persons in large populations. "Messages" include official messages, rumors and gossip, but also moods and sentiments,[7] and extend to activities like "lining-up contacts" for an acquaintance to achieve a substantial introduction to some remote person of importance.

Typically, a person is vastly overloaded in real time with messages of various sorts to which he could give attention. In societies with which we are familiar – as opposed to the segmentary societies of the anthropologist – each person is effectively unique. No two share an identical topological position in the full networks they live in. Even in direct ties two persons differ, in the number and attributes of friends, their demographic position in a family, their ties in organizational contexts, and so on; and there are so many relevant social categories that probably few people are even in the same cell of the multi-dimensional contingency table to which they are assigned by using merely standard sociological indicators. Hence only limited concrete guidance on choice of message to handle can be found from imitation, much less from accepted norms and rules.

It follows from the nature of the network context that a person receives messages of a given sort in quite erratic and unpredictable fashion, as well as being enormously overloaded, if one considers all active and latent messages of all sorts accepted by at least some of that society's members as real and relevant. Each of us lives under erratic bombardment of all kinds of messages in a large and complex web which yet is different from, though tied to, the web of any neighbor. Fundamentally, a person has to function as a service facility to stochastic streams of messages of various sorts. His problem, solved in large part implicitly, is to evolve a priority scheme to deal with these flows, a scheme which in real life is forced to be rather different from his neighbor's. A great many priority schemes for physical facilities have been analyzed, quite recently surveyed in a book by N.K. Jaiswal (1968). The most relevant schemes probably are in the alternating priority family (Jaiswal, 1968, VII. 2, VII. 5). The server, after completing one item, tends to give preference to another of the same type, if available; the cost of switching from one type of servicing to another being represented by a reorientation

[7] Diffusion of moods involves compounding of perceptions, which carries further Kleinrock's idea that message lengths change at every node. Modelling such phenomena would require more powerful structural mathematics: some suggestive leads can be found in Friedell (1969) and Lorrain and White (1971).

time. (Such schemes have been applied, for example, to the analysis of automobile traffic in city street networks, with or without explicit traffic control devices.)

Even at this point some qualitative conclusions are suggested. Just from the analysis of physical networks, one becomes convinced of the near-impossibility of effective centralized control and monitoring across all nodes involved in a stochastic flow. The situation of human beings in real time in their social networks reinforces this conclusion. Further, it becomes clear that all persons must, from their nature as service facilities for stochastic streams of messages, have a great deal of freedom and leisure, whether or not they desire them, recognize them, or use them – rather in conflict with the traditional economic view of the labor/leisure margin. Remember from the simple classical model that a server must operate well below its apparent average capacity if there is not to be enormous building of congestion and delays. The same principle applies to a server – or set of parallel servers if a person can cope simultaneously with several forms of message flow – in even the most complex queue model. Not only is a person overloaded with respect to the total of all message flows he might attend to, but he must pare down his attention span through a priority scheme so that he responds to fewer streams of messages than he could handle in a deterministic utopia. The inevitable corollary to matching demands to response in real time is an idleness quotient for the server. It simply is not possible to build a social system in which the priorities for a person's use of real time are effectively dictated elsewhere or one in which its members are deprived of access to considerable idle time (however it may be masked by codes of demeanor).

Node and Network

Turn to the relations between node and network. If network in the human case is to be more than a vague metaphor it must have some of the specificity of Kleinrock's type of model. Its topology, routing procedure, and link capacities must have some stability and be relatively divorced from the traffic flow matrix. In particular, there is no point to having a network which changes shape and hue depending on the kind of message then in it. Our obvious course as analysts is to recognize distinct networks for different general types of messages (though within each type there will remain many priority choices, and so on), and to grant that concrete persons are imbedded in various combinations of such abstract networks. Integration of the different types is defined by the usage of real time at the concrete nodes, their allocations of real time among types of networks.

I suggest that human society has long since evolved just such a scheme. The vague "general type" of network above corresponds to the "institution" and "role frame." These are much more than analytic ideas of recent vintage; they are in fact, the way human interaction in real time is factored out in our everyday practice.

Two decades ago in *The Theory of Social Structure* S.F. Nadel (1957) proposed a conundrum of fundamental importance: how can it happen that social structure is enacted through roles – perhaps our commonest concept – when these occur in frames which are logically disparate and hence cannot be interrelated in cultural terms. After a masterfully lucid dissection of the problem, Nadel had the insight to say he had no answer – though, of course, he showed how roles which explicitly transcended logical comparability, authority roles, in fact, together with recruitment patterns, held concrete systems together. The network analysis here suggests that a humble tool of long familiarity – the time budget – is a missing clue. Role frames correspond to analytic networks and what ties them together to become concrete social structure is the use of real time by concrete persons, who each appear in roles in different networks. Simple accounting for time spent will not help much, given stochastic flows; what is needed is knowledge of the priority schemes at a node, which switch it back and forth in real time among messages in different analytic networks.[8] This solution for Nadel's problem is intrinsically more satisfying than the idea of authority roles, for the solution is a homogeneous one dependent on a similar kind of activity carried on throughout the system. (Some fascinating leads for further research are suggested by some of the by-products of the international cooperative time-budget study associated with Szalai – in particular his study of how household time budgets are affected by moves to new locations requiring increased commuting time.)

---

[8] An obvious strategy is to contrast the practices of familiar, node types who appear very busy but in different ways: e.g., a housewife and an executive.

Role Frames

Consider now a network of a given analytic type, for a given role frame. Its nodes are concrete people, but only in one of their numerous role capacities. From the perspective of the given network, its nodes are highly unreliable in real time, since their priority schemes are often shifting them out of one network into another. There is a family of queuing models that deal with just the phenomenon of unreliability – these models trace the implications of given patterns of "breakdowns" which put the server facility out of operation (Jaiswal, 1968, IV; White and Christie, 1958).

Looking at a society as a whole, a number of dialectic relations become apparent. Even if one imagines a single role frame in isolation as the whole of some total institution society, actions will be decoupled from one another by congestion effects at the various nodes in the network. Different role frames are coupled together into an interacting whole, a society in real time, by the switching of nodes in real time from one to another; the obverse of this coupling is severe decoupling in any one role frame, as when the continuity of family life is disrupted by occupational emergencies and vice versa. The evolution of distinct role frames can be seen as a technical necessity: even networks of physical facilities would require some such factoring to cope with overloads of messages in kinds as well as amount. Empirical research should be relatively easy since the distinctness of frames is not just an analytic convenience, but rather is observable in the way people are socialized to perceive and act in their social world.

Network Growth

Next, contrast the properties of a human network, aside from the nature of their nodes, with those of Kleinrock's teletype network. The most essential difference is that no single "designer" can be invoked: rather, links often are spun and disappear under local pressures. The net evolves; in Kleinrock's terminology, the routing also is flexible and is dependent on the state of the set of messages in the network. Moreover, one cannot assume there is any given destination assigned to the message from its initiation. A "traffic matrix" is influenced by the topology of the network rather than the latter being selected to suit the former. Nor will all messages be handled – the idea of a given traffic density is less relevant than the view of a hierarchy of priority classes, there always being some message of the type to attend to when one has no more urgent call.

There are some suggestive empirical findings in the literature on human networks. Rapoport and various associates (1963) have mapped sociometric networks in high school populations, separately for ties of different choice priority and hence, presumably, of different intensity and, thus, transmittal capacity. Their basic finding is that the fraction of the population reached asymptotically through links of given priority tends to be (the outcome depending on the particular nodes chosen as initiators) substantially less, the higher the priority. Initially, a putative message spreads out to as many others as there are ties of the given priority to the initiators, but soon the familiar effect of inbreeding is manifest and the trace curve approaches an asymptote. Those linked by high priority ties tend to share mutual friends; so one is led into relatively isolated clumps of people with numerous indirect feedback loops linking one of them to another. Kleinrock's net designer does not seek to establish such inbred loops.

Bott (1957) and subsequent writers have looked intensively at inbreeding in networks – usually of adults in their whole range of domestic, leisure ties – in terms of its relation to members' styles of behavior, including the properties of conjugal and other particularly close ties in the network. One interpretation of her work is that patterns of behavior become shared by persons who live in a close-knit network.

Neither of these research lines has dealt with actual message flow; so it is interesting to try to meld their results with those of Kleinrock on stochastic flows in nets. Recall that Kleinrock's overall conclusion is that message delay is minimized by concentrating traffic in as few links as feasible; i.e., by a centralized network in which routing goes through a central node – the star network. "As feasible," is, however, a strong limitation when traffic intensity is high. In that case alternate routing schemes – however desirable to increase adaptability – have disastrous effects in routing messages through long and often circular bypaths: nodes are often so busy that a given message is often sent an alternate, longer way, but that means still more nodes are kept even busier, a vicious circle. When traffic density is high, one quickly reaches the point of requiring more and more links, so that a fully connected net gives lowest delays in spite of the otherwise inefficient dispersal of capacity.

One infers from Rapoport and Bott that neither the star nor the fully connected net is likely to emerge in human populations. One infers from Bott that highly inbred networks yield common patterns of behavior, which should lead to common ideas about priorities for messages and, hence, reduced delay in the messages deemed more important. But inbred networks are like neither the star nor the fully connected net required on topological grounds to minimize delay according to Kleinrock. This is one quandary – good agreement on priority rules is achieved only in a highly inbred network which tends to be ill-connected.

There is a second quandary at high message levels, probably the common situation in human nets. Kleinrock shows that then alternate routing rules are disastrous in delay terms, but alternate routing is inherent in the informal human network. One way out of the quandary is to deny the relevance of the engineer's performance criterion, minimizing delay. This way out is not satisfactory. Delay is necessarily correlated with congestion, with long waiting lines. In the human case one need not consider concrete inventory capacity at a node, but human memory is both limited and costly in terms of other mental activity so that minimizing delay is a reasonable criterion.

At low message levels it is possible that natural sociometric nets of weak ties (Granovetter, 1969) play a crucial role. They have little inbreeding and yield perhaps enough sociometric stars to resemble Kleinrock's star network. Reasonable message delays may depend on the existence and use of weak ties – much more simulation work and sociometric measurement both are needed on this point.[9]

The main problematic in a human network (of a given type) may be its performance under high traffic load. Perhaps formal organiza-

[9] In his first paper Granovetter (1969) shows how important may be sociometric links which are apparently so casual as to be trivial: without them there could not be effective integration of informal networks with social structure. In his thesis (1970) Granovetter demonstrates empirically that most new jobs are found through weak ties; he goes on to draw inferences of how one's inventory of casual ties, accumulated over decades, shapes one's future and by the same token the observable structure of informal social nets. Granovetter's work can be seen as an extension of Rapoport's (1963) work to realistic adult contexts over long time horizons, and it also owes much to the Bott (1957) tradition.

tions have evolved as a solution to this problem of high traffic density. Surely it is a commonplace that the formal "Table of Organization" with its inane tree structure is a mystification, an ideological fixation of managerial types. No tree could possibly support the traffic loads at higher nodes called for by the formal rule of communicating through the lowest common supervisor. Tom Burns (1961) is one of the most vivid of the writers who impress on us how essential direct communication is. Chester Barnard (1949) was not the first to say informal communication nets are the heart of organization, and the executive's job is really to shape and encourage and keep open these nets. Yet perhaps there is more to the "Table of Organization" than we think.

No informal human net with ties strong enough to sustain a common cognitive orientation and goals will spread far; rather, the close-tie network will also be the fragmented network. Kleinrock's star network has the minimum number of links necessary to guarantee connectivity in a population, through one central node: but no man could sustain several thousand communication links. A tree structure has no more links and is a natural extension of the star network. In Kleinrock's terms (though no simulations have as yet been run on trees) the tree will be costly in route length, but efficient in concentration of channel capacity.

Perhaps the tree of a classic table of organization is not best seen as a routing map for existing message traffic; on the contrary, it is a device for forcing the generation of messages where they are not natural to the informal human nets which necessarily carry the bulk of the message load. Its other function would naturally be as a route map for second-order messages, messages about maintenance and adjustment of priority schemes for substantive messages, priority schemes which must be held in common to accomplish much.

Conclusion

We are irritated by delays in everyday life as we move along networks of facilities and attend to messages in networks of acquaintances. Just these systems of delays may be crucial to our social order, and to the essential freedoms human beings retain. The properties of persons as nodes are so different from those of machines that the network ideas we have borrowed from engineering must be recast. As much attention must be given to how humans switch among different networks as to the topology of particular networks. Yet, analysis of machine networks can be highly suggestive. The astounding success of Kleinrock's assumption of independence suggests that decentralization and decoupling in social systems go deeper and are more pervasive than even their ideological proponents have suggested. Social systems seem remarkably impervious to deliberate manipulation, whether based on the insight of social analysts or of men as everyday members. Kleinrock's work may help to explain this imperviousness to insight.

REFERENCES

Barnard, Chester (1949). *The Functions of the Executive.* Cambridge: Harvard University Press.

Bott, E. (1957). *Family and Social Network.* London: Tavistock.

Burns, T., and Stalker, G. (1961). *The Management of Innovation.* London: Tavistock.

Cox, D.R. and Smith, W.L. (1961). *Queues.* London: Methuen & Co.

Friedell, M.F. (1969). "On the Structure of Shared Awareness." *Behavioral Science* 14:28–39.

Granovetter, M.S. (1969). "Alienation Reconsidered: The Strength of Weak Ties." Harvard University, Unpublished.

Granovetter, M.S. (1970). "Changing Jobs: Channels of Mobility Information in a Suburban Population." Ph.D. thesis, Harvard University.

Jaiswal, N.K. (1968). *Priority Queues.* New York: Academic Press.

Kleinrock, Leonard (1964). *Communication Nets: Stochastic Message Flow and Delay.* New York: McGraw-Hill.

Koopmans, T.C. (1964). "Economic Growth at a Maximal Rate." *The Quarterly Journal of Economics* 78:355–94.

Lorrain, François, and White, H.C. (1971). "Structural Equivalence of Individuals in Social Networks." *Journal of Mathematical Sociology* 1, No. 1.

Milgram, S., and Travers, J. (1969). "The Small World Problems." *Sociometry,* Dec.

Nadel, S.F. (1957). *The Theory of Social Structure.* London: Cohen and West.

Rapoport, Anatol (1963). "Mathematical Models of Social Interaction." In *Handbook of Mathematical Psychology*, Vol. 11. Ed. by R.D. Luce, *et al.* New York: Wiley.

White, Harrison, (1963). "Uses of Mathematics in Sociology." In *Mathematics and the Social Sciences, Annals of the American Academy of Political and Social Science*, June, pp. 77–94. Ed. by J.C. Charlesworth.

White, Harrison, (1970). "Search Parameters for the Small World." *Social Forces.* 49: 259–64.

White, Harrison, and Christie, L.S. (1958). "Queuing with Pre-emptive Priorities or with Breakdown." *Operations Research* 6:79-95.

Part Four:

Simulation Models

Introduction

In different ways, each of the papers in this section draws upon the intellectual traditions and approaches exemplified in the previous sections. Yet it can also be argued that they share a common theoretical or pretheoretical approach going beyond the fact that each simulation model is not analytically solvable but must be repeatedly operated if relevant deductions are to be made.

Thus Alker's uses of Simon's causal modelling approach and Hopkins' difference equation models seem very similar to Milstein's or Chadwick's use of a dynamic simultaneous equation system. Indeed Hopkins' paper does not differ methodologically from Milstein's when it uses least-squares forecasting methods; its suggestions as to a more complex realization of mobilization/assimilation theory do imply, however, a set of nonlinear mechanisms of the sort that cannot be easily estimated or analyzed by paper and pencil (analytic) methods. Smoker's discussion of correlational evidence in validity studies of international simulations also relies on statistical methodologies, such as Schwartzman employs. More profoundly, one can conceive of discrete simulations of the sort Smoker reviews so expertly as sets of complex difference equations, less stochastic than Milstein presents, more nonlinear than Chadwick's models, but not inherently very different from either of them.

Alker's use of the rational modelling tradition parallels that of Aranson, Hinich and Ordeshook, but with a statistical purpose more akin to that of Chadwick or Rapoport and his associates. He presents a general strategy for measuring political capabilities, which can be applied either to political actors or systems. Moreover, the use of ideal-type models of influence or integration relationships as norms against which to judge actual performances seems a practice not too distant from the intent of most rational theorists. In a more indirect way, most budget-oriented international simulations also imply or use (incrementally) rational allocation procedures. But only TEMPER among Smoker's models explicitly invokes "cost-effectiveness" rationales.

A further important feature of each of the simulations presented or outlined is its explicitly stated complex social structural character. Relations between different actors in different loci of interaction are explicitly modelled, particularly in the INS-IPS-WPS or TEMPER models reviewed by Smoker, but also the mobilization/assimilation model suggested by Hopkins and the multi-arena Brunner-Lipset model discussed by Alker. In this sense, the fascination of Charvát, Kučera, Soukup, and White with the structural patterns in social relationships is shared by many of their simulation-oriented colleagues. Moreover, Alker's or Chadwick's suggestions of probabilistic systems measures, like those of Charvat and his associates, all might profitably be used inductively to discover the more general and nonobvious significance of various simulation model assumptions. Would, for example, probabilistic dependency measures reveal some of the criticisms of TEMPER's structural assumptions cited by Smoker; would they show a more realistic pluripolar network structuring in IPS? Would Alker's power capability measures or Chadwick's transactional measures show a similar structure?

In what sense, then, do the papers in this section share any significant orientational unities? First, the above argument suggests that simulation modelling is an eclectic approach, not likely to be content with the limiting assumptions or substantive preoccupations of any one paradigmatic or preparadigmatic orientation.

Moreover, simulation blends the deductive use of mathematically stated theory via model operation with the methods of the more inductive statistical tradition, which need to be applied to model outputs for interpretive or validational purposes. Hopkins' use of model-based least-squares estimation methods further illustrates the close affinity of statistical and simulation methodologies for deductive forecasting or more inductive and synthetic theory-building purposes.

But in another sense, a certain focussing orientation (or constraining tradition) is evident in each of the models of the present section; when narrowly defined, this "process modelling" orientation can be as limiting in, and as revealing of, theoretical insights as any other single modelling approach. Whether developed by students of Deutsch or by the original Carnegie Technology group of organizational theorists (including Guetzkow, March, and Simon), process simulations tend to focus on incremental social change and satisficing behavior within given organizational systems. Granting the surprising intellectual power that such a realistic conceptualization helps to generate, we must still take care that other theoretical emphases are not entirely forgotten. Fortunately, the call for rationalistic analyses of alternate or selftransforming systems in Alker's presentation, Brunner and Hopkins' focus on structure-changing processes in developing-systems, and the strong tendency for man–machine simulations in the INS tradition to produce emergent, unpredicted structural transformations all lead away from such limiting preoccupations.

A second, potentially narrowing feature of process models is their penchant for richer behavioral detail joined with rather minimal attention to more complex cognitive processes such as psychoanalytic or rationalistic theories usually presuppose. Behavioral realism, even when joined to an explicit search for crucial causal mechanisms, can lose cognitive significance from both an empirical and a normative point of view. Such a problem is not inherent in the verbal theories of Lipset, Deutsch, Simon or Guetzkow, as discussed below – recall work by the Carnegie group, Deutsch and Lipset on valuational adaptation. Nor is it inherent in simulational methodology. Rather, it tends to result from too simple, algebraic representations of complex cognitive developments; sometimes this simplifying tendency is linked with data limitations. In this respect, only the fully programmed simulations like TEMPER or the Brunner-Lipset model have reasonably differentiated cognitive mechanisms. But again, the use of role-playing humans in the international man–machine simulations is the richest, if least explicit, process representation in any of the models of the present section.

In overviewing the potentialities of the simulation approach, as suggested by the papers of the present section, one more issue stands out: parsimony versus realism. The mathematical representations contained in most complex simulations are offered more in the name of realism than in the interests of elegance, generality, abstraction, or parsimony. Clearly aesthetic principles are at stake in such an issue and it ill behooves us to deny the controversies that exist on this point. Process models are as real, as powerful, and as provocative as the theoretical assumptions they contain, no more or no less. Should we use any other criterion for a comparative empirical assessment?

On Political Capabilities in a Schedule Sense: Measuring Power, Integration, and Development

*HAYWARD R. ALKER, Jr.**

Actualities are but low probability events. – Anon.

Introduction

What brings many to the study of politics is some kind of value-linked curiosity. Either they want to know how to change the world for the better, or they wonder if certain changes in their governments or their policies would really bring about a significant improvement. Sometimes the concern is a more urgent and negative one: how to stop or to prevent certain changes in system rules or policies thought to be threatening to basic values. More contemplatively, similar inquiries might be made into the values sustained by current practices or the possible damages associated with contemplated changes.

Whatever the orientation, the need to contemplate situations other than contemporary political actualities is clear. The empirical theorist of the present needs to search for cases unlike the present in some crucial aspect in order to introduce controls into his demonstrations of cause-effect relationships. Those dreading or desiring

*Department of Political Science, Massachusetts Institute of Technology, and Latin American School of Political Science and Public Administration, FLACSO, Santiago, Chile.
Research for the author's contributions to this volume has been partly financed by N.S.F. grant G.S. 2429 to the Center for International Studies, M.I.T.

some future actions or outcomes need some kind of theoretically relevant examples to suggest what might happen in such a yet unreal situation, such as the people's wishes in a fair election. Political activists use concepts like "undemocratic," "false consciousness," "demeaning compliance," "surplus repression," or "surplus integration" that assume as yet unrealized norms. The proverbial fascination of the historical imagination with similar hypothetical possibilities is certainly as well known.

The present paper attempts to link the actual and the possible, the desirable and the undesirable in a scientific yet voluntaristic way. It suggests formal measurement concepts for distinguishing attractive or unattractive system capabilities from those that are impossible to achieve. Since such capability concepts are in fact rather hard validly to measure, and the timeless applicability of socio-political laws cannot be taken for granted, the measures must be taken as tentative ones, only as good as the imperfect empirical theories they embody. Nonetheless, the need to have some conceptual equipment to grapple with the reality of unrealities, of counterfactual possibilities and impossibilities, and of actualities interpreted in such terms, seems compelling enough to justify the effort.

The values taken as illustrative examples of what appears to be a quite general approach to the measurement of political capabilities are topical ones: power, integration, and development. Their opposites have several names: powerlessness or dependence, disintegration or lack of effective coordination, underdevelopment or decay. Whether thought of as capabilities or incapacities, these properties are clearly related ones, a point that should become clearer with the more detailed discussion below. The essential idea there is that the abilities and inabilities of political actors or systems can usefully be thought of in a multidimensional schedule sense, a choice-oriented economic notion used by Harsanyi to summarize power potentials in terms of a schedule or graph or function linking opportunity costs to desirable performance possibilities. Once such schedules are available we can begin to delimit repertoires of attractive or unattractive performance possibilities.

The shift from primary concern with actualities to a focus on summary measures of opportunities and potentialities may seem a regression to the preoccupations of "nonoperational" political theorists or theoretical politicians just at a time when behavioral political scientists have developed a number of impressive examples of moderately powerful, explanatory empirical theory. Yet it can and will be argued that not until such complex, multivariate, dynamic, causal theories were rigorously developed, using contemporary data generation and analysis methodologies, was it possible rigorously to make and defend statements of relevance to values as complex and not completely observable as power, integration, and development. The first example of capability measurement will be largely a heuristic one, a rationalistic procedure based on Harsanyi's work on voluntaristically measuring unilateral power or influence (dependence) in a schedule sense. Then, moving into a different kind of formal statement, it will be shown how further manipulations of the Simon-Homans differential equation model of group interaction can be used to suggest multidimensional measures of dependency integration and autonomy applicable to a regional common market. The final set of capability measures will be based on an information-processing model, the Brunner–Lipset simulation of democratic political development. It is hoped that the diversity of these examples, and the timeliness of the problems they refer to, will lend credence to the value of the present approach.

On Measuring Unilateral Power.

Harsanyi's idea of measuring power in a schedule sense is based on Dahl's earlier work, adding to it opportunity cost notions that help *A* and *B* rationally assess their respective action/inaction and compliance/defiance possibilities.[1] Just as Dahl emphasized the *relational* aspect of power, so Harsanyi stresses the *multidimensional* schedule sense of power. Both authors are thus explicitly cautioning against a nonrelational form of power thinking which describes an actor's power only in terms of his resource levels or military strength and

[1] Three good reviews of much of the recent North American literature on power are: R. Dahl (1967); R. Bell, *et al.* (1969); and J. March (1968). It is interesting that Harsanyi's "Measurement of Social Power, Opportunity Costs, and the Theory of Two-Person Bargaining Games," reprinted in Bell, *et al.* (1969), escapes from March's usual argument that most theories of power relations are tautologous, and thus nothing more than definitional elaborations. In what follows it should become clear that Harsanyi's use of utility values and rationality assumptions produces powerful (statistically overidentified) and testible theories in those cases where utilities are independently assessible.

against a unidimensional relational conception which compares capacities in terms such as GNP differences or kill ratios.

We can distinguish at least seven distinct aspects of the idea that "*A* has power over *B*" in the common sense that "*A* can get *B* to do something that *B* would otherwise not do." Dahl and Harsanyi mention the following:

1) *A*'s power *bases* or resources;

2) *A*'s *means*, behaviors or actions, that employ these resources;

3) *A*'s opportunity *costs* in using such means to his own ends (we shall distinguish gross costs, gross gains, and net gains or costs below);

4) The *strength* of *A*'s power over *B*, i.e. *B*'s opportunity costs in not complying with *A*'s wishes in certain important respects;

5) the *scope* of *A*'s power over *B*, i.e. the set of *B*'s behaviors influenced by *A*;[2]

6) the *amount* of *A*'s power exercised over *B*, i.e. the probability change in a specific behavior of *B* within *A*'s scope;

and, when *B* is thought of as a plurality of actors,

7) the *extent* of *A*'s power over *B*, i.e. the set of actors over whom *A* exercises a certain amount of power.

Thus we can say that despite the impressive bases, means, scope, and extent of the United States' power over the Viet Cong and the forces of North Vietnam, its domestic opportunity costs in employing that power have been extremely high, and its coercive strength (roughly indicated by kill ratios) has not been sufficient to bring about the desired changes in the scope and amounts of the enemies' behaviors. Presumably, North Vietnam and the Viet Cong included the costs of future dependence in their own decisions not to

---

[2] As Dahl has noted, English lacks an adequate verb form corresponding to the noun "power." Thus, for this purpose we have used above "to influence" rather than "to empower," which has somewhat different connotations. In what follows we shall not try exhaustively to conceptualize all aspects of power and influence. Rather, we note: (*a*) that on some occasions, as above, we shall use "influence" to refer to the exercise of power; and (*b*) that this usage corresponds to the common meaning adopted by Dahl, in which power is an ability or capacity to get someone else to do something he otherwise would not do. And we recognize: (*c*) that sometimes influence (or power) is defined more broadly as capacities that need not rely on coercion or inducement for their realization; or (d) that power may be definitionally restricted beyond the mere notion of opposed wills or valuations to refer to (more or less) legitimated capacities exercised in a (more or less) coercive manner.

comply. Thus, at the same time, but in different ways, an actor can be powerful and powerless, or dependent and defiant.

A Rational Theory of Unilateral Influence Relations

The job of measuring desirable or undesirable political capabilities requires counterfactual theories of how political actors would behave in unreal situations, and it requires valuations with respect to such behavioral possibilities. (Note that such valuations are implicit in most of the seven aspects of a power relation cited above.) Perhaps the simplest and most discussed case of such relationships in political science is the unilateral power (or influence) relationship. Although most empirical situations, such as the Vietnam War, contain elements of reciprocal power relations, a focus on the unilateral case of *A*'s power over *B* has considerable expositional appeal. As the basis for valuations in this case we will simplify matters even further, but make the Dahl/Harsanyi list above somewhat longer, by using the utilities assigned by *A* and *B* to various of *B*'s actions and the cost coefficients with which *A* values his own power bases, given more or less explicit alternate use possibilities. The theoretical foundations of the argument will be the basic postulates that *both A and B are cost-consciously rational* in an actuarial sense in their decisions with respect to *A*'s attempts to influence *B* and that, within probabilistic limits, they are fully and accurately informed as to situational possibilities. Together with additional assumptions about *B*'s compliance possibilities and the causal effectiveness *of various of A's actions*, these allow us to calculate opportunity schedules for *A*'s influence possibilities and to measure *A*'s unilateral power over *B* in a testible fashion.[3]

[3] W. Riker's article on "Some Ambiguities in the Notion of Power," reprinted in Bell, *et al.* (1969), suggests that we are here defining power of influence in a logically incomplete, manipulative, or recipe sense that does not adequately comprehend an actor's capabilities: Thus, there is a direct parallelism (*a*) between ego-oriented power and necessary-and sufficient-condition causality (Riker's preferred interpretation), and (*b*) between other-oriented power and recipe causality. It is not surprising that this parallelism exists, for power and cause are closely related concepts. Power is potential cause; or, power is the ability to exercise influence while its actual excercise is causation (Bell, *et al.*, 1969, p. 117). Following the causal modeling approach first elaborated in H. Simon's earlier *Models of Man* (1957), we shall try to merge these two conceptions of power through the use of theoretically-based opportunity schedules and *ceteris paribus* assumptions. Since Simon uses *multiple*-cause regression–equation models with *ceteris paribus* assumptions, however, we will be content to describe power more voluntaristically as potential sufficient cause, because no one cause is necessary in a multivariable additive equation.

After presenting the outlines of a *causal model* of unilateral influence relations, we shall address the question of influence possibilities and power measurement in terms of a simplified realization of the model. Definitionally we assume influence to be the exercise of power and power to be a species of potential causation. A's power over B will be described in terms of previously mentioned situationally specific characteristics of a power relationship, including the utility maximization assumption applied to both influencer and influencee. Thus, a contextually relevant, voluntaristic notion of social causation is being proposed. In a preliminary, preoperational fashion the resulting model is schematized in Figure 1.

Perhaps the most striking feature of Figure 1 is its complexity. Even when the scope, amount, and extent of A's influence is limited to a single potential probabilistic behavioral change by B, ΔP_B, in spelling out Harsanyi's ideas we have found it necessary to assume random errors, otherwise perfect information, plus rational calculation abilities. Thus both A and B must calculate their expected net or maximum realizable utility gains.

$$\max \widehat{\Delta U_A} (\Delta p'_B, \Delta \, \text{base}'_A), \quad \max \widehat{\Delta U_B} (\Delta p'_B \; U'_B(\text{not}\Delta p'_B)),$$

before choosing any action. This suggests the important insight that until changes in structure or valuation occur, dependency may be rational for both A and B. In A's case we have made this actuarial calculation explicitly dependent on contemplated levels of change in p_B and the bases used by his influence means; for B it depends on the magnitude of the contemplated behavioral change and the cost of not making such a change. (As distinguished from unmarked, actual variable values, primed variables represent either contemplated possible or perceived actual values, while roofed variables, or those preceded by E's, represent actuarial expectations.) Again for simplicity, resource utilization is assumed to diminish A's supply of power bases, which are valued by A in an opportunity cost sense. Moreover, A must be seen as able to perceive, understand and simulate B's own utility maximizing calculations. Although B is also postulated to be a rational actor, his behavior is more parsimoniously represented in several respects. First, because he is assumed not to be contemplating an influence initiative, no specific means of B's actions are explicitly indicated (other than compliance or defiance, thought of as means to

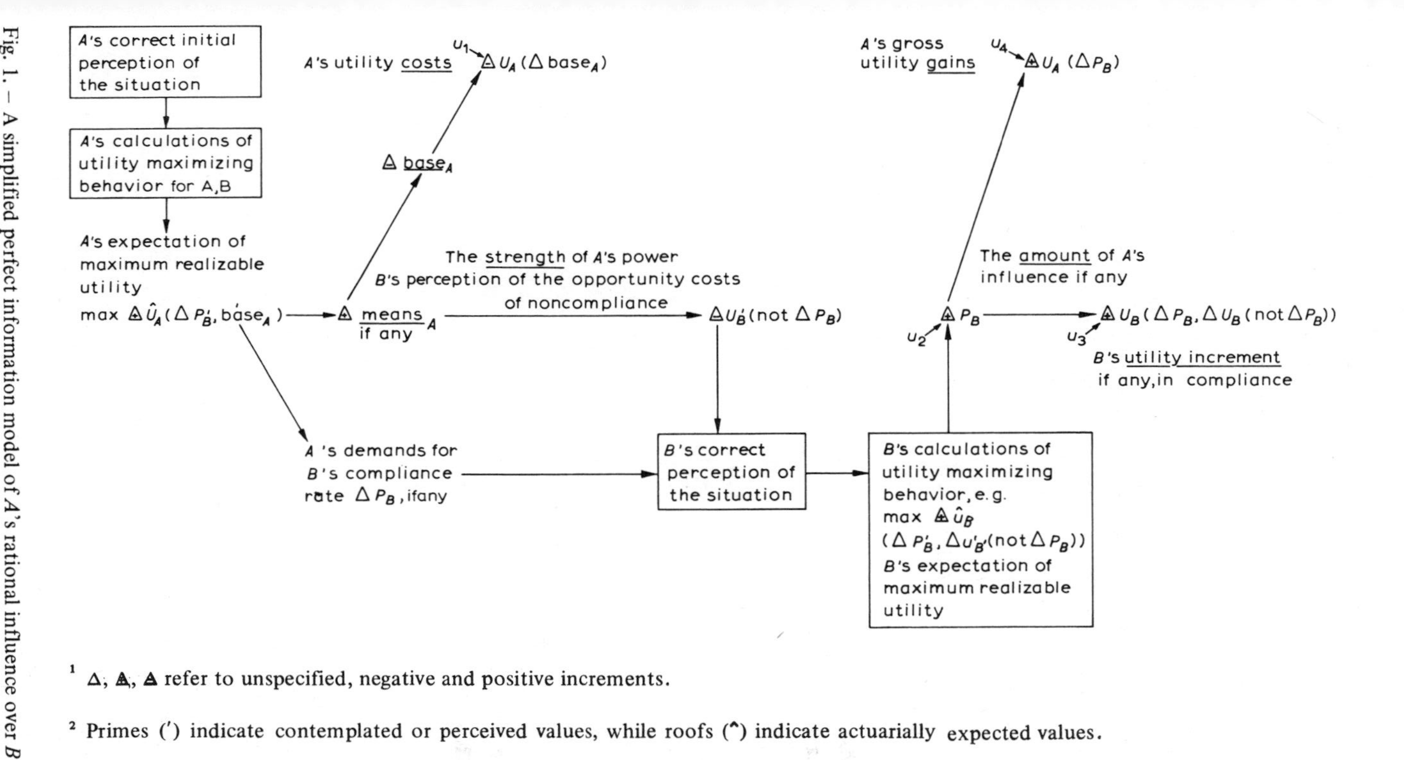

[1] Δ, $\blacktriangle$, $\blacktriangle$ refer to unspecified, negative and positive increments.

[2] Primes (′) indicate contemplated or perceived values, while roofs (^) indicate actuarially expected values.

[3] Arrows indicate causes and boxes indicate incompletely specified processes.

[4] The major simplifications of this model are its information, rationality and ceteris paribus assumptions together with the absence of structure changing mechanisms.

Fig. 1. – A simplified perfect information model of *A*'s rational influence over *B*

utility maximization).[4] Secondly, *B*'s cost calculations are more implicit than *A*'s because only his compliance/noncompliance behaviors are indicated and his cost functions on these actions and others are not explicitly given.

Despite these simplifications, the model of Figure 1 allows some interesting calculations. First, it suggests how to determine when *A*'s influence attempts will be successful. Because the model's rationality *cum* perfect information postulates imply that *A* will obey the "rule of anticipated reactions," *A* will only act when there is a positive net realizable expected utility to be gained by doing so. *Rational* influence acts are always successful, at least in a probabilistic sense. Thus the question: "When will it work? " becomes influencer centered: "When will he try? " Assuming inducements work through *B*'s utility calculus means that the cost to *B* of not going along with *A*'s influence attempts is sufficient to make *B*'s expectations of his *net* realizable utility positive when he probabilistically complies. Relaxing the rationality assumption of net gain for *A*, we can also calculate answers to a second kind of question: What are the conditions under which (irrational) influence attempts *would not* be successful, i.e. noncompliance would be visible? If probabilistic model assumptions are correct, data on successful influence attempts, rarer nonsuccessful efforts, and situations where no influence attempts were made (i.e. "nondecisions") can be used to estimate previously unspecified model parameters. The resulting functions can serve as schedules of counterfactual influence possibilities; thus a well-specified model of influence relations will allow us to answer past or future oriented versions of the more general speculative question: What would happen *if A were* to attempt such and such actions

---

[4] An intriguing alternative to the present approach would be the elaboration of this relationship of dependence from *B*'s perspective. Reciprocally, we could ask how much power does *B* have over *A* given his limited instruments: degrees of compliance and defiance. And we could turn what *A* considers "irrational defiance" into what *B* sees as the elimination of "demeaning compliance" because of a different perception of his utility components. Surely a more fundamental transformation of dependence takes place when *B* begins negatively to value future benefits of dependence, i.e. dependence in and of itself, and begins to make demands for structural change, such as independent means of action for himself. These possibilities would seem worth exploring in the integration example below. They also suggest adding a "systemic effects" category to the Dahl-Harsanyi framework, an idea pursued further in our discussion of contingent power schedules and Brunner's simulation models.

within his behavioral repertoire? And summary power measures could be constructed that delimit such repertorial possibilities.

For later reference, it will be convenient to summarize the major relationships implied by our model of perfect information and rational influence in algebraic form. It should be remembered that B's behavioral modifications indicated these are probabilistic changes and therefore are not observed in every actual case. For A's behavior, we have our first significant behavioral derivation from the rationality postulate:

$$\Delta\,\text{means}_A > 0 \text{ iff } \max \Delta\widehat{U_A}(\Delta p'_B, \Delta'\text{base}_A) > 0. \tag{1}$$

(A's means will be utilized and his demands communicated, if and only if his expectation of the maximum realizable utility associated with feasible levels of resource utilization and new amounts of B's compliance is positive.)

$$\Delta U_A^{(\prime)}(\Delta p_B, \Delta\,\text{base}_A) = \Delta U_A^{(\prime)}(\Delta p_B) + \Delta U_A^{(\prime)}(\Delta\,\text{base}_A). \tag{2 or 2$'$}$$

$$\Delta\widehat{U_A}(\Delta \overset{(\prime)}{p}_B, \overset{(\prime)}{\Delta}\text{base}_A) = \Delta\widehat{U_A}(\Delta \overset{(\prime)}{p}_B) + \Delta U_A(\overset{(\prime)}{\Delta}\text{base}_A). \tag{2a or 2a'}$$

(A's actual and expected realizable utilities, as calculated by A and perceived by B, are by definition actual or actuarial additive functions of the utility costs A places on consumed bases and the utility benefits associated with increases in B's performance probability.) Parenthetical primes are used, as in (2a$'$), to avoid another equation.

$$\Delta\,\text{base}_A = f_o(\Delta\,\text{means}_A). \tag{3}$$

$$\Delta\,\text{base}_A \leqslant \text{base}_A. \tag{3a}$$

(A's means, conceptualized as a multidimensional vector of actions, tend to use up his bases, conceptualized as a multidimensional resource vector of finite magnitude. Although not written out, exactly analogous, equally deterministic perceptual versions of (3) and (3a), i.e. (3$'$), and (3a'), are also assumed to hold true for either A or B.)

$$\Delta U_A^{(\prime)}(\Delta\,\text{base}_A) = f_1(\Delta\,\text{base}_A) + u_1 \tag{4 or 4$'$ for A and B}$$

$$\begin{aligned}\Delta\hat{U}_A(\Delta\,\text{base}_A) &= E_A(\Delta U_A(\Delta\,\text{base}_A)) \\ &= E_B(\Delta U_A(\Delta\,\text{base}_A)) = f_1(\Delta\,\text{base}_A).\end{aligned} \tag{4a}$$

(A's utility costs are an increasing function of the bases consumed, subject to an additive random error u_1; after the fact perceptions, by a perfect information assumption (4′), are perfectly accurate, while by assumption (4a) expected or anticipated utility changes ignore the error term.)
Similarly,

$$\Delta U_A^{(\prime)}(\Delta p_B) = f_4(\Delta p_B) + u_4 . \qquad (5 \text{ or } 5')$$

$$\Delta \hat{U}_A(\Delta p_B') = f_4(\Delta p_B'). \qquad (5a \text{ for } A \text{ or } B)$$

(A's gross utility gains are an increasing function of increases in B's specified compliance probability, subject to an additive, random error u_4; anticipated and perceived utility gains are calculated according to the assumptions derived from actuarial rationality and perfect information postulates, as above.)

Turning now to B's evaluations and behavior, we have:

$$\Delta U_B^{(\prime)}(\text{not}\Delta p_B) = f_5(\Delta^{(\prime)}\text{means}_A , \text{not}\Delta p_B^{(\prime)}). \qquad (6 \text{ and } 6' \text{ for } A \text{ and } B)$$

(As equally and perfectly perceived by A and B, B's utility costs [A's strength] in B's not complying with A's request for a behavioral change Δp_B is a function of the magnitude of the contemplated request for a behavioral change and the means employed by A to bring it about.)

$$\Delta p_B > 0 \text{ iff } \max \Delta \hat{U}_B(\Delta p_B) > 0. \qquad (7)$$

(B will rationally comply if and only if his maximum expected realizable utility is greater by doing so; it is assumed implicitly that when he expects a net utility gain, A will rationally use his available means to influence B, thus incurring the previously mentioned opportunity costs and presenting B with perceived costs for not complying that are greater than those for complying.) More precisely for contemplated $\Delta p'_B$:

$$\Delta p_B = f_2(\max(\Delta \hat{U}_B(\Delta p_B', \Delta U_B'(\text{not}\Delta p_B')))) + u_2 . \qquad (7a)$$

$$\hat{\Delta} p_B = E_A(\Delta p_B) = E_B(\Delta p_B)$$
$$= f_2(\max(\Delta \hat{U}_B(\Delta p_B, \Delta U_B'(\text{not}\Delta p_B)))). \qquad (7b)$$

(Because of perfect information and actuarial rationality on the part of both A and B, A's and B's expectations agree on the amount of change, if any, that B will make in response to A's actions or inaction; moreover subject to random fluctuations, the amount of A's influence, B's compliance rate, is a calculable function of B's maximum realizable utility gain or loss in changing his behavior to the extent requested.)

$$\Delta U_B(\Delta p'_B, U_B(\text{not}\,\Delta p'_B)) = f_3(\Delta p'_B, U_B(\text{not}\,\Delta p'_B)) + u_3. \tag{8}$$

(B's realized utility gain, if any, is a separable function of his changes in compliance probabilities and the opportunity costs of not complying at the new rate, subject to a random error u_3; analogous perception and expectation equations (8′) and (8*a*) could be stated for both A and B.)
An intriguing part of this model is A's ability to calculate just the right amount of change ΔP_B that, as jointly perceived, maximizes his own return while still giving B a compliance option that is slightly more attractive than noncompliance when A's means of "persuasion" are employed. But changes in compliance rates do have upper limits:

$$\Delta p_B \leqslant 1 - p_B \text{ and } \Delta\, p_B \leqslant 1 - p'_B. \qquad (7c \text{ and } 7c')$$

Even if the general functional forms indicated above are known, the above model specification is incomplete in two respects. First, we must complete our determination on the basis of the perfect information of the actual value of ΔP_B, ΔP^*_B, demanded by A. We have just assumed actuarial expectations to equal true variable values minus their additive random components, calculated from similar expectations when necessary. Relying on these assumptions, Δp^*_B, Δ^* means$_A$, Δ^* base$_A$ are calculable in terms of expressions for the all important maximum realizable utilities of A and B. From equations (1) thru (5a) we have:

$$\max \Delta \hat{U}_A(\Delta p'_B, \Delta'\text{base}_A) = E(\Delta U_A(\Delta p^*_B, \Delta^*\text{base}_A)) =$$
$$f_1(\Delta^*\text{base}_A) + f_4(\hat{\Delta} p^*_B). \tag{9}$$

Here Δp^*_B is that value of Δp_B which A sees as maximizing his expected utility payoff under the assumption that B will do likewise vis-à-vis A's actions. More simply, since both A and B are assumed able to calculate A's strength exactly, from equations (6′, 8) we have:

$$\max \Delta \hat{U}_B(\Delta p'_B, \Delta U'_B(\text{not } \Delta p'_B)) =$$
$$f_3(\Delta p^*_B, f_5(\Delta^* \text{means}_A, \text{not}\Delta p^*_B)). \tag{10}$$

Thus we have assumed that a Δp^*_B exists that simultaneously maximizes the expressions in (9) and (10). The idea that A and B agree, within random error, on what ΔP_B will actually be allows us to infer another important behavior prediction from Equations (7*a*), (7*b*), (7*c*), and (10):

$$\Delta P_B = f_2(f_3(\Delta P^*_B, f_5(\Delta^* \text{means}_A, \text{not}\Delta P^*_B))) + u_2. \tag{11}$$

(Except for a random element u_2, ΔP_B can be predicted from a complex function of A's original proposals if A and B are rational.)

Finally, we need to state this model in a way that allows other, nonmanipulated causes of B's and A's behavior, without destroying the possibility of causally estimating and interpreting influence and power relations. Given the initial situation facing A and B, the only exogenous causal variables in the model are the implicit causes, u_1, u_2, u_3 and u_4. If we are going to argue that they represent all other, nonmanipulated causes of ΔU_A, ΔP_B, ΔU_B and ΔU_A, surely a major simplification within our model is the further assumption that these implicit residual causal variables are random variables that are unrelated to each other. It turns out that just this *ceteris paribus* assumption is the basis of causal inference with regression type equations in the Simon-Blalock modelling tradition.[5]

[5] A fuller statement of the causal modelling approach is contained in A. Blalock and H. Blalock (1968). An updating of that approach in terms of probabilistic interpretations of regression coefficients is suggested by Henri Theil (1970). In the interests of brevity we shall not further complicate (and make more adequate) the present analysis; let it suffice to argue that the above formalization, from which follows a simple illustration, allows us to measure power in more than a mere recipe sense, as described in Note 3, because of the inclusion of implicit exogenous causes, the u's that A cannot manipulate. A natural extension would be to include *explicit* exogenous *nonvoluntaristic* causal variables in the model of Figure 1. Opportunity costs based on alternate possible actions could also have been used. There is no reason within the causal modelling tradition for not doing so; here expositional simplicity has again been our guide.

$$E(u_i, u_j) = 0 \quad \text{for } i, j = 1, \ldots 4, \; i \neq j \tag{12}$$

Although we shall not demonstrate how here, this assumption allows us to derive numerous predictions as to relations among model parameters above and beyond the already suggested predictions as to the magnitudes of behavioral and evaluational changes that A and B will experience.

A Simple Example

Rather than further elaborate the above model, we shall suggest a simple example of it, with specific functional forms for $f_0 \ldots f_4$.

This example will also allow us to illustrate the joint (but sequential) maximization calculations referred to above, for the special case where A uses inducements but not sanctions. We shall define variables and functions as they become necessary in a sequential exposition starting with A's utility definitions and situation perceptions; for simplicity, expectations, perceptions, actual values, and contemplated values will not always be distinctly indicated. We shall assume B is doing the desired act with probability P_1, $0 < P_1 < 1$ without any interference by A.

Similarly A's utility is a positive linear function of his single basic resource base, and B's action probability, P_B:

$$U_A(P_B, \text{base}) = C_1 \text{ base} + C_4 P_B + u_1 + u_4; (C_1, C_4 > 0). \tag{13}$$

From Equation (13) follows the contemplation of possible utility gains and losses associated with possible increasing B's action levels:

$$\Delta P_B \leqslant 1 - P_1. \tag{14 = 7c}$$

$$\Delta \hat{U}_A(\Delta P'_B, \Delta'\text{base}) = \underset{\text{costs}^6}{-C_1 \Delta'\text{base}} + \underset{\text{gains}}{C_4 \Delta P'_B}. \tag{15 = 2'a}$$

---

[6] Because we are assuming no costs for information processing or communication, a semicontingent always costly influence policy, and sanctions only in the sense of absent inducements, this expression concurs with Harsanyi's fuller definition of opportunity costs (Bell, *et al.*, 1969, p.227); more precisely, the *costs* of A's power over B will be defined as the *expected value* (actuarial value) of the costs of his attempt to influence B. If A could be irrational, they might be thought as a weighted average of the net total costs of rewarding B and of the net total costs if his attempt were unsuccessful, of punishing B).

Unfortunately, Equation (15) is indeterminant because it is not yet clear what the costs will be for A's basic resources, i.e. how much base will be used up by a given amount of ΔP_B. We assume action possibilities are, within resource limits, very simple yet costly, without random error:

$$\Delta\text{base} = C_0 K$$
$$\Delta\text{base} \leqslant \text{base}_{max} \qquad (16, 16a = 3, 3a)$$

where K is the (carrot-like) inducement that A can offer B for satisfactory compliance. But what action level will have an effect on B? Answering this question requires a knowledge of A's strength over B and more generally, of B's utility function U_B. Fortunately (for the exposition of the present example), this can be assumed to be a function of B's action level P_B, the magnitude of inducement means K and the accompanying suggestion of a $\Delta P'_B$ change in B's behavior.

$$U_B(P_B, K, \Delta P'_B) = U_1 + C_3 \log(1 + K)\, IC_B - P_B U_x + u_3 . \qquad (17)$$

$$\text{where } IC_B = \begin{cases} 1, \text{ if compliance: } \hat{P}_B = P_1 + \Delta P'_B. \\ 0 \text{ if defiance: } \hat{P}_B \neq P_1 + \Delta P'_B. \end{cases} \qquad (17a)$$

Hypothetical exploration of Equation (17) suggests the following:

$$U_B(P_1, 0, 0) = U_1 - P_1 U_x + u_3 \qquad (U_1 > 0, 0 < P_1 < 1, U_x > 0).$$
ordinary behavior

Except for random fluctuations, when A is not asking B to comply or take actions to that effect, B's utility is made up of an inherently negative disutility associated with compliance expectations, $-P_1 U_x$, and an exogenous set of social inducements, U_1, apparently unrelated to B's action rate.

$$U_B(P_1, K, \Delta P'_B) = U_1 - P_1 U_x + u_3 .$$
defiant behavior

Unlike many real world situations where both defiance and sanctions have absolute costs, this case shows noncompliance costs to equal those before A appeared on the scene. But if B were induced to comply, he would receive

$$U_B(P_1 + \Delta P'_B, K, \Delta P'_B) = U_1 + C_3 \log(1 + K) - (P_1 + \Delta P'_B)\, U_x + u_3$$
$(C_3 > 0)$.
induced compliance

This expression shows a utility carrot associated in a positive but marginally declining way with the magnitude of A's inducement activity K, along with an inherently negative cost for doing P_B more frequently, i.e. $-\Delta P'_B U_x$. Now we can almost calculate A's strength over B, defined in terms of the gross opportunity costs for B that A can manipulate using inducement K. The missing term is B's utility (presumably a disutility) in doing what A wants without A having to make any effort:

$$U_B(P_1 + \Delta P'_B, 0, \Delta P'_B) = U_1 - (P_1 + \Delta P'_B) U_x + u_3 .$$
noninduced compliance

From this expression we have an expression in C_3, an efficiency coefficient, and K:

$$\Delta \hat{U}_B(\text{not}\, \Delta P'_B) = U_B(P_1 + \Delta P'_B, K, \Delta P'_B) - U_B(P_1 + \Delta P'_B, 0, \Delta P'_B).$$

A's strength over B, B's gross opportunity costs in noncompliance	=	The utility of induced compliance	−	The utility of noninduced compliance

$$= C_3 \times \log(1 + K). \qquad (18 = 6b)$$

= efficiency coefficient × effective action magnitude

Equation (18) suggests, appropriately enough, that B's (gross) opportunity costs are a marginally diminishing function of A's inducement action: means and ends are beginning to come together.[7]

[7] Our usage corresponds to Harsanyi's model (Bell, *et al.*, 1969, p. 230), but not necessarily his own language. Thus, in the unilateral model that he sketches, he discusses how "the strength of A's power is measured in *utility* terms, i.e. in terms of the disutility costs to B of noncompliance." But when A is trying to get B to change p_B from p_1 to p_2 with inherent disutility$-\Delta p_B U_x$, Harsanyi refers to "the *strength* of A's power over B" as "the difference $U_2 - U_1$," meaning the change in B's socially manipulable utility evalution. If we want the amount of A's power and the strength of B's power to be intuitively related, as in Harsanyi's own paper, then the strength of A's power should not be measured in terms of the just noticeable utility incentive for B that would be lost in noncompliance, but in terms of the total magnitude of A's impact on B's utility, as perceived by B.

At this point it is natural for A again to ask what he has to do in using his strength to make B comply. Since, by assumption, A can assume B is actuarially rational, the answer is a simple one: B will comply *when* his expected utility in complying just noticeably exceeds his utility expectations associated with noncompliance. We shall call a just noticeable utility difference, *JNUD*, assuming it to be a physiological constant. Then compliance means

$$\widehat{U}_B(P_1 + \Delta P'_B, K, \Delta P'_B) = \widehat{U}_B(P_1, K, \Delta P'_B) + JNUD \quad (19)$$

compliance utility expectation > noncompliance utility expectation
just

Thus the carrot that A must throw B may cost A a lot, but it only just whets B's appetite. By setting up the inducement system of Equations (17), (17a), which just barely pays off when B performs as A wants him to, A can pretty well control B's behavior for any feasible request, $\Delta P'_B$, if he tries hard enough:

$$\Delta U_B(\Delta P'_B, \Delta U_B(\text{not}\,\Delta P'_B)) = C_3 \log(1+K) - (\Delta P'_B)U_x = JNUD > 0. \quad (20)$$

Of course, if A's inducements do not produce a $\Delta\widehat{U_B}$ that is noticeably positive and he is irrational enough to ask for compliance, B can not be expected to comply with A's wishes: defiance results.

But to what extent would such an effort be worth while for A? Is some degree of defiance or noncompliance *ever* likely? Given that his inducements have a declining marginal effectiveness in changing B's opportunity costs, several calculation outcomes may suggest foregoing or limiting an influence attempt. But in each case, since A will rationally temper his demands, only random noncompliance will occur. First, of course, it may be that no change in B's behavior is worth the cost in basic resource; secondly, only a certain level of K might be "cost-effective" up to a point where ΔP_B is less than, and not equal to $1-P_1$. Finally, inducement resources may run out even before K actions stop becoming productive for A.

To see which outcome will occur, we need to return to A's over all cost/benefit calculation. In order to find the action that maximizes his expected utility gain, we need a function for his utility gain in terms of his action level. Once the optimal non-zero action level, if any, is calculated, we can figure out how much compliance this brings, and what benefits and losses result for A and B. From the definition of U_A and Equations (13)–(15), we can calculate $\Delta\widehat{U_A}$ for various possible $\Delta P'_B$ and $\Delta'\text{base}_A$'s:

$$\Delta\widehat{U_A}(\Delta P'_B, \Delta'\text{base}_A) = C_4 \Delta P'_B - C_1 \Delta'\text{base}_A . \tag{15a}$$

Expressing the last term as a function of K follows immediately from Equation (16); assuming B is rational with respect to just noticeable utility differences allows the use of Equation (20), after transposition, as a way of restating $\Delta P'_B$ as a function of K:

$$\Delta\widehat{U_A}(\Delta P'_B, \Delta'\text{base}_A) = -\frac{C_4\, JNUD}{U_x} + \frac{C_4 C_3 \log(1+K)}{U_x} - C_o C_1 K. \tag{15b}$$

Equation (15b) uses the following useful expressions as its main components:

$$\Delta P'_B = -\frac{JNUD}{U_x} + \frac{C_3 \log(1+K)}{U_x} \quad \text{for } \Delta P_B \leqslant 1 - P_1 . \tag{20a}$$

$$\Delta'\text{base}_A = C_o K. \tag{16}$$

Now maximizing this expression by taking the first derivate and setting it equal to zero gives:

$$\frac{C_4 C_3}{U_x(1 + K\text{max})} = C_o C_1 \text{, or}$$

$$K\text{max} = \frac{C_4 C_3 - U_x C_o C_1}{U_x C_o C_1}. \tag{21}$$

And equations (20), (20a) and (16) above give:

$$\Delta'\text{base}_{\text{max}} = \frac{C_4 C_3 - U_x C_o C_1}{U_x C_1}. \tag{21a}$$

$$\Delta\widehat{P'}_{B\,\text{max}} = -\frac{JNUD}{U_x} + \frac{C_3 \log(1 + K\text{max})}{U_x}. \tag{21b}$$

$$\max \Delta\widehat{U_A}(\Delta P'_B, \Delta'\text{base}_A) = C_4 \Delta P'_{B\,\text{max}} - C_1 \Delta'\text{base}_{\text{max}}. \tag{21c = 9}$$

The actual ΔP_B^*, $\Delta^*\text{base}_A$, K^* advocated by A in his proposal to B depend on some further calculations in terms of the options and constraints noted above:

$$\text{Aspects of compliance demand by } A \text{ to } B = \left\{\begin{array}{l} \Delta P_B^* = \Delta^*\text{base}_A = \max\Delta\hat{U}_B = \Delta\hat{U}_B(\text{not}\Delta P^*) = K^* \\ = 0 \text{ if } \max\Delta\hat{U}_A \leqslant 0 \\ \left.\begin{array}{l} \Delta^*\text{base}_A = \min(\text{base}_{\max}, \Delta\ \text{base}_{\max}) \\ K^* = \min(K_{\max}, \text{base}_{\max/C_0}) \\ \Delta P_B^* = \dfrac{-JNUD}{U_x} + \dfrac{C_3 \log(1 + K^*)}{U_x} \\ \Delta U_B(\text{not}\Delta P_B^*) = C_3 \log(1 + K^*) \\ \max\Delta\widehat{U_B}(\Delta P_B^*, \Delta U_B^*(\text{not}\Delta P^*) \\ = JNUD. \end{array}\right\} \begin{array}{l} \text{if } \max\Delta\hat{U}_A \\ = C_4\Delta P_B^* - \\ C_1\Delta^*\text{base}_A \\ > 0 \end{array} \end{array}\right.$$

The rationality postulate applied to B's behavior insures actuarial compliance because of the specific control that A exercises over B's utility. One can easily show that the *JNUD* payoff increase for compliance indicated in Equation (20) above maximizes B's utility. It is first necessary to remember that, by assumption, before A did anything, B's utility was maximized by $P_B = P_1$; moreover, the form of the Equation (17), B's utility function, indicates that influences other than A's inducements and the intrinsic disutility of increasing P_B are constant or random. Thus an inducement just greater than this intrinsic disutility is going to be effective; therefore Equations (8), (20), (22) imply:

$$\begin{array}{l} \Delta\widehat{P_B} = \Delta P_B^*. \\ \Delta P_B = \Delta P_B^* + u_2. \end{array} \qquad (23, 23a, = 7b, 11)$$

For a causal interpretation, we must of course add to the above

$$E(u_i, u_j) = 0 \text{ for } i, j = 1, \ldots 4, (i \neq j). \qquad (24 = 12)$$

From Modelling Influence to Measuring Power

Harsanyi's essential insight into measuring power is the superiority of a theory-based functional specification of influence possibilities. Thus abilities, capacities, inabilities, and incapacities should be stated or measured in terms of influence models. But even the quasi-economic interpretation of A's abilities in terms of a "mere" production function or supply schedule has limitations in his view. He prefers schedules defined in terms of opportunity costs, not merely basic materials:

> ...[*A*] given individual's power can be described not only by stating the specific values of the five [definitionally most important, i.e. cost, strength, amount, scope, and extent] dimensions of his power (whether as single numbers, or as vectors, or as lists of specific items), but also by specifying the mathematical *functions* or *schedules* that connect the cost of his power with the other four dimensions. When power is defined in terms of the specific values of the five power variables we should speak of power in a *point* sense, and when power is defined in terms of the functions or schedules connecting the other four power variables with the costs of power we shall speak of power in a *schedule* sense.
>
> Power in a schedule sense can [also] be regarded as a "production function" describing how a given individual can "transform" different amounts of his resources... into social power of various... strength, scopes, amounts and extensions...
>
> It seems to me that [the common-sense] notion of power as an ability is better captured by our concept of power in a schedule sense...[while the point sense better corresponds] to the common-sense notion of actually exerted *influence*...
>
> If a person's power is given in a mere schedule sense [defined in terms of resources], then we can state the specific values of his five power dimensions only if we were also told how much of his different resources he is actually prepared to use in order to obtain social power... Whereas his power defined in a [mere] schedule sense indicates the conditions under which his environment is ready to "supply" power to him, it is his *utility function* which determines his "demand" for power under various alternative conditions.[8]

In the context of the present concern with action possibilities and structural potentialities – changes in policies or governments – a careful reading of Harsanyi suggests a somewhat expanded list of approaches to power measurement. Table 1 summarized such a non-

[8] Harsanyi in Bell, *et al.*, 1969, pp. 231–2. I have added the phrases in brackets and emphasized "utility function" in attempting to be faithful to Harsanyi's meaning. Only when resources are interchangeable and linear in their utility values (the case of the simple example detailed above), do Harsanyi's distinct concepts of power in a "schedule sense" and a "mere schedule sense" begin to coincide.

TABLE 1

FIVE APPROACHES TO POWER MEASUREMENT

Approach	*Description and Comment*
1. Power or influence in an incomplete point sense	Possibly atheoretical and incomplete descriptions of power/influence situations in terms of power bases or means or influence outcomes (amounts, scopes, extents) that lack explicit opportunity costs measurements for both A and B.
2. Power or influence in a (complete) point sense	Possibly atheoretical descriptions of the aspects of a power/influence situation that rely on utility gains, power costs, strengths, amounts, scopes, extents, and effects (see Table 2 for a realistic example). Aggregate measures in either a complete or incomplete point sense can also be derived by (probabilistically) combining measurements for various situations.
3. Power in a mere schedule sense	Functional models of relationships between power or influence amounts, scopes, extents (and possibly strengths or net inducements), and the means or bases employed. These give falsifiable but incomplete specifications of action or influence possibilities, and as such, are very useful for exploring counter-factual possibilities and measuring actor capabilities, conceived of as performance repertoires.
4. Power in a schedule sense	Functional specifications of relationships between power amounts, effects, scopes, extents, strengths, net inducements, net gains, and influencer costs. Like 3 above, but more completely, this approach allows prediction of situation possibilities in a point sense. Utility functions for both influencer and influencee also allow aggregate power measures like generic power (see note 10). Nonetheless of limited use for exploring power repertoires, conceived of as *alternate* scenarios (power/influence situations with *alternate* specifications of initial conditions, behavioral rules, functional forms, or parameters).
5. Power in a contingent schedule sense	Functional relationships in either sense 3 or 4, or derivative influence measures in either sense 1 or 2, based on contingent assumptions as to which model parameters (or functional forms) have been changed. These make possible the power analysis of alternative scenarios as well as parameter-contingent repertorial measures of future potentialities, but are only as good as their implicit (or explicit) theories of structural alternatives.

exhaustive extension of his distinctions among power measurements in a "point sense," and a (complete or orthodox) "schedule sense." Several considerations call for such an elaboration and expansion of Harsanyi's own useful and pioneering reconceptualizations of work by Dahl, March, Shapley and Shubik.

First of all, the unavailability of data on opportunity costs for influencer or influencee in many real situations means that incomplete influence or power measurements in a point sense or "mere" functional specifications will continue to be frequent tools for political analysis. One need not subscribe to a "behavioristic" bias against subjective variables like utilities when admitting the difficulty *in practice* of utility measurement. Observing a wide enough range of appropriate behaviors by influencer or influencee is usually hard to do. More than in economics, information is power, and good information is hard to get. And, as Harsanyi among others has reminded us, adequate utility measurements must exist *before* attempting to assess power relationships in terms of a nontautological rational theory of utility-maximizing behavior.

A second argument for paying more attention to theoretically less complete models of influence in a "mere schedule sense" is that they encourage speculation as to alternate action possibilities or aggregate measures based on them of actor capabilities. Such speculation is, of course, crucial for someone interested in the desirable and undesirable possibilities and impossibilities within a particular situation, all but one of which must remain counterfactual or unreal. Adding utility functions for both influencer and influencee in the interest of getting unique predictions can lead too quickly into the identity of the actual, the rational, and the possible and of the unreal, the irrational, and the impossible, when rationality is next assumed. Political surprises resulting from either incompletely rational behavior, structural or valuational transformations are then more rarely anticipated. Costs are frequently unstable, changing or manipulable. Moreover, the common-sense idea of power as *capability, ability*, or *capacity* suggests a situation-specific point measure or a cross-situation aggregated measure of action possibilities inferred from "mere" schedules, relating different bases and means to (strengths) amounts scopes and extents.

This perspective also suggests an important reason for emphasizing point measures of power bases, means or costs, and influence measures of strength, amount, scope and extent. The very notion of theoretically based power schedules or influence models calls for situation-specific point interpretations. As powerful theories with behavioral implications, both incomplete and complete power schedules lead via mathematical deduction (or simulation) to general or specific point predictions of situational outcomes. These in turn can be used to test and amend empirical theories of power and influence relationships and more philosophically to comprehend emergent situational possibilities. The major thrust of the present section stems from just this observation: *if we really think of power as a capability, ability or capacity, to measure it we should move from functional or schedule-like theories of influence behavior to their implicit concepts of power capacities and incapacities.* Some such characterizations will be functional; others might well be specific multidimensional point measurements or aggregate repertorial indices.

The contemplation of alternate action possibilities and emergent governmental potentialities within given influence structures leads to the need for a richer language of cross-situational possibilities. As indicated in Table I, three such suggestions are the ideas of a power/influence *scenario*, a power *repertoire*, and a *contingent power schedule*.

Like their modern counterparts in GNP differences or kill ratios, classical unitary measures of national power were sometimes based on implicit scenarios of possible and likely inter-nation influence attempts, sometimes limited to military possibilities. Powerful nations were those with the larger repertoires of expected successful performances. [9] Implicit in such arguments are theories of situational outcomes.

Thus, on occasion, it would seem appropriate to think of different behavioral theories governing encounters in various military or non-military contexts. We may then define *scenarios* not just as political or military "situations" characterized in a point sense in terms of power/influence aspects, but more generally as power/influence situations characterized additionally by situation-specific environmental regularities and sometimes, as well, the (utility-increasing) strategies of their various actors. In a phrase, scenarios are situations plus opportunity schedules of either a complete or incomplete sort.

[9] The most suggestive source on this point has been H. and M. Sprout (1965).

Evidently, an actor's or an army's capabilities have something to do with the set or *repertoire* of scenarios for which he can give poor or credible performances. Conjoined with lists of various possible scenarios, we need to think of contingent power schedules. Such schedules may differ from arena to arena just as battles might have to be fought on land or on sea using different heuristic rules. And especially in situations evidencing considerable structural change, schedules with differing strategies, valuational revolutions or technological developments need to be contemplated as well. *Only in a probability-weighted contingent, repertory sense might classical unitary measures have some validity; we intend further to explore this approach, without expecting any single measure to be totally adequate.*

A convenient mathematical way of expressing alternate power schedules is to present generalized functional forms, variations in which are indicated by parameter changes. A simple example might be the various "constants" requiring empirical estimation in the utility functions and production relationships of the previously described model of unilateral influence. More complex changes in model structure, such as from a dependence to a reciprocal influence situation, may require the activation of new functional relationships or "second-level" functions describing changes in "first-level" relationships. Theories of development and decay, integration and disintegration, power institutionalization and power dispersal clearly tell us, for example, about changes in ordinary, first level, political behavior. If such mechanisms affect only decisional values and structures, "mere" opportunity schedules need not be made contingent on such changes in parameters or functions. Complete schedules are more likely to require *contingent* restatements in terms of appropriate structure-modifying or structure-maintaining variables or functions. In any case, however, discussions of emergent political potentialities will depend on explicit or implicit theories of structural change. And contingent power schedules will only be as valid as the theories they assume.

Some Illustrative Power Measures

For concreteness, we shall now illustrate the range of power measurement approaches summarized in Table 1. The basis of this exercise will be the probabilistic rational model of unilateral influence graphed in Figure 1, formalized in Equations (1)–(12), and exemplified in Equations (13)–(24) above. Since that model further simplifies reality by ignoring (or subsuming) situational differences in power scope and extent, there follows a focus on aggregate probabilistic measurements in terms of power means, bases, costs, strengths, and amounts. Surely a more complex and complete set of illustrative power measures could be derived in an analogous fashion. Since the present purpose is to flesh out the more abstract discussion of previous sections, consideration of measurement alternatives will be limited to already mentioned suggestions. As in the previous remarks, perceptions, expected or anticipated values, and actual values may be only implicitly distinguished.

Incomplete Point Sense Power or Influence Measures

Previously mentioned incomplete point measures of power or influence (essentially those available without complete opportunity cost information or even mere power schedules) include:

a) descriptions of power bases, means, amounts, scopes, and extents;

b) rates or levels of utilization, success or failure, based on incomplete utility assumptions, e.g. influence attempt levels, compliance rates, noncompliance (defiance) likelihoods;

c) partly ordered comparisons between various actors or across situations in terms of any of the above, e.g. "*A* seems to be more powerful than *D* because he exhibits higher kill ratios in combat"; "*C* is more powerful than *D* because he can get more people to do what he wants by using (or using up) his larger resource bases."

The utilities and limitations of such measures should not need elaboration at this point.

Measures that assume rational behavior and/or measurable opportunity costs on the part of the influence allow considerably more insight; we shall now focus on schedule-based point measures, as indicated in approaches 3 and 4 of Table 1. For example, we have discussed rational compliance rates, rational noncompliance rates, "irrational defiance" and "demeaning compliance." The last two labels result from a divergence in perceptions of *B*'s utility components. Ranges of potentially controllable behavior amounts, scopes, and extents (at whatever cost to the influencer, as long as they are basically feasible) also belong in this category of schedule-based point measures.

More specifically, influences, abilities, or power capacities may be defined in a mere schedule sense (to be illustrated below), but they may also be defined in terms of some aggregation of influence possibilities. For example, among many variants, consider:

The amount of A's *influence ability with respect to* b's *scope* i $= \max \Delta\widehat{P_{bi}}$ for which $\Delta\widehat{U_b}(\Delta P_{bi}, \text{not}\,\Delta P_{bi}) > 0$. (25*a*)

The scope of A's *influence ability* = the number of b's behavior scopes for which $\Delta P_{bi} > 0$, given $P_{bi} < 1$. (25*b*)

The extent of A's *influence ability with respect to scope* i = the number of actors b for which $\Delta P_{bi} > 0$, given $P_{bi} < 1$. (25*c*)

An overall influence ability index for A, IA_A

$$\text{IA}_A = \frac{\max \sum_{\text{actors}_b} I_b \sum_{\text{scopes}_i} S_i \dfrac{\Delta P_{bi}}{1 - P_{bi}}}{\sum_{\text{actors}_b} I_b \sum_{\text{scopes}_i} S_i} \begin{pmatrix}\text{jointly feasible}\\ \text{amounts} > 0\end{pmatrix} \tag{25d}$$

Rather similar measures of *inabilities* could be defined in an analogous repertorial fashion. In each case we are assuming rational behavior on the part of the influencee; in the last equation we require both subjective weights S_i for the importance of various of B's behavioral scopes and cross-influencee importance coefficients I_b. Because a variety of ways of using A's resources is possible, we have chosen the index maximizing value in the interests of uniqueness and repertorial suggestiveness.

Since the example of a previous section is extremely simplified, only the scope-specific amount of (schedule-based) influence ability can actually be calculated. Nonetheless, it shows in principle how one might proceed in measuring other capability aspects. According to the rationality assumption, B's behavior is governed by Equation (20*a*):

$$\Delta\widehat{P'_B} = -\frac{JNUD}{U_x} + \frac{C_3 \log(1+K)}{U_x}. \tag{20a}$$

Therefore any change in $\Delta P_{B.}$ up to $1-P_1$ is possible if A takes enough action K. Ignoring cost constraints on A's request, the only other possible constraint on A's influencing B is resource exhaustion, which Equations (16′ and 16a) tell us will not happen when K is less than what we shall define as K_{base}:

$$K \leqslant \frac{\text{base}_{max}}{C_o} = K_{\text{base}}. \tag{16a}$$

Thus:

$$\begin{array}{l}A\text{'s influence}\\ \text{ability amount}\end{array} = \min\left(1 - P_1, -\frac{JNUD}{U_x} + \frac{C_3 \log\left(1 + \frac{\text{base}_{max}}{C_o}\right)}{U_x}\right). \tag{25a}$$

Point Sense Measures of Power or Influence

Once we assume the existence of opportunity cost measures for both influencer and influencee in the sense of paragraph 2 of Table 1, it is very tempting to take one further step and assume both A and B are rational, thus moving to the schedule-based point sense measures mentioned in paragraph 4. In this way most (complete) point sense measures are likely to measure the success and failure of influence attempts (exercised power). And fewer action possibilities may be considered. But logically, behavior is not completely determinant even with rationality assumptions if, for example, we assume weak rationality notions, such as "A will not necessarily maximize his expected realizable utility, but he will avoid taking actions leading to an expected net loss." Nonetheless, assuming that expected values of amount changes can be uniquely calculated from some a priori resource distribution assumptions, we could develop another set of capability measures similar in forms to Equations (25a, b, c, d).

For example:

$$NLIC\begin{pmatrix}\text{A no-loss}\\ \text{influence}\\ \text{capacity}\\ \text{index}\end{pmatrix} = \frac{\max \sum_{\text{actors}_b} I_b \sum_{\text{scopes}_i} S_i \frac{\Delta P_{bi}}{1 - P_{bi}}}{\sum_{\text{actors}_b} I_b \sum_{\text{scopes}_i} S_i} \quad \text{(jointly feasible no-loss amounts).} \tag{26}$$

Clearly, alternative repertorial measures are available for both optimal and expected influencer's capacities and incapacities. A weakening of requirements that every amount change be "no loss" in its own right leads, for example, to the following repertorial measure based on some kind of model expectations that include rules for initial resource allocations. Were no such behavioral theory available, a maximum numerator value could be calculated.

$$UWECI\begin{pmatrix}A\text{'s utility-}\\ \text{weighted}\\ \text{expected}\\ \text{capacity}\\ \text{index}\end{pmatrix} = \frac{\sum\limits_{\text{actors}_b}\sum\limits_{\text{scopes}_i} \Delta\widehat{U_A}(\Delta\hat{P}_{bi})\cdot\dfrac{\Delta\widehat{P_{bi}}}{1-P_{bi}}}{\sum\limits_{\text{actors}_b}\sum\limits_{\text{scopes}_i} \Delta\widehat{U_A}(\Delta P_{bi})} \tag{27}$$

(assuming jointly feasible amount changes > 0).

Again we have normalized our index, i.e. divided it by its maximum value, in order to facilitate cross-actor and cross-situation comparison. For some purposes, comparisons in less general terms may also be desirable.

We complete the transition to schedule-based point measures of exercised power with two more suggestions, leaving to the reader the derivation of the actual values of these coefficients in the simple case of unilateral influence detailed above.

A useful way of bringing the utility maximizing assumption into an analysis is to use it as a norm against which to compare actual performance. Thus *one can turn the frequent criticism that power measurement in terms of bases or means is nonpredictive into a virtue; admit to constructing capacity measures, whose indicated power potentials may rarely be realized in practice*. As a step in that direction, the capability measures of Equations (25*d*), (26), and (27) can be thought of in such terms, although the use of expected values in measure (27) may mean that the implied norm could in practice be exceeded. As these measures use maximum or importance-weighted expected payoff amounts, it is also possible to use utilities themselves as major index components. Using maximum rather than expected values for an unnormed utility increasing capacity index, for example, gives:

$$UICI\begin{pmatrix}A\text{'s utility}\\ \text{increasing}\\ \text{capacity}\\ \text{index}\end{pmatrix} = \max \sum_{\substack{\text{actors}\\ b}} \sum_{\substack{\text{scopes}\\ i}} \Delta U_A(\Delta P_{bi}). \qquad (28)$$

As with so many capacity indices, obvious alternatives exist, including data-based measures of actually realized utilities.

For cases where theories predict the probabilities p of various differently valued outcomes, Harsanyi suggests and expected satisfaction measure of "generic power" substantially like:

$$UWEI\begin{pmatrix}\text{a utility-weighted}\\ \text{expected influence}\\ \text{index of } A\text{'s}\\ \text{generic power}\end{pmatrix} = \frac{\sum_{\substack{\text{actors}\\ j}} \sum_{\substack{\text{scopes}\\ i}} \sum_{\substack{\text{amounts}\\ k}} \widehat{P(\Delta P_{jik})} \Delta U_A(\Delta P_{jik})}{\sum_{j} \sum_{i} \sum_{k} \Delta U_A(\Delta P_{jik})}. \qquad (29)$$

This measure tells roughly how often the influencer is likely to get especially pleasing outcomes; a "maximum achievable" version of the same concept, as well as related measures of actual performances, implied failures or missed opportunities, can easily be envisioned.[10]

Power Measures in a Mere Schedule Sense

Turning from a small set of schedule-independent and schedule-based performance and capability measures, it is worth exploring Harsanyi's schedule notions of power measurement somewhat

[10] Harsanyi, in "Measurement of Social Power in n–Person Reciprocal Power Situations," reprinted in part in Bell, *et al.* (1969, pp. 239–48), actually defines his concept of generic power over a collective decisional outcome using utility differences between actual and worst conceivable payoffs. Whereas the amount of A's specific power is the probability that he will get exactly his preferred policy adopted, the index for his generic power weights outcome probabilities with utility differences. Since the example of this section does not involve reciprocal power and collectively generated goals, we have not followed up the obviously interesting study of influence on collective goal allocations.

further. Because of the great range of such schedules derivable from any reasonably complex theory of influence supply and/or demand, we shall not yet assume specific or complete scenarios joining behavioral rules for A and B with opportunity schedules, but we shall

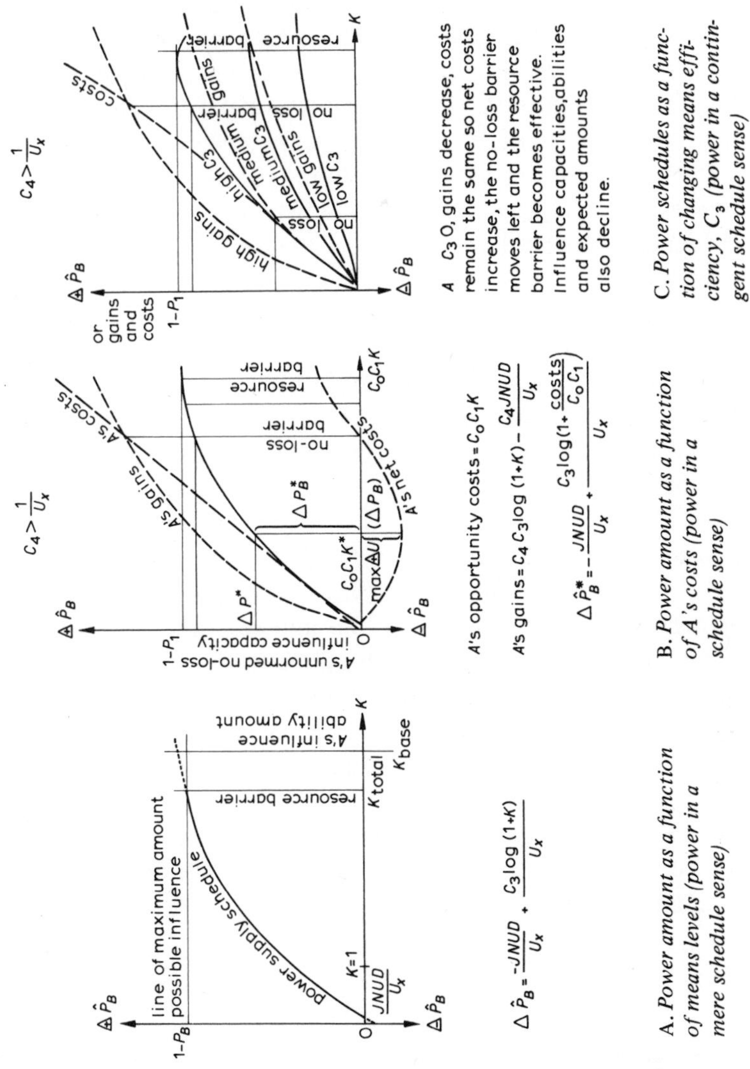

A. *Power amount as a function of means levels (power in a mere schedule sense)*

B. *Power amount as a function of A's costs (power in a schedule sense)*

C. *Power schedules as a function of changing means efficiency, C_3 (power in a contingent schedule sense)*

Figure 2: Three Power Schedules Derived from a Unilateral Influence Model

[1] **Basic equations for expected values of ΔP_B are derived in the text. Analogous schedules in** terms of action levels, bases used, base costs, net costs or other "constants" are possible.

[2] **A number of graphically convenient assumptions, $C_4 > \frac{1}{U_x}$, no binding resource** constraints in 2A and 2B, are not essential to the basic presentation.

[3] For the figure on the left only A is assumed rational; in the other two cases both A and B are assumed so.

selectively focus on the power amount schedules of Figure 2. As previously emphasized the intent will be illustrative, with an eye for value-relevant counterfactual and contingent possibilities.

Figure 2*A* plots a power or influence supply schedule derived from Equation (20*a*) of the example of the section "A simple Example." Assuming *B* rationality complies in appropriate circumstances, it shows the previously mentioned diminishing effectiveness of influence actions of magnitude *K*. But, because we have assumed the means efficiency coefficient, C_3, is large, the resource barrier of Equation (16*a*) is not constraining. For total control only $K_{total} < K_{base}$ is needed. Thus the power schedule intersects the maximum possible influence amount barrier before intersecting the resource barrier, revealing a wide range of *A*'s action possibilities. Note how, according to Equation (25a), *A*'s total potential control of the situation is indicated by the magnitude of *A*'s influence ability amount. Rather than explore other such mere supply schedules, e.g. for *A*'s strength, scope, extent, or net inducements as a function of means or bases, we move on to power schedules based on the assumption that *A* and *B* are both rational.

Power Measures in a Schedule Sense

Turning to Figure 2*B*, the simplifying nature of our model's assumption regarding cost, Equation (15), and resource utilization, (16), becomes clear. Opportunity costs associated with *K* action units are merely $C_0 C_1 K$. Thus a simple transformation of Equation (20*a*) into cost units and a relabeling of the horizontal axis transforms the "mere" power schedule of Figure 2*A* into the orthodox power schedule of Figure 2*B*.

Scenarios with rationality assumptions also constrain and reduce the range of (desirable) action capacities. Using the formulas associated with Equations (15) and (16) shows that

$$\Delta\widehat{U_A} = \underbrace{-\frac{C_4\, JNUD}{U_x} + \frac{C_4 C_3 \log\left(1 + \frac{\text{costs}}{C_0 C_1}\right)}{U_x}}_{\text{gains}} - \text{costs}. \tag{15a}$$

where costs = $C_0 C_1 K$. A no-loss barrier exists for $C_0 C_1 K$ increases; it is implied by the equation:

$\Delta U_A = 0,$

no-loss barrier, (15*b*)

and the intersection of gain and loss lines based on Equation (15a). As suggested by *NLIC*, the no-loss influence capacity index, this barrier shows how rationality-based repertorial measures tend to be smaller than resource- or means-based abilities in the senses we have defined these terms. In fact, the unnormed no-loss influence capacity indicated in Figure 2*B* is the numerator of a special case of the *NLIC* index of Equation (26).

Within the rational modelling tradition, some other scenarios are, of course, possible. Through the application of a utility maximization notion of rationality, the actually demanded (and expected) compliance rate, $\widehat{\Delta P_B^*}$ (= $\widehat{\Delta} P_B$) is even smaller than the no-loss maximum. Thus stronger rationality assumptions make more and more power scenario alternatives seem unreal. In terms of the graphically implied values for the coefficients of Equations (22) and (28), $C_0 C_1 K$ is seen to be not much more than half its possible range, a feature of this power/influence scenario that would show in the utility-weighted expected capacity index, *UWECI*, of Equation (27).

The actual calculations for capacity index values are simple enough not to repeat here, especially since for the case of Figure 2*B* a nonbinding resource constraint has graphically been assumed. Two other graphical features of Figure 2*B* are also worth noting. First, both the utility gain expression and the influence amount increase expressions have similar forms: this should not be surprising when the linearity of utility gains in ΔP_B and the ease of axis relabeling are recalled. As a further result, the gross gain curve will be higher than the supply schedule in a joint plot such as Figure 2*B* whenever, as we have assumed, $C_4 > \frac{1}{\bar{U}x}$. The dependency of the form of the supply schedule of Figure 2*B* on C_3 and the related gross gain curve on C_4 suggests a further look at these and other "constants" within the unilateral influence model. Since the magnitudes of these coefficients are not fixed theoretically, but only estimated from empirical data, alternative scenarios should be conceivable in terms of different values for them.

Power Measures in a Contingent Schedule Sense

For the sake of expositional simplicity, we shall only explore one such possibility, variations in the means effectiveness coefficient C_3. Recalling the previous discussion of the need to explore changes in the parameters of assumed behavioral regularities, we shall limit ourselves further to such plausible hypotheses as "the decrease through aging of *A*'s means effectiveness," or the related phenomena of "*B*'s growing autonomy," or "*B*'s increasing immunity to *A*'s strength" as they would appear in *B*'s utility function, Equation (17). Suggestions of some consequences of an efficiency decrease are indicated in the contingent power schedule of Figure 2*C*.

We leave as an exercise the algebraic demonstration of the geometrically evident consequences of decreasing means efficiency. Both gross gains and net gains decrease while opportunity costs remain the same. The no-loss barrier moves left, decreasing influence abilities, capacities and expected amounts (as we have defined them), while the previously superfluous resource barrier constraint becomes effective for those irrationally willing to pay the costs. Problems seem to multiply each other as actor *A* loses his total control possibilities.

Can we catch any of these counterfactual possibilities that are so graphically arresting in a contingent power schedule in terms of the previously defined point measures? It appears possible to do so, with the ironic consequence that these point measures become schedules again! The basic strategy would be to introduce C_3*-contingent* definitions of the abilities, capacities, and amounts defined in Equations (25)–(29). After all, each of those measures is based on a model that assumes a particular value for C_3.

Thus Figure 2*C* suggests power schedules for three different values of C_3; these might be interpreted as due to *A*'s aging or imperial disintegration along with *B*'s growing immunity and autonomy. But this thought implies either moving to a three-dimensional contingent power schedule (which except for graphic limitations seems an entirely appropriate multidimensional concept) or to a *second-order power schedule* relating influence amounts to structural changes in means efficiency. As a result, point ability, capacity or amount measures could also be given a second-order or contingent interpretation in terms of *capability index schedules relating index values to changing structural parameters.* Such a schedule is implicit, for example in Figure 2*C*. Note how as C_3 diminishes, the horizontal line defining the limits of an (unnormed) influence capacity measure moves down. A *capability index schedule* would only make this relation more graphically exact by plotting changing capability (ability or capacity) index values, such as those in Equations (25)–(29), against decaying structural parameters.

Finally, we turn to the problem of measuring a special kind of capability, a system's capability to transform itself. Since structural changes in power schedules or implied system capabilities amount to changing power scenarios, it appears plausible to suggest *second-order capability indices* for measuring the growth or decay capabilities or incapabilities inherent in contingent power schedules or derivative capability index schedules. Based on some theory or theoretical possibilities of growth or decay, *such indices of potentialities or actualities* would be measures of cross-scenario capabilities. They could, for example, depend on changing structural "constants." A single example, suggested by the above discussion of growth or decay in means of effectiveness, is an index of (self-) transformation possibilities, given by Equation (30):

$$\begin{array}{l}A\text{'s systemic (self-)}\\ \text{transformability index}\\ \text{with respect to}\\ \text{parameter } C_i\end{array} = \max \sum_{\substack{\text{all } C_i \text{ values}\\ \text{feasible within}\\ \text{a certain period}}} IA_A(C_i) \qquad (30)$$

where $IA_A(C_i)$ is a C_i-contingent index schedule version of the overall influence ability defined in Equation (25*d*).

We have come a long way from atheoretical measures of actual influence behaviors to schedule-based assessments of systemic self-transformation capabilities. Yet in terms of an extremely simple formalized model of unilateral influence relations, we have only begun the exploration of structural changes, of development or decay, in power and influence relationships, from states like dependence to independence, or integration to disintegration. Higher-order causal theories of structural change in lower-order behavioral regularities have been found a necessary prerequisite for such a preliminary understanding of political capabilities. But perhaps these elementary explorations sufficiently reveal theory-based contingent power schedules and contingent repertorial measures based on them as both manageable and suggestive vehicles for exploring the political consequences of structural change.

On Measuring Integration

Integration can be thought of as a process of transferring political loyalties, expectations, and activities from old political units toward new, larger decision-making centers with varying degrees of power, legitimacy, and authority. In the context of recent experiences with various international common markets, voluntaristic regional integration (the subject of special interest here) refers more specifically to the voluntaristic restructuring of a regional international system that increases the collective capabilities of member states to achieve common goals and to resolve common disputes without the expectation of appeals to collective violence against other members. The capabilities of such systems may be defined inwardly with respect to their members or outwardly, with respect to their environments.

Our selective approach to problems of measuring regional integration is very much in the spirit of the previous analysis of power. First of all, it too depends on a relatively simple, perhaps paradigmatic causal model. The model of integration processes is, in fact, a reinterpreted version of the Simon-Homans model of social interaction in small groups subject to external demands.

Secondly, this model is similarly sensitive to structural transformations. Our focus will be primarily on such system changes. Because voluntaristic regional integration is already a "second-order" process modifying the mechanisms of ordinary transactional relationships, we in effect will be continuing the discussion of contingent opportunity schedules within growth and decay processes. Points that are obvious by analogy with previous remarks will, therefore, not require as much elaboration.

Moreover, the Simon-Homans causal model that we shall use has some important dynamic properties that allow us to treat it from one perspective as a model of unilateral dependence of a regional system on a more influential external one. As such, it may prove a useful vehicle for interpreting super-power roles in East and West European and Latin American common markets. Perhaps a more appropriate valuational orientation would be the perspective of integration-oriented actors in such a system as they strive to meet members' demands or to gain greater authority and self-determination: the model also allows such an interpretation. Although neither perspective seems unimportant, we shall find it necessary to augment the

Simon-Homans model with various utility functions in order to explore the possibilities and impossibilities of such perspectives in a value-relevant way, just as Harsanyi suggested adding utilities and opportunity costs to Dahl's probabilistic calculations.

Finally, it is worth noting at the outset that the integration literature contains an important distinction between integration as a process and integration as a condition.[11] This distinction, like the one between power and influence, seems obvious enough until one asks what the process is and how we should characterize its condition and potentialities at some point. Yet, through time, it has generally become recognized in the literature on measuring regional integration that the state or condition of an integration/disintegration process should be conceived of in multidimensional terms: the European Common Market was not obviously integrating or disintegrating when gross income and world-wide trade volumes were going up, relative trade partnerships were leveling off, the French were vetoing British membership, the Commission of the market was helping to solve major agricultural crises but failing to increase its scope, legitimacy, or authority in regional transportation matters.

Thus, a multidimensional conception of decision-maker opportunity schedules within integration and disintegration processes in terms of resources, costs, scopes, amounts, and extents is appropriate. Surely these remarks bring to mind the above discussion of the need for describing power potential and power exercise in both a multidimensional point and a multidimensional schedule sense. Power and integration should prove to be closely related concepts, even if they differ in important referential aspects.

After a review of the Simon-Homans model, we shall talk about measuring capabilities in its terms. The first interpretation will be from the perspective of an external, driving power; the second, from

---

[11] The major approaches to modelling and measuring regional integration are for present purposes usefully summarized in articles by Alker, Lindberg, Nye, Puchala, and Schmitter in L. Lindberg and S. Scheingold (1970). To avoid unnecessary duplication, references to this literature will be brief and without extensive footnotes. A fairly detailed discussion of the Simon-Homans model in particular, as well as alternatives to it, is given in Alker's paper in Lindberg-Scheingold (1970), entitled "Integration Logics: A Review, Extension and Critique."

Simon's basic analysis, on which the present discussion heavily depends, is reprinted in Chap. 6 of his *Models of Man* (1957). In particular, his concept of "integration surplus" was historically crucial in stimulating the perception that the Simon-Homans model could be treated in a power-like schedule sense.

a within-system viewpoint. These capabilities can be used, of course, to bring about integration and disintegration, or to maintain integration at a desired level in the interest of, or opposed to the interests of external actors.

The Simon-Homans Model

The differential equation model forming the basis for our discussion is governed by three linear causal relations, which involve four basic variables and seven parameters. Yet because they are ingeniously conceptualized in a realistic and dynamic way, these constructions by Simon allow various interpretations and suggest numerous subsequent analyses.

Working, for simplicity, at the aggregate system level for a regional common market, we first define the following variables:

$T(t)$ = the average level of economically meaningful (rewarding) *transactions*, defined with a zero value equal to pre-integration market levels;

$S(t)$ = the average level of *support* (or authority – legitimacy sharing) at time t for centrally coordinated market decision-making;

$I(t)$ = the *integration* (or task-fulfillment) level of allocative or regulative central common market decision-making at time t;

$D(t)$ = task or integration-related *demands* directed toward central market institutions.

Even at the outset it should be clear from this list that $I(t)$ will function very much like P_B in the previous model, except that it should be thought of as a multidimensional index like those of Equations (25*d*), (26)–(29), summing over various amounts, scopes, and extents.[12]

---

[12] Since the Simon-Homans model is not disaggregated with respect to separate within-system actors, this suggestion will only be briefly touched upon here, in part because the "Integration Logics" paper cited before goes further into a multi-actor approach susceptible to computer simulation. Speaking in terms of an incompletely articulated "no cost" approach to the study of system repertoires, I there proposed measures which could be thought of as indices of collective demand processing success levels or capacities. For example:

$$\textit{DPSI}\ \text{Demand-processing success index} = \frac{\sum_{\text{actors}_i}^{N} \text{Base}_i \sum_{\text{demands}_v}^{V} S_{vi} D_{vi}}{\sum_{i}^{N} \text{Base}_i \sum_{v}^{V} D_{vi}} \qquad (31a)$$

The basic model relating interpretation levels to demands, support, and transaction levels is:

$$\begin{aligned} T(t) &= a_1 S(t) + a_2 I(t) \\ \frac{dS(t)}{dt} &= b_1 [T(t) - \beta S(t)] \\ \frac{dI(t)}{dt} &= c_1 [S(t) - \alpha I(t)] + c_2 [D(t) - I(t)] \end{aligned} \qquad (32a, b, c)$$

(All coefficients are assumed to be positive.)

Simply, but less precisely put, any (excess) level of rewarding transactions is assumed to be caused in a linear, approximately simultaneous way by positive support and positive integration levels (a_1,

---

Here the system's integration success level or capacity is measured in terms of the scope, extent, and amount of demands by resourceful within-system groups that are successfully met or diminished, in theory (S_{vi} would then be model based) or in practice, without lowering the relevant actors' support for the common market. As stated here, the measure is implicitly a schedule dependent on *demand values*, which themselves might be made more determinant on the basis of theoretical expectations. Expansions of this approach in terms of *cross-scenario* successes based on various demand possibilities were also proposed.

Speaking also from the perspective of system coordinators or leaders, closely related measures in terms of *member* utilities might look like

$$IUWIS \begin{pmatrix} \text{a system's} \\ \text{utility weighted} \\ \text{integration satis-} \\ \text{faction index} \end{pmatrix} = \frac{\sum_{\text{actors}_j} \sum_{\text{scopes}_i} \Delta U_{ji} \quad (\text{system response to } \widehat{D_{ji}})}{\max \sum_{\text{actors}_j} \sum_{\text{scopes}_i} \Delta U_{ji}} \qquad (31b)$$

Here D_{ji} is a scope specific demand magnitude and ΔU_{ji} is the utility j gains from unspecified responses to expected demand magnitudes. From the leader's perspective it might be more natural to measure how he could do to meet his own demands rather than service those of others. The result would correspond more exactly to a simple power capacity measure in terms of a leadership's own costs or resources. Thus, for example,

$$NLIGC \begin{pmatrix} \text{A no-loss} \\ \text{integration} \\ \text{capacity} \\ \text{index} \end{pmatrix} = \frac{\max \sum_{\text{actors}_j} \sum_{\text{scopes}_i} \hat{S}_{ji} \hat{D}_{ji}}{\sum_j \sum_i \hat{D}_{ji}} \qquad (31c)$$

might be useful for repertorially assessing how many expected demands could be met without net costs by leaders ($\widehat{S_{ji}}$=1) rather than at a loss ($\widehat{S_{ji}}$=0). A formula even closer to (26), (27), or (28) might be useful given a focus on leadership utilities, actions, and accomplishments.

$a_2 > 0$). And the rate of change of the support level depends positively on whether excess transaction levels exceed those "expected" via a calibration coefficient β on the basis of a given support level. Finally, increases in integration levels are seen as responses to two kinds of political pressures: exogenous demands for more integration activities than currently exist, and bureaucratic initiatives based on support levels for control institutions above those needed, *ceteris paribus*, to maintain the current integration level, i.e. $S(t) > \alpha I(t)$. In this model only demand is exogenous, and other variables are excluded; this assumption amounts to a *ceteris paribus* hypothesis that could (and perhaps should) be replaced by a more stochastic treatment more like the one given above.

Regional Integration as a Dependent System

An important introductory observation about model (32) is the decisive nature of the exogenous demand variable, $D(t)$, in the long run. In this sense, we can think of regional integration or disintegration as unilaterally responsive to pressures external to the system. Such an observation follows directly from the mathematical assumptions of Equations (32). To demonstrate it, we shall explore the amount of causal impact of the exogenous, demand generating actor, call him A, on $I(t)$, $S(t)$ and $T(t)$ as t becomes large ($t \to \infty$). The resulting equilibrium system of ($I(\infty)$, $S(\infty)$, $T(\infty)$ given $D(\infty)$), derived by setting the change rates of Equations (32), to zero, clearly shows the long-term dependence of I, S, and T on D.

After some algebraic manipulations of the equations causally determining T, S, and I respectively, we derive:

$$T(\infty) = a_1 S(\infty) + a_2 I(\infty)$$

$$S(\infty) = \frac{b_1}{\beta} T(\infty) \qquad (33a, b, c)$$

$$I(\infty) = \frac{C_2}{C_1 \alpha - C_2} D(\infty) + \frac{C_1}{C_1 \alpha - C_2} S(\infty).$$

Difference equation versions of these "equilibrium causal relations" are graphically represented in Figure 3*A*. For present purposes, we go one step further to derive an expression for $I(\infty)$ as a function of $D(\infty)$, its only exogenous driving variable; the result of such manipu-

A. Unilateral Dependence (Equations 33)

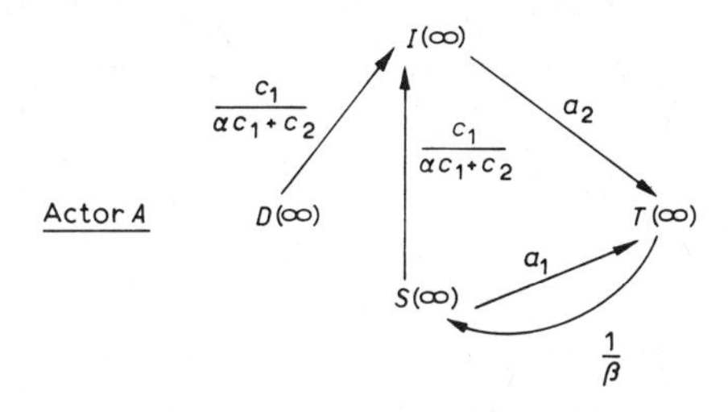

B. Partial Autonomy (Equations 40)

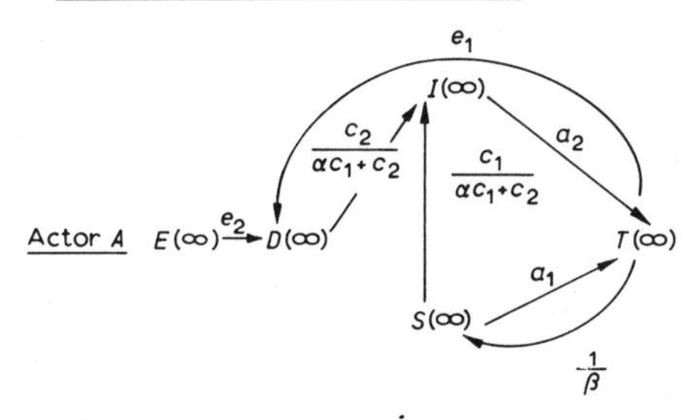

Equilibrium dependency coefficients are derived from reduced equilibrium difference equation versions of (32). It is possible further to construct indirect as well as direct dependencies from these diagrams.

Fig. 3. – Equilibrium patterns of dependency for two regional integration models

lations of (33*a*, *b*, *c*) is (33*d*):

$$I(\infty) = \left[\frac{C_2(\beta - a_1)}{C_2(\beta - a_1) + C_1(\alpha(\beta - a_1) - a_2)}\right] D(\infty) = K_1 D(\infty). \quad (33d)$$

Thus a common market's long-term integration level is seen to be controlled by external forces. Similarly satisfying (or depressing) equilibrium interpretations show how *A* affects *B*'s support and transaction levels.

Having established a long-term kind of causal dependency of the hypothesized common market systen (*B*) on exogenous forces (*A*), how can we interpret this in a schedule sense? Clearly, we first need suggestions as to utility functions and cost measures for *A* and *B*, followed by further discussions as to means and bases. If *D*(*t*) is totally exogenous to the system, we might infer that the system would not exist except for pressures from *A*, who presumably is rational in his demands for integration or disintegration. Note how, in the long run, $I(\infty) = S(\infty) = T(\infty) = 0$ if $D(\infty)$ is zero as well. Thus, if desired, total disintegration can be obtained, or a certain desired stable integration level might be approximated. To express this kind of preference pattern:

$$U_A(I, t) = -d_1(I(t) - D(t))^2 \tag{34}$$

seems appropriate, with $d_1 > 0$. A appears equally unhappy when $I(t)$ is above $D(t)$ or below it, in a quadratically increasing way.

As with most external actors, we shall assume that A also prefers stability of equilibrium in the system it more or less adequately controls. For the present model, stability in performance is a structural property dependent on the values of its structural "constants." It means that small accidental departures from equilibrium will not produce a run-away system. Following Simon, it is possible to show, using methods of advanced calculus, that

$$\text{System (32) is stable} \quad \text{iff} \quad \begin{cases} \beta > a_1 \\ b_1[(\beta - a_1)(c_1\alpha + c_2) - a_2c_1] > 0. \end{cases} \tag{35a, b}$$

Because β, a_1, b_1, c_1, c_2, α, and a_2 are by assumption positive, a measure of equilibrium stability is given by the stability index, $\dot{I}S$, derived from (35b):

$$IS = (\beta - a_1)(c_1\alpha + c_2) - a_2c_1. \tag{35c}$$

IS must be positive if stability is to occur.

To complete a rationalistic calculus for the external actor A, we need a costing of resource utilization options. Presumably effective, costly and resource exhausting sanctions or inducements are associated with the making of demands of magnitude $D(t)$ – otherwise the causal interpretation of Equations (32) would be invalid. Rather than elaborate assumptions about this process, we shall leave it implicit in terms like (34) for A's utility function. But we will assume it possible for A, with quadratically increasing costs, to alter integration scenarios by manipulating c_2 (or the ratio c_2/c_1, the structural measure of the relative influence of external versus internal sources of changes in integration levels). Such a possibility is plausible, given that c_2 is the coefficient of the one term in model (32) that A controls; it is desirable from A's perspective to influence c_2 apparently for two reasons: the system stability index IS if positive, increases with c_2, and $D(t)$ becomes a more effective determinant of integration levels when the c_2/c_1 ratio increases.

A utility function that contains each of the assumptions mentioned above, is the following:

$$U_A(I(t), D(t), c_2', SI) = \frac{-d_1(I(t) - D(t))^2 - d_2(c_2' - c_2)^2}{SI}. \quad (34a)$$

$$\text{where } d_1, d_2 > 0$$

Notice how (34*a*) becomes infinitely negative whenever SI is 0 unless, as is unlikely, both the I–D and $c'_2 - c_2$ gaps are perfectly zero.

Next, for B, let us assume a simple utility function:

$$U_B(I) = -d_3 I. \quad (36)$$

Should we necessarily assume that, because A can totally disintegrate the system when $D(\infty)$ is zero, B places no value on integration? From A's perspective, it would seem logical: "If they really wanted integration, why not do it themselves even when I don't want any? " Such a question assumes that B is powerful enough to do what it wants even if A does not want it. In its presuppositions, it violates our basic assumption of B's dependency on A, with its implied lack of structure-changing or demand-making capabilities on B's part. At a later point, therefore, we may explore alternate utility functions for B; but for now, we shall assume that the psychological tendency to devalue what others control has become dominant for B.

Let us return to A's perspective. *Equations (32a, b, c; 34a, 36) give us*, except for the determinants of D, *a reasonably complete model from which could be derived mere opportunity schedules, power schedules, and contingent power schedules that are a function of* c_2, the magnitude of external causes of integration change. Rather than present such schedules fully, let us explore A's influence/integration options, before discussing a different model more in concord with B's perspective and our desire to measure integration capabilities.

Cost-conscious decision-making is trivial unless there are some kinds of choice dilemmas involved. For example, from A's perspective, doesn't the utility function of Equation (34*a*) suggest setting the two variables he controls, $D(t)$ and c_2', at their desired values and enjoying the resultant utility satisfaction as the system gradually settles down into its equilibrium values? Assuming, for the moment, that c_2' is set at c_2, it is possible to show that when $D(t)$ is maintained at the desired $D(\infty)$, *B*'s utility is not necessarily maximized. *$I(t)$ does not necessarily converge to A's desired $D(\infty)$ as $t \to \infty$*. The resulting phenomena Simon calls a kind of "integration surplus" or "integration deficit" which we interpret as due to within-system resistance by *B* to total capitulation to *A*'s demands. Note how this characterization is appropriate only from *A*'s perspective: by (36) *any* excess of $I(\infty)$ over zero is a "surplus" according to *B*.

A's basic opportunity schedule is already implicitly at hand. Recall Equation (33*d*). From it we can derive the structural relationships determining integration surplus or deficit results of equilibrium. Let us define, *from A's perspective*:

$$\text{integration surplus}_A \Leftrightarrow I(\infty) > D(\infty).$$
$$\text{integration deficit}_A \Leftrightarrow I(\infty) < D(\infty). \qquad (37a, b)$$

Algebraic manipulation of Equation (33*d*) immediately shows that, if $(\beta - a_1) > 0$, as stability requires:

$$\text{integration surplus}_A \Leftrightarrow c_1(\alpha(\beta - a_1) - a_2) > 0. \qquad (37c)$$

Moreover, from Equation (32*c*) we can derive at equilibrium that:

$$\underset{\text{integration surplus}_A\text{ level}}{I(\infty) - D(\infty)} = \frac{c_1}{c_2} \underset{\text{support surplus level}}{[S(\infty) - \alpha I(\infty)]}. \qquad (37d)$$

High levels of system support go together with an integration surplus$_A$, but a demand surplus and a support surplus are mutually antithetical possibilities.

The basic dilemma facing *A* is now explicit, even though it has taken considerable analysis of the implications of different scenarios to make it so. Equilibrium integration levels in the system will be higher than desired when, and if, a support surplus exists according to Equation (37*d*). The phenomenon of positive integration support levels can be attributed, at a deeper level, to structural tendencies in the system of concern. According to (37*d*) and Figure 3*A*, higher external dependencies (c_2), and higher internal regime support requirements, (α) will, up to an appropriate level, help "correct" this surplus. Higher c_2's and α's will also increase system stability (35*c*). But the problems are cost (34*a*) and accessibility: changing the degree of dependency within a system is hard; support level requirements are assumed too expensive to be accessible. Thus a trade-off between cost and benefits must be made. The principal derivative schedules of interest have already been functionally implied. Because *B*'s utility is linear in integration levels, *A*'s strength is linear in *I* while his capacities are limited by a quadratic cost that for some ranges exceeds the benefits of structural "readjustments." The main substantive conclusions from a detailed examination of such capabilities, as measured in terms of c_2–contingent power schedules, would be similar to those in the previous case. *B*'s dependence on *A* is not complete, as the feedback loop of Figure 3*A* suggests. Both *A*'s costs and structural constraints summarized in the complex coefficient of Equation (33*d*) limit total external control of the integration/disintegration process, even in the long run. Yet from *B*'s valuational perspective, as we have described it, any positive integration, whether a "surplus" or "deficit," may remain a permanent frustration.

Towards Greater Autonomy in Regional Integration Systems

Implicit in the above model is a possible standard for *B*'s evaluations of integration that is not so entirely negative. If we can avoid a reflexive identification of *B*'s utilities with *A*'s disutilities, a better source for endogenous utility determination might be found and new integration scenarios constructed. A key link in such a rethinking on *B*'s part would be the establishment of an endogenously derived demand for integration. As suggested by Figure 3*A*, the most appropriate source for such "within-system demand" would seem to be some function of the system support variable *S*, or perhaps a function of *T*, the only direct equilibrium cause of *S*. After all, Equation (32*c*) suggests an adjustment mechanism for integration levels based on support levels as well as demands, and support derives from exceptional transactional performance.

Provisionally then, we suggest a new demand function for B:

$$U_B(\alpha, I, S, t) = -d_4(S(t) - \alpha I(t))^2 + d_5. \tag{38}$$

As before, we shall need to make cost-specific additions to this expression. The constant d_5 emphasizes the fact that some net positive utility might be associated with a utility-maximizing integration level. Preparatory to discussions about structural change options, we have also made this expression an explicit function of the structural parameter α. Conceptually, αI is the support level needed to maintain integration at a constant level in the absence of demand-related pressures for more integration or disintegration.

If utilities are reformulated within a regional integration-system striving for greater autonomy, means for integrating or disintegrating the system should be also. As the previous analysis has shown, the major variable in the system leading to its long-run integration or disintegration is the demand level. Therefore, it would appear appropriate to redefine the model's basic equations to allow for internal sources of demand as well as external ones. Because integration processes develop or decay through the pressures of internal contradictions, we shall not assume demands are simply a function of support levels. Rather, it would be more realistic to make them a function of rewarding transaction levels. Thus, a new set of basic model equations would be

$$T(t) = a_1 S(t) + a_2 I(t) \tag{39a = 32a}$$

$$\frac{dS(t)}{dt} = b_1[T(t) - \beta S(t)] \tag{39b = 32b}$$

$$\frac{dI(t)}{dt} = c_1[S(t) - \alpha I(t)] + c_2[D(t) - I(t)] \tag{39c = 32c}$$

$$D(t) = e_1 T(t) + e_2 E(t) \tag{39d}$$

(all coefficients > 0).

Here we still have an exogenous demand variable, $E(t)$, but introduce an endogenous demand component $e_1 T(t)$. The closer e_2 is to zero (or the larger e_1/e_2 is), the greater autonomy the system enjoys, at least in the short run.

Does this new model (39) escape from the kind of long-run dependence on external forces evidenced by the old one (32)? Solving for equilibrium and stability conditions shows an increased independence of D from E without changing the basic long-range dependency of the regional system on actor A's demands, i.e. variable E. Thus, equilibrium conditions, which we group collectively under the label of Equations (40) are the same as (33*a, b, c*) adding (40*d*):

$$D(\infty) = e_1 T(\infty) + e_2 E(\infty). \tag{40d}$$

The addition of another equilibrium feedback arrow in Figure 3*B* shows the existence of more within-system influences on I. But, solving Equations (40*a, b, c, d*) for $D(\infty)$ as a function of $I(\infty)$ and $E(\infty)$ gives:

$$\begin{aligned} D(\infty) &= \frac{e_1 a_1 + (\beta - a_1) e_1 a_2}{\beta - a_1} I(\infty) + e_2 E(\infty) \\ &= K_2 I(\infty) + e_2 E(\infty); \end{aligned} \tag{40e}$$

and then, solving for $I(\infty)$ as a function of $E(\infty)$ alone leads to:

$$I(\infty) = \frac{K_1 e_2}{1 - K_1 K_2} E(\infty), \tag{40f}$$

where K_1 is the coefficient expression of Equation (33*d*). Note how these mean that $I(\infty)$ will be zero when $E(\infty)$ is zero, even though within-system sources of demand have not disappeared, a case of "integration deficit" at equilibrium.

Stability requirements can be derived as before.[13] After simplification, they lead to three stability conditions:

$$\begin{aligned} &(\beta - a_1) > 0 \\ &c_1 \alpha + c_2 > c_2 e_1 a_2 \\ &(\beta - a_1)(c_1 \alpha + c_2 - c_2 e_1 a_2) > a_2 (c_1 + c_2 e_1 a_1). \end{aligned} \tag{41a, b, c}$$

Except for the case where (41*a*) and (41*b*) are both invalid, we can again summarize these conditions in a simple index, IS_1:

$$IS_1 = (\beta - a_1)(c_1 \alpha + c_2 - c_2 e_1 a_2) - a_2 (c_1 + c_2 e_1 a_1). \tag{41d}$$

---

[13] The actual mathematics is that suggested by Simon (1957, p. 104), who cites P.A. Samuelson (1947, p.271).

Paralleling our previous investigation, does it appear possible that an integration surplus and a support surplus coexist? The answer is "yes" because the relationship between these two variables, (37*d*), is still a valid derivation from the present model, in particular Equation (40*c*). Moreover, a new relationship, (40*e*), shows that the $(I(\infty)-D(\infty))$ integration surplus depends on both an endogenous integration-generated demand and an external demand. Reconceptualizing the integration surplus concept *from B's perspective* so as to concentrate on the extent to which integration levels exceed or fall below system-generated needs or demands for them, leads to two new concepts. From Equation (40*d* and 40*e*)

demand surplus$_B$ effective	$\Leftrightarrow D(\infty) - K_2 I(\infty) > 0$	(42)
exogenous demand$_A$	$\Leftrightarrow e_2 E(\infty) > 0$	
integration surplus$_B$	$\Leftrightarrow I(\infty) - e_1 T(\infty) > 0.$	

Comparing (42) with (37) we see that *B*'s perspective leads to a new definition of integration surplus equal to a similarly novel demand surplus concept. Without going through some fairly complicated algebra, we are now in a position to discuss the basic characteristics of *B*'s opportunity schedules and self-determining capabilities. In order to concretize *B*'s options and dilemmas, we suggest the perspective of a reasonably responsive institutional elite within a regional common market system. Institutional elites frequently strive to increase their own capabilities beyond endogenous support levels without being totally irresponsive to them. Moreover, they too, like external elites, prefer the systems they help control to be stable ones. Assuming the behavioral responses of Equations (39) already represent rational expenditures of effort, what plausible structural change might pro-integration elites consider?

First of all, system leaders might want to increase system autonomy by increasing e_1 and c_1 and decreasing c_2 and e_2, as suggested by another look at Figure 3*B*. Moreover, in the long run, if these changes are not too costly, they might consider increasing the transaction-producing efficiency of their own activities (a_2 in (39*a*)). Or assuming institutional support mechanisms remain unchanged, they might look within the terms of Equations (42) and (37*d*). Even though they help reduce unwanted integrations surpluses, it is clear that, at equilibrium, external pressures create a surplus of endogenous unsatisfied demand. Increasing α to diminish unsupported integration makes integration increases harder to achieve when the system is not at equilibrium (39*c*). Moreover, trying to increase production efficiencies a_2 runs counter to stability (cf. 41*d*) and generates more frustrated equilibrium demands (42). And worst of all, increasing e_1 clearly endangers stability even when it tends to increase autonomy. Changing c_1 is not clearly likely to enhance stability either (41*d*).

When we try to envision the capabilities of within-system integration elites, one positive source of satisfaction we have not yet mentioned is the greater extent to which the schedule of (42) suggests an ability, on the basis of internal demands, to frustrate external actor's equilibrium demands. But this strength can be costly in structural terms for both actors, especially *B*, because c_1, c_2 and e_1 increases can all, in certain circumstances, generate unsatisfied equilibrium demands, unsupported integration surpluses, and increased instabilities.

How would we measure *B*'s capabilities in such circumstances? First of all, we need a revised version of (38). Although it is probably unrealistic, the next formula:

$$U_B(S, I, \alpha, a_1', e_1', c_1', t) = \frac{-d_4(S(t) - \alpha I(t))^2 - d_6(a_2' - a_2)^2 - d_7(e_1' - e_1)^2 - d_8(c_1' - c_1)^2}{SI_1(t)} + d_5 I(t) SI_1(t) \tag{38a}$$

$$\Delta a_2' \leqslant \Delta a_{2\,\max}, \Delta e_1' \leqslant \Delta e_{1\,\max}, \Delta c_1' \leqslant \Delta c_{1\,\max}, \tag{38b}$$

where resource constraints set $\Delta a_2'$, $\Delta e_1'$, $\Delta c_1'$ maxima, is one such possibility. Next we shall solve Equations (34*a*), (39*a*–39*d*) with or without (38*a*) and (38*b*) for utility maximizing behaviors.[14] Then a

[14] A full maximization treatment would require the discovery of optimal utility-increasing paths through time. The appropriate mathematics, optimal control theory, is more complex than the level of discussion of the present effort. It, too, becomes inadequate the more *A* and *B* behave like dynamic game players in their move choices. Then differential gaming mathematics becomes relevant. A relevant recent summary of the appropriate literature, with a good bibliography, is R.E. Kalman, *et al.* (1969).

number of cost-specific contingent schedules could be constructed, embodying the choice dilemmas already mentioned. From the resulting schedules, various capability measures would be computable. Each step in the analysis would follow the more detailed, but simpler, example of the previous discussion of power measurement.

Would such an exercise really measure regional integration capabilities? One argument is that the measures already proposed in Equations (31), note 12, are better measures of a system's integration level and capability. Were our present model more disaggregated than the B vs. A-interpretation implies, a multi-actor, no-net-cost, demand-satisfaction, repertorial approach would be a clearly appropriate measurement strategy. In such a sense, integration is just the opposite of power: it refers to a *system's ability to get for member actors what they want but otherwise could not get*. System B enables its members rather than disabling them. Integration thus means the capacity of a system to satisfy demands, achieve common goals, and resolve inter-member disputes, in a way that exceeds the sum of individual capabilities.

But in another sense, integration in a schedule sense is like power, the *power of regional integration system B to get external actor A to tolerate non-optimal integration levels which for its own reasons B finds more desirable*. Then B's autonomy to do what *it* wants to, irregardless of A's demands, becomes a relevant component of the integration concept. This transformation of perspective amounts to studying, in all the previously mentioned senses, the power of an integration system vis-à-vis its environments.

For example, consider the following several indices, each especially attentive to one of the terms in B's utility function (38*a*). In each case we assume that behavior summarized by Equations (39) already represents efficient resource allocations and that separate resources go into structural manipulations. (A fuller and more realistic treatment of resources and means is beyond the scope of the paper.) Let $E\max(\delta, T)$ = the maximum range of model-based external demands $E(t)$ over a period T within which, by judicious structural readjustments, integration system B can maintain

$$(S(t) - I(t))^2 < \delta. \tag{43a}$$

This is clearly a Deutschian adaptive capability index that emphasizes system autonomy. It assumes A is rational according to (34a), without assuming B makes the least costly a'_2, c'_1, e'_1, adjustments, just the most effective, feasible ones. More constrained autonomy indices, with respect to levels of integration, unsupported integration, and demand surplus could easily be devised along similar lines, as could repertorial equilibrium potentialities.

We prefer here to suggest some alternative measures of goal achievement, self-determination and self-transformation more like Equation (30). The first assumes optimizing behavior by both A and B with respect to structural manipulations as well as routine behaviors:

$$BUMCT\begin{pmatrix}\text{B's utility}\\ \text{maximizing}\\ \text{capacity}\\ \text{in } T\end{pmatrix} = \max \sum_{t=0}^{T} U_B(c'_1, a'_2, e'_1, t, E(t), \hat{c}_2) \quad (43b)$$

Note that until $E(t)$ values are well specified, this is an implicit function of $E(t)$.

The second index is a no-loss repertorial index of integration enhancement abilities, where again c'_1, a'_2, e'_1 values may vary through time.

$$BNLIAT\begin{pmatrix}\text{B's no-loss}\\ \text{integration}\\ \text{enhancement}\\ \text{ability in } T\end{pmatrix} = \max \sum_{t=0}^{T} \Delta I(c'_1, a'_2, e'_1, t, \hat{E}(t), \hat{c}_2) \quad (43c)$$
$$\text{where } U_B(t) \geqslant 0$$

This index presupposes, it should be noted, that the $d_5 I(t)$ term in (38a) is big enough in at least some situations to offset the negative cost terms in the numerator of (38a). Finally, as a rather different kind of integration capability measure, we could study system stability as it is affected by the external actor, who is assumed to be efficiently manipulating c_2. Through time:

$$MEIT\begin{pmatrix}\text{minimum}\\ \text{expected}\\ \text{instability}\\ \text{within } T\end{pmatrix} = \min\,(IS_1(E(t), \hat{c}_2, \hat{c}_1, \hat{a}_2, \hat{e}_1, t)) \text{ for } t \in T \quad (43d)$$

It should be clear that low values of these capability indices imply poor performance, the lack of regional autonomy, a kind of disintegration, or even systemic political decay.

Measuring Political Development

At several points, the previous discussion of integration and disintegration has used concepts, such as autonomy, dependence, responsiveness, institutional power, and nonviolent conflict resolution, which have clear correspondences in the literature on national political development and decay.[15] Thus, some close analogies are likely to exist between these two literatures and that on national power and weakness: all three refer to systemic capabilities or incapabilities.

Moreover, a cluster of questions and distinctions have arisen as to the multidimensional nature of development in what we would call a point or schedule sense. Scholarly characterizations have included equality, capacity, differentiation; consensus, legitimacy, tolerance, stability, democracy; autonomy, differentiation, secularization; adaptability, autonomy, complexity, coherence; and power-sharing, executive stability, the absence of domestic violence, participant political socialization, territorial integrity. Polemical claims have used many of these terms (or their opposites) in descriptive *cum* evaluative ways. Given the obviously controversial nature of development evaluations and the vagueness inherent in many such conceptual distinctions, some authors have preferred to concentrate on developing empirical process models of social change.

In general, such process models employ language analogous to our distinctions regarding the aspects of power/influence situations or scenarios. And they incorporate or suggest how other measures of potential or exercised political capabilities might be defined. Such an approach, of course, does not deny the importance of the value questions implied by the earlier literature; rather, it helps provide better scientific grounds for exploring such issues.

As a basis for extending the present conception of capability measurement in a schedule sense to the study of political development, we shall limit the discussion to part of one simulational model,

---

[15] As before, our literature review will be sharply limited to points essential to the present discussion. Two helpful reviews have been R.F. Hopkins (1969) and S.P. Huntington (1972).

the party responsiveness subroutine within the Brunner-Lipset simulation model of political development.[16] The treatment will obviously not be an exhaustive one, given Lipset's particular interests in one subset of developmental characterizations and Brunner's work on other aspects of the ideas of Lerner, Deutsch, Lipset, and Huntington. Within Lipset's work on how parties process group demands, Brunner has focused on the legitimacy of political institutions and the tolerance of political actors for one another in a system responding with more or less consensus or cleavage to issues arising out of economic and other aspects of the modernization process.

After a restatement of the Brunner-Lipset party system subroutine from a power analysis perspective, we will point to the meaning of opportunity schedules implicit therein, but again without completing the necessary calculations. On this basis, illustrative unitary measures of various developmental aspects of a party system will be proposed.

The Brunner-Lipset Model of Party Responsiveness

In his thesis, Brunner frequently uses concepts from Lasswell and Kaplan's classic *Power and Society*. Because this work has informed almost all subsequent discussion in the power literature, including Dahl and Harsanyi's, one should be able to fit the basic variables of the Brunner-Lipset model of party responsiveness into our previously elaborated power analysis framework. The key variables in the Dahl-Harsanyi treatment are the cost and benefits derived from a utility function; in the Brunner-Lipset model an analogous role is played by stress variables, which can be thought of as disutilities generated by gaps between expectations (aspirations) and achieved value positions in various political arenas. As a moment's reflection should make clear, motivating aspiration-achievement gaps need not depend on full-information, anticipatory, rational calculation procedures. Models without such calculating powers may well prove to be more realistic, and they lend themselves to provocative analysis in terms of differences between actual and optimal possible performances calculated on the basis of stress-minimizing assumptions.

Table 2 suggests a power analysis framework for reviewing the

[16]Earlier versions of this model were discussed in R. Brunner, "Some Comments on Simulating Theories of Political Development," in W. Coplin (1968); and H.R. Alker, Jr. (1971). An introduction to the process-modelling approach to political development is given in R.D. Brunner and G.D. Brewer (1971b). The source for the present discussion is R.D. Brunner (1971a).

TABLE 2

VARIABLES IN THE BRUNNER-LIPSET PARTY RESPONSIVENESS SUBROUTINE, CHARACTERIZED IN THE TERMS OF POWER ANALYSIS

Variable Types	*Group Characteristics*	*Party Characteristics*	*Party System Characteristics, Including Governing Party Systemic Effects*
Actors	Groups $I, .. G, IG, .. NG$.	parties $I, IP, P .. NP$.	NPP, an index for sums over all parties; IGP, an index for the governing party.
Bases	access to party positions on value issues, including media access, $AP(G, V, P)$: $AP(G, V, NPP) = \sum_{P=1}^{NP} AP(G, V, P)$ a group's share of the crisis-regulated number of significant demands within a quarter.	governmental access on value issues, including media access $AG(P, V)$; access in electoral support arena, $AE(P, G)$; party's share of a quarter's significant demands.	$AG(IGP, V)$, $AG(NPP, V)$; legitimacy of party arena for groups, $LEG1(G, 1)$; legitimacy of support arena $LEG1(G, 2)$; inter-actor tolerance pattern, $TLF(G, I)$, where $1 .. G, I, .. NA = NG+NP$. The number of processed demands within a quarter = $NDS \times ND$.
Means, Including the Making of Demands and Granting of Access	party access demands to revalue $AP(G, V, P)$; changing party support, $\Delta AE(P, G)$; changing group expectations of parties in support arena, $\Delta EP(IG, V)$.	$XAT(p)$ = party p's adaptability; granting of access, $\Delta AP(G, V, P)$.	governmental (in)effectiveness for group G in the current and previous quarters, $GEF(G)$, $GEP(G)$; $GEF(G) = \sum_{V=1}^{NV} \frac{EP(G, V) - AP(G, V, IGP)}{AP(G, V, IGP)}$ redistribution of access in support, party legislative arenas.
Opportunity Costs	chance of stress increase through $\Delta EP(IG, V)$; expectation (aspiration) increase through alienation in party arena or mobilizations in the support arenas.	chance of stress increase in governmental arena through group-induced expectation (aspiration) increase in support or party arenas.	chance of stress increase within governing party; change in crisis level=SSS=sum of all stresses in support, party, governmental, and military arenas.

Positive or Negative Influence Amounts	$\Delta AP(G, V, P)$, increased group representation in a party, and $\Delta EG(P, V)$, increased representation of these aspirations in the legislative arena.	changes in party support, $\Delta AE(P, G)$, and in governmental access, $\Delta AG(P, V)$.	$\Delta LEG1(G, 1)$, $\Delta LEG1(G, 2)$ positive or negative changes in G's legitimacy evaluation of the party and support arenas; changing, and renormalized access levels; $\Delta TLF(G, I)$, changing tolerance patterns.
Strength	party support stresses if groups with old support.	group access stress in party arena if party access is not given.	party stresses in governmental arena if party access demands not met.
Scopes	value domains $V = 1, \ldots IV, \ldots NV$.	$V = 1, \ldots, IV, \ldots NV$.	$V = 1, \ldots IV, \ldots NV$.
Extents (and arenas)	parties, including governing party in party (P) and governmental (G) arenas.	groups, governing party in electoral support (E) and legislative, i.e. governmental (G) arenas.	groups, parties in all arenas: (E), (P), (G) and military (M).
Benefits	$\Delta SP(G, V)$, stress reductions.	$\Delta SG(P, V)$ and $\Delta SE(P, G)$, stress reductions.	ΔSSS, crisis reductions.
(Dis)Utilities	$SP(G, V)$ group stress w.r. to values = $\dfrac{EP(G, V) - AP(G, V, NPP)}{AP(G, V, NPP)}$; $GEF(G)$, $GEP(G)$, previously defined as system means.	$SG(P, V)$ party value stress in legislative arena, $= \dfrac{EG(P, V) - AG(P, V)}{AG(P, V)}$; in support arena, $SE(P, G)$, similarly defined; salience, $SAL = \dfrac{SG(P, V)}{\sum_{IV=1}^{NV} SG(P, IV)}$.	total stress across systems, i.e. crisis level, SSS.

definitions essential to an understanding of the Brunner-Lipset party system subroutine. Although some of the variables there appear in routines specifying relevant actions or outcomes in other arenas, viz., the electoral support, governmental (legislative) action, and military support arenas, the table is not a complete summary of the Brunner-Lipset model.[17] When reasonably exact correspondences exist between the concepts of our extended Dahl-Harsanyi power analysis framework and Brunner FORTRAN variables, a symbolic expression used by Brunner is given. Using the "stress equals disutility" equivalence mentioned previously, a reasonably good fit in concepts is suggested in the table, except that Brunner does not explicitly use power *strengths* nor do his actors explicitly calculate the expected opportunity costs or stresses associated with various action possibilities in an actuarial way. Nonetheless, nearly complete point sense measures of system power or development would be easily available in applications of the present approach to the Brunner-Lipset model.

Table 2 illustrates a useful pretheoretical formula in the power (and development) literature that *actors use means that depend on resources, at various costs to themselves and others, through time to achieve desired amounts of behavioral, attitudinal or systematic change in different value contexts or arenas.* In the party system subroutine, and the closely related electoral support arena, the major actors are *NG* socio-economic groups and *NP* political parties, while the major objectives are changing degrees of access to *NV* distinct, important political values. Specifically, in the Turkish case, agricultural, trade, professional, official, and religious groups are seeking access to policy positions in the legislative, governmental arena of the three major parties; the Republican Peoples Party, the Democratic Party, and the National Party. The principal issues of concern are the distribution of wealth and income, religious practice, press censorship, and the use of the state radio.

A fuller appreciation of the bases, means, costs, and amounts of exercised power in the Brunner-Lipset party responsiveness sub-

[17] Nor should the present review be considered a generally adequate exposition or defense of Brunner's work. As far as I am aware, his thesis provides the clearest specifications to date of significant theories within the political development area. They are combined with an interesting, comparative empirical application to Turkey, 1950–60, in a way which exhibits considerable sophistication in the analysis of model properties as well as a clear awareness of their limitations.

routine requires discussion of the flow chart of Figure 4, as well as the remaining items in Table 2. In general, the flow of actions suggested by Figure 4 is that stressed actors will seek access in arenas they consider legitimate or effective and make demands of those toward which they have sufficient tolerance. Parties are clearly limited interest aggregators. Thus, a number of appropriate thresh-

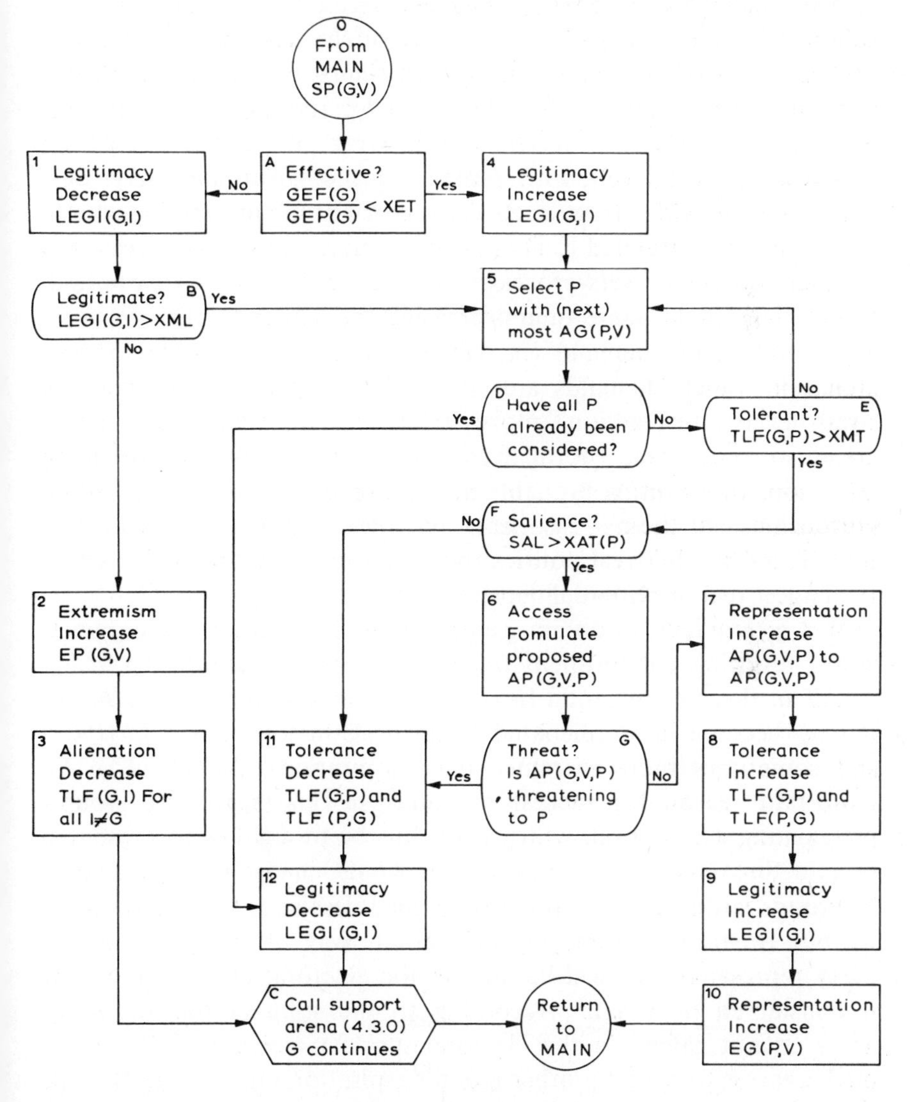

Fig. 4. – The Brunner-Lipset Party Responsiveness Subroutine

olds have to be passed before a stressed group actually makes or has accepted an access demand for more say concerning a party's position regarding a particular value. $AP(G, V,P)$ is G's access in the party arena to party P's position on value or issue V; $AP(G, V,P)$ is the related demand, and $EP(G, V)$ the group's originating aspiration or expectation level.

A normalized stress $SP(G, V)$ between access and expectation levels summed over all parties is at the root of the demand and response process. First of all, the governing party must be seen as effective – note the definition in Table 2 of perceived party system (in)effectiveness variables $GEF(G)$ and $GEP(G)$, in terms of a group's perceived cross-value stress levels with respect to the governing party. Secondly, system-wide stress levels are important in determining whether a demand is attended to at all, because total stress can increase the number of demand sets processed within a quarter of a year period, NDS, while at the same time decreasing the demands treated as part of a simultaneous demand set, ND. Moreover, the sequences and the arenas in which demands are attended to depend on comparative stress levels: the "action" moves from issue to issue and arena to arena, so some group (normalized) stress levels do not receive much attention. Interpreting probable unrequired expectations or stress increases as costs seems reasonable and plausible in the present context: it means that real politics focus on those issues associated with the largest real or potential deprivations.

If a group fails to obtain greater representation in P regarding V and a resulting commitment by P to increase representation in V's behalf in the governmental (legislative or policy) arena ($\Delta EG(P, V)$), it may become more alienated (a decrease in tolerance, $TLF(P,G)$) and sometimes more extremist in its aspirations ($\Delta EP(G, V)$). An important reason for success or failure in this regard is a group's pre-existing access level, which may thus be thought of as a resource base: a threatening demand, one that would change the access ranks of groups within a party, is always denied. In the case of an attended to, but frustrated aspiration, an alternate way of trying to increase party representations will be used in the electoral support arena if it is considered legitimate. According to the support routine, party access is not gained in the electoral support arena, but the use of media access to whip up other group's aspiration (and demand) levels may bring about the desired $\Delta EG(P, V)$, even if the unmodelled *content* of the party's demands may differ to some extent.[18]

Parties, on the other hand, are selectively active in party, government, support, and military arenas according to processes not all explicitly portrayed in Figure 4, but in part summarized in Table 2. They responsively attend to certain group stresses in the party system arena, for example, only if relevant demands are made that affect salient enough values – if their own salience index *SAL* of stress exceeds an adaptability threshold $XAT(P)$ in a nonthreatening way. In the governmental arena, legitimate coalitions with tolerated partners may be necessary to achieve policy access, and frustrations may also lead to support appeals. As for the support arena, parties there sometimes unilaterally grant access to their supporters, but not in a simple *quid pro quo* manner; only expectation increases can be

---

[18] Whether or not they show access to decision-making processes with respect to the values concerned, the absence of an explicit analysis of the extent to which interests of model actors are actually opposed has several ramifications. First, it makes us wonder about the realism of an assumption that electoral support appeals cannot be specifically tailored to particular population subgroups. That such demands in an electoral arena do cause *some* degree of heating up of the general electorate is, of course extremely plausible.

Secondly, the absence of content-specific measures of value access – other than Brunner's use of groups' per capita incomes and party voting strengths – makes "consensus" hard to define. Should we say, for example, that consensus means that everyone agrees to disagree about the same stressful problems?

$$IPCNS1\begin{pmatrix}\text{first}\\ \text{index of}\\ \text{party}\\ \text{consensus}\end{pmatrix} = \frac{\displaystyle\sum_{\substack{\text{all distinct}\\ \text{party pairs } P,\,P'}} r(SG(P,V),SG(P',V))}{\#\text{ distinct party pairs}} \tag{44a}$$

where the product-moment correlations r are taken across all values and *IPCNS1* has a maximum of unity in the frightful case where everyone agrees that they are lacking access to the same things. If the generated outcome of an access redistribution were to produce public goods (e.g. economic growth or an end to corruption) more nearly enjoyable by everyone, conflicts of interest might not be so total as in the case of disputes over *shares* of the same pie. Perhaps a better index of consensus would use legitimacy weights for groups or parties, evidencing the idea of agreement on where and how to resolve differences or communalities in interest on issues jointly perceived to be stressful. For example:

$$IPCNS2\begin{pmatrix}\text{second}\\ \text{index of}\\ \text{party}\\ \text{consensus}\end{pmatrix} = \frac{\displaystyle\sum_{\substack{\text{all distinct}\\ \text{party pairs } P,\,P'}} r(LEG2(P,1)SG(P,V),LEG(P',V)SG(P',V))}{\#\text{ distinct party pairs}} \tag{44b}$$

where conventions are the same as above and $LEG2(P,1)$ is the legitimacy party P accords to the party arena.

obtained there in a reasonably direct way, but that involves raising other group's aspirations as well, which may mean more sharing within a party's decision process of any resulting increases in legislative access ($AG(P, V)$). Brunner's model also encompasses the appeal by various political parties for control of military decision-making. Changes in activity into this arena, when others are considered illegitimate, allow us to study breakdowns in nonviolent decision-making capabilities and they allow Brunner to model the system breakdown that occurred in Turkey around 1960. Because these mechanisms are not directly relevant to the party responsiveness process, however, we shall not dwell on them in detail here.

An important emphasis in the Lasswell-Kaplan scheme of power analysis, not yet included in the augmented Dahl-Harsanyi list of the present paper, is on political effects. Political effects are those post-outcome or post-influence consequences within an exercised power relationship that affect the system of relationships themselves. One interpretation, based on contingent schedule ideas, describes effects as "system-changing or maintaining feedbacks," such as changes in the parameters of the various models we have examined. Another related interpretation is emphasized by Brunner, who focuses on slowly changing constraints within a system model, including the legitimacy and tolerance levels evident in Figure 4. From a system's level perspective, we have tried to incorporate a related interpretation within Table 2.

The last column of the table suggests some of the more important variables of use in studying systemic development capabilities and incapabilities. Without trying to reify the system being discussed, we have somewhat augmented Brunner's emphasis on effects such as changing patterns of legitimacy and tolerance in order to incorporate his similarly fascinating aggregate stress-crisis relationships, some of which were mentioned above in the discussion of time processes. Changing levels of demand and access also seem appropriate bases for a study of system democracy, stability, or responsiveness and have, therefore, been included in the system-level column of Table 2 as well.

Development Schedules and Capability Measures

Given the classifications of Table 2 and the model of Figure 4, what would correspond to development schedules in a mere, a full, or a contingent sense? In answering this question, we are again immediately forced to define our perspective. We might emphasize the capabilities of a developing system vis-à-vis its external environment, or vis-à-vis its social system as modelled by Brunner, but the above treatment of the autonomy of an integrating or disintegrating system will be assumed suggestive enough in this regard. And we could emphasize a single actor's goal achievement opportunities, because of, or in spite of, some other actor's wishes, but here too, earlier treatments of unilateral influence or dependence relations should serve as adequate examples of such an approach.

Thus, the opportunity presents itself of taking a system's level focus from which one can tackle the problem of defining relevant evaluative concepts in a measurable way. In the present case, then, the appropriate development opportunity schedules would seem to be positive ones: they would tell how means (demands) or opportunity costs (actual or expected stress increases) made the achievement of desired objectives more or less possible. In this sense development and integration would be very analogous concepts. Contingent development schedules might thus indicate how, demands → amounts, stress → access schedules varied as a function of system legitimacies, revaluations, tolerances, or adaptabilities. Either vector functions, with separate entries for each group or party, or aggregate system measures, like access successes or alienation rates as a function of crisis levels, could be computed and graphed in appropriate ways. Access rates for optimal demand strategies, if calculable, would be very useful, especially if actual system performances fell below them appreciably.[19] Surely such schedules would help us better

[19] The meaning of optimal strategies in the present context is one of the many unexplored questions that our approach forces us to raise. In conventional differential equation systems or econometric causal modelling, policy effects and benefit-optimizing policy choices can often be uncovered by reasonably standard model analysis strategies, including the analysis of compound paths or final forms. The extension of such techniques to more realistic simulation models is not yet a well-defined or clearly feasible procedure. Yet current developments in nonlinear econometric estimation and nonlinear control theory might soon make optimization calculations possible for subroutines like that of Figure 4 – I have in mind the TROLL system developed by Edwin Kuh and Mark Eisner at M.I.T.

Until such calculations are available, our discussion of development opportunities can only take place in a "mere schedule sense," since it would be counter-productive, I feel, to here make the assumption, as was done for the Simon-Homans models, that behavioral regularities reflected rational behavior. The very real and provocative tension between model performances and the best or worst feasible alternatives to them would thereby be lost.

understand system potentialities and policy possibilities.

Rather than pursue further such tempting possibilities, which would require considerable efforts at model analysis that are beyond the scope of the present paper, let us now turn to various schedule-based point measurements of developing or decaying system capabilities. Although most of the indices we proposed will be limited to time-specific scenarios, cross-time versions or plots of these statistics would surely allow us to explore development and decay possibilities in a dynamic way. Relevant illustrative measures include Equation (43) of the above treatment of the integration/disintegration process. Our focus will again be illustrative, not exhaustive, with special emphasis on the explicitly and implicitly evaluative concepts used in the Brunner-Lipset party-system analysis.

Brunner treats tolerance, legitimacy, and consensus in what we could call an incomplete point sense. Rather than explore obvious ways of aggregating or averaging such vectors and matrices through time and across actors, we suggest that a system's political capabilities develop when its legitimacy and tolerance levels are expected to be, at least in the aggregate, self-sustaining. The demand-processing success index of Equation (31*a*) is an obviously appropriate schedule-based repertorial measure of such a concept. Equations (44*a,b*) have already exemplified the consensus measurement problem. Another approach, which might be implicitly more critical of partially sequential model satisficing practices, is suggested by

$$ILEE\begin{pmatrix}\text{index of legitimacy-}\\ \text{enhancement}\\ \text{efficiency for given}\\ \text{stress levels}\end{pmatrix} = \frac{\sum_{G=1}^{NG} \Delta \widehat{LEGI(G, 1)}}{\max \sum_{G=1}^{NG} \Delta \widehat{LEGI(G,1}\begin{pmatrix}\text{different}\\ \text{stress-linked}\\ \text{demand}\\ \text{practices}\end{pmatrix}} \quad (45)$$

where it is assumed that the maximization calculation allows the recognition of different demand magnitudes or sequences without, however, a change in other model parameters or inputs, including limiting stress levels. Legitimacy changes within the party arena are assumed to cover a single, quarterly time period.

Turning to system democracy and responsiveness, a number of

measures suggest themselves. Analogous to Equation (27) of our power analysis treatment is a stress-weighted access redistribution covariation index focused on the party arena:

$$SACI\begin{pmatrix}\text{stress-access}\\ \text{adjustment}\\ \text{covariation}\\ \text{index}\end{pmatrix} =$$

$$\frac{1}{\#\Delta\text{'s}} \sum_{\substack{\text{groups}\\ G}} \sum_{\substack{\text{parties}\\ P}} \sum_{\substack{\text{values}\\ V}} \Delta\widehat{AP(G, V, P)}\widehat{SP(GV)}. \qquad (46)$$

Obvious standardizations of model-based covariations are possible, including a stress-access adjustment correlation which might be a useful evaluative performance measure. Restatements in terms of party access in the governmental arena also seem attractive. Presumably, all systems changes increasing such indices would be considered more responsive, while negative *SACI* values would provide an intensity-weighted kind of frustration index.

In the same vein, an expected frustration index, perhaps more sensitive to model irresponsiveness than merely the overall stress (crisis) level, would be the following, calculable from a system model such as Brunner-Lipset, but not from point observations:

$$MRSG\begin{pmatrix}\text{Marginal}\\ \text{rate of stress}\\ \text{generation}\end{pmatrix} = \sum_{\text{groups}_G} \sum_{\text{values}_V} \frac{\Delta\widehat{SP}(G, V)}{\Delta EP(G, V)} \qquad (47)$$

where the expectation in the numerator is a model-based response to a small, exogenously induced aspiration increase. (Note how implicitly this is a hypothetical, schedule-based, cross-scenario measure: small equivalent changes in all aspirations are not likely, but the concept is nonetheless attractive.) Again obvious refinements could be made extending or normalizing the above measure.

How could one argue that a system was becoming increasingly undemocratic? What might democracy mean in the present context? One simple, normalized point index might be a measure of correspondence between party electoral support and party governmental access:

$$DEM1 \begin{pmatrix} \text{first} \\ \text{democracy} \\ \text{index} \end{pmatrix} =$$

$$\frac{\displaystyle\sum_{\text{groups}_G} \sum_{\text{parties}_P} AE(P, G) \sum_{\text{values}_V} AP(G, V, P) AG(P, V)}{\displaystyle\sum_G \sum_P AE(P, G)^2}. \tag{48}$$

When each party delivers an aggregate share of policy determinations equal to electoral support levels, this index approaches unity. Given the somewhat arbitrary way in which the Brunner-Lipset model allocates value accesses, and not values, more precise democratic responsiveness measures may be hard to develop and apply, although a tougher standard than (48), involving value-specific, policy-access shares would clearly seem desirable. One counterfactual possibility of particular interest when compared to *DEM*1 might be:

$$DEM2 \text{ (equal media access)} = \widehat{DEM1} \text{ (based on initial equal media positions.)} \tag{48a}$$

This contingent schedule-based measure might control for the effects of unequal media access; thus it would seem a truer measure of premanipulation correspondences between popular wishes and representative actions, but again, only obtainable from development schedules, not point data. Party performance assessments in a similar hypothetical fashion should be equally of interest for believers in the validating appeal of democratically "fair" elections or of an underlying consensus or a general will. Thus, one could appraise how well the Brunner-Lipset system model would perform in other unreal, ideal type cases of special interest, e.g. those with high consensus and competition in the sense of Equation (44*b*).

As for stability measures, two possibilities seem especially appropriate in light of Lipset's concerns. One would simply be the expected rate with which demands or aspirations leave their "proper" arena and enter the controversy-enhancing support process:

$$PSAEI\begin{pmatrix}\text{party system}\\ \text{aggregation}\\ \text{efficiency index}\end{pmatrix} = \frac{\begin{matrix}\text{model predictions as to}\\ \text{no. of uses of support arena/quarter}\end{matrix}}{\text{no. of demands } (=ND \times NDS)\text{/quarter}}. \tag{49}$$

Besides being a scenario-specific measure, this index suffers, in its labelling at least, from a kind of anti-electoral bias. More profound, in a schedule sense, would be some repertorial measure of the stress-volume likely to be handled without appeals to the military arena, which in turn depends on perception of arena legitimacies. As in the above case, if subroutines are not run for every case, some probabilistic basis for evaluating possible scenario variations might need to be employed. Consider for example:

$$NMSCI\begin{pmatrix}\text{non-militaristic}\\ \text{stress-handling}\\ \text{capacity index}\end{pmatrix} = \frac{\sum\limits_{G}\sum\limits_{V}\widehat{M(G, V)}\widehat{SP(G, V)}}{\sum\limits_{G}\sum\limits_{V}\widehat{SP(G, V)}}. \tag{50}$$

Here $M(G,V)$ is a zero or one model-base index depending on whether or not stress by G for V is likely within, say, the next year to lead to party demands in the military arena. Clearly a *NMSCI* of 1.0 is the least militaristic development attribute.

These equations complete our illustrative review of development capability measures. As Brunner's analysis makes clear, many other value-relevant measurement possibilities exist; our varied but incomplete treatment of several of these has attempted to encourage recognition of such diversity, even within the framework of an opportunity-schedule approach. Calculating correlations across repertorial measures might help reveal which of the proposed measured or their alternatives are empirically distinct. Indices calculated from contingent schedules relating desirable properties to parameter changes should be further explored. Clearly those measures that highlight unrealized, but potentially realizable system states of a desirable or undesirable sort are the ones most likely to survive in the literature on policy possibilities and system potentialities.

Recapitulation

As is appropriate in a paper on measuring the capabilities of political systems, we have attempted a lot, but so far accomplished only a little.

Our initial motivating premise was that scholarly interests in politics often stem from value-based concern with system potentialities and/or policy possibilities. Since few such aspirations or fears are ever perfectly realized, atheoretical factual point measurements of system performance cannot answer many of the important questions we want to ask about system capabilities or limitations. Nor can we evaluate actual performances or proposed policies vis-à-vis value relevant ideals using simple, behavioral measures.

As students of power, integration, and development have lately come to discover, the measurement of important capacities or abilities, if it is ever to go beyond informed judgements, must rely on explicitly stated, realistic, verifiable, causal models of influence, integration, and development processes. A number of such models, mostly stated as computer simulations, now exist.[20] As a way of illustrating a quite general approach to capability (or incapability) measurement, we have taken some pains to illustrate diverse, often counterfactual measurement possibilities vis-à-vis three differently conceived formal models of development, integration, and the exercise of power. Unless at least one of these examples appeals to the reader, little is likely to come from reading the present paper: it is a statement of measurement possibilities, few of which have even been used in empirical or evaluative research.

Yet, at least a few points of general significance we may claim to have established, because of our efforts. First of all, we have demonstrated the compatibility of very different theoretical concerns, such as the extent of international dependence, the autonomy of regional integration systems, or the responsiveness of party systems, with an extended, nontautological power-analysis approach, which we prefer to call "capability analysis." Far from being nearly dead, weak, or

---

[20] A good review of the literature up until about 1967 is W. Coplin (1968). A more recent review is J. Laponce and P. Smoker. As Harsanyi's own work with analytical game-theory models makes clear, capability analysis does not *require* the relevant process model to be a nonanalytic simulation: it only requires determinative (or counterfactual, predictive) schedules relating the appropriate process elements, as for example, in Figure 1 and Table 2.

inadequate as some critics have implied,[21] power measurement has just begun to be realized. Because the capability to get things done *despite* other actors or *for* other actors is a potentiality, it must be described as a partly unobservable, counterfactual property of a complex system. Until one has reasonably sophisticated cost-specific process models of power accumulation, exercise, and depletion processes, it is hard to think how adequate conceptualizations of power in a Dahl-Harsanyi-Lasswell sense could be formulated. Now, the availability of a variety of process models makes this provisionally possible. Since many of the enduring questions of political analysis require measures of capabilities, we must conclude that schedule-sense measures of manifold possibilities will continue to be a relevant way of integrating normative and empirical concerns.

Secondly, we have demonstrated, and applied with reasonable but not perfect consistency, the role of at least three kinds of opportunity schedules – mere schedules, full schedules, and contingent schedules – in the study of political capabilities. Although discussion of the Harsanyi model emphasizes cost-conscious (full) rationality opportunity schedules, that of Simon-Homans focuses on contingent schedules, and our remarks about Brunner-Lipset were much more limited to mere schedules not based on maximization assumptions; each of these constructs could be applied more fully in the other cases as well. Capabilities described in a schedule sense allow us to delineate repertoires of multidimensional *possibilities* and *impossibilities* for actors and systems in a parsimonious, yet value-relevant way.

But in another sense, our emphasis on schedules, derived from reasonably complex models of rational or stress-motivated behavior,

[21] Recall the previously cited articles by Riker and March (1968). Of course, some of the reasons for the greater adequacy of the present approach may be our greater attentiveness to the problems and possibilities they have discussed. Thus, note that most of our opportunity schedules or repertorial measures solve (or fail to solve) the measurement and model problems "at the same time," as March would have it. March and Riker's hesitations about the generality or sufficiency of a power approach seem less justified with respect to a differentiated set of ego- or other-oriented capability concepts which can be applied to many different processes. Moreover, the process models we have used as examples incorporate many of the force-activation, depletion, and conditioning mechanisms that March suggests they might. An a priori Shapley-Shubik approach to capability measurement when actors' motivating stresses or optimal strategies are unknown would be to assume all orderings of demands as equally likely inputs to such process models and to calculate resulting success rates.

justifies an eclipse of power analysis, at least in its pretheoretical phases. We have found various kinds of capability analysis in terms of appropriate process models to be a more general approach than classic preoccupations with "getting *B* to do what he otherwise would not do." Here Riker's suggestion, implicit also in Harsanyi's and Simon's work, of treating power as potential cause within a model structure seems especially germane. The idea is again quite general and we have used it to study more or less structurally-contingent opportunities or potentialities within influence, integration, and development systems.

At a less general level of analysis, some important similarities and differences within these literatures have emerged. Some measures, e.g. the nonmilitaristic stress-handling index (50) or the systemic demand-processing success index (31*a*), are relevant to all three areas of concern. But when evaluations are explicitly included in measurement indices, one is sensitized to the need for choice from among distinct analytical vantage points, viz. observer, influencer, influencee, or some system level combination of the three. Capabilities exercised for, or against someone, in the presence of, or ignoring external actors, are distinct concepts in each of the literatures we have investigated. Equilibrium, contemporary, optimal, lawful, or other ideal-type norms all suggest useful bases for evaluating policies or systems. The realization that power, integration, and development, as well as their opposites, are multidimensional in their aspects, as well as their component variables and relationships, can be a liberating, as well as a humbling, lesson for the student of political analysis.

REFERENCES

Alker, H.R. (1971). "Le Comportement Directeur [Directive Behavior]." *Revue Française de Sociologie*.

Bell, R.; Edwards, D.; Wagner, R. (Eds.) (1969). *Political Power: A Reader in Theory and Research*. New York: Free Press.

Blalock, A., and Blalock, H. (Eds.) (1968). *Methodology in Social Research*. New York: Holt, Rinehart and Winston.

Brunner, R.D.(1971*a*). Processes in Political Development: Simulating Theories of Political Systems. Ph.D. Dissertation, Department of Political Science, Yale University, especially Chap. 3–5.

Brunner, R.D., and Brewer, G.D. (1971*b*). *Organized Complexity: Empirical Theories of Political Development*. New York: Free Press.

Coplin, W. (Ed.) (1968). *Simulation in the Study of Politics.* Chicago: Markham Press.

Dahl, R. (1967). "The Power Approach to the Study of Politics." In *International Encyclopedia of the Social Sciences.* Ed. by D. Sills. New York: Macmillan.

Hopkins, R.F. (1969). "Aggregate Data and the Study of Political Development." *The Journal of Politics* 31: 71–94.

Huntington, S.P. (1972). "The Change to Change." Forthcoming.

Kalman, R.E.; Falb, P.L.; Arbib, M.A. (Eds.) (1969). *Topics in Mathematical Systems Theory.* New York: McGraw-Hill.

Laponce, J. and Smoker, P. (Eds.) (1972). *Experimentation and Simulation in Political Science.* Toronto: University of Toronto Press.

Lindberg, L., and Scheingold, S. (Eds.) (1970). "Regional Integration: Theory and Research." A special issue of *International Organization* 24, No. 4. Also published separately by Harvard University Press, as a book.

March, J. (1968). "The Power of Power." In *Varieties of Political Theory.* Ed. by D. Easton, Englewood Cliffs, New Jersey: Prentice-Hall.

Samuelson, P.A. (1947). *Foundations of Economic Analysis.* Cambridge, Mass.: Harvard University Press.

Simon, H. (1957) *Models of Man.* New York: Wiley.

Sprout, H., and Sprout, M. (1965). *The Ecological Perspective on Human Affairs.* Princeton: Princeton University Press.

Theil, Henri (1970). "On the Estimation of Relationships Involving Qualitative Variables." *American Journal of Sociology* 76: 103–54.

[illegible]
Dahl, R. A. [illegible] "The Power Approach to the Study of Politics," in: International [illegible] of the Social Sciences [illegible]. New York: Macmillan.
[illegible]
Huntington, S. P. [illegible]
Kahn, H. [illegible] New York: [illegible]
[illegible] Toronto: University of Toronto [illegible]
Lindberg, [illegible] and Scheingold, [illegible]
[illegible]
[illegible]
[illegible]
[illegible]
[illegible]

Mathematical Modelling of Mobilization and Assimilation Processes

*RAYMOND F. HOPKINS**

The interplay of two *general processes*, social mobilization and assimilation, is the prime determinant of the growth and decay of various communal, ethnic, and nationality groups. Karl Deutsch has described how these two basic social processes shape communal conflict and the rise of nationalism (Deutsch, 1966). Communal tensions underlie a large portion of the conflict that exists in the modern world – violence in Nigeria, Malaysia, and Pakistan are recent examples of the conflict that is possible when two or more differentiated groups exist within a common political framework. Changes in the population characteristics of a particular territory with respect to these two processes, therefore, are of substantial theoretical and practical interest to students of political conflict and national development (*see* Horowitz, 1969).

* I want to thank Professor Karl Deutsch who both inspired this research and supported it during the summer of 1969 from his research funds. I am indebted for research assistance in collating data for this project to Sheldon Kravitz and Yung Kim at Harvard and to Arlene Zarembka at Swarthmore. The results of their work are reflected in a fairly complete data handbook. I also want to acknowledge my gratitude to Ronald D. Brunner who both suggested ideas during the project and made many helpful comments on an earlier draft and to George J. Stolnitz and the International Development Research Center of Indiana University who provided guidance and support in revising this essay. Most especially I am indebted to my wife, Carol, who assisted in every stage of this study.

This essay discusses some approaches to quantitative analysis of mobilization and assimilation processes. Its basic purposes are to explore the conceptual problems arising in quantitative analysis of mobilization and assimilation processes, to search for more satisfactory ways to simplify techniques for projecting future population configurations, and to suggest a possible approach to organizing both theory and data through a simulation model. In particular, it reports on a simple model to represent these processes and the problems that such model building encountered. The conceptual tasks needed both to represent the processes in a model and to use the model for statistical projections were found to be divergent in the first two parts of this paper. As a result, two directions were pursued. In part three a more complex model for simulating mobilization and assimilation is described, and its attendant assumptions, strengths, and weaknesses are discussed. Then, using time-series data specifically collated for this project, the fourth part describes three cases that illustrate the potential application of some of the theoretical propositions about what shapes mobilization and assimilation. These studies also utilize extrapolation of population trends, using simple least-squares equations, and speculate on the possible political consequences of the projected outcomes.

The succeeding work, by Paul Werbos in collaboration with Karl Deutsch to extend the quantitative study of mobilization and assimilation discussed in this essay, deals with the problems of predicting population trends with respect to mobilization and assimilation. Werbos, using the data I initially collated, describes various techniques for projection which he undertook and reports results that appear to successfully (with low error) project population change, at least over limited time periods. Werbos, in his essay, also offers a number of methodological suggestions that relate to the problems he encountered in his work. While his purposes were essentially different from those in this essay, a number of his methodological comments complement my point that greater sophistication is needed in quantitative analysis by political scientists, both in relating theory to quantitative techniques, and, as Werbos suggests, in selecting and using quantitative tools.

Introduction: The Theoretical Perspective

Social mobilization refers to the changes that occur as people move into more urban, industrialized, and literate modes of life.[1] This process generates new tastes and demands and increases individual resources and group consciousness. Social mobilization is a universal feature of twentieth century society, as exposure to mass media, literacy campaigns, and the spread of technology have altered work and life styles, induced migration, and facilitated the acquisition of expanded capabilities. Social mobilization does not always guarantee modernization. Role orientations may remain ascriptive and diffuse, and modern institutions may fail to develop even though sizable mobilization occurs. Geertz (1963), Huntington (1968), and others have described how the rise of literacy, increased economic interdependence, and other elements of the mobilization syndrome have promoted political instability, weakened institutions, and generated linguistic, religious or cultural conflicts. As people shift from fairly constricted and parochial life-styles, their aspirations, interdependence, and degree of interaction may increase faster than their economic satisfaction, toleration for "modern" institutions, and acceptance of "strangers."

> Social mobilization thus means potential politicization, and quite likely it means politicization along the lines of language and ethnic culture, that is, nationalism intermingled with and reinforced by elements of rising expectations and frustrations and of social discontent (Deutsch, 1967, p. 211).

While the mobilization process may shift people with different cultures and languages into a more integrated social framework, in which they may work in the same industry and depend upon the same market system, it is the process of assimilation that will determine whether they play similar or merely complementary roles in the economy and enjoy identical or separate housing, education, and social services.

Assimilation is the process by which individuals come to share

[1] At the aggregate level, such mobilization is marked by a rise in literacy, increased exposure to mass media and modernity, urbanization, and a movement out of agricultural employment (*see* Deutsch, 1961).

common identities, usually reinforced by common languages, values, and codes of conduct. People may be said to be assimilated when both they and others share inclusive identities with respect to major group activities. The movement of individuals from a differentiated to an assimilated portion of a population is difficult to measure, even crudely. Investigators have used different criteria to designate assimilated or differentiated groups depending upon the population being studied and the purposes of the investigation. However, distinctions are salient for determining how differentiated one group is from another to the degree that important behavioral consequences are associated with them. In many cases distinctions seem clear, for example, most Chinese are culturally, linguistically, and religiously differentiated from Malays in Malaysia. These differences are associated with a variety of consequences in the behavior of each group and in the indulgences they enjoy. For the purpose of this essay, assimilation is considered as a very general phenomenom – a process of change that increases the homogeneity of two or more groups. While we can and will refer to particular forms of assimilation, indexed by language (or ethnicity), this is for the sake of concreteness; the particular application of the techniques and analyses subsequently discussed should be applicable to a variety of contexts.

The interplay of the two processes of social mobilization and assimilation provides a critical balance in situations of change. Greenberg is optimistic that mobilization, which normally occurs first, will spur assimilation, at least linguistic assimilation. He expects that

> the increase of communication that goes with greater economic productivity and more extensive political organization will lead typically to the spread of a *lingua franca*, whether indigenous or imported, resulting in widespread bilingualism and the ultimate disappearance of all except a single dominant language (cited in Pool, 1969, p. 15).

However, assimilation into a new language or culture usually involves the slow learning of many new habits and the unlearning of old ones; "its changes are counted in decades and generations" (Deutsch, 1966, p. 125).

Mobilization, on the other hand, tends to be more rapid and may force people into new and inescapable contacts with each other as workers, customers, and neigbors – contacts far narrower, perhaps, than the range of human relations than can be communicated in the absence of a common culture to outsiders. Linguistically and culturally, then, members of each group are outsiders for the other . . . and more conspicuous differentiation and conflict may result (Deutsch, 1966, pp. 125–6).

If a mobilized but differentiated group has distinctive cultural traits that it prizes and feels are threatened by another, "foreign" group, its members are more likely to become supporters of and recruits to separatist or nationalist political movements. In short, when mobilization exceeds assimilation, communal conflict is likely, especially in societies that are less developed.[2]

If the assimilation process does fall behind mobilization, as Deutsch typically expects, linguistic, cultural, or religious identities may be excited. Such "primordial sentiments" (as Geertz refers to these resurgent communal identities) may produce a politics of governmental immobilism. The alternatives "would seem to be either Balkanization, *Herrenvolk* fanaticism, or the forcible suppression of ethnic assertion by a leviathan state . . ." (Geertz, 1963, p. 187).

Assimilation between politically relevant groups, therefore, can be vital in shaping the capacity of a political system to cope with the burdens of government. Yet, despite its recognized importance and a fairly rich body of theory, there has been relatively little systematic comparative study of the qualitative and quantitative impact of assimilation on political behavior. (*See* Deutsch, 1961, 1966; Fishman, 1968; and Rustow, 1967.) Despite a plethora of case studies discussing assimilation, and general agreement on both the centrality and complexity of language in shaping and reflecting assimilation (*see* Fishman, 1968, and Grimshaw, 1969), few systematic comparative and diachronic investigations of language have been completed (Fishman, 1966, pp. 420–58). Other elements in assimilation have received even less attention. Yet such studies would be both possible and worth while if appropriate simplifying assumptions are made.

[2] *See* Fishman (1968, pp. 53–68) and Inglehart and Woodward (1967, pp. 40–45). Relying on cross-national data, they found a high correlation between linguistic pluralism and instability among "transitional" states.

Although rates of assimilation and mobilization vary in different countries and regions, and in different historical time periods, it seems reasonable to assume that the factors underlying shifts or maintenance of linguistic or other identities are largely the same. What we wish to investigate, therefore, is a general model of mobilization and assimilation, which would depict trends and shifts that have already occurred, be applicable to a wide variety of situations, and yield projections about future population configurations. This may be the first step towards simulating political outcomes which thus far no one has been able to do, at least directly.

From Qualitative to Quantitative Modelling: A First Approximation

In *Nationalism and Social Communication*, Karl Deutsch has described mobilization and assimilation processes theoretically, and, in an appendix, provided a "crude mathematical model" to express these changing population characteristics over time. The model consists of a series of differential equations in which sizes of the subpopulations of a country are the variables, and rates of change and natural increase, assumed to be relatively constant, are parameters. The model assumes exponential growth. It represents changes in the size of an assimilated (A) or mobilized (M) populations as composed of growth (excess of births over deaths) plus a *shift* from "differentiated" (D) or "underlying non-mobilized" (U) population, respectively. Although Deutsch described verbally four interrelated populations in his book, his differential equation model treats assimilation and mobilization as two distinct processes (only related by the fact that $A + D$ and $D + U$ both must equal total population).[3]

The formulas he proposed for these processes were

$$\frac{dA}{dt} = (a + c)A, \frac{dD}{dt} = (d)D - cA, \frac{dM}{dt} = (b + m)M \text{ and } U(t) = A(t) + D(t) - M(t)$$

where a, b and d represent rates of per capita natural increase of A, M, and D, and c and m represent rates of per capita net entry of outsiders into A and M as of the initial period examined.

[3] *See* Karl W. Deutsch (1966, Chap. 6 and Appendix V, pp. 123–52 and 235–39).

With time-series data for two or more points and *independent estimates of rates of natural increase*, it is possible to use this model to project the size of the mobilized or assimilated population and to estimate the rates of change.

The model as outlined by Deutsch (with the assistance of Robert Solow) best serves as a starting point for the empirical investigations. His equations, when incorporated in a computer program using historical time-series data to project future or prior population trends for a country,[4] pose problems, since their solutions indicate "explosive" population growth and require that at least one of the parameters for growth and shift rates be exogenously estimated (most reasonably, the natural increase in one of the populations). For example, in solving for growth formula for the assimilated population $\frac{dA}{dt} = (a + a)A$, the natural growth in the assimilated populations (a), and the change due to shifts from other groups (c) should be calculated separately. Since this cannot be done from census data, it is difficult or impossible to determine accurately whether change in the portion of a population which is assimilated (or mobilized) is due to different net rates of growth or to shifts of population from one group to another. Another limitation is that the model assumes that increases in the mobilized or assimilated population due to shifts can be expressed as a function of the size of the "receiving" (mobilized or assimilated) population. Consequently, the absolute shift from, say, the underlying to the mobilized population may continuously increase even when the underlying population becomes quite small.[5] As a result of these limitations, an altered formulation has been developed as a base for quantification. In this model, drawing upon Deutsch's verbal analysis, the population of a country is specified to be composed of the four mutually exclusive subgroups shown in Figure 1.

Most countries have populations with more complex differences among their major groups than a simple dichotomous one – for instance, India. However, this particular assumption seemed reasonable for simplifying nationality and assimilation problems in many

---

[4] *See* Carol R. and Raymond F. Hopkins, "Projections of Population Change by Mobilization and Assimilation," forthcoming in *Behavioral Science* in the computer program abstract section.

[5] This problem was noted by Deutsch (1966, Appendix V, Point 4).

states, hopefully without great distortion. The assimilated *versus* differentiated populations might refer, for example, to whites and blacks in the United States, the Flemish and Walloons in Belgium, or Greeks and Turks in Cyprus. The mobilized population might be based on various indices such as functional literacy or urbanization. Since in each case specific criteria would have to be reviewed, for our purposes crude indices suffice to illustrate the ways that modelling might proceed. A link between the assimilation and mobilization processes is established by a set of difference equations and it is possible to solve for all the parameters using census data for four time periods. [6] The solutions, it was hypothesized initially, could be used to project future population characteristics, as well as discover "rates" of shift in populations, at least as a first approximation. At the same time, the projections could be expected to yield rough estimates of the future only, since they depend on two major unrealistic assumptions: (1) the model truly represents the actual processes of change in particular, and (2) it specifies *constant* proportional natural growth and shifts in the population. Consequently,

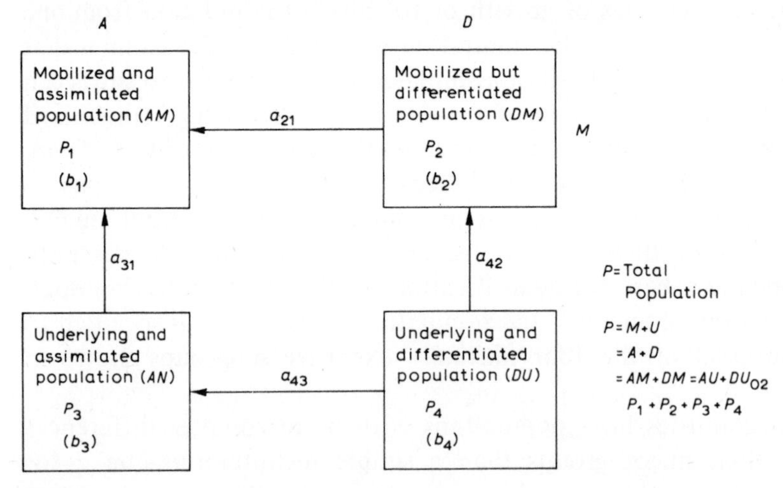

Fig. 1.*

*Deutsch labeled these four subpopulations differently; the populations above labeled P_1, P_2, P_3 and P_4 he refers to as *N*, *H*, *Q* and *R*, and b_1, b_2, b_3 and b_4, the rates of natural increase, as *n*, *h*, *g* and *r* (Deutsch, 1966, p. 126).

[6] The use of difference equations changed slightly the assumptions about the process from continuous exponential growth to discontinuous geometric growth. In practice, the results should be quite similar (*see* Goldberg, 1961).

parameters estimated from the period for which census data are available yield fixed rates of change into future or historical periods.

Each of the arrowed paths in Figure 1 indicates an assumed shift in the direction of mobilization and assimilation. The "a_{ij}" are positive coefficients and refer to the proportion of the people who leave subpopulation P_i and move to P_j. It is assumed that these rates change rather slowly over time and can, therefore, be considered constant, and that the psychological and social *distance* traveled in shifting from one subpopulation to another, either in becoming mobilized or in assimilating, was also constant, and, therefore, absorbed by the parameter estimates. The "b_i" coefficients refer to the natural growth rate of subpopulation i. Thus, the total amount of change involved in becoming mobilized or assimilated is, by assumption, roughly the same at all points in time.

The model represented in Figure 1 may be expressed by Equations (1) through (4) below.[7]

$$P_1(t+1) - P_1(t) = b_1 P_1(t) + a_{21} P_2(t) + a_{31} P_3(t) \tag{1}$$

This equation states that the mobilized and assimilated population (P_1) will increase from time t to t+1 by natural growth ($b_1 P_1(t)$), plus the assimilation of the proportion a_{21} of the mobilized but differentiated population, P_2, and the mobilization of the proportion a_{31} of the assimilated but underlying population, P_3.
Similarly:

$$P_2(t+1) - P_2(t) = b_2 P_2(t) + a_{42} P_4(t) - a_{21} P_2(t) \tag{2}$$

$$P_3(t+1) - P_3(t) = b_3 P_3(t) + a_{43} P_4(t) - a_{31} P_3(t) \tag{3}$$

$$P_4(t+1) - P_4(t) = b_4 P_4(t) - a_{42} P_4(t) - a_{43} P_4(t) \tag{4}$$

With four points in time, at equal intervals, it is possible to solve for the parameters (coefficients) of the difference equation model. In this approach, by choosing a subset, either early or late, of census figures for those equations which are overidentified, an exactly identified or unique solution is possible.[8] Where historical data for

---

[7] These equations are shown without constant or stochastic terms. These terms were later introduced in computer runs using least-square solutions; they did not substantially affect the results.

[8] *See* Hopkins and Hopkins (1969) for the formal solution of these equations.

more than four censuses are available, a least-squares solution can also be used to estimate the parameters.

Time-series population statistics were gathered to use with this model. Two indices of mobilization, urbanization, and literacy were chosen, as were two indices of assimilation, language, and ethnicity. These indices were selected because they can be considered relatively good proxy aggregate indicators of the complex social phenomena under study, while also likely to be available for a variety of countries over a span of at least several decades. From an initial list of forty-three countries selected as tentatively worth investigating, data for twenty-one political units were gathered.[9] Census estimates, for four subpopulations whenever possible, were chosen on the basis of these indicators, i.e. urban-Malays are P_1, urban-non-Malays are P_2, and so forth.

Data from Finland, Canada, and Malaysia were used to test the usefulness of the model for deriving rates of assimilation and population increase and for making projections. Both exact and least-squares estimates were calculated for the parameters of the difference equations. Under both approaches, coefficients for natural increase and for population shifts were derived that on their face seemed unreasonable. Negative growth rates – contrary to the assumptions of the model – and explosive growth rates (as high as 10 percent per annum), coupled with equally unreasonable estimates of population shifts, resulted. Data from Finland, which has extensive census records for the Finnish and Swedish populations, were used to derive both exactly identified (as in Figure 1) and least-squares estimates for the parameters of the difference equations. Not only were "wild" parameters calculated, but these procedures produced ludicrous population figures when projected very far beyond the time periods from which they were derived.[10] These results, shown

[9] In drawing up the initial list, countries were used with "nationism" problems owing either to low mobilization or multiple languages that make difficult a single nationality or language community (*see* Fishman, 1968, pp. 30–47). Rustow's (1967, pp. 384–6) survey of linguistic homogeneity was helpful in making selections. There are several reasons why some countries were excluded from the data collection. The most frequent was the paucity of national statistics. Data from at least three censuses have been collected for: Argentina, Belgium, Brazil, Canada-Quebec, Ceylon, Cyprus, Czechoslovakia, Finland, India, Israel, Japan, Malaysia, Peru, Philippines, Scotland, Taiwan, Thailand, USA, USSR, and Yugoslavia. *See* "Interim Report on Mobilization/Assimilation Project," unpublished report, Swarthmore, Pa. and Cambridge, Mass., March, 1970.

[10] Footnote see page 385.

TABLE 1

PARAMETER ESTIMATES FOR FOUR-EQUATION MODEL
(FINNISH DATA, TEN-YEAR INTERVALS 1820–1950)

Exactly Identified Estimates (EIE) (based on 1820–1850 data)		*Least-Squares Estimates (LSE) (based on 1880–1950 data)*
	Natural Growth Parameters	
1.96	b_1	.93
3.79	b_2	–0.02
–1.67	b_3	–0.05
10.34	b_4	–0.03
	Population Shift Parameters	
3.62	a_{21}	–10.20
–0.18	a_{31}	0.42
–0.02	a_{42}	0.06
10.26	a_{43}	1.02

	Urban		*Rural*		
	Finns	*Swedes*	*Finns*	*Swedes*	*Total*
Populations projected in 1960. . .	P_1	P_2	P_3	P_4	P
Using EIE from 1820	1,626,178,000	34,000	3,685,000	569,000	1,630,467,000
Using LSE from 1880	–5,987,700	540,486	9,045,710	667,103	4,265,592
Census Data*	1,553,151	148,873	2,557,557	181,665	4,446,222

*From the *Statistical Yearbook of Finland*, 1968.

[10] Ronald D. Brunner, using similar techniques in an unpublished paper, derived interpretable coefficients from a three equation model representing language assimilation in Quebec. Although his results yielded plausible projections, this may be due in part to the simpler model and a closer approximation of the assumption of constant change in the real world (*see* Brunner, 1966). I am grateful to him for showing me his paper.

in Table 1, were among the "worst" found as the long projection time exaggerates discrepancies between real and simulated data. Nevertheless, the results make the point; the model, assuming constant shift rates and interrelated processes, does not provide credible results. In the case of natural population increase (birth rates minus death rates) least-squares led to little improvement.[11]

This suggests that the difference equation model (Figure 1) is inadequate for both projections and for representation of the phenomena involved. Its results challenge the validity of the two assumptions listed above. Apparently fairly simple formulas are needed for calculating projections alone (as developed by Hopkins and Hopkins, 1971, and Werbos, 1971) which might be even simpler than the four-equation model initially proposed. For other purposes, we need more sophisticated models in order to represent real world complexities. As a simulation model, the above four-equation first approximation would appear to be of essentially heuristic utility pointing to difficult problems that mathematical modelling must take into account, such as feedback effects, and the effects of variable value structures in the different subpopulations.

In conclusion, I would suggest that more complex mathematical models for studying the actual processes of mobilization and assimilation are indicated. One can make some simplifying assumptions about "fixed" rates of change (which, whether constant or varying, would not be altered by threshold changes or feedback) and use these as calculating routines just for projections. Proceeding from this conclusion, Paul Werbos was able to derive population estimates fairly close to the actual data using least-squares techniques and equations that treated each process as independent with *separate* equations for each process. His projections for the year 2000 do not yield parameter estimates for *growth and shift rates*; they do provide useful base projections of trends, if not for actual modelling of the processes.[12] This is equivalent to using Deutsch's "crude" model

---

[11] These judgements are based on over twenty-five trials with different versions of the model using the "TROLL" system for modelling and simulation developed at M.I.T. I am grateful to Edwin Kuh for his helpfulness and to Jonathan Shane for his assistance in programming.

[12] Werbos (1971) was interested in equations that would yield the best "fit," while my principal concern is to model the processes, using theoretical propositions suggested by Deutsch and others.

without trying to calculate rates of shift. Projections that I made in this fashion are discussed in conjunction with the four case studies presented in the fourth section. But parameters calculated from census data do not necessarily represent *valid* estimates of growth and shift rates and frequently yield poor projections. Simple models to estimate "real" parameters, therefore, seem unwarranted.[13] If the assumptions of the model are unrealistic, the parameters are likely to be untrustworthy. To understand the complexity that underlies the "true" processes, more complex models that go beyond accounting and estimating techniques will be required.

A More Complex Model

Theorists who have discussed mobilization and assimilation have proposed a number of factors that could be added to a model of these processes. In this section, some further factors will be incorporated into a verbal "model" that might represent a first step towards developing a computer simulation. By positing a simulation model as a goal, criteria for evaluating theoretical propositions sharpen the formulation of the verbal model. While this model is still quite simplified, it is too complex to be tested in its entirety by any conventional statistical procedure.

We begin by adding four additional shift parameters and three measures of the socio-political structure to the earlier model (*see* Figure 2). All the shift rates, in fact, become variables affected by changes in other variables according to relationships specified in a new, larger set of parameters (which are largely undetailed here). The new rates represent demobilization and dis-assimilation. Movement in these directions does, in fact, occur. In Malaysia, for instance, age-specific literacy figures from the 1930 and 1947 censuses suggest that as the population aged from their twenties to their forties, literacy (reported as the ability to read) declined. Similarly, with respect to linguistic assimilation, reversals occur. In Montreal, Lieberson suggests that French-speaking residents frequently learn English in school or in connection with employment but lose this

[13] Werbos, by assuming no interdependence, thus reducing the number of parameters to be calculated and introducing error terms, was able to produce more *reliable* parameters and fits for most data series, those where changes were fairly regular.

ability later in life, since few homes are bilingual (Lieberson, 1965, pp. 10–12). In the United States, among blacks who became assimilated into middle class values and status ("black Anglo-Saxons"), efforts to increase their feelings of differentiation and militancy met with some success (Hare, 1965).

The three structural variables to be added are the *inequality* of the communal populations, the *interaction* among them, and the *distance* between them. Inequality would exist when mobilization brought more rewards for one group than another. If the per capita income of P_1 were greater than that of P_2, for instance, even though both were "mobilized" equally, then assimilation would be affected. Amount of interaction, or contact among different groups occasioned by work, transportation, and other life patterns, is difficult to simulate directly but can be represented as a product of mobilization. Generally, the greater the mobilization and the less the physical separation of different groups, the more interactions among them will occur. "Distance" represents the amount of change that would be required in the values, habits, language and other features of one group in order for it to be assimilated into another group. Distance impedes assimilation; initially determined according to the circumstances, it should be represented as varying over time by endogenously generated effects. The distance for the differentiated group to travel to assimilate, shown as d below, need not be the same for the reversed process (a_{12}), or any mixture of the two leading to mutual assimilation.

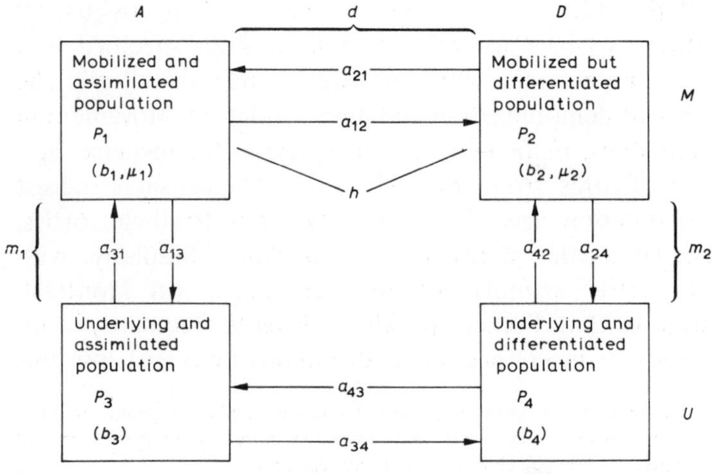

Fig. 2.

Before describing the assumptions within this proposed model, three major caveats need to be mentioned. First, "assimilation" has purposely been defined vaguely. For some situations, language acquisition might be an adequate indicator. As Deutsch has argued, this is a critical factor in complementary communication patterns and is associated with shared learning, such that two groups acquiring a common language are more prone to respond similarly to identical stimuli. However, a variety of other tests of assimilation, including some rather stringent definitions, such as no association between housing, income and other values, and ethnicity, have been proposed.[14] Ideally, any model should be serviceable in encompassing different criteria for assimilation. As I noted earlier, assimilation is surely multi-dimensional and occurs in degrees rather than in either or fashion; for simplifying purposes, however, individuals may be dichotomized into simple assimilated/unassimilated categories. The boxes in Figure 2, then, assume two fairly compact or uniformly similar groups, with a fixed distance between them, although this may be a gross simplification in some instances.[15] Some students of assimilation in fact prefer terms such as integration or absorption in order not to assume complete homogenization as a goal. A UNESCO report on immigration discussing the process of assimilation suggests that

> perhaps it might be said that the process, however denominated, involves a moving equilibrium of conformity, varying with time and social conditions. In every society there is a point up to which conformity with the given cultural configuration is demanded, and beyond which – unless it is fixed at the extreme of total conformity to a rigidly homogeneous culture (imagined or real) – it is not required. (Borrie, 1959, p. 98)

---

[14] Lieberson, for instance, in studying ethnic assimilation in the United States, concludes that assimilation occurs when knowledge of a group's prior ethnic (linguistic, cultural) origin "in no way gives a better prediction or estimate of their relevant social characteristics than does knowledge of the behavior of the total population of the community or nation involved" (Lieberson, 1963, p. 10). In this case, inequality or segregation reflects a lack of assimilation, while in the model schematized in Figure 4 below, they affect it. In general, we expect that a similar environment will shape similar response predispositions. Thus, differences in responses in a similar context could also be used as an indicator of lack of assimilation.

[15] A series of concentric circles around a core group representing various layers of assimilation might be a more realistic way to schematize separate groups of people.

In the proposed model, we retain the loose notion of assimilation as movement from one group to another, even though this view may be inaccurate in some contexts. Essentially, three structural types of assimilation, as outlined in Figure 3, might occur: conformity, synthesis, and pluralism. Although one type almost always predominates in a given situation, all three are usually present.[16]

Type		Example
Conformity (acculturation)	$P_1 \longleftarrow P_2$	Soviet Union*
Synthesis (emergent monoculture)	$P_1 \longrightarrow P_3 \longleftarrow P_2$	Tanzania
Pluralism (bilingualism/biculturalism)	$P_1 \longrightarrow P_{3(1,2)} \longleftarrow P_2$	Canada

Fig. 3. *See Vardys (1969, pp. 14–16) on the efforts to acculturate to Russian other nationalities.

With minor alterations, the model could be adjusted to accommodate other assimilation patterns such as emergent language groups (Swahili in Tanzania) or bilingual groups (as in Canada), while changes in the distance variable could indicate growing synthesis.[17] The notion of shift or acculturation (as employed by Deutsch and others) should be sufficient to use in verbally outlining our proposed more complex model.

A second qualification about the model is that the political system is not represented. A rise in demands and/or conflict frequently accompanies mobilization of differentiated populations. Government policy regarding segregation in housing and schools, discrimination in employment, and the use of "official" languages in legal affairs and educational institutions could have important consequences. For some purposes, adding government policy options would be desirable. However, this seems likely to be a confusing rather than a clarifying complication at this stage of theorizing. It should be possible, moreover, to study some political variables more simply by comparing outputs of the model, such as changes in the mobilized

[16] *See* Gordon (1964, pp. 84–159), who argues that in the United States, these types occur, but that pluralism predominates. In comparison with other states, this judgement would probably be modified.

[17] For example, in Canada, one could model assimilation into and out of the bilingual community from the communities speaking English or French only. Since the linguistic patterns in some states are varied and include indigenous and foreign languages and a range of formal and informal policies toward each group, to model the Philippines, Ethiopia or India, for instance, could require more extensive adjustments (*See* Fishman, 1968).

differentiated populations of a country, with indices of conflict or variations in government policy over time.

Finally, migration and the behavior of children have not been accounted for. In many cases, permanent migration is not large enough to be a problem, but for some states, where immigration has been large, such as Canada or Israel, it could be important.[18] And children are a problem with respect to literacy and language until they are old enough to have had some education.[19] Because of these and other factors, models as in Figure 2, while incorporating more complex factors than simple projection equations, are still basically accounting schemes and data organizing devices with limited theoretical content.

In order to incorporate multivariate theories into a model, we may have to consider questions of causes of change in birth rates, death rates, mobilization rates, and assimilation rates. For example, we may want to consider the effects of inequality, where a dominant population enjoys favorable incomes and employment status as well as other values such as greater political power. Relative deprivations, more readily perceived by the mobilized portion of the unassimilated population, can generate conflicting pressures both for change in order to enjoy greater privileges, and against change to "close ranks" within the differentiated group. A privileged assimilated population may grow faster in some historical periods because of its declining death rates (due to better health care), but slower in later periods when "mobilized" life styles depress its birth rate.

The reason population forecasts are often disappointing to policy scientists is that demographers seldom consider causes of change (particularly nondemographic causes in birth and death rates). The more complex mathematical systems of demographers have primarily moved in the direction of using more elaborate age/cohort breakdowns, age-specific fertility patterns, and assumptions about stable population characteristics. These essentially more elaborate formal schemes cannot provide reliable forecasts when the processes in-

---

[18] Twice as many Italians in Quebec, for instance, have assimilated to French as have assimilated to English (*Report of the Royal Commission*, 1967, p. 32). In Israel, immigrants constituted nearly half the Jewish population during the 1950's.

[19] The offspring of mixed marriages until they have acquired their own characteristics are also a problem in determining assimilation.

volved are likely to be affected by causes exogenous to their model.[20]

Figure 4 outlines proposed relationships between the components of the mobilization/assimilation processes presented in Figure 2. In it we propose to let rates of population shift into or out of mobilized and assimilated populations vary, affected by changes in other variables according to a set of parameters crudely indicated by plus (+) and minus (–) estimates in the diagram. The flow of consequences from one variable to another in this schematized model are based on at least nine major sets of assumptions.

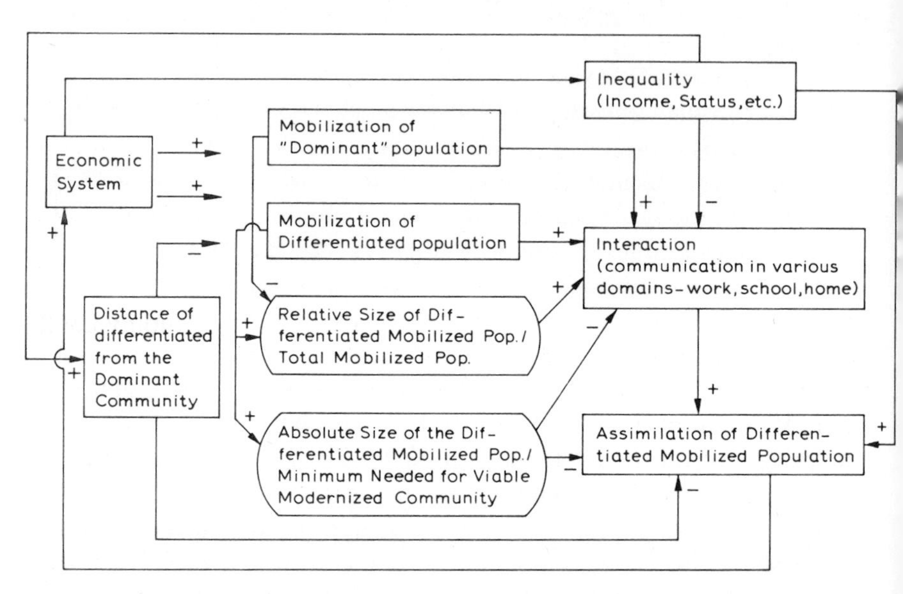

Fig. 4. – Schematic representation of a model for Mobilization/Assimilation Processes (Read + as increase, – as decrease)

1. The economic system is essentially independent of these processes and acts to stimulate change exogenously, except for some feedback effects of assimilation (which should improve the economy by reducing costly artificial barriers to employment). It determines both mobilization rates and rates of natural increase. The incentives and opportunities which the economy offers for a rural population

[20] *See* Keyfitz (1968). I am indebted to Ronald Brunner who brought this point to my attention.

to migrate to cities or otherwise undergo mobilization are the principal determinants of the mobilization rates. Natural increase rates are also affected by the level of economic development, as the decrease in death rates and then birth rates in Europe, and more recently elsewhere, has suggested. Religion, birth control devices, and education also have some impact, but often not substantial. For example, birth rates among the predominantly Catholic French Canadians, now that most are mobilized, are substantially the same as English Canadians, although their growth rates were higher in earlier periods (*Report of the Royal Commission*, 1967, p. 22). While b_1, b_2, b_3 and b_4 would be set by a state's vital statistics (where available), they would be altered by the effects of economic development, perhaps represented by GNP per capita of each subpopulation. The mobilization rates, a_{31}, a_{13}, a_{24} and a_{42}, at least for indicators such as urbanization, would be established by the relative income and future prospects of urban and rural sectors. These rates could be checked against historical indicators and the formula for their calculation adjusted appropriately.

The effects of the economic system would need to be disaggregated for different linguistic or cultural groups. The economy could be modelled using equations similar to those used by Brunner and Brewer for their model of development, which disaggregated for rural-urban sectors (*see* Brunner and Brewer, 1971).

2. It is assumed that rates of natural increase are affected solely by the various social subsystems, especially the economy, and not by assimilation rates or by the relative size of the communities. More generally the full range of indulgences and deprivations in relevant values would affect these, and might be measured both by social accounting data as well as by content analysis, for instance, for information on status deprivation.

3. Little assimilation is assumed to occur among the underlying (traditional, rural) population. In the notation of Figure 2, $a_{43}=a_{34}=0$, and in Figure 4 no account of this conceivable shift is made.[21]

---

[21] Fishman (1966, p. 443), states: "Whereas small rural groups may have been more successful in establishing relative selfcontained communities which reveal language maintenance through the preservation of traditional interaction patterns and social structures, urban groups, exposed to interaction in more fragmented and specialized networks, reveal more conscious, organized and novel attempts to preserve, revive or change their traditional language."

4. Mobilization of the "dominant" population would proceed faster than for the differentiated group. The dominance would be determined by initial size of the population's mobilized sector and by its control of values relative to its size. The greater the "distance" of the differentiated from the dominant population, the more its rate of mobilization would be slowed. This assumption would be reflected in varying intensities of demand of mobilized attributes. If the two populations were equal in status and skills, the distance between the two would be slight. Reference to a dominant linguistic or cultural group might be unfair where groups were relatively equal, but in most cases, this characterization seems reasonable.[22]

5. Changes in the relative and absolute size of the mobilized but differentiated population have diverse consequences. Increases in its *relative size* (in Figure 2 this would be $P_2/(P_1+P_2)$) generally raise interactions with the dominant population as the probability of random cross-group interactions between P_2 and P_1 (the dominant population) rises. When $P_2 > P_1$, the proportion of intergroup contacts is likely to decline, but the absolute number would increase as long as the size of P_1 did not shrink.

Increases in the *absolute size* of P_2 would make it more capable of self-maintenance and decrease felt pressures to assimilate. As Deutsch remarks in suggesting alterations for his model, "Refinements would have to include changes in the rate of assimilation a as a function of changes in the mobilization rate, and particularly as functions of the rise of the mobilized but unassimilated group H [P_2 in our notation]. Generally, if H is large, and its rate of growth h is also large, a may tend to decline, at least for considerable periods" (Deutsch, 1966, p. 239). The minimum population needed for a viable mobilized community would vary somewhat according to a country's size and population distribution.

6. *Inequality* in the values shared by the dominant and differentiated populations would be calculated by differences generated in the economy. Inequality exists when, in the life space of people in a differentiated community, the ratio of their "inputs" (such as ex-

---

[22] Fishman objects to aggregate labeling of dominance. He disagrees with Weinrich who, though against using the notion of a "dominance configuration" at "any cost," accepted as expedient (as we do) restricting "the term dominant to languages in contact situations where the difference in mother tongues is coupled with a significant difference in social status" (*see* Fishman, 1966, p. 435).

perience, training, and physical effort) to their "outcomes" (income, position, status) is greater than the comparative ratio for the dominant population. Obviously, respect and other intangible values included in inequality might result from religious or cultural practices independent of economic rewards, but occupation and income are probably the best indicators of inequality. In some countries, Malaysia for instance, economic factors might need to be supplemented by additional considerations, since the Chinese are economically dominant while the Malays are politically dominant.

Inequity tends to increase feelings of discontent and hostility in contact situations; hence in the envisaged model, greater inequality increases the distance between the two linguistic or cultural groups (Adams, 1963, and Heider, 1958). It is also assumed that inequality decreases trans-group interactions, since members of P_1 and P_2 are less likely to share interlocking roles except in superior–inferior relationships (which often restrict social intercourse), and increases assimilation, by offering enhanced rewards to those who enter the dominant population. Assimilation is stimulated by a motivation for equality, primarily reflected in the balance of material rewards, though associated psychic rewards may also be important. The material rewards for assimilation, according to Deutsch, include "employment, promotion, higher income, freedom of choice, security, and prestige. Such rewards would tend to speed up assimilation, whereas penalties would have the opposite effect. Penalties for assimilation may be loss of previous employment or loss of social status," especially when the old culture provided fairly high income or status (Deutsch, 1966, p. 158). Although inequity acts to increase incentives to integrate, it also has a negative effect on assimilation indirectly through its effect on distance.

7. *Distance* is a summary variable representing the barriers between two cultures in terms of degrees of similarity, difficulty of learning the other's speech and life patterns, and the consensus on values and symbols. Changes in distance can change the "learning" rate of a group, which in turn determines its capacity to assimilate. In general, similarity of alphabets, codes of ethics, or personal experiences would decrease distance. Distance is increased by greater inequality. Its major effect in the model is to slow assimilation. It is perhaps the strongest factor affecting assimilation and, because it is relatively constant, is the prime reason why assimilation is a slow or

nonexistent process, even when economic incentives and interactions would promote it.[23]

8. *Interaction* refers to those situations in which individuals of the differentiated community communicate, either among themselves or with others, within various domains of action as diverse as a business conference or "over the back fence." Fishman points out that interactions can be of varying significance depending on the role relationships of those interacting (Fishman, 1966, pp. 431–4). For instance, Kenya settlers who learned "kitchen Swahili" were hardly assimilating toward an African language or culture. However, the effects of inequality on the interaction variable in our model might control for this obvious consideration without requiring disaggregation of interactions by "domain."

Mobilization, we assume, increases interaction – indeed, this is one of the principal theories in the literature. Urbanization as an element in mobilization certainly increases the potential for interaction. Philip Hauser describes the consequences of urban density thus:

> In aboriginal America, a person moving within the ten-mile circle could potentially make only 313 different contacts with other human beings. In contrast, the density of the United States as a whole today would make possible 15,699 contacts in the same land area. The density of the average central city in the United States would permit over 2.5 million contacts, the density of Chicago over 5.3 million contacts, the density of New York City over 7.8 million contacts, and the density of Manhattan over 23.5 million contacts in the same land area. The potential number of contacts, when considered as a measure of potential human interaction, provides, in a simplistic way to be sure, a basis for understanding the difference that city living makes. (Hauser, 1968, p. 194)

Interaction, in turn, increases the salience of language and cultural loyalties. Interaction would represent cross-group communications, that for some might override the noise of "local" messages. The

[23] *See* Deutsch (1966, pp. 156–63); Kloss (1966, pp. 209–12) argues that distance has mixed effects since it can reduce incentives to assimilate among similar groups.

common language of cross-group communication would be the common code toward which assimilation would occur. (*See* the discussion on Quebec in the fourth section below.)

9. The last variable in the model is the net assimilation that occurs ($a_{21}P_2 - a_{12}P_1$). The model indicates that this is directly or indirectly influenced by all the other variables. It is assumed that "distance" establishes barriers, while inequality and interaction generate pressures to assimilate. Those, in turn, are shaped by the performance of the economy and the changes in mobilized populations.

This description of a model for mobilization/assimilation processes clearly requires further specification and testing.[24] It is presented here in tentative fashion in order to enrich the discussion of specific cases in the next section of the paper and to elicit criticisms and comments on its adequacy. The model will be under-identified, hence, parameters (indicated by the arrows between boxes in the model in Figure 4) would have to be derived by initial subjective estimates. Such parameters represent the strength of relationships between variables, for instance, indicating whether changes in inequality have a greater net direct or indirect (through distance) effect on assimilation.

Although the schematized model has variables with multiple and ambiguous effects upon assimilation, it still lacks the conceptual complexity recommended by some sociolinguists. Fishman states: "Our current state of generalizable knowledge in the area of language maintenance and language shift is insufficient for the positing of relationships of cross-cultural or diachronic validity" (Fishman, 1966, p. 441). Heinz Kloss, for example, has elaborated a much more complete list of fifteen interrelated factors, nine of which had mixed effects on linguistic shifts (Kloss, 1966). In response, it can only be noted again that additional variables and feedback loops could be incorporated into the model; however, since it is complex enough already to yield an enormous variety of outcomes when fitted to different contexts, this does not seem necessary. Moreover, the research directions recommended by Fishman, who deplores the "primitive level of scientific generalization," are disaggregated analysis and the study of controlled comparative situations using data

---

[24] The most obvious problem will be collecting data and modelling the economic system. Ronald Brunner and I have explored the possibility of modelling these processes in Quebec for which a good deal of data is available.

analysis. This suggestion seems doomed to failure because most data analyses tend to be static and yield only descriptive generalizations. They often fail to take advantage of the uniform and conceptually relevant cross-national (and diachronic) data sets that Fishman concludes are needed. As Jonathan Pool, who himself has worked on cross-national data analysis, concludes: "The planner needs predictive, dynamic hypotheses: good guesses about how a country's value on one variable would change if he changed its value on the other. Knowledge of this kind does not and cannot follow logically from static description." (Pool, 1969, pp. 13–14). What is needed, then, at least in a fashion similar to the outlined model, is to choose seemingly important sociocultural variables and let them interact in an operating model or simulation of the process being studied (Fishman, 1966, pp. 446–8).

Three Case Studies

Three case studies, using simple projections of future population configurations, illustrate some of the general points of the outlined model. Belgium, Canada, and Malaysia each contain two major linguistic and cultural groups, and in each, communal tensions and political problems are created by mutual antagonisms. Before discussing these cases, however, two problems in the application to concrete situations should be noted. These are the selection of the territorial unit and choice of indices of mobilization and assimilation. Both should take into account the particular characteristics of the case under study.

Thus, focusing on a nation-state can sometimes disguise important subnational contrasts. When the English and French communities in Canada, for instance, are examined, the factors shaping assimilation would seem to indicate a gradual decline of the French-speaking minority. However, since French speakers are not dispersed randomly but rather are concentrated (80 percent) in one province, Quebec, *national* pressures to assimilate to English are diffused for most French speakers; indeed counter-pressures to maintain the French language and culture are much enhanced. These differences are illustrated in Table 2, which shows an increase in the ability to speak English in Canada as a whole, but not in Quebec. Thus, the national assimilation figures are a composite of two very different rates, high in the English-dominated provinces, such as Ontario, and low or negative in Quebec, where more people may assimilate to French than leave it (*Report of the Royal Commission*, 1967, pp. 22–23). It may be important, therefore, to study other areas than those provided by national limits, say, separate provinces or regions. For Canada we will examine only one subunit, Quebec. Indeed, focusing on Montreal alone might have been reasonable, since what happens there is critical for French to English assimilation in all of Quebec.

TABLE 2

ETHNICITY, MOTHER TONGUE AND UNILINGUAL LANGUAGE ABILITY SPEAKING, CANADA AND QUEBEC, 1961

CANADA	*Ethnic Origin*	*Mother Tongue*	*Unilingual*
English	44%	58%	67%
French	30%	28%	19%
QUEBEC			
English	11%	13%	12%
French	80%	81%	62%

> If the French Canadians lose their numerical preponderance in the Montreal area, which accounts for 40 per cent of Quebec's population and wields vastly disproportionate economic and cultural influence, the chances for even the cultural survival of the rest of French Canada will be drastically reduced (Corbett, 1967, p. 85).

A second generic problem in the quantitative analysis of a specific case is the choice of indicators. While data for a single index, such as urbanization or literacy may be adequate and also be more probably available for four or more censuses, more complex and reliable measures would be possible and desirable for research in greater depth. With respect to assimilation data, language usage is perhaps the best single index. But census data frequently do not contain the most applicable information and virtually no census statistics contain information of this kind.[25]

[25] The Canadian census which asked about "mother tongue" – the language first learned and still familiar – comes closest to this sort of information. The United Nations, for instance, has not been able to secure data of this kind, though it has been interested in doing so according to officials.

Linguistically, the country is divided into two major areas: Flanders in the north, inhabited by the Dutch-speaking Flemish, and the southern area, bordering France, where Walloons speak French. Communes along the linguistic frontier and Brussels are linguistically mixed.

Although a minority, the French-speaking group was dominant until recently. French was the language of the elite throughout the country, including those in the north, and thus reflected class differences. Industry developed first in the French-speaking south, and the Roman Catholics of this region had more liberal religious and political views. As the Flemish population mobilized, it became bilingual at a rate nearly double that of the Walloons.[26] Since the French-speaking group has displayed reluctance to learn Dutch, the government, influenced by growing political demands by the Flemish for recognition of Dutch, has insulated the linguistic areas so that schools and administrative services in each area are unilingual, with special bilingual arrangements for Brussels and the mixed communes along the linguistic border. Although this practice of separate but equal may reduce tensions between the two communities, it is also likely to slow assimilation into a bilingual community by encouraging the maintenance of the dominant language in each area. Projections to the year 2000 of the trend between 1880 and 1930, the latter being the last census year with adequate data,[27] are given in Table 3 below. These show a gradual decline for those who speak French only, an increase in urbanization to over three-fourths of the population and growth of literacy to over 96 percent. The projections use least-squares to estimate growth parameters essentially as Deutsch outlined in his original model, except that the natural growth and assimilation components are not separated.[28] The in-

[26] Based on estimates from the 1930 and 1947 censuses that showed nearly seven out of ten bilinguals were Flemish.

[27] Apparently owing to sensitivity over language and communal practices, recent censuses have not reported linguistic information.

[28] A difference equation, $M_t - M_{t-1} = kM_{t-1}$, was substituted for Deutsch's equation $dM/dt = (b+m)M$. The TROLL system at M.I.T. made estimates for the summary parameter k and then projected each population's growth with the constraint that Deutsch mentions, namely that total population $P = M_t + U_t = A_t + D$. Errors were less than 5 percent on the

TABLE 3

TRENDS AND PROJECTIONS OF TOTAL, ASSIMILATED AND MOBILIZED POPULATIONS, BELGIUM, 1880–2000 (In 1000's)

Year	*Total*		*Assimilated* *(French Speaking Only)*			*Mobilized (Urbanized)**		
	Actual	*Estimated*	*Actual*	*Estimated*	*%*	*Actual*	*Estimated*	*%*
1880	5520	5520	2230	2230	40	2377	2377	43
1890	6069	5931	2485	2365	40	2895	2735	46
1900	6674	6374	2575	2507	39	3500	3136	49
1910	7424	6851	2833	2658	39	4194	3471	52
1920**	7406	7365	2850	2818	38	4260	4076	55
1930	8092	7917	3039	2988	38	4894	4622	58
1940		8513		3168	37		5222	61
1950	8512+	9154		3359	37		5870	64
1960	9189++	9844		3561	36	6102++	6599	67
1970		10588		3775	36		7380	70
1980		11389		4003	35		8225	72
1990		12253		4244	35		9147	75
2000		13183		4499	34		10104	77

*Population in communes of 5000 or more.

**Figures for 1920 based on territory included in 1920 census report. The 1947 census report gives slightly altered figures for 1920.

+1947 census.

++1961 figures. Urbanization was 66% according to the census.

SOURCES: Publications of the Belgium Government

Statistique de la Belgique Population Recensement Général.

(15 Octobre 1846)

(31 Décembre 1856) (31 Décembre 1900)

(31 Décembre 1880) (31 Décembre 1910)

(31 Décembre 1890) (31 Décembre 1920)

Royaume de Belgique Population

Recensement Géneral au 31 Décembre 1930

Recensement Géneral de la Population, de l'Industrie et du Commerce au 31 Décembre 1947.

Recensement de la Population, 31 Décembre 1961.

average. By adding a constant term, this was reduced. The results were substantially the same, however, and the additional term added nothing; it merely shifted some of the unexplained variation between actual and simulated data from discrepancies in results to an unaccounted factor.

creased mobilization indicated by these trends would probably increase political participation and demands of the Flemish, who have been the more rural population. The language picture seems likely to remain relatively static, while mobilization continues as the urban population grows.

Unless the inequalities between the dominant French-speaking population and the less privileged Flemish are reduced, we may see increased conflict as the mobilized Flemish continue to withdraw support from policies and governments that perpetuate the status quo.

Malaysia

When the Federation of Malaysia became independent in 1957, it contained nearly equal portions of Malays and Chinese.[29] In addition, there was a sizeable Indian minority of about 10 percent and a tiny, but elite, English community.

Conflict between the communities has remained one of the central problems facing the state. The communities are separated by different languages, religions (Malays are Islamic), cultures, and economic position. The Chinese are more urbanized and control large portions of the economy, particularly retail trade. The Indians, although many are in the civil service or wage employment, are largely outside the main arena of communal conflict. Data on language usage are not available, but the only official language (as of 1967) is Malay. English, however, is still an important medium of communication among the elite, especially since it can connect the Malay and other communities. Government policy favors Malay and aims that it should gradually become the medium of instruction (Allen, 1968, p. 257). The Malays, in spite of their political control – based on disproportionate representation of the rural areas, where they are in the majority, and insured through their predominance in the police and armed forces – recognize the Chinese, with their greater economic resources, as dangerous rivals (*see* Rabushka, 1970, and Ratnam, 1965). Militant Chinese have demanded equal political rights and the recognition of Chinese as an official language. Until 1969, the Alliance, a coalition of parties from each of the three

[29] Census figures vary somewhat. *The Official Year Book, 1963* (p. 11) lists 46 percent indigenous Malays and 42 percent Chinese and 10 percent Indians and Pakistanis (Cited in Allen, 1968, p. 204).

major communities under Malay leadership, attempted to mute communal issues and stress "national" concerns, working out compromises in private. In May 1969 communal rioting in Kuala Lumpur and several other cities led to a state of emergency and suspension of the constitution. The rioting followed increased political support among Chinese for more militant candidates for Parliament. The prospect for future peaceful relations between the communities seems dim.

The population trends in Malaysia projected in Table 4 show a steady growth in the mobilized Malay population and a slow decline in the relative sizes of the differentiated Chinese and Indians. These figures exclude Singapore, the city-state that briefly (1963-1965) was a part of the Federation. Singapore is approximately 80 percent Chinese; when it was in the Federation, the Malays lost their edge in population.[30] Here again, changing rates of natural increase (or any other change in the process) are not shown.

TABLE 4

TRENDS AND PROJECTIONS OF TOTAL MOBILIZED AND ASSIMILATED* POPULATIONS, MALAYSIA, 1931–2000 (In 1000's)

Year	*Total*		*Mobilized*						*Underlying*					
			Mobi/Assimi.			*Mobi/Diffe.*			*Under/Assimi.*			*Under/Diffe.*		
	Act.	*Est.*	*Act.*	*Est.*	*%*	*Act.*	*Est.*	*%*	*Act.*	*Est.*	*%*	*Act.*	*Est.*	*%*
1931	3786		324		9	720		19	1540		41	1202		31
1947	4908	5046	728	763	15	1196	1215	24	1699	1698	34	1385	1370	27
1957	6256	6279	1291	1303	21	1649	1674	27	1835	1808	29	1381	1494	24
1960		6705		1521	23		1830	27		1830	27		1524	23
1970		8342		2483	30		2410	29		1862	22		1588	19
1980		10380		3905	38		3057	29		1825	18		1594	15
1990		12917		5918	46		3735	29		1723	13		1541	12
2000		16072		8658	54		4406	27		1570	10		1426	9

*Mobilization is literacy; Assimilation is based on census records for ethnic identification.

SOURCES: 1931–1957 *Censuses*, Government of Malaya, Kuala Lumpur. Berzina. *The Population of Indonesia, Malaya and the Philippines*, U.S. Department of Commerce, Washington, D.C., 1963.

[30] Singapore remains closely tied economically to the Federation and is regarded as a part of Malaysia by many Malays in spite of the Chinese dominance there. These trends including the increase in the mobilized, assimilated population (literate Malays) are based essentially on a high rate of natural increase among Malays and not on assimilation. *See* Smith (1952, pp. 59–61, 78–81) for an analysis of earlier population trends that seem to have accurately anticipated a more rapid increase of Malays.

The projected expansion of mobilized Malays (which may be exaggerated) should increase the proportion of Malays in the modern economy, especially in well paid posts, and thereby make Malays more secure. This might reduce the pressure to continue the political inequities experienced by Malaysian Chinese who "have been systematically discriminated against, disfranchised or otherwise reduced to a low level of political efficacy" (Rabushka, 1970, p. 178). Malays have used legislation to carefully preserve their political dominance in the past, but this may be felt to be less necessary once they have clear majorities in both urban and rural areas. However, communal tension and hostility might not be reduced unless the distribution of economic rewards becomes more equitable.

At present, the distance between the communities is great. Assimilation in Malaysia between the Malays and the Chinese is apparently nil. Hostility is a product of the unequal economic status of the two groups, important cultural differences, and an accumulation of reciprocally negative images based on experiences in World War II, the communist insurgency, the practices of Chinese secret societies, favoritism shown by the British toward the Malay population, and the treatment each has received from the other (Ratnam, 1965).[31]

Rural Malays, the largest population group in Malaysia, have an extremely negative and stereotyped image of Chinese. Peter Wilson reports that in one rural village, Malays who have lived among the Chinese in Singapore depicted themselves as being:

> a minority oppressed and discriminated against, forced to live in the poorest parts of the island and the city, unable to gain access to good housing, welfare, and other benefits, and steadily economically strangled by the Chinese. One may (felt). . . the only solution. . . was either the expulsion or the slaughter of the Chinese, and he personally favored the latter course. . . This Malay's account seems to reflect the more general analyses offered of the riots between Malays and Chinese in Singapore. . . And it is this opinion and outlook that they (villagers) absorb and use to analyze the general situation as it comes to them over the radio and in newspapers (Wilson, 1967, p. 50).

[31] This distance seems to permeate the broadest considerations. For instance, Wilson (1967, p. 55) reports that Malay villagers feel that Jawi (Arabic) script is superior to Rumi (Roman) script in written Malay because it is "incomprehensible to non-Malays (i.e. Chinese)."

This communal distance has dampened interaction; Malays and Chinese live in separate *kampongs* (wards) and attend separate schools. Rural villagers can carry hatred for the Chinese into a more mobilized life in which greater interaction is required; if so, racial riots are not likely to abate.

Northern Ireland, in 1969–70, has demonstrated that fairly bloody communal conflict can be based on religious and socio-economic differences alone. In Malaysia, where linguistic and cultural differences also exist, increasing mobilization promises greater conflict unless the Chinese dominance in the economy is overturned. This may be possible if, as the projections indicate, Chinese numerical strength declines. However, if the Chinese position becomes more tenuous, they may offer violent resistance rather than yield.

Quebec

The situation in Canada and the concentration of French Canadians in Quebec has already been mentioned in discussing some factors important in the assimilation process. Recalling that language is a key indicator of general assimilation and represents a critical feature of assimilation itself, it should be noted that bilingualism declined in Canada from 17 percent in 1931 to 12 percent in 1961, while French-only speakers increased from 17 percent to 19 percent, and English-only speakers remained virtually unchanged at 67 percent. These statistics reflect a number of underlying factors, including a high rate of natural growth among the French population and assimilation to English among immigrant groups (*Report of the Royal Commission*, 1967, pp. 24–46).

Communal strife has been practically as old as the country. After various struggles enduring into the nineteenth century, the British North American Act of 1867 established English and French as the two official languages of Canada. In the next century, use of French outside of Quebec declined and French Canadians experienced a declining role in the federal civil service, from 27 percent in 1918 to 15 percent in 1963 (it was even lower in the preceding decade) (Corbett, 1967, pp. 102–3). A carefully documented study in the 1930's found discrimination toward French Canadians moving into an industrial society created increasing social pressure against French aspirations (Hughes, 1942).

Mobilization has increased the French Canadians' rate of interaction with other literate, urban dwellers, and with this their awareness of English dominance. Occupations available in the industrialized parts of the economy have created for French speakers "unequal opportunities for work. . . (and) a limited utilization of the potential skills of those who do not know the dominant language perfectly."[32] French spokesmen often refer to a lack of respect and, in some cases, even contempt among their English-speaking countrymen (*See* Corbett, 1967, pp. 260–62). In the decade of the 1960's, French-speaking people of Quebec responded to this situation by demands for greater recognition of French or for the independence of Quebec; they succeeded in gaining renewed attention to the rights of the French Canadians.[33]

Except in Quebec, French speakers are in a clear minority, and schools, unions, and social activities are conducted largely in English. Only Quebec has a dual language policy, and even here in business affairs English is often needed to advance. Thus, it is not surprising to find that political violence expressing discontent and separatist demands has erupted.

Outside of Quebec, assimilation to English has been frequent among those of French origin. In 1961, for instance, 38 percent of those of French origin in Ontario reported that English was their mother tongue and 65 percent reported similarly in British Columbia. In Quebec, however, only 1.6 percent of those of French origin gave English as their mother tongue, whereas 9.4 percent of English origin reported French as mother tongue. As the Royal Commission on Bilingualism and Biculturalism reports:

> Anglicization of those of French mother tongue is negligible in Quebec, little to be found in New Brunswick, and strongest in Ontario; yet in Ontario the situation varies greatly from one region to another. On the other hand, such assimilation is more rapid in all the other provinces. . . As a general rule, the further a community of French origin is from Quebec, the higher the rate of assimilation and, as a corollary, the larger the group, the lower the

[32] From a study by Jacques Brazeau in the *Canadian Journal of Economics and Political Science*, cited in *The Report of the Royal Commission* (1967).

[33] The Royal Commission on Bilingualism and Biculturalism was established in 1963.

rate of assimilation (*Report of the Royal Commission*, 1967, p. 32).

This demonstrates how increased concentration of size can decrease the effect of interaction (as suggested in Figure 4). Similarly for the British population in Quebec,

> . . . just as for the French in other provinces, smallness of numbers and degree of isolation are factors in assimilation. On the whole, the minority of British origin in Quebec escapes the assimilation process, because of its concentration in the Montreal district and southeastern counties of the province (*Report of the Royal Commission*, 1967, p. 33).

In spite of increasing heterogeneity of national origin among Canadians, there is increasing homogeneity of mother tongue. About one out of six Canadians has changed from the language of origin, with 93 percent changed to English representing nearly three million Canadians. Table 5, showing the 1961 distribution of mother tongue by ethnic origin, indicates that English is clearly dominant and the language into which nearly all assimilation occurs.

TABLE 5

DISTRIBUTION BY MOTHER TONGUE BY ETHNIC ORIGIN, CANADA, 1961*

Ethnic Origin	*Mother Tongue*	
	English	*French*
British	98.6	1.0
French	10.0	89.6
German	59.0	0.8
Italian	22.2	3.7
Jewish	57.9	1.3
Dutch	51.8	0.3
Polish	40.4	0.9
Scandinavian	69.7	0.6
Ukrainian	33.9	0.3

**Report of the Royal Commission*, 1967, Table 2, p. 23.

Although four-fifths of all French Canadians live in Quebec and their majority position reduces pressures to assimilate to English, two counter trends were predicted for all of Canada by the Royal Commission studying bilingualism and biculturalism: "a reduction in the relative size of the group of French origin can reasonably be expected within a relatively short time, other things being equal," and a steady increase in Canadians with English as their mother tongue (*Report of the Royal Commission*, 1967, p. 22).

A national survey in 1966 illustrates how increasing interactions in urban environments, coupled with incentives created by a relatively indulged dominant English population, have induced assimilation to English. Table 6 shows that among those who live in urban areas, where pressure for interaction is higher, the percentage of those of French ancestry who now speak English only is considerably higher than in rural areas. This change apparently takes some time since it is true for those who were born in cities, but not for those who move there. Among those who "assimilate" in the opposite direction – from English ancestry to French speaking only – the same pattern may be found.

TABLE 6*

LINGUISTIC ASSIMILATION AMONG CANADIANS, 1965

Percent with French Ancestry who Speak English Only (total is 3.4%)

		Place of Residence	
		Rural	**Urban**
Place of Birth	**Rural**	2.7	2.7
	Urban	2.1	4.5

Percent with British Ancestry who Speak French Only (total is 0.9%)

		Place of Residence	
		Rural	**Urban**
Place of Birth	**Rural**	1.0	0.7
	Urban	0.2	1.1

*I am grateful to William P. Irvine of Queens University, Kingston, Ontario, for sending me these results from his study of social change in Canada. His survey data are based on 4069 respondents, age twenty-one or older (Personal communication, Jan. 14, 1971).

The situation in Quebec, however, where the number of those who speak only English declined, is the opposite of that for the country as a whole. French seems likely to maintain its dominance there. Table 7 projects the population trend of 1931–61 to the year 2001. Since the English-speaking population has higher status in Quebec and is dominant in Canada, those reported as speaking English only are stipulated to be the "assimilated" population. They were 11.6

percent of the population (compared to 13.3 percent of English ethnicity) in 1961, and are projected to decline slightly to 9 percent in 2001 if the trend is steady. The major outcome expected is the continued mobilization of French-speaking Canadians.

TABLE 7

TRENDS AND PROJECTIONS OF TOTAL, ASSIMILATED AND MOBILIZED POPULATIONS*, QUEBEC, 1931–2001 (In 1000's)

Year	*Total*		*Mobilized*						*Underlying*					
	Act.	*Est.*	*Mobi/Assimi.*			*Mobi/Diffe.*			*Under/Assimi.*			*Under/Diffe.*		
			Act.	*Est.*	*%*	*Act.*	*Est.*	*%*	*Act.*	*Est.*	*%*	*Act.*	*Est.*	*%*
1931	2875		318		11	1476		52	78		3	983		34
1941	3332	3566	335	389	11	1774	2035	57	75	77	2	1147	1064	30
1951	4056	4422	383	470	11	2314	2737	62	80	76	2	1279	1139	26
1961	5259	5485	532	561	10	3374	3644	66	76	74	1	1276	1206	22
1971		6804		664	10		4803	71		72	1		1264	19
1981		8439		779	9		6277	74		69	1		1314	16
1991		10467		907	9		8139	78		66	1		1355	13
2001		12982		1049	8		10483	81		62	1		1383	11

*Mobilization is urbanization in towns of 1000 or more, assimilation is English only (official tongue).

SOURCES: *Censuses of Canada* for 1931, 1941, 1951, 1961, Ottawa, Canadian Government.

Those trends suggest that some "indigestible" English will remain in Quebec, but that French-speaking Quebec will be unassimilatable into a unilingual English Canada. In order to reduce the tensions which such trends portend, the Royal Commission's first recommendations were aimed at creating new educational and legal practices to counter the trends by preserving and promoting a bilingual community in eastern Canada.

The developmental dynamics of both communities, however, are obscured by the simple projections. These are partially a product of the distance between the groups and the interaction that an increasingly technical society fosters. Fortunately, a recent survey among Canadian youth, thirteen to twenty years of age, provides some helpful evidence on the character of these two social variables.

Distance was indicated by two questions. One asked the respondents to rate how much various juxtaposed groups would agree on Canada's future. Of the six possible cleavages, by region, religion, birthplace, wealth, urbanization and language, all groups agreed that least consensus would be found in the last type. A second question elicited that English Canadians were perceived as closer to Americans than French Canadians (overwhelmingly by English speakers themselves), and English and French speakers were seen as alike in their food and occupations but different in the importance they attached to religion and the kind of government they want (Johnstone, 1969, pp. 23–36, 45–50).

Interactions were calculated by asking the respondent the frequency of his intergroup contacts in language use, residence, school, or close personal friends. High positive relationships existed among both French and English speakers between frequency of contacts and commitment to a bilingual culture. However, daily language exposure had much less effect in Quebec than outside. "This result suggests that the demographic rather than the interpersonal environment has the more powerful influence on dispositions regarding bilingualism," Johnstone concludes (1969, p. 71). It is further evidence for the importance of taking into account the geographic dispersal and location of language communities, possibly by disaggregating a country into key units. In Quebec, compared to all of Canada, the probabilities of random interaction are for more contacts in either English or French (0.26 vs. 0.20), many more in French only (0.44 vs. 0.03), but also more contacts could occur in neither (0.19 vs. 0.10) (Johnstone, 1969, p. 74). While interactions seem to increase commitment to mutual assimilation, the pressure to assimilate generated by interaction would be toward French in Quebec and English in the remainder of Canada.[34]

In each of the three countries surveyed (Belgium, Malaysia, and Canada (Quebec)) equality, distance, and interactions are important in shaping assimilation patterns. In Belgium and Malaysia, territorial or residential separation coupled with government policies that promoted unilingualism have reduced assimilation. In Malaysia, communal hostility and physical identity probably prevent all but the slightest assimilation, while in Canada, distance between major groups is far less and assimilation to English is widespread (and could

[34] The French, partially as a result, are considerably more bilingual than the English.

eventually lead to a unilingual state were it not for the concentration of French speakers in Quebec). In these case studies, similar variables shaping the transformation of linguistic and cultural communities were depicted. While the processes in each seem to operate in a similar manner, varying values for the parameters in the different situations combine to produce different outcomes. These, in turn, promote different political climates and different responses to the demands of mobilized but differentiated groups.

Conclusion: Toward Theoretical Significance and Policy Relevance

Efforts to depict through models such complex and broadscale processes as mobilization and assimilation have not made much progress. As a result, insights that might result from an understanding of these processes, of the shifts in population that they are likely to produce, and the consequences that such shifts are likely to bring, have not been available to assist policy-makers. Since government policy might alter these processes, one major justification for investigating them is to learn about the likely consequences of different mobilization and assimilation rates for conflict and the formation of political communities. How might we progress in achieving clearer and more concrete concepts and theories for mobilization and assimilation?

This question can only be approached by exploring the avenues for further work now available and the purposes which can be served by various research strategies. First, we need to clarify the concepts of mobilization and assimilation, perhaps by defining more narrowly and rigorously what is meant. Deutsch has emphasized the relevance of communication in fostering similar values and modes of life, but language may be a poor surrogate to indicate communication patterns among individuals, at least in some contexts. Urbanization is also not fully satisfactory as an index of mobilization. As Arriaga notes, relying on the percentage of population that is urbanized can be misleading, especially for comparative purposes. Moreover, we are really interested in the socio-economic characteristics of urbanism – which may be hard to quantify (Arriaga, 1971).

A second task would be to expand relevant data collections. Gaps in existing time-series data could be closed, as well as additional units added to data collections.[35] As the case studies here illustrate, aggregate time-series census data can be supplemented usefully by survey information. Content analysis would also be an important tool for generating relevant data, by supplying measurement on variables such as group hostility and political demands. It is important for model builders focusing on general or macro phenomena to avoid relying on a single type of data. By gathering different types of data, and data on more than single indicators, more satisfactory indicators are likely to emerge.

A third avenue for further work would be theory clarification and more formal specification of models. The flow diagram in Figure 4 would require considerably more specification in order to indicate the difference equations of a simulation model. Common dimensions among related variables would be needed, as well as careful stipulation of multiplicative relationships. In such a model, it should be possible to consider various "assimilation" outcomes (as in Figure 3). Bilingualism/biculturalism as an alternative outcome to that of outright shifting from one to another subpopulation should be encompassed in future models. Various *assumptions* about change should also be accommodated by future theoretical elaboration.

The actual techniques to be used in estimating parameters should also be considered. In general, regression estimates will be satisfactory if the model stipulated is either simple enough for purposes of pure extrapolation, or accurate enough so that its complexity, combined with possible errors in data, will not yield misleading results. When there are "noisy" data, a complex model tends to be inferior to a simple one using ordinary least-squares regression. Even though a more complex model may more accurately reflect "reality," the simpler model may yield better predictions.[36] To use more complex (and hence more satisfying) models, hypotheses about noise in the data may eventually be needed for solving the problem of errors in the real data that are used to assess a model's performance.

Finally, the consequences for political behavior or other social concerns should be considered. Discussions of mobilization and assimilation processes have been particularly remiss concerning their impact on political behavior; this essay is no exception. We might

---

[35] *World Handbook II* (Yale Press, forthcoming) and the *Cross-Polity Time-Series Survey* (Cambridge : MIT Press, 1971) are useful steps in this direction.

[36] *See* "Appendix A" of Werbos (1971).

begin at a more or less demographic level, by making projections of likely future population configurations, and then trying to separate different rates of change among different groups, still relying on simple projections. For example, an "underlying" population is likely to undergo periods of rapid growth at least several decades later than that of the dominant population, as the life expectancies associated with better health care and work demands spread, and cultural patterns of family life and reproduction may adjust still later. We can use such analyses to propose different growth rates for different populations at the same point in time or, using simple projection techniques, entire sequences of future predictions.[37]

Then, especially if we can develop process models along the lines already suggested, we can begin to estimate changes in the rates of population shifts and growth, and their social and political consequences. Government policies, thresholds of interaction intensity, and size of "viable" communities, can all be included in principle as factors in policy relevant studies, since these are part of the forces shaping political identities and the push and pull toward homogeneity or separation among groups.

At this more advanced level, we might be able to compare derived measures among different units. For instance, comparisons of similar mobilization and assimilation processes in different countries and at different periods could assist in clarifying structural properties of satisfactory models and, in addition, clarify the range of political outcomes that may reasonably be associated with these processes. Moreover, we could investigate whether and how the "clock" of change varies in different historical periods.

These and other possibilities exist for developing theoretically relevant and rich models. Such models should eventually allow policy alternatives to be assessed as to their potential effect upon rates of change, and subsequently on group differentiation or assimilation. Our purpose in the long run is to generate policy relevant hypotheses and assess their validity. In the shorter run, however, enormous work will be required to clarify more precisely concepts and theories about these processes, relating them to various empirical contexts, and to develop or acquire quantitative techniques suitable to the limitation of the data and the complexity of the phenomena.

---

[37] This point was suggested to me by Karl W. Deutsch.

REFERENCES

Adams, J.S. (1963). "Toward an Understanding of Equity." *Journal of Abnormal and Social Psychology*, pp. 422–36.

Arriaga, Eduardo E. (1971). "A New Approach to the Measurement of Urbanization." *Economic Development and Cultural Change* 18:206–18.

Borrie, W.D. (1959). *The Cultural Integration of Immigrants*. Paris: UNESCO.

Brunner, Ronald D. (1966). On Assimilation. Yale University, Unpublished paper.

Brunner, Ronald D. and Brewer, Garry D. (1971). *Organized Complexity: Empirical Theories of Political Development*. New York: Free Press.

Corbett, Edward M. (1967). *Quebec Confronts Canada*. Baltimore: The Johns Hopkins Press.

Daedulus (1967). "The Nature and Limits of Forecasting," 96, Summer.

Deutsch, Karl W. (1961). "Social Mobilization and Political Development." *The American Political Science Review*, Sept.

Deutsch, Karl W. (1966). *Nationalism and Social Communication*. Cambridge: M.I.T. Press, Rev. Ed.

Deutsch, Karl W. (1967). "Nation and World." In *Contemporary Political Science: Toward Political Theory*. Ed. by Ithiel DeSola Pool. New York: McGraw-Hill.

Fishman, Joshua A., *et al.* (1966). *Language Loyalty in the United States*. The Hague: Mouton and Co.

Fishman, Joshua A., Ed. (1968). *Language Problems of Developing Nations*. New York: John Wiley.

Geertz, Clifford (1963). "The Integrative Revolution." In *Old Societies and New States*. Ed. by Geertz. New York: Free Press (reprinted in *Political Modernization*. Ed. by Claude Welch. Belmont, Calif.: Wadsworth, 1967).

Goldberg, Samuel (1961). *Introduction to Difference Equations*. New York: Science Editions, Inc.

Gordon, Milton M. (1964). *Assimilation in American Life*. New York: Oxford University Press.

Grimshaw, Allen D. (1969). "Language as an Obstacle and as Data in Sociological Research." *Items*. New York: Social Science Research Council, June.

Gullick, J.M. (1969). *Malaysia*. New York: Praeger.

Hare, Nathan (1965). *The Black Anglo-Saxons*. New York: Marazini and Munsell.

Hauser, Philip (1968). "Urbanization – Problems of High Density Living." In *World Population: The View Ahead*. Ed. by Richard N. Farmer, *et al.* Bloomington, Ind.: Bureau of Business Research, pp. 187–215.

Heider, Fritz (1958). *The Psychology of Interpersonal Relations*. New York: John Wiley.

Hopkins, Carol R., and Raymond F. (1969). A Difference Equation Model for Mobilization and Assimilation Processes. Unpublished paper.

Hopkins, Carol R., and Raymond F. (1972). "Projections of Population Change by Mobilization and Assimilation." *Behavioral Science*, forthcoming.

Horowitz, Donald L. (1969). Multi-Racial Politics in the New States: Toward a Theory of Conflict. Paper delivered at the American Political Science Association Meetings, New York, Sept.

Hughes, Everett C. (1943). *French Canada in Transition*. Chicago: University of Chicago Press.

Huntington, Samuel P. (1968). *Political Order in Changing Societies*. New Haven: Yale University Press.

Inglehart, Ronald F., and Woodward, Margaret (1967). "Language Conflicts and Political Community." *Comparative Studies in Society and History* X: 27–45.

Johnstone, John C. (1969). *Young Peoples Images of Canadian Society*. No. 2, Studies of the Royal Commission on Bilingualism and Biculturalism. Ottawa: Queens Printer.

Keyfitz, Nathan (1968). *Introduction to the Mathematics of Population*. Reading, Mass.: Addison-Wesley.

Kloss, Heinz (1966). "German-American Language Maintenance Efforts." In *Language Loyalty*. Fishman, pp. 206–52.

Lieberson, Stanley (1963). *Ethnic Patterns in American Cities*. New York: Free Press.

Lieberson, Stanley (1965). "Bilingualism in Montreal: A Demographic Analysis." *American Journal of Sociology* 71, July.

Pool, Jonathan (1969). National Development and Language Diversity. A paper read at the American Political Science Association Meetings in New York, Sept. 2–6.

Rabushka, Alvin (1970). "A Note on Overseas Chinese Political Participation." *American Political Science Review*, March, pp. 197–8.

Ratnam, R.J. (1965). *Communalism and the Political Process in Malaya*. Kuala Lumpur: University of Malaya Press.

Report of the Royal Commission on Bilingualism and Biculturalism, Vol. 1. (1967). "The Official Languages." Ottawa: Queens Printer.

Rustow, Dankwart (1967). *A World of Nations*. Washington: The Brookings Institution.

Smith, T.E. (1952). *Population Growth in Malaya*. London: Royal Institute of International Affairs.

Vardys, V. Stanley (1969). Communism and Nationalities in Soviet Nation Building. A paper read at the American Political Science Association Meetings, New York, Sept. 2–6.

Werbos, Paul (1971). Successful Prediction of Assimilation and Mobilization: A Case Study of Methodology in Political Science. Draft paper, Harvard University, April.

Wilson, Peter J. (1967). *A Malay Village and Malaysia: Social Values and Rural Development*. New Haven: HRAF Press.

International Relations Simulations: A Summary

*PAUL SMOKER**

Introduction

The study of politics and affairs of states dates back many centuries – the use of simulation in international relations just over a decade. Although it is possible to trace the evolution of international relations simulations from primitive war games, the starting point for modern simulations is marked by constructions such as Oliver Benson's Simple Diplomatic Game (Benson, 1961, 1963), Harold Guetzkow's Inter-Nation Simulation (INS) (Guetzkow, 1959, 1965) (Guetzkow, *et al.*, 1962) and Lincoln Bloomfield's Political Military Exercise (PME) (Bloomfield and Padelford, 1959) (Bloomfield and Whaley, 1965). These pathbreaking constructions inspired further developments in the field, including the all-computer Technological, Military, Political Evaluation Routine (TEMPER) (Raytheon, 1965) (Gorden, 1967, 1968), and two second-generation constructions: the World Politics Simulation (WPS) and the International Processes Simulation (IPS). William Coplin's WPS (Coplin, 1969) is a man-computer construction that uses on-line computing facilities and is

---

*I would like to thank Northwestern University Research Coordination Committee for partial support in the writing of this report.

currently in its third format (ICAF, 1969, 1969 ii). Paul Smoker's IPS (Smoker, 1968) also uses interactive computing (Smoker, 1970) and is in its second format (Smoker, 1970 ii). This review will discuss each of these simulations and its place in the field. Reference will also be made to modifications of these basic models and to other lesser-known simulations of international relations.

Definition

Each discipline defines simulation according to its own purposes; and even within disciplines, opinions differ. According to Webster's *New World Dictionary*, "to simulate" means "to give a false indication or appearance of, as in 'to simulate interest'" and "to have the external characteristics of, to look or act like, as in 'the insect simulated a twig.'" Certainly simulation is false in the sense that it is not "the reality." The same can be said of purely verbal analyses of social phenomena; yet one would hesitate to ascribe the label "simulation" to such endeavors. Guetzkow has progressively defined simulation as:

> . . . an operating representation of central features of reality. . . (Guetzkow, 1959, p. 183)

and

> . . . a theoretical construction consisting not only of words, not only of words and mathematical symbols, but of words, mathematical symbols and surrogate or replicate components all set in operation over time to represent the phenomena being studied. (Guetzkow, 1968, p. 203)

While some social science simulators have distinguished "games" from "simulations" using the criteria that simulations usually become games when human decision-makers are involved (Ackoff, 1962) (Shubik, 1960), Guetzkow does not make this distinction. A "surrogate or replicate component" in Guetzkow's framework could be a human being or a subroutine in a computer program.

For some purposes, it might be considered desirable to replace all human decision-makers by computer routines so that many options can be considered relatively quickly. From this perspective, the use of human beings as surrogates in simulations such as INS, WPS, and IPS might be considered an admission of failure with regard to theories of the situation. Thus faced with a lack of adequate explicit theory concerning the processes involved, human beings can be used as "black box" components on the assumption that their behavior in the simulated environment will, at least in part, correspond to "the reality."

For other purposes, such as training foreign service officers or Peace Corps personnel, human decision-makers use the simulation environment – an environment that includes other human decision-makers – as an experience which may at some later date be relevant to a practical problem. Such a procedure enables the trainee to accumulate a "personal experience bank" in a relatively short time. Some simulators of international relations have seen simulation as a model, while others stress experimentation on a model. Brody (1963) defines a model as a collection of assertions about some reality – past, present, or predicted – and classifies models into four distinct types: pictorial, verbal, mathematical, and simulational. MacRae and Smoker (1967) on the other hand, adopt Ackoff's view that models are representations of systems, objects and events, are idealized since they are simplifications that consider only relevant properties of reality, and hopefully demonstrate the nature of a reality. Further, they argue that simulations may be considered as experimentation on models, and that it is useful to distinguish between a model and experimentation on a model.

While it may be possible to achieve consensus in defining simulations of international relations, it is questionable whether such consensus is desirable at this time. Simulation is still creatively evolving as a technique and any premature closure upon a single formulation in the simulation of international processes could be disfunctional (Guetzkow, 1968, p. 257).

Some Uses of Simulation in International Relations

Because simulation can involve relatively complex models with a number of different "component parts" operating at many levels, it has been used in a wide variety of ways in the study of international relations. Some researchers have used simulation as an environment in which to study the behavior of individuals, a classic concern being the relationship between various personality characteristics and decision-making in crisis situations. Two good reviews of simulation crisis research have been published (Hermann, 1969) (Robinson *et al.*, 1969). Charles F. Hermann (1965, 1967 i) has considered crisis decision-making, threat, time, and surprise in an Inter-Nation Simulation; Margaret G. Hermann (Hermann, M. 1965, 1966) has used INS to study stress, self-esteem, and defensiveness; David Schwartz has analyzed threat, hostility, and behavior preferences in crisis decision-making, again using INS (Schwartz, n.d.). Brody, Benham, and Milstein have analyzed hostile international communication, arms production, and perception of threat (Brody *et al*, 1966); Shapiro has considered cognitive rigidity and moral judgements (Shapiro, 1966); Druckman has studied ethnocentrism and intergroup relations in an Inter-Nation Simulation (Druckman, 1968); while Driver and his associates have developed from structural studies of aggression, stress, and personality in an Inter-Nation Simulation (Driver, 1962, 1965) to a long and detailed series of studies using the Tactical and Negotiations Game (TNG) (Streufert *et al.*, 1965 i, 1967) (Streufert, 1968). The Streufert/Driver TNG experiments use a relatively simple all-man format where the use of nation teams is a device for studying complex decision-making in individuals and groups (Streufert *et al.*, 1965 ii, 1969 i, 1969 ii) (Streufert, 1969). While the TNG has been used to compare perceptual differences between Chinese and American nationals (Streufert and Sandler, 1969), the central focus of this in-depth series of games has been complex decision-making (Streufert, 1969 ii) and testing complexity theory with regard to individual personality (Streufert and Castore, 1968), rather than international relations theory. Of course, personal characteristics of real world decision-makers appear to be important (Raser, 1965) and certainly there is ample evidence to suggest important differences of behavior in international relations simulations that are associated with individual characteristics (Crow and Noel, 1965) (Smoker, 1968 ii, 1971) (Coplin, 1969). However for the purposes of this review, the TNG is regarded as a small group simulation or experiment rather than an international relations simulation. It would require a separate review to include all the relevant work in social psychological and psychological experimentation. Moreover, although many of these studies cover relevant topics such as pacifist strategies (Shure *et al.*, 1965), mediation and arbitration (Pruitt and Johnson, 1969) (Johnson and Pruitt, 1969), negotiation (Mushakoji, 1968, 1971) (Pruit, 1968), boredom (Pilisuk *et al.*, 1967), and cooperation (Pruitt, 1966, 1969), none of these simulations focuses directly on international relations and international relations theory. As Streufert recognizes (Streufert, 1968 ii, p. 17), the results from these experiments should be interpreted cautiously even if face-validity (Hermann, 1967 ii) is present. This is not to suggest that such studies are less important than simulations of international relations, as defined here, but to limit the scope of this article to those constructions that attempt to construct model world systems, or directly to relate psychological characteristics to international relations in such systems.

For example, Charles and Margaret Hermann, in their attempt to simulate the outbreak of World War I using a modified Inter-Nation Simulation, selected participants on the basis of the California Psychological Inventory in such a way that personality characteristics matched those of the real world decision-makers at the time of the crisis (Hermann and Hermann, 1963, 1967). Real world personality characteristics were inferred using a complex content analysis procedure. Dina Zinnes' comparative study of hostile behavior of decision-makers in simulate and historical data, again the World War I crisis, provides a second example of international relations simulation study that includes personality variables as central to its design (Zinnes, 1966).

The studies of Cappello (1971), Crow and Raser (1964) and Ruge (1969) represent attempts to use the Inter-Nation Simulation as a cross-cultural research device and to relate cultural and personality factors to aspects of international relations. This use of simulation may, as Ruge points out (Ruge, 1969, p. 21), reveal relevant factors for inclusion in future theory concerning international relations.

A second use of simulation in international relations has been to study particular situations such as the outbreak of World War I (Hermann and Hermann, 1967) (MacRae, 1967), nuclear proliferation in the 1960's (Brody, 1963), inspection for weapons production (Singer and Hinomoto, 1965), the Vietnam war (MacRae and Smoker, 1967) (Milstein and Mitchell, 1968), the Taiwan Straights crisis (Pelowski, 1971), the East-West disarmament negotiations of the mid-1950's (Bonham, 1967), the Mid-East situation (DeWeerd, 1968), international events of the early 1960's (Meier and Stickgold, 1965), and the patterns of cohesion of NATO (Forcese, 1968). All-computer simulations such as *CRISISCOM* (Pool and Kessler, 1965) have been of particular value in this use of simulation.

A third use of simulation has been as an educational device (Guetzkow, 1964 i). Many scholars have used simulation in this fashion. On occasion, systematic research has been undertaken to check the validity of educational simulations, be they at the elementary school level (Targ, 1967, 1968 i, 1968 ii), in high schools (Cherryholmes, 1965), or in colleges and universities (Robinson *et al.*, 1966) (Cohen, 1962). More often than not, the educational value is hypothesized on the grounds of participant involvement and face validity (Judge, n.d.) (Burton, 1966) (Smoker and Martin, 1968). Simulations such as the PSW simulation developed by John Parker, Clifford Smith, and Marshall Whithed (Parker and Whithed, 1969) (Smith and Whithed, 1968 i) are justified by the designers by arguing for the practical experience given to students of international relations as a result of participation. Again, if the focus is broadened from international relations simulations to educational simulations in general, a massive literature is found for instructional uses of simulation. This area is beyond the scope of this review, but an interested reader might consult some standard works (Twelker and Wallen, 1967) (Boocock and Schild, 1968) (Tansey, 1970).

A fourth use of simulation in international relations is the attempt to consider a particular theoretical or functional aspect of the international system. For example, collective decision-making and coalition behavior have been important topics in the study of international relations, and a number of simulation endeavors have attempted to investigate these phenomena (Alker, 1969) (Browning, 1969). Another central focus of much international relations theory has been the concepts of balance of power and deterrence. Deterrence has been studied by Raser and Crow (1969), while balance of power is being investigated by Dina Zinnes and her associates (Zinnes *et al.*, 1969) using a Simscript format. Other non-national aspects of international relations, such as multinational corporations and international organizations, have been receiving increasing attention in the theoretical literature, and this focus is reflected in the work of simulation researchers. Smith and Whithed have tried to study international business decision-making in a political setting using a number of game-type simulations (Smith and Whithed, 1968 ii, 1969); Frank Hoole has simulated budgetary decision-making in an international organization using a computer model (Hoole, 1970); while Pelowski has considered the problems of an all-computer simulation module of multinational corporate futures (Pelowski, 1969). The Pelowski approach is typical of the growing commitment to modular simulations in international relations research. Scholars with this perspective argue that full-blown simulations of international relations can be developed by progressively linking an increasing number of modular simulations as they develop. Each modular is a representation of some component part of international relations theory and can be inserted into the nest of modulars or replaced by an improved modular. In this way, fine-grain computer simulations of localized revolutionary processes, such as the Cornblit all-computer model of short-run political change (Cornblit, 1971), might in principle be related to coarse-grain modules of international processes, such as Oliver Benson's Simple Diplomatic Game in its new modular format (Krend, 1971), through a common data base.

A central use of simulation is described by Harold Guetzkow in his article "Simulations in the Consolidation and Utilization of Knowledge about International Relations" (Guetzkow, 1969). This perspective views simulation as a format for theory and distinguishes at least three thrusts for the simulation enterprise. To begin with, simulations are seen as vehicles for differentiating and amalgamating theories of international relations. Islands of theory, for example, might be progressively linked through a dynamic modular approach. A second aspect stresses simulations as vehicles in the validation of theories of international relations. Here, empirical findings are organized so that the validity of their theoretical contents may by assessed. Finally, the role of simulations in the utilization of knowledge for policy-making in international affairs can be considered, including the complex questions associated with exploring alternative policy futures The policy aspect of simulation has attracted the interest of a number of scholars (Ausland and Richardson, 1966) (Bailey, 1967) (Bobrow and Schwartz, 1968) (Bobrow, 1969), and this trend is likely to continue.

Other reviews of simulation in international relations adopt alternative typologies for considering various uses of simulation (Hermann,

1968) (Krend, 1968) (Crow, 1966) (Abt Associates, 1965) (Guetzkow and Jensen, 1966). The multiple uses of simulation in international relations (SIP, 1966 i, 1966 ii, 1968) and the wide variety of theoretical perspectives (Guetzkow, 1964, ii) (Coplin, 1966) (Chadwick, 1969) has led to considerable conceptual diversification amongst simulators of international relations. This diversification is also apparent in such documents as the Gomer master list of simulation variables, where some hundreds of simulation variables currently in use are listed (Gomer, 1968). Many of these variables from different simulation experiments have been recorded on IBM cards and microfilm, and a considerable volume of textual and numerical data is stored in a simulation data bank (Busse, 1969). In addition, a number of bibliographic and abstracted bibliographic sources are available which include material dealing with simulation in international relations (Myers, 1968), thus complementing existing information sources in international relations (Park, 1968).

The variety of uses of simulation is, to some extent, related to the theoretical diversification of the users of simulation. In fact, the theoretical underpinnings of simulations in international relations can be used to differentiate important aspects of the major simulation models. Given a concern with military and power factors, it is not surprising to find the ensuing simulation, as in the case of TEMPER, has relatively fine-grain representation of military characteristics and relatively coarse-grain political characteristics. Similarly, given a concern with the influence of domestic political questions on foreign policy decisions, the World Politics Simulation is relatively fine grain for domestic political structures of nations, and relatively coarse grain with regard to the international system (ICAF, 1969 iii). The International Processes Simulation, because of a concern with the international system and its consequences on national, subnational and transnational behavior, has relatively fine-grain modelling at the international system level (Pfaltzgraff, 1969).

There seem to be at least two procedures that may in the future be used to overcome this problem of partial modelling. The most obvious, but perhaps least practical, is somehow to construct one simulation that is homogeneous in terms of multilevel theory. This is to argue for multilevel theory that is equally well- (or poorly-) developed for every relevant component part and relationship. At the present time, this appears to be a rather difficult proposition since theory is still relatively fragmented and insular, and there are considerable – and legitimate – differences of opinion concerning basic concepts and frameworks.

An alternative approach would nest simulations in a modular fashion in such a way that only "undistorted" output from one modular was used as input to the total network. Given the partial and lumpy nature of theory in international relations, this procedure is appealing. As theory develops in a particular section, modulars can be replaced. As new theory evolves in previously unmapped areas, new modulars can be added to the nest. As meta-theory changes, theory concerning the relationships between modulars, the executive procedures in the computer programs, can be adapted.

The problem of meta-theory is, of course, very important. Such "theory" might be developed using monte-carlo approaches to "fit" output from the nest of modulars to some data-set alleged to be representative of "reality." But implicit in this approach are the assumptions that social reality is constant in terms of laws of human behavior, that the data-set is somehow representative of "reality," and that correspondence of output is a necessary condition for correspondence of structure and process. The first and last of these assumptions require a discussion of validity; the second, a consideration of relevance.

On Validity of Simulations of International Relations

Hermann, in his now-classic discussion of validation problems in simulations of international relations (Hermann, 1967 ii), discusses the relationship between the purpose of a simulation and the question of validity. While other theorists had considered the problems in some detail (Campbell and Fiske, 1959) (Kress, 1966) (Crow and Noel, 1965), the validity criteria developed by Hermann have become important referents in considering performance characteristics of simulations of international relations. The five criteria suggested by Hermann use different aspects of simulation performance to evaluate its validity:

1. internal validity, after Campbell (Campbell, 1957), demands replication of performance characteristics over repeated runs;
2. face validity results from surface realism from the point of view of experimenter or participants;

3. variable parameter validity involves comparisons of the simulation variables and parameters with their assumed counterparts in the referent system;

4. event validity requires prediction of discrete events using simulation; and

5. hypothesis validity compares the performance characteristics of simulations to theoretical or hypothesized relationships.

Internal validity has had limited use (Elder and Pendley, 1966), and some criticism (MacRae and Smoker, 1967, p. 5), but the other formulations are used more often. Recently, other scholars have developed alternative perspectives (Evans *et al.*, 1967) (Martin, 1968) (Grant, 1970), some of them specifically related to simulation of international relations (Guetzkow, 1968) (Smoker, 1969) and some to problems of organizational research and design (Sullivan, 1969) (Vertinsky, 1971).

Guetzkow sees validity as homomorphism of theory and empirical analyses (Guetzkow, 1968, p. 206) and suggests

> ... by using some systematic rigor in making comparisons between simulations and "realities," by taking reference data largely from extant international systems rather than laboratory and field research about non international phenomena, and by finding in simulations internal processes and outputs which correspond to reference processes as well as reference outcomes, a convergence of evidence is gained which increases the credibility of the theoretical constructions of simulations. (Guetzkow, 1968, p. 208)

Smoker adds an additional dimension when he argues:

> All of the studies so far surveyed define simulation validity as a function of the predicted and actual correspondences between simulation and "reality." The "real world" is regarded as given, and the "model world" is regarded as an attempt to demonstrate or show or reveal aspects of reality. If there is a lack of validity, the model world is altered in an attempt to increase the validity of the simulation.
>
> It is possible to take the complementary position and to evaluate the "real world" relative to the "model world" incorporated in a

simulation. With this perspective the model world becomes an attempt to demonstrate or show or reveal the way parts of reality could or should be, and differences between the two worlds are rectified by changing aspects of reality through social and political action. (Smoker, 1969, p. 11)

This definition of complementary validity raises more questions than it answers, but it may be of value as simulations of international relations are increasingly used for practical military and political ends.

In the following sections of this paper where a number of international relations simulations are evaluated, problems of validity constantly arise. The last section of the paper considers problems of relevance and possible future developments.

Evaluations of International Relations Simulations

The Technological, Economic, Military, Political Evaluation Routine

Relatively little is published in book or journal form describing the TEMPER simulation, considering the voluminous mimeographed material available; but the best single article in generally-available format is Abt and Gorden's report on project TEMPER (Abt and Gorden, 1969). This article describes the structure of TEMPER in terms of the actors, nation groups, and how they act. Of particular interest is the section of the article dealing with the intellectual basis for TEMPER and the resulting set of theoretical assumptions. A central, and subsequently critical, theoretical assumption is that:

> Nation actors are treated as highly aggregated decision-making units that attempt to minimize the discrepancy between their ideal state and reality by allocating political, military, and economic resources within acceptable costs. The two super powers and their allies, the United States and its allies and the USSR and its allies, compete for the political loyalty, economic cooperation and military alliance of the neutral nations. (Abt and Gorden, 1969, p. 248)

Elsewhere (Raytheon, 1965), considerable detail is given regarding the initial TEMPER model. According to this documentation source, TEMPER attempts "to describe global cold war conflict and simulates it with a digital computer program." The TEMPER simulation program is written in a subset of Fortran common to Fortran IV, CDC Fortran 62, and Fortran 63. To run the simulation, the minimum computer system must have a 32 thousand-word memory, a card reader, three magnetic-tape drives, an on-line printer and, of course, a Fortran compiler. A more efficient system could use an off-line printer and about six magnetic-tape drives, while to use all features of the simulation requires eleven magnetic-tape drives.

The overall-flow diagram for the simulation is shown in Figure 1. This diagram is extracted from analyses of TEMPER (MARK II) undertaken at the Industrial College of the Armed Forces in Washington, D.C. (De La Mater *et al.*, 1966). Four sets of components make up the computer program. They are the psychological submodel, four subroutines; the economic submodel, six subroutines; the war submodel, seven subroutines; and the decision-making submodel, twelve subroutines. Each submodel is time dependant, some sub-

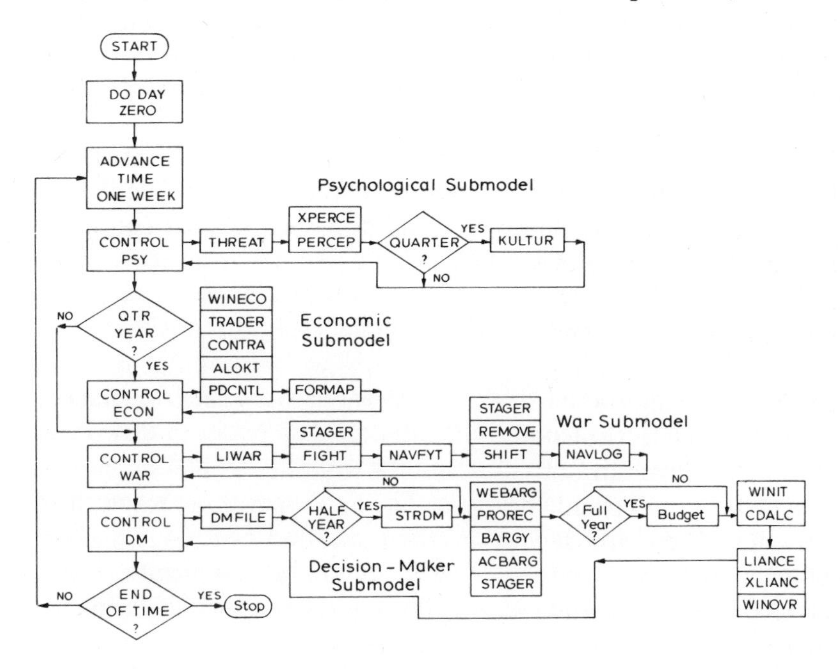

Fig. 1. – Sequencing of Temper subroutines

routines being weekly, some quarterly, some semi-annually, and some yearly.

The psychological submodel consists of a threat subroutine (THREAT), a perception subroutine (PERCEP), an experience subroutine (XPERCE) and a cultural subroutine (KULTUR). PERCEP and XPERCE simulate "the distortion that would occur in the receipt of tactical, strategic, and budget information from one country by another through diplomatic, intelligence, and communication channels" (De La Mater *et al.*, 1966, p. 31). Similarly, it is argued that THREAT computes the various elements of military and political threat which tend to modify normal cultural motivations, while KULTUR introduces and updates the cultural motivations which are considered most significant in influencing a nation in its relations with others.

As an example of TEMPER logic, it is of interest to consider KULTUR and the variables involved in defining these "most significant" cultural motivations. Six alleged motivations are included in the model; they are: internal initiative; military coercion; military initiative; propensity to tax; external dynamism; and military power ratio. These motivations are affected only by the various components of THREAT. THREAT itself has two major components: military threat, and political threat – military threat being subdivided into tactical threat and strategic threat; and political threat being subdivided into global threat, threat from allies, and threat from neutrals. At the lowest level of aggregation, military threat uses concepts of counter-force units, nuclear credibility, level of military operations, population loss, and maximum military operations; while political threat boils down to alliances (either East, West or Neutral), alignment, land desire, and external dynamism.

To start the simulation at "Day Zero," the cultural motivation values are set using the data base values modified slightly in four of the six cases by tactical threat. After "Day Zero," KULTUR is not re-entered until the end of a quarter year (simulation time). Then, as initially, Military Power Ratio is set between its no-threat and maximum-threat limit, depending on the level of threat (which, in turn, depends upon the relative military power of East and West). Similarly, internal initiative, military coercion, military initiative, and propensity to tax are updated by a function where threat drives the motivation either up or down toward its maximum threat limit. External dynamism is computed using a formula which lowers it in the face of military threat and raises it for a political threat.

A casual consideration of "the cultural motivations which are considered most significant in influencing a nation in its relations with others" suggests that the theory underlying TEMPER assumes great importance to military and threat factors in international relations and international relations theory. This observation is supported when the nature of the variables used in TEMPER is considered. Approximately 160 variables are listed as having unique representation in the Fortran program as a whole. Of these variables, ninety are concerned directly with military factors; thirty with economic resources/population factors; thirteen with geographic factors; twelve with escalation, threat and bargaining factors; nine with political factors; and the rest with such things as recording simulation time. When it is realized that nearly all the geographic factors are military in the sense that they are variables (such as fraction of land held), this means that approximately two-thirds of the variables in TEMPER are military variables while 6 percent are political, most of the remainder being economic.

Since the simulation is alleged to be more than a war game, and since "the fundamental theoretical assumption about world conflict on which the TEMPER Model is based is that the overall nature of the current world conflict and the national strategies designed for dealing with it are best defined in the comprehensive terms of global military, political and economic interactions" (Abt and Gorden, 1969, p. 251), a more detailed consideration of the international relations theory in the TEMPER simulation seems in order.

A scouring of the voluminous mimeographed literature concerning TEMPER reveals a number of international relations assumptions which, even if they were the only assumptions in the simulation, place grave doubts on the hypothesis-validity of the model as a vehicle to study international relations. As a vehicle for war gaming, it may be extremely valid; but this review is not concerned with war games. The assumption is that TEMPER's reputation as a simulation of international relations, as propounded by Abt and Gorden – two of the major architects of TEMPER – must be considered with regard to various validity standards for international relations simulations.

The TEMPER data base includes data for 117 nations, and these data are recorded and aggregated by three TEMPER routines (TEMPO, TEMPET, and T-PUNCH), such that there are thirty-nine nation groups and twenty conflict regions on the TEMPER map; thirteen land and seven sea. These thirty-nine nation groups are further sub-divided into an East Block and a West Block. The left-over nation groups, such as Israel and Egypt, are placed in a neutral block whose power ratio is zero, since power ratio is calculated by dividing east by west and vice-versa. Thus TEMPER assumes there is one western block, one eastern block and a neutral block. An actual TEMPER map of the world as used in the 1966 evaluation of TEMPER is shown in Figure 2. An almost identical map has been used in subsequent years in the man-computer format discussed below (ICAF, 1966, 1967, 1968 i, 1968 ii). In addition, TEMPER

CONFLICT REGION	WEST	EAST	NEUTRAL
1	S. Vietnam	N. Vietnam	Laos
2	Thailand	Cambodia	Burma/Ceylon
3		Red China	
4	Pakistan	Mongolia	India
5	S. Korea	N. Korea	
6	Japan		
7		USSR	
8	USA/Canada		
9	Australia		African Nations
10	Turkey/Iran		Middle East
11	NATO Europe	Red Europe	Neutral Europe
12	Brazil/Venezuela	Cuba	Neutral America
13	Malaysia	Indonesia	

Fig. 2. – Temper map

includes just nations in its model and assumes each nation group acts with a common purpose, since no internal dissention or subversion is allowed in the model, and no political or other interest groups are present. Similarly, no international organizations, multinational business or other components of the international system are included.

This set of assumptions runs counter to many international relations theorists. It is difficult to grant much hypothesis-validity to these assumptions, given the impressive array of theorists who do not share the view of TEMPER (McClelland, 1966) (Burton, 1967) (Waltz, 1967) (Deutsch, 1968) (Galtung, 1968) (Angell, 1969) (Alger, 1970). Of course TEMPER, in its newer man-computer format, is mainly an educational device for members of a United States military establishment, and it may be argued that the question of hypothesis-validity is of less value than the educational usage. An alternative perspective would argue that it is not very desirable for many hundreds of military officers to be exposed to an image of international relations which is theoretically not very credible. Of course, if international relations is viewed as a war game, then TEMPER might be seen as a means toward that goal, as individuals exposed to it might tend to act in accordance with the socializing experience involved. This is to take the notion of complementary validity seriously and to try to create a reality in the image of a model.

Other reviews of TEMPER have concluded that:

> Indirect benefits notwithstanding, in our opinion TEMPER is a failure. TEMPER could not succeed at the present state of knowledge; it cannot be repaired. Our recommendation, therefore, is to abandon TEMPER. This should be done quickly since any further time or money spent on TEMPER is wasted.

The reasons why we have arrived at this conclusion are spelled out in detail in subsequent sections. Briefly, they are:

1. In comparison with the real world of the cold war, the TEMPER world is fatally distorted.
2. The relation between TEMPER's inputs, design features and outputs renders it invalid as a simulation.
3. The design of TEMPER makes it practically useless as a subsidiary tool for the conduct of political gaming.

4. The distortions in the TEMPER world render it unsuitable for any attempt to construct a new simulation or gaming model (Balinski *et al.*, 1966, p. 2).

And elsewhere:

> The TEMPER map, around which the theory is structured, is too restrictive for any significant improvement to the present model. Further development will require an approach that permits more realistic and flexible international relations simulation.
>
> The data base is inadequately described. No standard of measurement is provided for the dynamic simulation variables. There exists no theoretical justification for the methods of aggregation. Much of the "theory" of the model is embodied in the values assigned to the data base variables, but this "theory" has not been discussed in any of the documentation.
>
> It is concluded that the data base must be adequately described to the player and researchers before the simulation outputs will gain any respect.
>
> Research into TEMPER must begin with a study that results in acceptance or rejection of the basic assumptions. Subsequent studies must determine if the basic assumptions have been, or in fact can be programmed. Any research into the micro aspects of the simulation, however interesting, will be of little value unless it can be correlated to the basic assumptions of the model, and viewed in the light of a specific use; eminence of the researchers notwithstanding (Draper, 1966, p. 39).

Draper's comments concerning the basic assumptions in the TEMPER model support the earlier discussion of inadequate international relations theory. Unfortunately, it is not at this time possible to give any objective evaluation of TEMPER in terms of empirical comparisons of real world performance to TEMPER. No empirical validity studies have been undertaken on the model and, objectively speaking, its performance characteristics are unknown. Some output from TEMPER has been published (ICAF, 1968 iii) giving print-out from runs of the simulation conducted during 1968.

Many of the variables published are strictly military; but some, such as trade, provide an opportunity for at least an "eye-ball" validity study of this variable. A first thing that becomes apparent when inspecting the trade tables is that trade is defined in an unorthodox fashion. Two types of trade exist: political trade (or exports) which occurs in TEMPER to regain declining friendship, and residual trade (or imports) which is defined as trade to meet unsatisfied demand. When the trade tables are inspected for these total categories, it becomes apparent that most of the trade links between nations in TEMPER are zero. The greatest amount of trade is manifested by the USACAN group in TEMPER where trade links exist with the other nations in about 12 percent of all possible cases. The average for USACAN, NATOEU, and JAPAN is nearer 10 percent. In the real world for these nations with the others in the sample, the average is over 90 percent. Something is wrong, it would seem, with the performance characteristics of TEMPER with regard to trade; and this is, in part, acknowledged in the previously-mentioned ICAF report (De La Mater *et al.*, 1966). In the preceding two sections of this report, the authors point out that there can be no trade between blocs in the TEMPER model, since West and East Blocks do not award Ally Value (the degree to which a nation group values its alliance with another nation group) to each other. The authors then point out that since, in the real world, such trade does exist, "provision probably should be made to accommodate this real world situation" by modifying two of the subroutines, or through a major modification of TEMPER. It seems reasonable to suppose that this particular flaw in performance is associated with the archaic conceptual framework incorporated in the model. It does not seem unreasonable to suppose that many other performance characteristics of the model are likely to be similarly distorted. Before leaving the trade discrepancy, it should be pointed out that not all the discrepancy occurs because of the peculiar assumptions associated with the bipolar structure of the simulation. An inspection of the print-out reveals that, for example, in more than half the cases, the USACAN nation group has no trade at all with South Vietnam, and either no imports or no exports with the European NATO countries. Even if TEMPER is just a war game, this is a little hard to take.

The behavior of TEMPER has been compared to INS and to DETEX 11, a variant of PME (Alker and Brunner, 1969), and some criticism is levied at the debatable economic relationships and the aggregation procedures in TEMPER's bipolar world. Thus, they write:

> Even if its implications need to be explored by many more operating runs the TEMPER model is especially suggestive of debatable relationships, partly because of its explicit nature. Thus we have already noted the considerable overlap of DETEX and TEMPER problem components, but the rather implausible relationships govern the aggregation in TEMPER. The projection of cost effectiveness decision making rules onto the Soviet Union, East and West Germany is also controversial, especially when various kinds of deterrent capabilities are considered. A lot of psychological variables, such as misperception tendencies are included in TEMPER, but their impact on problem definitions and magnitudes in TEMPER does not correspond to their impact in DETEX 11 or INS (Alker and Brunner, 1969, p. 109).

It is true that the explicit nature of the TEMPER equations renders the simulation vulnerable to criticism where less formal all-man or man-computer representations might avoid embarrassing questions. However, the basic criteria of adequate international relations theory applies to all representations, and it is on this point – not the particular details of particular equations – that the present reviewer considers the TEMPER simulation not only inadequate, but dangerous as a teaching device for military officers. In the absence of any validity studies concerned with real world performance characteristics, the only remaining criteria applicable to evaluating TEMPER are the criteria of hypothesis validity. On this score, the fundamental assumptions about internationals incorporated in the model are sufficiently in error to throw the validity of the whole simulation into serious question. It does not seem unreasonable to demand that those who use a simulation of international relations over a number of years as part of an educational experience for some hundreds of military officers are under obligation to present evidence as to the validity of the model and the resulting image of international relations it incorporates. Even if the simulation is used, from the parochial perspective of "the management of our (USA) national resources and the interrelation of economic, military, and political factors on an international level, from our (USA) national perspective" (Westfall and Draper, 1966, p. 1), some of the conclusions of an earlier review still appear to hold, notably

> TEMPER has design deficiencies which make it unsuited for other than experimental use without major modification.

and

> The interplay of many variables used to describe a country and its relations with other countries has not been tuned to the point where results are valid and convincing. This tuning, to be effective, will require reforming of many of the equations, restructuring of the relationships between subroutines and extensive testing of results of computer runs (ICAF, 1966 ii. p. 11).

In summary, TEMPER may represent a brave first attempt at all-computer simulation of international relations when considered from the technical point of view; but from the theoretical and substantive viewpoint, it is seriously invalid unless it is being used deliberately, or otherwise, as a socializing device to demonstrate the way things could be or should be. Its validity then might be measured relative to actions of the United States military in the real world. This is a complex and controversial question, best left to the final discussion of relevance.

The RAND/M.I.T. Political Military Exercise (PME)

The PME has its roots in the work of Herbert Goldhamer at the RAND Corporation (Goldhamer and Speier, 1961, p. 499). Goldhamer's games incorporated political decision-making and policy formulation into limited war games, and were played by the RAND Corporation from 1955 onward (Averch and Lavin, 1964) (Giffin, 1965, pp. 65–68). Using this experience, Lincoln Bloomfield and his associates developed the Political Military Exercise in its various forms (Bloomfield and Padelford, 1959) (Bloomfield, 1960). The POLEX 1 exercise was run in 1958 using academic and U.S. government experts as players; and subsequently, other series were run by

Bloomfield, including the POLEX-DAIS and DETEX series (Bloomfield and Whaley, 1965 i, 1965 ii). The EXDET series of games used only student decision-makers (Whaley and Seidman, 1964) (Whaley *et al*, 1964), and several United States government agencies have used variants of the PME for training, policy, and research purposes (Barringer and Whaley, 1965, p. 456). More recently, the CONEX-EXCON series of games has been run, using a modified form of PME (Bloomfield, 1968) known as GENEX. Similar experiments have been run by Michael Banks, A.J. Gromm, and A.N. Oppenheim in Europe (Banks *et al*, 1968).

The PME is an all-man exercise in which there are a number of nation teams and a control team. The nation teams represent particular political entities within a nation (such as the National Security Council for the United States team and the Politburo in the Soviet Union team) and make moves simulating actions of the team they represent. Initially, all interteam communications are written, and pass through the control team, the only exceptions being face-to-face conferences between particular decision-makers or groups of decision-makers which are held subject to the credibility evaluations of the control team. Teams can only take action during the well-defined move periods. The control team has several roles. It checks for credibility and only allows moves that it believes to be possible; it acts as "nature" in deciding physical outcomes of particular actions of particular teams; it simulates all important or relevant groups not represented by teams in the simulation such as particular international organizations or domestic pressure groups. Thus, the teams represent particular decision-making groups in the situation, and control tries to represent all other relevant factors. A control team might, for example, introduce an accidental nuclear explosion or an earthquake or an assassination. Certainly, the control team is able to manipulate the direction of the game to some extent and can be selected specifically for the particular goals of the research experiment. A PME crisis simulation of the Mid-East situation might, for example, include regional experts on Mid-East affairs, military experts on conventional and guerrilla strategies, economic experts on important industries such as oil, and experts on crisis behavior. Some aspects of the control team's work can be preprogrammed, such as preprogramming all or nearly all of the essential messages sent from control in the early stages.

Nation teams are sometimes small – two or three people in particular roles – and sometimes large – up to eight or so people. For some situations (such as simulating a Mid-Eastern crisis), domestic pressure groups (such as Palestinian guerrillas) can be represented separately by a team. Decision-making positions within the team can be assigned by control prior to the game, or can be self-selected by individuals in the teams. Move periods usually last about one to one-and-a-half hours, although much depends on the research interest of the exercise. Similarly, the relationship of game time to real world time can be varied, as can the duration of the game. Features such as intelligence facilities and leaks are often introduced in the game, and "hot line" facilities are sometimes provided, again depending on the topic being simulated. The scenario, or world history, is particularly important in these games when some possible future is being simulated. Each participant is given some time to study the game scenario before the game.

Because of the wide variety of formats in which PME has been used and because of the policy-oriented perspective of many of its users, relatively little concern has been given to questions of validity. Since PME is, to a large extent, seen as a crisis game by its users where the focus is on "crudely simulating the decision making process at the top governmental level" (Bloomfield and Whaley, 1965, p. 857), evidence of validity is focused on actors and the decision-making process rather than longer-term aspects of the international system. Lucas Fischer has considered the hypothesis validity of PME with regard to aspects of the decision-making process (Fischer, 1968). He argues, for instance, that the question of rationality in decision-making is dealt with more adequately in the PME than in many verbal models since, although the game rules encourage rationality, great scope is given for irrational behavior in crisis situations, especially in the form of selective perception of issues, information, and alternatives. Moreover, certain structural aspects of the game, such as time pressure, incomplete and ambiguous information, and high threat to values, tend to impede rationality in an analogous way to real world decisions. Fischer also concludes that while time is extremely important in both PME and reality with regard to crisis decision-making, the sharp differentiation between domestic and external politics differs from some theorists who see mutual penetration of domestic and foreign policies (Rosenau, 1966) (Scott, 1967).

Fischer also argues that a great variety of organizational structures can be adopted within each team, and this makes possible many different forms of decision-making. On the other hand, organizational norms, sanctions, and rewards are less well represented, although at crisis times, such incentives may be less important. Fischer also suggests that factors related to time and uncertainty can produce tension in players which is related to that hypothesized for real world situations.

Fischer discusses instruments of national policy in PME, including alliance patterns and the use of violence, and patterns of international action, including power and international organization. Unfortunately, all the comparisons are conjectural and no supporting data from the simulation is presented in any systematic fashion. Nevertheless, Fischer argues that the PME is a valuable heuristic device and many important theoretical assumptions have been built into the exercise.

Alker and Brunner, in their comparison of TEMPER, PME and INS, point out that of these three simulations, PME is the least likely to undergo major long-term changes in the international system and, as suggested by Fischer, has some built-in tendencies operating against going to war (Alker and Brunner, 1969, p. 104).

Any evaluation of performance characteristics of PME at this time is purely subjective, since no rigorous empirical attempt has been made to compare its behavior to real world behavior. Many of the arguments presented by Fischer are quite appealing, but not necessarily valid. For example, he argues that PME players are a relatively uniform group, and that this can be interpreted as a statement of the game model to the effect that cultural and other sociological differences are not important in determining individual and group behavior; or as a statement that foreign policy decision-making elites, during crisis, tend to behave similarly in similar circumstances, regardless of their personal or national background (Fischer, 1968, p. 22). There are a number of empirical studies of real world (McClelland *et al.*, 1965) (McClelland, 1968) (Corson, 1970) and simulation (Smoker, 1968 ii, 1969) (Coplin, 1969) behavior which suggest that cultural, national, and personal differences are important in regard to conflict behavior in general, and crisis behavior in particular, in both simulations and realities. It is to Fischer's credit that he acknowledges that alternative theories exist, and also that the Stanford crisis studies (Holsti *et al.*, 1968), for example, have opposite assumptions to that of the PME in this regard (Fischer, 1968, p. 24). But this does not resolve the problem that most, if not all, of the empirical studies go against the particular set of theories chosen for validation purposes by Fischer.

On another point, the control team is central to the processes in the PME since the explicit and implicit assumptions it holds about reality are critical in the subsequent course of events. Some research might be undertaken with PME using different types of control teams for the same scenario. It does not seem an unreasonable hypothesis to suggest that the various outcomes from such a series of runs might be strongly related to the particular theoretical positions of those in control.

Until empirical analyses of performance are undertaken with output from the PME, it is difficult, if not impossible, to evaluate its validity. It could be that the nature of the control team and the nature of the crisis problems tackled are such that PME acts as a reinforcer of basically incorrect perceptions of reality and incorrect theory in much the way that TEMPER does. Certainly, there is no compelling empirical evidence to suggest that results from PME should be taken seriously, and there is some cause for concern that the exercise has been used by United States government agencies with, apparently, no particular concern as to its real world validity as a policy device, other than subjective, untestable propositions about output from the simulations.

To some extent, this lack of concern with evaluating reality performance is understandable, given the foreign policy focus of the simulation and the relative difficulty of undertaking rigorous empirical analyses in such an area (Jensen, 1966 i) (Jensen, 1966 ii). However, methodological developments in the quantification of events data have been made (Azar *et al.*, 1970) such that definition and measurement of a foreign policy event are possible in some detail (Hermann, 1970) (McGowan, 1970) and with some measure of reliability (Sigler, 1970) (Leng and Singer, 1970). Given these developments, relatively "hard" analyses might now be made in the comparison of the output and real world events. Such comparisons could assist considerably in providing an empirical base for evaluating reality performance.

The Inter-Nation Simulation (INS)

The INS is perhaps the best-known simulation of international relations. It was developed by Harold Guetzkow and his associates at Northwestern University and first reported on in book form early in the decade (Guetzkow *et al.*, 1963). Subsequently, it has been reviewed from several perspectives (Verba, 1964) (Raser, 1969) and has been subjected to a wide range of validity studies (Guetzkow, 1968).

INS is a man-computer model – sometimes the computations being conducted by hand during the pause between game periods, sometimes by computer (Pendley, 1966) (Smoker, 1966). Figure 3 gives the decision and information cycle for a typical INS. For this diagram, it has been assumed that the calculations are performed by hand and not by a computer program. Each period lasts roughly seventy-five minutes, although, of course, great variation exists in different formats of INS. For example, the INSKIT for use in schools has one time schedule for a ninety-minute simulation period, and another for a forty-five-minute session (Guetzkow and Cherryholmes, 1966 i, p. 19). In this case, the decision forms used by participants are designed in such a way that they are self-calculating.

Typically, the participants are divided into nation teams, each team comprising a number of decision-making positions. In the INSKIT, for example, each prototypic nation may have a head of state, a foreign policy adviser, an official domestic adviser, a foreign affairs diplomat, and a domestic opposition leader. Additionally, an international organization is often included under the direction of a secretary general (Guetzkow and Cherryholmes, 1966 ii).

In Figure 3, the schedule calls for the main set of economic and political decisions to be made after half an hour in each period. These decisions are used in the programmed environment to calculate the state of each nation at the start of the next period. Of course, during the period, participants can communicate with each other by messages or in conferences and can undertake a number of political activities, such as forming alliances or signing cultural agreements. If an international organization is present, then it has, as a rule, a regularly scheduled meeting at the end of each period.

The unprogrammed part of INS is very analogous to the PME. Great flexibility exists for adapting the model to suit particular

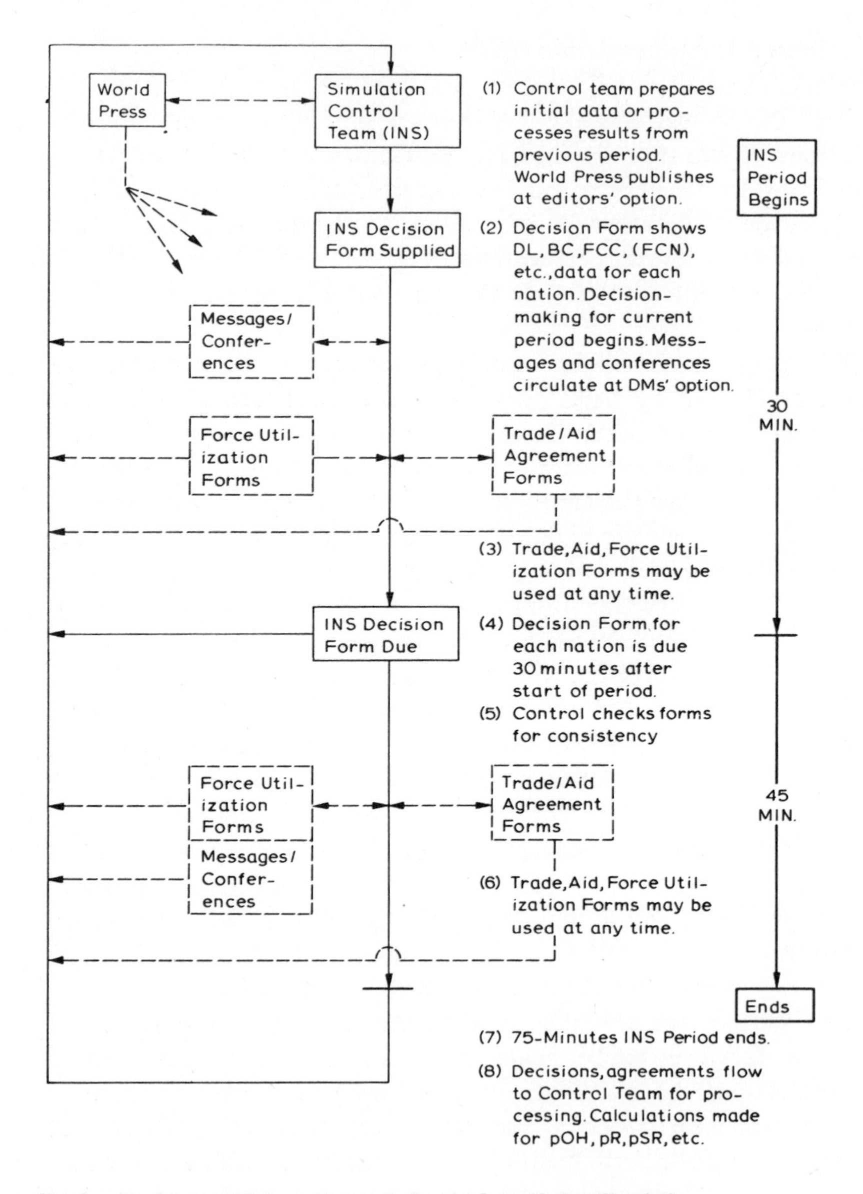

Fig. 3. – Decision and information cycle for the Inter-Nation Simulation

research interests. For example, controlled intervention has been used on a number of occasions to test certain hypotheses such as the spread of nuclear weapons and its consequence on alliance structure (Brody, 1963), and the consequences of implementing Osgood's graduated, independent tensions-reduction initiatives (Crow, 1963). Unlike PME, INS has been used to consider both short-term crisis situations, such as the outbreak of World War I (Hermann and Hermann, 1967), and longer-term patterns in international relations (Narding and Cutler, 1969) (Chadwick, 1969).

The programmed part of INS is analogous to the control team in PME in certain regards. The programmed part consists of a series of equations relating various political and economic factors (Guetzkow *et al.*, 1963) (Guetzkow, 1965). For example, in the original INS model, the satisfaction of consumers with the standard of living depended upon the minimum level of consumer goods necessary and the amount of consumer goods over and above this minimum figure in a diminishing-returns fashion. Thus, successive increases in the quantity of consumer goods available result in decreasing amounts of extra consumer satisfaction. The equation for expressing this set of assumptions in INS is a quadratic equation (Guetzkow *et al.*, 1963, p. 125), and subsequently it was found to be in error by Elder and Pendley (Elder and Pendley, 1966 ii).

In effect, the programmed assumptions in INS represent a simple computer simulation of aspects of international relations. These assumptions were originally made by expressing aspects of theory about international relations in terms of simple equations. Coplin has compared INS theory to theories of international relations and concludes that:

> If there is one obvious conclusion from the preceding discussion, it is that the Inter-Nation Simulation is a theory building exercise conducted not by a number of unsophisticated psychologists who have run out of experiments, but rather by a group of scholars who are well acquainted with the verbal theories of international relations. Moreover the creators of the simulation have been eclectic in their approach. Their model has as much in common with "traditional" as with "non traditional" theoretical positions. (Coplin, 1966, p. 577)

INS differs from most other simulations of international relations in one extremely important fashion. Apart from comparisons of the assumptions incorporated in the model to assumptions about international relations (Coplin, 1966) (Gottheil, 1966), a considerable number of empirical studies have been undertaken in which reality and simulation are compared. Some of these studies consider one or a few variables (Caspary, 1965) (Pendley and Elder, 1966), some focus on specific events (Targ and Nardin, 1965) (Hermann and Hermann, 1967), while others consider the associations between a larger number of variables (Chadwick, 1966, 1967).

The various studies of INS have been independently reviewed by Harold Guetzkow and George Modelski (Guetzkow, 1968) (Modelski, 1969) and an evaluation of the validity of INS is best based on the critical work of these two scholars. Modelski and Guetzkow independently considered twenty-four specific studies using INS, the studies being authored by twenty-nine investigators. From these twenty-four studies, Guetzkow selected fifty-five instances for which he made a judgement of correspondence between simulation and international realities. Guetzkow, on the basis of the empirical evidence, assigned a rating of "much," "some," "little," "none," or "incongruent" for the correspondence in each of the fifty-five cases. He discovered that thirty-eight out of fifty-five comparisons carried a rating of "much" or "some," thirteen a ranking of "little" and four an assigned ranking of "incongruent" (Guetzkow, 1968, p. 253).

Modelski independently concluded that thirty of the fifty-five cases merited "much" or "some," and in only four cases did the Modelski scores differ by more than one degree. An independent comparison of the Modelski and Guetzkow comparisons (Krend, 1969) gave a correlation of 0.95 between the two sets of ratings, the agreement being highest for studies concerned with the use of humans as surrogate decision-makers and lowest for studies of relations among nations.

In his critique of INS, Modelski argues that INS is essentially a nation-state model of world politics and is, as such, one special case of world politics. He discusses four basic assumptions of INS in some detail, namely:

1. that nations are the basic unit of analysis;
2. that nations are essentially self-sufficient;
3. that validators of national decision-making are individuals and groups in the nation's political system; and
4. that central decision-makers control the basic national capabilities and their allocation.

Modelski's penetrating analysis concludes that a generalized simulation system of world politics should be able to cope with a universe of possible world politics that is multi-organizational, significantly interdependent, equipped with global validation procedures and, at the same time, with politicians sensitive to various publics. All of his suggestions argue for greater complexity in terms of role positions and organizational structures. Modelski observes that the second generation IPS goes some way towards meeting his objections.

Although the reality performance of INS leaves much to be desired, the willingness of INS researchers to subject their results and models to rigorous empirical analyses has led to the creation of two second generation man-computer simulations of international relations. Each of these simulations is based on INS, but attempts to rectify errors and omissions in the former INS model. This section of the article ends with a review of these two models: the World Politics Simulation (WPS) and the International Processes Simulation (IPS).

The World Politics Simulation (WPS)

The World Politics Simulation, like INS, is a man-computer representation of aspects of international relations. The decision and information cycle for WPS is illustrated in Figure 4. WPS is currently in its third format and is designed to create an operating environment somewhat similar to that in which national foreign policymakers act and interact (ICAF, 1969 i, p. 1). Up to nine nations are included in WPS and each is represented through an economic submodel, a demographic submodel, and a political submodel. From the point of view of foreign policy, the political submodel is most innovative and contains the most interesting set of theoretical assumptions. The model assumes that a number of domestic pressure groups (known as policy influencers) exert pressure on decision-makers, and that decision-makers are motivated by a desire to stay in office. The participant's manual for WPS places considerable emphasis on the policy influencers (ICAF, 1969 iv), and the background materials for the simulation give examples of particular policy influencers for particular nations (ICAF, 1969 v). In Israel, for example, the policy influencers are assumed to be the center socialist parties, the center right parties, the center left parties, the foreign ministry, public opinion, organized labor, agrarian federations, industrial managers, the military moderates and the military radicals.

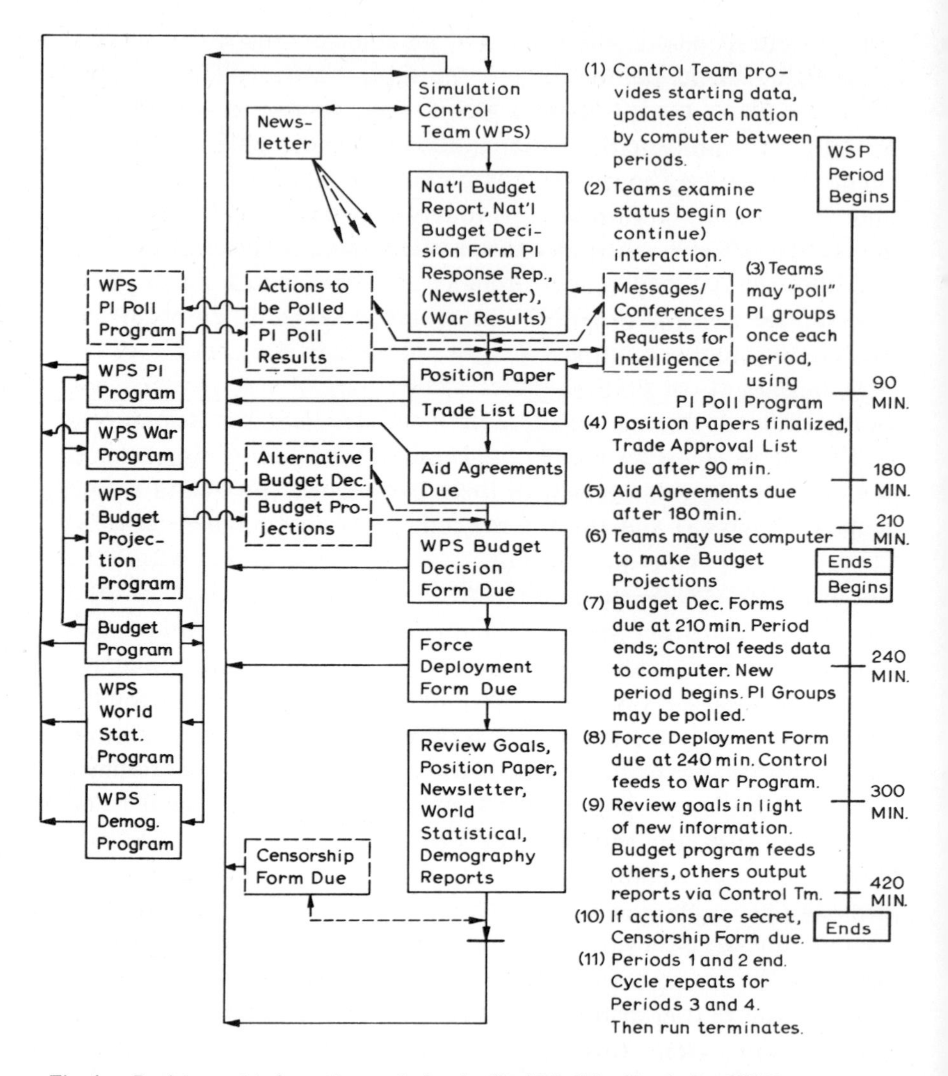

Fig. 4. – Decision and information cycle for the World Politics Simulation III/69

Figure 4 shows how WPS is organized in groups of two periods, and illustrates some of the novel man-computer interactions introduced into the simulation. WPS uses an on-line terminal to speed up the man-machine interface, and provides a limited look-ahead capability with regard to trying out policies and gaining an estimate of the consequences on the policy influencers. Feedback to participants, as in the case of INS, is between periods when consequences of human decisions on the simulated international environment may be calculated (ICAF, 1969 vi).

Like INS, the United Nations is often represented by participants; but like PME, other nations not represented by teams and the U.N. can be simulated by control if necessary to the purpose of the experiment. WPS in this regard is sometimes more vulnerable to the criticism of Modelski concerning other organizations in world politics, although its relatively fine-grain modelling of domestic processes is quite superior to the programmed domestic model in INS or IPS in terms of hypothesis validity.

As in the case of PME and TEMPER, it is at this time difficult to evaluate the model on other than hypothesis-validity grounds. No empirical studies of its performance characteristics relative to international relations have been undertaken, although a comparative study of diplomat and student behavior in WPS has been published (Coplin, 1969). This study reports on a series of four runs with WPS, two with United States state department personnel and two with high school students. Strong differences were found for investment and performance in economic growth, foreign aid patterns, meeting frequency, message frequency, alliances, and activities involving the international organization. A mixture of differences and similarities was found for satisfaction of the policy influencers, uses of military force, foreign trade patterns, use of communications media, and patterns of hostility and friendship. Strong similarities of behavior were found for economic interest in trade, and domestic versus foreign policy actions as sources of policy influencer satisfaction.

Coplin's analysis leads him to the conclusion that rather than view INS or WPS as a theory of political phenomena, it is more appropriate to say that each run *represents* a theory of political phenomena. To some extent, this disaggregated view of particular outcomes is consistent with the outlook of many foreign policy analysts, and is complementary to the social scientific view that is concerned with within- and between-run variance and its distribution. The various uses of simulation in the study of politics reflect these perspectives (Coplin, 1968, 1970).

In the absence of further evidence concerning the performance characteristics of WPS, it seems reasonable to suggest considerable caution in interpreting results from any of the runs with WPS, although hypothesis-validity would suggest that the linkage between policy influencers and foreign policy is clearly superior to any other existing simulation of international relations. The international system component of the model is severely underdeveloped, and the focus on foreign policy may well have introduced distortions at other levels of analysis.

Certainly, it does not seem unreasonable to suggest that because of its continuous use as an educational device for officers in the armed forces of the United States of America, some effort should be made by those using it to present evidence as to its reality performance. While the theoretical assumptions incorporated in WPS seem reasonable – unlike those of TEMPER – the relatively strong emphasis of domestic influence on foreign policy and the relatively underdeveloped nature of the rest of the simulation theory suggest the possibility of lack of correspondence in, for example, the interaction between governments and the political aspects of the international system. Hopefully, those placing credence in WPS as an educational device for military officers will begin to require objective evidence concerning the performance characteristics of international relations simulations. In the absence of such evidence, a healthy skeptic might be forgiven for suspecting a manipulative and training goal, rather than an educational motive in the use of TEMPER and WPS by the Industrial College of the Armed Forces in Washington, D.C., U.S.A. There is, after all, some evidence to support the assumption that a currently dominant military view equates international relations with a war game, tempered by the constraints of domestic policy influencers.

The International Processes Simulation (IPS)

The International Processes Simulation was developed by Paul Smoker at Northwestern and Lancaster Universities. Like the WPS, it represents a second generation man-computer simulation; but unlike WPS, it is particularly focused on the international system. The basic model is described elsewhere (Smoker, 1968 i) and differs from all the other models so far in its overall image of international relations. After Galtung, Alger and others, an attempt is made in IPS to introduce an international system containing international governmental organization, international nongovernmental organization, multinational corporations, nations, and national corporations. The decision-making positions in the human part of the simulation reflect this structure as in addition to governmental decision-makers (such as heads of state and foreign affairs ministers), nongovernmental decision-makers (such as citizens, managing directors of nation-based and

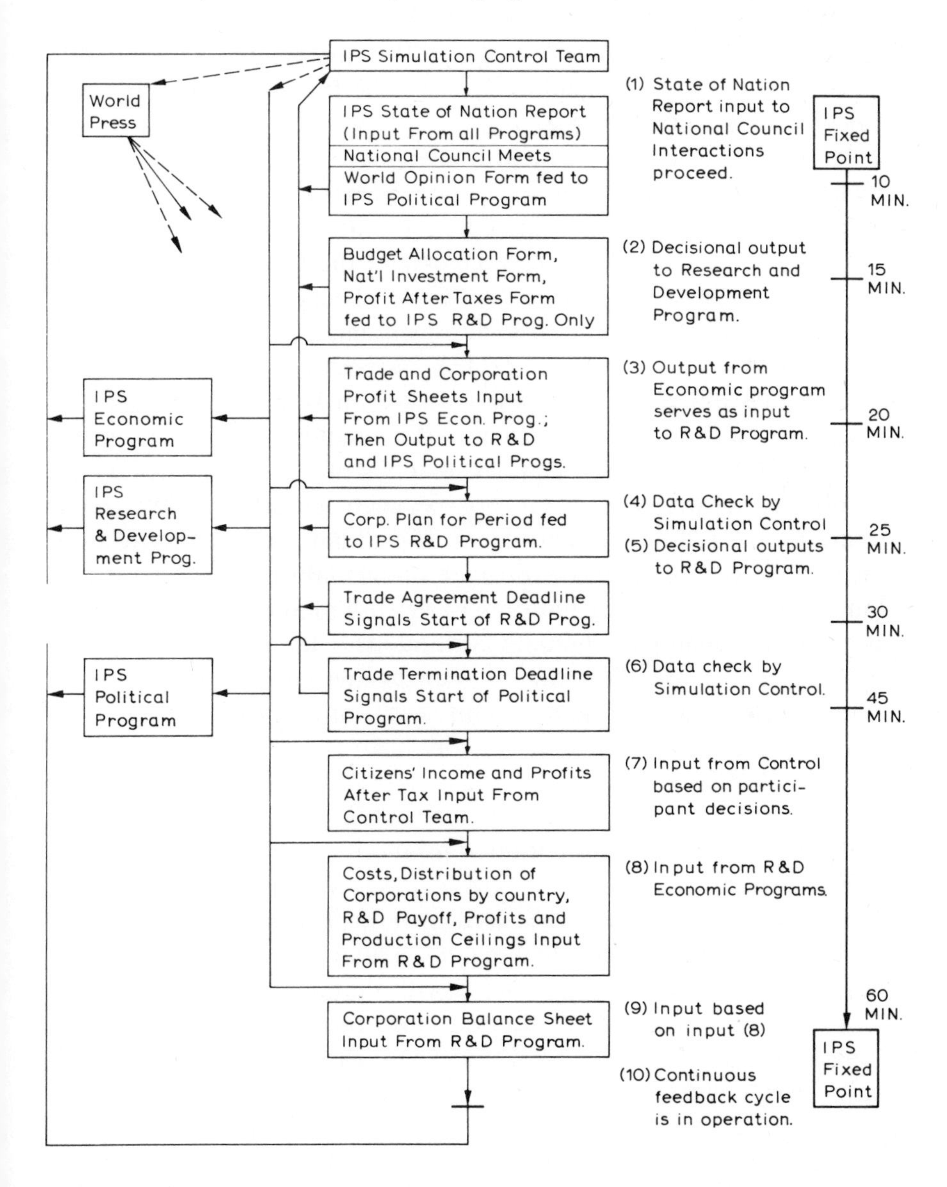

Fig. 5. – Decision and information cycle (Part 2) for International Processes Simulation

multinational corporations), and officers and representatives of international organizations are included. In fact, the actual structure of a particular simulation run can be changed by varying a nation-state component and an international component. Thus, using the same model, a variety of worlds can be generated changing from a nation-state type structure of the early 1900's to an international type structure of the 1970's and 80's. The decision and information cycle for IPS is shown in Figure 5.

It must be stressed that, although multinational business is included in IPS, IPS is not a business game after the style of the International Operations Simulation (Thorelli and Graves, 1964); similarly, the international nongovernmental organization component is present in IPS as a part of an international system rather than a valid representation of such organization (Judge, 1967).

The computer component of IPS, like the human component, is developed from INS. There are, however, a number of differences, which are fully explained elsewhere (Smoker, 1968 i). The programs are modular and contain approximately 130 variables, including a number of additional political variables such as world opinion, public opinion, and political effectiveness. Like WPS, the program is interfaced with the participants through on-line equipment. There is no look-ahead capability in the present version of IPS; but unlike WPS, there is an attempt to simulate continuous feedback of information to the participants. This can be seen by the fairly regularly-spaced left to right arrows in Figure 5. This is critical to the operation of the simulation as an impression of continuity is created by fast and frequent feedback from the environment to the participants. As a result, there is no need to halt the simulation as in the case of INS or PME, and the end of the period is no more significant than the end of a real world year.

The latest version of IPS used two on-line terminals and two separate systems of interlocking programs (Smoker, 1968 iii). A choice of two data bases is included with the programs.

A number of validity studies have been conducted on IPS (Smoker, 1968 ii, 1969, 1971), and comparative studies with INS have been undertaken whenever possible. The validity studies have been selected to test the model in terms of conflict behavior by replicating some of the studies of Rummel and Tanter concerning domestic and foreign conflict properties of nations (Rummel, 1963)

(Tanter, 1966); alliance and cooperative behavior of governments by replicating the studies of Singer and Small concerning over time alliance behavior of nations (Singer and Small, 1966); and general systemic properties by replicating and extending the Chadwick studies of INS and the international system (Chadwick, 1966, 1967).

To summarize these studies for thirty-three discrete types of domestic and foreign conflict behavior aggregated into fourteen categories using the Rummel coding scheme, the performance characteristics of IPS show strong correspondence to the international system of 1955–60 in terms of generating the same structures when subjected to factor analytical procedures. Additionally, the future world exhibits significantly different patterns of behavior than the past simulated world, and these patterns are consistent with the predictions of prominent peace theorists (Galtung, 1968). Similarly, professional decision-makers exhibit significantly different patterns of behavior than high school decision-makers. The high school and future worlds are also less conflictual.

For the Singer-Small alliance studies, when comparisons of 130 separate simulation and international system correlations of alliance patterns are undertaken, the IPS correlations correspond to the international system correlations in roughly two-thirds of the cases.

For the Chadwick replication of the intercorrelations between seventeen separate variables ranging from economic and trade variables to political, alliance and conflict variables, roughly two-thirds of the 136 correlations were similar in IPS and referent systems, whereas less than half were similar for the INS.

The evidence from these studies suggests that IPS demonstrates stronger correspondence to the referent international systems considered than does INS for these variables. Although this is the case, care is required in the use of IPS as an educational technique since, on hypothesis-validity grounds, it seems reasonable to suggest the focus of IPS is almost exclusively at the international system level. While domestic processes within nations are represented in the programmed and unprogrammed parts, relative to WPS, the model is poorly developed here. IPS has been used as an educational device (Biery, 1969), but until more evidence is accumulated (Busse, 1968) (Soroos, 1969), care should be taken to explain its as yet limited confirmed validity.

On the other hand, relatively few theorists have models that transcend the "ping-pong-ball" view of planet Earth, and an exposure to IPS may be of value from this point of view. Relative to other simulations of international relations, the performance characteristics are at least tolerable, given the primitive state of the art; and in addition, rudimentary multilevel theory is incorporated in the model.

Within the context of future requirements, however, there are serious errors in structure and theory. There are no structural components in the simulation that relate the ecological and technological global environment to economic, political, and social variables. There is no built-in procedure for participants to change the rules of the environment under certain conditions. And there is an inadequate understanding of social time and over time processes such that it seems possible that different parts of the simulation are working on different time scales.

Each of these problems requires a considerable amount of work and some drastic overhauling of international relations theory. The next generation of man-computer simulations will, hopefully, make some progress in this regard.

Summary and Prospects

Guetzkow has conceptualized the INS as a self-organizing system (Guetzkow, 1963); and the community of international relations simulators can be seen in a similar way, to a large extent. Particular models, such as the INS, are taken and adapted in extremely innovative ways by different scholars in different parts of the world for different research purposes (Laulicht, 1967) (Seki, 1966) (Cappello, 1971). As a vehicle for theory and development of theory in a cumulative fashion, the simulation endeavor, despite many problems (Schwartz, 1965), has been amongst the most rigorous and sustained during the last decade of international relations research (Guetzkow, 1970). Basic models, such as INS, have been progressively developed into constructions such as WPS (Coplin, 1969) and IPS (Smoker, 1968 i). At the micro level, individual decision-makers in INS have been computerized (Bremer, 1970) and detailed analyses of individual equations have led to revisions and improvements (Elder and Pendley, 1966 ii).

The problem of validity is still one of the most difficult questions facing all models in international relations, but there appears to be an increasing concern with this question among simulators. It is no longer enough to have a model unless some sort of validation is considered as a part of the continual process of model creation. Similarly, the question of relevance is likely to become increasingly important as different views on what is relevant confront one another. For example, both WPS with its focus on policy influencers, and IPS with its concentration on the international system, can be conceived as theoretical statements of relevance. An objective observer might conclude that both viewpoints need to be incorporated in a next generation simulation.

Of course, relevance considerations bring many important value questions into focus and, in this way, raise issues concerning the validity of aspects of reality. Those simulators concerned with practical policy may increasingly seek to change reality as a result of some experience with a relevant model. A lively and hopefully productive debate between simulators and practitioners may be anticipated in the next decade of activity.

Early in the past decade, it seemed useful to differentiate between all-computer and man-computer simulations; but the advent of on-line equipment and almost immediate feedback has in some way blurred this previously clear distinction. An all-computer simulation has now become a situation with one experimenter interacting with one computerized environment, often modifying his experiments as a result of the response (or should we say "stimulus") from the computer. A man-computer simulation simply involves more than one experimenter, with the experimenters themselves interacting with each other. As we know from the beginning effect in simulations such as IPS, it takes a little while before the participants' behavior is conditioned by the computerized environment, and the same may be true for the all-computer experiment.

Whatever distinctions subsequently emerge in a typology of international relations simulations it seems clear that increasing use will be made of computer approaches in the study of international relations, and a number of third generation constructions are likely to emerge in the next decade. These constructions may incorporate whole new ranges of variables, such as those relevant to global ecosystems and survival, and may explore many more properties of world politics with a concern for validity and a sensitivity for relevance far in excess of all our present simulations.

REFERENCES

Abt Associates, Inc. (1965). *Survey of the State of the Art: Social, Political, and Economic Models and Simulations.* Cambridge, Mass.: Abt Associates, Inc.

Abt, Clark C., and Gorden, Morton (1969). "Report on Project TEMPER." In Dean G. Pruitt and Richard C. Snyder, Eds. *Theory and Research on the Causes of War.* Englewood Cliffs, New Jersey: Prentice-Hall, Inc., pp. 245–62.

Ackoff, Russell; Gupta, Shiv K.; and Minas, J. Sayer (1962). *Scientific Method: Optimizing Applied Research Decisions.* New York, N. Y.: John Wiley & Sons, Inc.

Alger, Chadwick F. (1970). "Trends in International Relations Research." In James C. Charlesworth, Ed. *Annals, American Academy of Political and Social Sciences Meeting,* "Design for the Discipline of International Relations: Scope, Objectives, and Methods," March 14, 1969.

Alker, Hayward, R., Jr. (1969). "Computer Simulations, Conceptual Frameworks and Coalition Behavior." In Goennings, Kelly, and Leiserson, Eds. *The Study of Coalition Behavior: Theoretical Perspectives and Cases from Four Continents.* New York, N.Y.: Holt, Rinehart, and Winston.

Alker, Jr., Hayward R., and Brunner, Ronald D. (1969). "Simulating International Conflict: A Comparison of Three Approaches." *International Studies Quarterly* XIII, 1: 70–110.

* Angell, Robert C. (1969). *Peace on the March: Transnational Participation.* New York, N.Y.: Van Nostrand Reinhold Company.

Ausland, John, and Richardson, Hugh (1966). "Crisis Management: Berlin, Cyprus and Laos." *Foreign Affairs* 44: 291–303.

Averch, H., and Lavin, M.M. (1964). *Simulation of Decision Making in Crises: Three Manual Gaming Experiments.* RAND Report RM-4202-Pr. Santa Monica, Calif.: RAND Corporation.

* Azar, Edward; Cohen, Stanley; Jukam, Thomas; and McCormick, James (1970). Methodological Developments in the Quantification of Events Data. East Lansing, Mich.: Cooperation/Conflict Research Group, Michigan State University.

Bailey, Gerald (1967). *Utilizing Simulation of International Behavior in Political-Military Affairs: A Preliminary Analysis.* Arlington, Virginia: Human Sciences Research, Inc.

Balinski, Michel; Knorr, Klauss; Morgenstern, Oskar,; Sand, Francis; and Shubik, Martin (1966). *Review of TEMPER Model* (Final Report Draft). Princeton, N.J.: Mathematica.

Banks, Michael; Groom, A.J.R.; and Oppenheim, A.N. (1968). "Gaming and Simulation in International Relations." *Political Studies* XVI: 1–17.

Barringer, Richard E., and Whaley, Barton (1965). "The MIT Political Military Gaming Experience." *Orbis, A Quarterly Journal of World Affairs* IX, 2: 437–58.

Benson, Oliver (1961). "A Simple Diplomatic Game." In J.N. Rosenau, Ed. *International Politics and Foreign Policy: A Reader in Research and Theory.* New York, N.Y.: Free Press of Glencoe, Inc., pp. 504–11.

Benson, Oliver (1963). "Simulation of International Relations and Diplomacy." In Harold Borko, Ed. *Computer Application in the Behavioral Science.* Englewood Cliffs, N.J.: Prentice-Hall, Inc., pp. 574–95.

Biery, James (1969). "Playing Games with the Future." *Northwestern Review.* Evanston, Ill.: Northwestern University, pp. 18–23.

Bloomfield, Lincoln P. (1960). "Political Gaming." *United States Naval Institute Proceedings* LXXXVI, 9: 57–64.

Bloomfield, Lincoln P. (1968). *Report on CONEX 1.* Cambridge, Mass.: Center for International Studies, Massachusetts Institute of Technology.

Bloomfield, Lincoln P., and Padelford, N.J. (1959). "Three Experiments in Political Gaming." *The American Political Science Review* LIII, 4: 1105–15.

Bloomfield, Lincoln, and Whaley, Barton (1965 i). "The Political-Military Exercise: A Progress Report." *Orbis, A Quarterly Journal of World Affairs* VIII, 4: 854–70.
Bloomfield, Lincoln P., and Whaley, Barton (1965 ii). "POLEX: The Political Military Exercise." *The Military Review: Professional Journal of the U.S. Army*. Fort Leavenworth, Kansas, pp. 65–71.
Bobrow, Davis B. (1969). Computers and a Normative Model of the Policy Process. Paper presented at the 1969 Meeting of the American Association for the Advancement of Science, Boston, Mass., December 26–31.
Bobrow, Davis B., and Schwartz, Judah L. (1968). *Computers and the Policy-Making Community*. Englewood Cliffs, N.J.: Prentice-Hall, Inc.
Bonham, Gaylor (1967). Aspects of the Validity of Two Simulations of Phenomena in International Relations. Ph.D. Dissertation, Department of Political Science, Massachusetts Institute of Technology.
Boocock, Sarane, and Schild,E.O. (1968). *Simulation Games in Learning*. Beverley Hills, Calif.: Sage Publications.
Bremer, Stuart A. (1970). The Validation and Evaluation of the Siper Computer Simulation Model. Chap. 7 in National and International Systems: A Computer Simulation. Draft, Ph.D. Dissertation, Department of Political Science, Michigan State University.
Brody, Richard A. (1963). "Some Systemic Effects of the Spread of Nuclear Weapons Technology: A Study through Simulation of a Multi-Nuclear Future." *Journal of Conflict Resolution* VII, 4: 663–753.
Brody, Richard A.; Benham, Alexandra H.; and Milstein, Jeffrey S. (1966). Hostile International Communication, Arms Production, and Perception of Threat: A Simulation Study. Stanford, Calif.: Institute of Political Studies, Stanford University, July.
Browning, Rufus P. (1969). Quality of Collective Decisions, Some Theory and Computer Simulations. East Lansing, Mich.: Michigan State University, June.
Burton, John W. (1966). International Relations Simulations on the Cheap. Evanston, Ill.: Simulated International Processes project, Northwestern University, July.
* Burton, John W. (1967). *International Relations*. Cambridge: Cambridge University Press.
Busse, Walter R. (1968). Negotiation in the International Processes Simulation. Dissertation Proposal, Northwestern University, November.
Busse, Walter R. (1969). The Northwestern Simulation Archives: Man-Computer Models of International Relations. Evanston, Ill.: Simulated International Processes project, Northwestern University.
Campbell, Donald T. (1957). "Factors Relevant to the Validity of Experiments in Social Settings." *Psychological Bulletin* 54: 297–312.
Campbell, Donald T., and Fiske, D.W. (1959). "Convergent and Discriminant Validation by the Multitrait-Multimethod Matrix." *Psychological Bulletin* 56: 81–105.
Cappello, Hector (1972). "International Tension as a Function of Reduced Communication (A Simulation Study)." In J. Laponce and P. Smoker, Eds. *The Vancouver Papers on Experimentation and Simulation*. Toronto: University of Toronto Press.
Caspary, William (1965). The Causes of War in Inter-Nation Simulation. Evanston, Ill.: Northwestern University.
Chadwick, Richard W. (1966). Developments in a Partial Theory of International Behavior: A Test and Extension of Inter-Nation Simulation Theory. Ph.D. Dissertation, Department of Political Science, Northwestern University.
Chadwick, Richard W.(1967). "An Empirical Test of Five Assumptions in an Inter-Nation Simulation about National Political Systems." *General Systems* XII: 177–92.
Chadwick, Richard W. (1969). "An Inductive, Empirical Analysis of Intra and International Behavior, Aimed at a Partial Extension of Inter-Nation Simulation Theory." *Journal of Peace Research* VI, 3: 193–214.

Cherryholmes, Cleo (1965). "Developments in Simulation of International Relations in High School Teaching." *Phi Delta Kappa* January, pp. 227–31.

Cohen, Bernard D. (1962). "Political Gaming in the Classroom." *Journal of Politics* XXIV, 2: 367–80.

Coplin, William (1966). "Inter-Nation Simulation and Contemporary Theories of International Relations." *The American Political Science Review* LX, 3: 562–78.

Coplin, William, Ed. (1968). *Simulation in the Study of Politics.* Chicago, Ill.: Markham Publishing Co.

Coplin, William (1969). "Man-Computer Simulation as an Approach to the Study of Politics: Implications from a Comparison of State Department and High School Runs of the World Politics Simulation." *Proceedings, National Gaming Council, Eighth Symposium.*

Coplin, William (1970). "Approaches to the Social Sciences through Man-Computer Simulations." *Simulation and Games* Vol. I, Beverly Hills, Calif.: Sage Publications, December.

Cornblit, Oscar (1972). "A Model of Short Run Political Change." In J. Laponce and P. Smoker, Eds. *The Vancouver Papers on Experimentation and Simulation.* Toronto: University of Toronto Press.

* Corson, Walter (1970). Conflict and Cooperation in East-West Crises: Measurement and Prediction. Ann Arbor, Mich.: Institute for Social Research, University of Michigan, April.

Crow, Wayman J. (1963). "A Study of Strategic Doctrines using Inter-Nation Simulation." *Journal of Arms Control* I, 4: 674–83.

Crow, Wayman J. (1966). "Simulation: The Construction and Use of Functioning Models in International Relations." In K.R. Hammond, Ed. *Egon Brunswiks Psychology.* New York, N.Y.: Holt, Rinehart and Winston, pp. 340–48.

Crow, Wayman, J. and Noel, Robert C. (1965). *The Valid Use of Simulation Results.* La Jolla, Calif.: Western Behavioral Sciences Institute, June.

Crow, Wayman J., and Raser, John (1964). A Cross Cultural Simulation Study. La Jolla, Calif.: Western Behavioral Sciences Institute, November, pp. 12–18.

*Deutsch, Karl W. (1968). *The Analysis of International Relations.* Englewood Cliffs, N.J.: Prentice-Hall, Inc.

De La Mater, Stephen T.; Dunham, Jack V.; Granston, Robert W.; Schulke, Herbert H.; Smith, Chester R.; and Westfall, Frederick R. (1966). *ICAF Analysis of TEMPER MARK II.* Washington, D.C.: Industrial College for the Armed Forces.

DeWeerd, Harvey (1968). An Israeli Scenario for a Laboratory Simulation. Santa Monica, Calif.: System Development Corporation, April.

Draper, George (1966). Technological, Economic, Military and Political Evaluation Routine (TEMPER) – an Evaluation. Washington, D.C.: National Military Command Systems Support Center, July.

Driver, Michael J. (1962). Conceptual Structure and Group Processes in an Inter-Nation Simulation. Part One: The Perception of Simulated Nations. Princeton, N.J.: Princeton University and Educational Testing Service.

Driver, Michael J. (1965). A Structural Analysis of Aggression, Stress, and Personality in an Inter-Nation Simulation. Lafayette, Ind.: Purdue University, January.

Druckman, Daniel (1968). "Ethnocentrism in the Inter-Nation Simulation." *Journal of Conflict Resolution* XII, 1: 45–68.

Elder, Charles D., and Pendley, Robert E. (1966 i). Simulation as Theory Building in the Study of International Relations. Evanston, Ill.: Northwestern University, July.

Elder, Charles D. (1966 ii). An Analysis of Consumption Standards and Validation Satisfactions in the Inter-Nation Simulation in Terms of Contemporary Economic Theory and Data. Evanston, Ill.: Northwestern University, November.

Evans, George W.; Wallace, Graham F.; and Sutherland, Georgia L. (1967). *Simulation Using Digital Computers.* Englewood Cliffs, N.J.: Prentice-Hall, Inc.

Fischer, R. Lucas (1968). The Rand/MIT Political-Military Exercise and International Relations Theory. Evanston, Ill.: Northwestern University.

Forcese, Dennis (1968). Power and Military Alliance Cohesion: Thirteen Simulation Experiments. Ph.D. Dissertation, Department of Sociology, Washington University, St. Louis, Mo.

* Galtung, Johan (1968). "Entropy and the General Theory of Peace." *Proceedings, Second International Peace Research Association General Conference.* Vol. I, Assen: Van Gorcum & Comp.

Giffen, Sydney F. (1965). *The Crisis Game: Simulating International Conflict.* Garden City, N.Y.: Doubleday and Company.

Goldhamer, Herbert, and Speier, Hans (1961). "Some Observations on Political Gaming." In James N. Rosenau, Ed. *International Politics and Foreign Policy.* New York, N.Y.: The Free Press of Glencoe, Inc., pp. 498–503.

Gomer, Louise C. (1968). Master List of Variables in the Simulation of International Processes. Evanston, Ill.: Simulated International Processes project, Northwestern University, March.

Gorden, Morton (1967). International Relations Theory in the TEMPER Simulation. Evanston, Ill.: Northwestern University.

Gorden, Morton (1968). "Burdens for the Designer of a Computer Simulation of International Relations: The Case of TEMPER." In Davis B. Bobrow and Judah L. Schwartz, Eds. *Computers and the Policy-Making Community.* Englewood Cliffs, N.J.: Prentice-Hall, Inc., pp. 222–45.

Gottheil, Diane Levitt (1966). A Method for Comparing Verbal and Simulation Theory, with Its Application to an Essay on Alliances by Wolfers. Evanston, Ill.: Northwestern University, April.

Grant, Lawrence (1970). The Problem of Validity for Computer Simulation. Ames, Iowa: Iowa State University, January.

Guetzkow, Harold (1959). "A Use of Simulation in the Study of International Relations." *Behavioral Science* 4, 3: 183–91.

Guetzkow, Harold (1962). "Inter-Nation Simulation: An Example of a Self-Organizing System." In Marshall C. Yovits, George T. Jacobi, and Gordon D. Goldstein, Eds. *Self-Organizing Systems.* Washington, D.C.: Spartan Books, pp. 79–92.

Guetzkow, Harold (1964 i). "Evaluation of the Inter-Nation Simulation as a Teaching Aid." *Proceedings of the American Society of International Law* 58: 78–79.

Guetzkow, Harold (1964 ii). "Simulation in International Relations." *Proceedings of the IBM Scientific Computing Symposium on Simulation Models and Gaming.* Yorktown Heights, New York: Thomas J. Watson Research Center, December 7–9, pp. 249–278.

Guetzkow, Harold (1965). "Some Uses of Mathematics in Simulation of International Relations." In John M. Claunch, Ed. *Mathematical Applications in Political Science.* Dallas, Texas: The Arnold Foundation (Southern Methodist University), pp. 21–40.

Guetzkow, Harold (1968). "Some Correspondence between Simulations and 'Realities' in International Relations." In Morton A. Kaplan, Ed. *New Approaches to International Relations.* New York, N.Y.: St. Martin's Press, pp. 202–69.

Guetzkow, Harold (1969). "Simulations in the Consolidation and Utilization of Knowledge about International Relations." In Dean G. Pruitt and Richard C. Snyder, Eds. *Theory and Research on the Causes of War.* Englewood Cliffs, N.J.: Prentice-Hall, Inc., pp. 284–300.

Guetzkow, Harold (1970). "A Decade of Life with the Inter-Nation Simulation." In Ralph G. Stogdill, Ed. *The Process of Model-Building in the Behavioral Sciences.* Columbus, Ohio: Ohio State University Press.

Guetzkow, Harold; Alger, Chadwick F.; Brody, Richard A.; Noel, Robert C.; and Snyder, Richard C. (1963). *Simulation in International Relations: Developments for Research and Teaching.* Englewood Cliffs, N.J.: Prentice-Hall, Inc.

Guetzkow, Harold, and Cherryholmes, Cleo (1966 i). *Inter-Nation Simulation Kit: Instructor's Manual.* Chicago, Ill.: Science Research Associates, Inc.

Guetzkow, Harold (1966 ii). *Inter-Nation Simulation Kit: Participant's Manual.* Chicago, Ill.: Science Research Associates, Inc.

Guetzkow, Harold, and Jensen, Lloyd (1966). "Research Activities on Simulated International Processes." *Background: Journal of the International Studies Association*, IX, 4 (Feb. 1966), 261–74.

Hermann, Charles F. (1965). Crises in Foreign Policy Making: A Simulation of International Politics. Ph.D. Dissertation, Department of Political Science, Northwestern University.

Hermann, Charles F. (1967 i). Threat, Time and Surprise: A Simulation of International Crisis. Princeton, N.J.: Princeton University, April.

Hermann, Charles F. (1967 ii). "Critique and Comment: Validation Problems in Games and Simulations with Special Reference to Models of International Politics." *Behavioral Science* XII, 3: 216–31.

Hermann, Charles F. (1968). "Games and Simulations of Political Processes." In *International Encyclopedia of the Social Sciences* Vol. 14, New York, N.Y.: The Free Press, pp. 247–81.

Hermann, Charles F. (1969). *Crises in Foreign Policy: A Simulational Analysis.* Indianapolis, Indiana: The Bobbs-Merrill Company, Inc.

* Hermann, Charles F. (1970). What is a Foreign Policy Event? A paper prepared for the Events Data Measurement Conference, Michigan State University, East Lansing, Michigan, April 15–16.

Hermann, Charles F., and Hermann, Margaret G. (1963). Validation Studies of the Inter-Nation Simulation. China Lake, Calif.: U.S. Naval Ordnance Test Station, December.

Hermann, Charles F., and Hermann, Margaret G. (1967). "An Attempt to Simulate the Outbreak of World War I." *The American Political Science Review* LXI, 2: 400–416.

Hermann, Margaret G. (1965). Stress, Self-Esteem, and Defensiveness in an Inter-Nation Simulation. Ph.D. Dissertation, Department of Psychology, Northwestern University.

Hermann, Margaret G. (1966). "Testing a Model of Psychological Stress." *Journal of Personality* 34, 3: 381–96.

* Holsti, Ole R.; North, Robert C.; and Brody, Richard A. (1968). "Perception and Action in the 1914 Crisis." In J. David Singer, Ed. *Quantitative International Politics: Insights and Evidence.* New York, N.Y.: The Free Press, pp. 123–58.

Hoole, Frank (1970). Decision Making in the World Health Organization: The Budgetary Process. Draft, Ph.D. Dissertation, Department of Political Science, Northwestern University, April.

Industrial College of the Armed Forces (ICAF) (1966 i). *The Player Handbook: TEMPER – 66.* Washington, D.C.: Industrial College of the Armed Forces.

Industrial College of the Armed Forces (ICAF) (1966 ii). *A Study and Evaluation of the Technological, Economic, Military and Political Evaluation Routine (TEMPER).* Washington, D.C.: Resistant School 1965–66 – TEMPER Committee Report, Industrial College of the Armed Forces.

Industrial College of the Armed Forces (ICAF) (1967). *The Player Handbook: TEMPER – 67.* Washington, D.C.: Industrial College of the Armed Forces.

Industrial College of the Armed Forces (ICAF) (1968 i). *The Player Handbook: TEMPER –*

68. Washington, D.C.: Industrial College of the Armed Forces.
Industrial College of the Armed Forces (ICAF) (1968 ii). *The Player Handbook: Addendum TEMPER – 68.* Washington, D.C.: Industrial College of the Armed Forces.
Industrial College of the Armed Forces (ICAF) (1968 iii). *TEMPER ICAF 1968 Reports,* Volumes 1 and 2. Washington, D.C.: Industrial College of the Armed Forces.
Industrial College of the Armed Forces (ICAF) (1969 i). *World Politics Simulation: Description of Model.* Washington, D.C.: Industrial College of the Armed Forces.
Industrial College of the Armed Forces (ICAF) (1969 ii). *Briefing Manual: World Politics Simulation III/ICAF.* Washington, D.C.: Industrial College of the Armed Forces.
Industrial College of the Armed Forces (ICAF) (1969 iii). *World Politics Simulation: Computer Program Listings.* Washington, D.C.: Industrial College of the Armed Forces, February.
Industrial College of the Armed Forces (ICAF) (1969 iv). *World Politics Simulation: Participant's Manual.* Washington, D.C.: Industrial College of the Armed Forces.
Industrial College of the Armed Forces (ICAF) (1969 v). *World Politics Simulation: Background Materials.* Washington D.C.: Industrial College of the Armed Forces.
Industrial College of the Armed Forces (ICAF) (1969 vi). *World Politics Simulation: Administrative Manual.* Washington, D.C.: Industrial College of the Armed Forces.
* Jensen, Lloyd (1966 i). United States Elites and Their Perceptions of the Determinants of Foreign Policy Behavior. Evanston, Ill.: Northwestern University, April.
* Jensen, Lloyd (1966 ii). "Foreign Policy Elites and the Prediction of International Events." *Papers, Peace Research Society (International)* V.
Johnson, Douglas F., and Pruitt, Dean G. (1969). Pre-Intervention Effects of Mediation versus Arbitration. Buffalo, N.Y.: Department of Psychology, State University of New York, August.
Judge, A.J.N. (n.d.). Proposal for the Development of a "World Game" as a Long-Term Education Technique. Brussels: Union of International Associations.
Judge, A.J.N. (n.d.) (1967). "Management Game Techniques and International NGO's." *Associations Internationales* 10: 659–65.
Krend, Jeff (1968). A Typology for Ordering the Simulation and Gaming Literature (Draft). Evanston, Ill.: Northwestern University, March.
Krend, Jeff (1972). "A Reconstruction of Oliver Benson's 'Simple Diplomatic Game'." In J. Laponce and P. Smoker, Eds. *The Vancouver Papers on Experimentation and Simulation.* Toronto: University of Toronto Press.
Krend, Jeff (1969). A comparison of Guetzkow-Modelski Correspondence Ratings. Evanston, Ill.: Simulated International Processes project, Northwestern University.
Kress, Paul (1966). On Validating Simulation: with Special Attention to Simulation of International Politics. Evanston, Ill.: Northwestern University, April.
Laulicht, Jerome (1967). "A Vietnam Peace Game: Computer-Assisted Simulation of Complex Relations in International Relations." *Computers and Automation* XVI, 3: 14–18.
* Leng, Russell J., and Singer, J. David (1970). Toward a Multi-Theoretical Typology of International Behavior. A paper prepared for the Events Data Conference, Michigan State University, East Lansing, Michigan, April.
* McClelland, Charles A. (1966). *Theory and the International System.* New York, N.Y.: The Macmillan Co.
* McClelland, Charles A. (1968). "The Access to Berlin: The Quantity and Variety of Events, 1948–63." In J. David Singer, Ed. *Quantitative International Politics: Insights and Evidence.* New York, N.Y.: The Free Press, pp. 159–186.
* McClelland, Charles A., *et al.* (1965). The Communist Chinese Performance in Crisis and Non Crisis; Quantitative Studies of the Taiwan Straits Confrontation, 1950–64. China

Lake, Calif.: Behavioral Sciences Group, Naval Ordnance Test Station.
* McGowan, Patrick (1970). The Unit of Analysis Problem in the Comparative Study of Foreign Policy. A paper prepared for the Events Data Measurement Conference, Michigan State University, East Lansing, Michigan, April.
MacRae, John (1967). Bosnian Crisis Simulation (Participants' Manual and Scenario). Lancaster: University of Lancaster.
MacRae, John, and Smoker, Paul (1967). "A Vietnam Simulation: A Report on the Canadian/English Joint Project." *Journal of Peace Research* IV, 1: 1–25.
Martin, Francis F. (1968). *Computer Modeling and Simulation.* New York, N.Y.: John Wiley & Sons, Inc.
Meier, Dorothy, and Stickgold, Arthur (1965). Progress Report: Event Simulation Project (INS-16) (Draft). St. Louis, Mo.: Washington University.
Milstein, Jeffrey S. and Mitchell, William Charles (1968). Computer Simulation of International Processes: The Vietnam War and the Pre-World War I Naval Race. Sixth North American Peace Research Conference, November.
Modelski, George (1969). Simulations, "Realities" and International Relations Theory. Evanston, Ill.: Simulated International Processes project, Northwestern University.
Mushakoji, Kinhide (1968). "Negotiations between the West and the Non-West – Cultural Problems in Conflict Resolution." *Proceedings, Second International Peace Research Association General Conference.* Vol. I, Assen: Van Gorcum & Comp.
Mushakoji, Kinhide (1972). "The Strategies of Negotiation." In J. Laponce and P. Smoker, Eds. *The Vancouver Papers on Experimentation and Simulation*. Toronto: University of Toronto Press.
Myers, Mary Lynn (1968). Bibliographic and Abstracted Bibliographic Sources: An Annotated Listing of Sources which Include Materials Dealing with Simulation in the Social Sciences, Especially Those Concerned with the Simulation of International Processes. Evanston, Ill.: Simulated International Processes project, Northwestern University.
Nardin, Terry, and Cutler, Neal E. (1969). "Reliability and Validity of Some Patterns of International Interaction in an Inter-Nation Simulation." *Journal of Peace Research* VI, 1: 1-12.
* Park, Tong-Whan (1968). A Guide to Data Sources in International Relations: Annotated Bibliography with Lists of Variables. Evanston, Ill.: Northwestern University.
Parker, John, and Whithed, Marshall (1969). Developing an International Mutual Response System through Political Simulation Techniques. Troy, N.Y.: Department of Political Science, Rensselaer Polytechnic Institute.
Pelowski, Al (1969). Multi-National Corporate Futures: An Approach to Simulation Module Construction in International Relations. Evanston, Ill.: Simulated International Processes project, Northwestern University.
Pelowski, Al (1972). "Preliminary Simulation of the Taiwan Straits Crises: An Event-Based Probability Model." In J. Laponce and P. Smoker, Eds. *The Vancouver Papers on Experimentation and Simulation.* Toronto: University of Toronto Press.
Pendley, Robert E. (1966). INSCAL: A Fortran Program for Performing the Calculations for the Inter-Nation Simulation. Evanston, Ill.: Northwestern University.
Pendley, Robert E., and Elder, Charles D. (1966). An Analysis of Officeholding in the Inter-Nation Simulation in Terms of Contemporary Political Theory and Data on the Stability of Regimes and Governments. Evanston, III: Northwestern University.
Pfalzgraff, Robert L. (1969). Simulation and International Relations Theory: A Comparison of Simulation Models and International Relations Literature. Philadelphia, Penn.: University of Pennsylvania.
Pilisuk, Marc; Skolnick, Paul; Thomas, Kenneth; and Chapman, Reuben (1967). "Boredom vs. Cognitive Reappraisal in the Development of Cooperative Strategy." *Journal of Conflict Resolution* XI, 1: 110–16.

Pool, Ithiel de Sola, and Kessler, Allan (1965). "The Kaiser, the Tsar and the Computer: Information Processing in a Crisis." *American Behavioral Scientist* VIII, 9: 31–8.
Pruitt, Dean G. (1966). "Reward Structure and Its Effect on Cooperation." *Papers, Peace Research Society (International)* V: 73–85.
Pruitt, Dean G. (1968). Negotiation as a Form of Social Behavior. Buffalo, N.Y.: State University of New York, October.
Pruitt, Dean G. (1969) "Reward Structure and Cooperation Part II: Motivational Processes in the Decomposed Prisoners's Dilemma Game" Buffalo, N.Y.: Department of Psychology, State University of New York.
Pruitt, Dean G., and Johnson, Douglas (1969). Meditation as an Aid to Face-Saving in Negotiation. Buffalo, N.Y.: Department of Psychology, State University of New York, January.
* Raser, John R. (1965). Personal Characteristics of Political Decision Makers: A Literature Review. La Jolla, Calif.: Western Behavioral Sciences Institute.
Raser, John R. (1969). *Simulation and Society*. Boston, Mass.: Allyn & Bacon.
Raser, John R., and Crow, Wayman J. (1969). "A Simulation Study of Deterrence Theories." In Dean G. Pruitt and Richard C. Snyder, Eds. *Theory and Research on the Causes of War*. Englewood Cliffs, N.J.: Prentice-Hall, Inc., pp. 136–49.
Raytheon Company (1965). *Technological, Economic, Military and Political Evaluation Routine (TEMPER)*.
Vol. I *Orientation Manual*, July, 1965.
Vol. II *The Theory of the Model*, August, 1965.
Vol. III *Game Handbook*, July, 1965.
Vol. IV *Technical Manual*, September 1965.
Vol. V *Operations Manual*, July, 1965.
Vol. VI *Reference Manual*, July, 1965.
Vol. VII *Data Collection Manual*, July, 1965.
Bedford, Massachusetts: Raytheon Company.
Robinson, James A.; Anderson, Lee F.; Hermann, Margaret; and Snyder, Richard C. (1966). "Teaching with the Inter-Nation Simulation and Case Studies." *The American Political Science Review* LX, 1: 53–65.
Robinson, James A.; Hermann, Charles F.; and Hermann, Margaret (1969). "Search Under Crisis in Political Gaming and Simulation." In Dean G. Pruitt and Richard C. Snyder, *Theory and Research on the Causes of War*. Englewood Cliffs, N.J.: Prentice-Hall, Inc., pp. 80–94.
* Rosenau, James N. (1966). "Pre Theories and Theories of Foreign Policy." In R. Barry Farrell, Ed. *Approaches to Comparative and International Politics*. Evanston, Ill.: Northwestern University Press.
Ruge, Mari Holmboe (1969). Decision Makers as Human Beings: An Analysis of Perception and Behavior in Cross-Cultural Simulation Experiment. Oslo: Institute of Political Science, University of Oslo, and International Peace Research Institute.
* Rummel, Rudolph J. (1963). "Dimensions of Conflict: Behavior Within and Between Nations." *General Systems Year Book* 8: 1–50.
Schwartz David C. (n.d.). Threat, Hostility and Behavior Preferences in Crisis Decision Making: A Further Comparison of Historical and Simulation Data. Philadelphia, Penn.: University of Pennsylvania.
Schwartz David C. (1965). "Problems in Political Gaming." *Orbis: A Quarterly Journal of World Affairs* IX, 3: 677–93.
* Scott, Jr., Andrew M., (1967). *The Functioning of the International Political System*. New York, N.Y.: The Macmillan Co.

Seki, Hiroharu (1966). "Kokusai Taikei No Simulation – INS-J-4 No Modern Ni Tsuite" [The Simulation of the International System – on the Model of INS-J-4]. *Kodokagaku Kenkyu* [*The Journal of Behavioral Science*] I, 2. Tokai Daigaku Kiso Shakaikagaku Kenkyujo.

Shapiro, Michael (1966). Cognitive Rigidity and Moral Judgments in an Inter-Nation Simulation. Evanston, Ill.: Northwestern University, September.

Shubik, Martin (1960). "Bibliography on Simulation, Gaming, Artificial Intelligence and Allied Topics." *Journal of the American Statistical Association*, December: 736–51.

* Sigler, John, 1970. Reliability Problems in the Measurement of International Events in the Elite Press. A paper prepared for the Events Data Measurement Conference, Michigan State University, East Lansing, Michigan, April.

Singer, J. David, and Hinomoto, Hirohide (1965). "Inspecting for Weapons Production: A Modest Computer Simulation." *Journal of Peace Research* 2, 1: 18–38.

* Singer, J. David, and Small, Melvin (1966). "Formal Alliances, 1815–1939." *Journal of Peace Research* 3, 1: 1–32.

Simulated International Processes project (SIP) (1966 i). Studies Related to the Simulation of International Political and Military Processes: Collection of Abstracts. Evanstan, Ill.: Northwestern University.

Simulated International Processes project (SIP) (1966 ii). Simulations and Gaming of International Military Political Behaviors: Survey of Activities. Evanston, Ill.: Northwestern University.

Simulated International Processes project (SIP) (1968). Another Partial Bibliography on Simulation in International Relations. Evanston Ill.: Northwestern University.

Smith, Clifford Neal (1968 ii). International Business Decision-Making in a Political Setting: The SW-1 Simulation. DeKalb, Ill.: Northern Illinois University.

Smith, Clifford Neal (1969)."International Business Decision-Making in a Political Setting: The Model SW-2 Simulation." *Proceedings, National Gaming Council, Eighth Symposium.*

Smith, Clifford Neal, and Whithed, Marshall Hale (1968 i). PSW-1 Simulation. DeKalb, Ill.: Northern Illninois University.

Smoker, Paul (1966). Fortran Program for Vietnam Simulation. Lancaster: Peace Research Centre.

Smoker, Paul (1968 i). International Processes Simulation: A Man-Computer Model. Evanston, Ill.: Northwestern University.

Smoker, Paul (1968 ii). Analyses of Conflict Behaviours in an International Processes Simulation and an International System 1955–60. Evanston, Ill.: Northwestern University.

Smoker, Paul (1968 iii). *IPS Program Pack.* Evanston, Ill.: Northwestern University.

Smoker, Paul (1969). "Social Research for Social Anticipation." *American Behavioral Scientist* XII, 6: 7–13.

Smoker, Paul (1970 i). "Simulating the World." *Science Journal.* London, July.

Smoker, Paul (1970 ii). "International Relations Simulations." In Pat Tansey, Ed. *Aspects of Simulations in Education.* London: McGraw-Hill.

Smoker, Paul (1971). "International Processes Simulation: An Evaluation." *Peace Research Reviews*, 3: 6.

Smoker, Paul and Martin, John (1968). *Simulation and Games: an Overview.* Chicago, Ill.: Modern Trends in Education Series, Science Research Associates.

Soroos, Marvin (1969). International Involvement and Foreign Conflict in the International Processes Simulation and the "Real" World. Ph.D. Dissertation Proposal, Northwestern University, May.

Stewart, Edward C. (1966). "The Simulation of Cultural Differences." *The Journal of Communication* XVI, 4: 291–304.
Streufert, Siegried (1968 i). The Components of a Simulation of Local Conflict: An Analysis of the Tactical and Negotiations Game. Evanston, Ill.: Northwestern University.
Streufert, Siegfried (1968 ii). The Tactical and Negotiations Game: A Simulation of Local Conflict: An Analysis of Some Psychopolitical and Applied Implications of TNG Simulation Research. Lafayette, Ind.: Purdue University, January.
Streufert, Siegfried (1969 i). "Increasing Failure and Response Rate in Complex Decision Making." *Journal of Experimental Social Psychology* 5: 310–23.
Streufert, Siegfried (1969 ii). Complexity and Complex Decision Making. Lafayette, Ind.: Purdue University, March.
Streufert, Siegfried; Clardy, M.; Driver, M.; Karlins, M.; Schroder, M.; and Suedfeld, P. (1965 i). "A Tactical Game for the Analysis of Complex Decision Making in Individuals and Groups." *Psychological Reports* 17: 723–29.
Streufert, Siegfried; Suedfeld, Peter; and Driver, Michael (1965 ii). "Conceptual Structure, Information Search and Information Utilization." *Journal of Personality and Social Psychology* II, 5: 736–40.
Streufert, Siegfried, and Castore, Carl H. (1968). Information Search and the Effects of Failure: A Test of Complexity Theory. Lafayette, Ind.: Purdue University, December.
Streufert, Siegfried, and Streufert, Susan (1969 i). "Effects of Conceptual Structure, Failure and Success on Attribution of Causality and Interpersonal Attitudes." *Journal of Personality and Social Psychology* II, 2: 138–147.
Streufert, Siegfried, and Sandler, Sandra (1969). Information Availability and Complex Perceptions of Americans and Chinese. Lafayette, Ind.: Purdue University, July.
Streufert, Siegfried; Castore, Carl H.; and Kilger, Susan (1967). A Tactical and Negotiations Game: Rationale, Method and Analysis. Lafayette, Ind.: Purdue University, June.
Streufert, Siegfried; Streufert, Susan; and Castore, Carl H. (1969). "Complexity, Increasing Failure and Decision Making." *Journal of Experimental Research in Personality* III, 4: 293–300.
Sullivan, Edward M. (1969). Simulation as a Tool for Organizational Research and Design. Evanston, Ill.: Department of Industrial Engineering and Management Sciences, Northwestern University, January.
Tansey, Pat, Ed. (1970). *Aspects of Simulation in Education.* London: McGraw-Hill.
* Tanter, Raymond (1966). "Dimensions of Conflict Behavior Within and Between Nations, 1958–60." *Journal of Conflict Resolution* X, 1: 41–64.
Targ, Harry (1967). The Inter-Nation Simulation: An Elementary School Exercise. Evanston, Ill.: Northwestern University.
Targ, Harry (1968 i). Impacts of an Elementary School Inter-Nation Simulation on Developing Orientations to International Politics. Lafayette, Ind.: Purdue University.
Targ, Harry (1968 ii). Children's Developing Orientations to International Politics. Lafayette, Ind.: Purdue University.
Targ, Harry, and Nardin, Terry (1965). The Inter-Nation Simulation as a Predictor of Contemporary Events. Evanston, Ill.: Simulated International Processes project, Northwestern University, August.
Thorelli, Hans B., and Graves, Robert L. (1964). *International Operations Simulation, with Comments on Design and Use of Management Games.* New York, N.Y.: The Free Press (Collier-Macmillan).
Twelker, Paul A., and Wallen, Carl J. (1967). *Instructional Uses of Simulation; A Selected Bibliography.* Portland, Oregon: Teaching Research Division, Oregon State System of Higher Education in cooperation with Northwest Regional Educational Laboratory.

Verba, Sidney (1964). "Simulation, Reality, and Theory in International Relations." *World Politics* XVI, 3: 490–519.

Vertinsky, Ilan (1971). "Methodology of Simulation and Experimentation for Social Planning." In J. Laponce and P. Smoker, Eds., *The Vancouver Papers on Experimentation and Simulation.*

* Waltz, Kenneth N. (1967). *Foreign Policy and Democratic Politics.* Boston, Mass.: Little, Brown & Co.

Westfall, F., and Draper, G. (1966). The Initial Use of TEMPER. Washington, D.C.: Industrial College of the Armed Forces, April.

Whaley, Barton; Ordeshook, Peter C.; and Scott, Robert H. (1964). EXDET III: A Student-Level Experimental Simulation on Problems of Deterrence. Cambridge, Mass.: Center for International Studies, Massachusetts Institute of Technology.

Whaley, Barton, and Seidman, Aaron (1964). EXDET II. Cambridge, Mass.: Center for International Studies, Massachusetts Institute of Technology, November.

Zinnes, Dina A. (1966). "A Comparison of Hostile Behavior of Decison-Makers in Simulate and Historical Data." *World Politics* XVIII, 3: 474–502.

Zinnes, Dina A.; Van Howeling, Douglas; and Van Atta, Richard (1969). A Test of Some Properties of the Balance of Power Theory in a Computer Simulation. Evanston, Ill.: Simulated International Processes project, Northwestern University, Summer.

*These items are not directly relevant to simulation but are referred to in the text.

Author Index

Subject Index